Modern Chinese Counter-Enlightenment

Modern Chinese Counter-Enlightenment

Affect, Reason, and the Transcultural Lexicon

Peng Hsiao-yen

Hong Kong University Press
The University of Hong Kong
Pok Fu Lam Road
Hong Kong
https://hkupress.hku.hk

ISBN 978-988-8805-69-3 (*Hardback*)

British Library Cataloguing-in-Publication Data
A catalogue record for this book is available from the British Library.

Digitally printed

To Patrick Hanan (1927–2014)

Contents

Figures

Preface

Modern Chinese Counter-Enlightenment from a Transcultural Stance

The Enlightenment propelling modernity as a global event in modern history has gained critics' attention in recent years. They cautioned against "a Eurocentric mythology" that is obsessed with the Enlightenment's European origins in the eighteenth century. Instead, as Sebastian Conrad points out in 2012, Enlightenment had many authors in many places, and it should be engaged with "comparatively and globally." In addition, its global impact, rather than merely a diffusion of the ideas of the French *philosophes*, is "the work of many actors and the product of global interactions" (Conrad 2012).[1] By contrast, Matthijs Lok and Joris van Eijnatten's 2019 article advocates studies of "a global Counter-Enlightenment across space, time and culture." Furthermore, the idea of multiple modernities and the "global opposition" to Westernization across history and places indicate that "there is no escaping Counter-Enlightenment." For them, comparisons between Johann Gottfried Herder (1744–1803) and Johann Georg Hamann (1730–1788) with "leading non-European but often Western-trained intellectuals," such as the Hindu Rabindranath Tagore (1861–1941), the Muslim Muhammad Iqbal (1877–1938), and the Confucian Liang Shuming 梁漱溟 (1893–1988), show that they saw Western, Enlightened modernity as "an assault on tradition and 'Eastern' values" (Lok and van Eijnatten 2019). To me, the attitude of the "enemies of Enlightenment" is much more complex than seeing it as "an assault" on tradition. My investigation indicates that the Counter-Enlightenment discourses embracing their own cultural heritage, rather than denouncing Enlightenment, were intended to carry on a dialogue with its agenda. They believed that Enlightenment rationality should be supplemented by affective Enlightenment.

The trend of Counter-Enlightenment, which traces to Jean-Jacque Rousseau (1712–1778) in the age of Enlightenment and culminated in the life philosophy movement flourishing at the turn of the twentieth century, should indeed be studied

1. In "Enlightenment in Global History: A Historiographical Critique," Sebastian Conrad Draws on Tipu Sultan (1750–1799) of the southern Indian city Mysore, Meiji Japan, modern China, and Korea to illustrate his idea of a global Enlightenment.

in global history. This book is devoted to this topic. In addition to the European and Asian philosophers connected to the movement, their Anglo-American counterparts such as Bertrand Russell (1872–1970) and John Dewey (1859–1952), who were invited to China in the early 1920s to lecture on Henri Bergson's (1859–1941) life philosophy, also figure prominently. This shows that the global reach of Counter-Enlightenment cannot be ignored. However, rather than from a comparative perspective, this book emphasizes the transcultural connectivity of the global Counter-Enlightenment discourses and attributes the networking of related ideas to transcultural players linking like-minded people from countries oceans apart, including Zhang Taiyan 章太炎 (1868–1936), Lu Xun 魯迅 (1881–1936), Liang Qichao 梁啟超 (1873–1929), Liang Shuming, and Cai Yuanpei 蔡元培 (1868–1940) from China; Inoue Tetzujirō 井上哲次郎 (1856–1944) and Nishida Kitarō 西田幾多郎 (1870–1945) from Japan; Rabindranath Tagore (1861–1941) from India; Rudolf Eucken (1846–1926) and Hans Driesch (1867–1941) from Germany; Bergson from France; Russell from England; and Dewey from the United States. It is about the stories of their transcultural interactions that activated the global Counter-Enlightenment network. To put it simply, my perspective is transcultural rather than comparative. As I have stated elsewhere, transcultural studies highlight the self-transformation of a culture as a result of its inception of other cultures. Interaction with others provides a key to self-renewal (Peng 2010).

The May Fourth period has been dubbed an Enlightenment era, as Vera Schwarz demonstrates in *The Chinese Enlightenment: Intellectuals and the Legacy of the May Fourth Movement of 1919* (Schwarcz 1986).[2] Her view constitutes in fact the mainstream May Fourth interpretation in mainland China and elsewhere since the 1930s. Since the late Qing dynasty, China had been humiliated by unequal treaties and obsessed with national survival at the continuing onslaught of foreign invaders. Disappointments with the socio-political instability during the two world wars led to the belief in the radical overhauling of feudal traditions. This period of national crises entangled with global calamity was a breeding ground for epistemic as well as cultural, ideological, and socio-political contentions. Schwarcz's book recounts how at the time Enlightenment rationality—modeled on European Enlightenment rationalism—and the establishment of science and democracy

2. The May Fourth movement turned the 1910s–1920s New Culture movement, which called for the modernization of Chinese language and culture, into a political movement. A game changer, it grew out of a student protest that began in Beijing on 4 May 1919. The students were protesting Western imperialism and the Chinese government's apparent inability to negotiate the Treaty of Versailles, which proposed to allow Japan, rather than China, to retain the province of Shandong after Germany's control of the territory during World War I. The ramifications of the event on cultural and political dimensions forced China to speed up modernization on all fronts. Often compared with the European Enlightenment, the May Fourth era, roughly from the 1910s to the 1920s, was dubbed "the May Fourth Enlightenment" or "The Chinese Enlightenment" by critics (Chow 1960; Schwartz 1986).

became prized as a cure-all for the country's setbacks on all fronts. My book, by contrast, intends to show that the same period also saw the burgeoning of the Chinese Counter-Enlightenment movement. While Enlightenment rhetoric stressed the power of reason, Counter-Enlightenment underlined the significance of the affective cultivation of the whole nation in solving China's problems. It emphasized the capabilities of the affects, a concept that would be made famous by Deleuze's 1980s study of Spinoza.[3] This book studies how the Counter-Enlightenment discourses in modern China, roughly beginning in the 1900s, peaking in the late 1920s, and continuing until the 1940s, put into relief the traditional Chinese concept of *qing* (情), which I equate with "the affects," to dialogue with Enlightenment rationality.

In Chinese, the word *qing* often appears in the saying *renqing shili* 人情事理, which literally means "human affective relations and the order of things" (see the conclusion). For the Chinese, not only does *qing* indicate emotions, feelings, "pre-individual bodily forces," and "automatic responses," but it denotes the relational forces that connect humans, living and non-living beings, atmospheric elements, and everything in the universe as a whole. In other words, the concept of *qing* constitutes the cosmological truth—a relational ontology that includes all living bodies, matter, and the cosmos in an affiliative entirety. While the perspective of the affects is called "an ontology of the human" in *The Affective Turn: Theorizing the Social* (Clough and Halley 2007, x), it is also indeed about such a relational ontology although its cosmological aspect was generally neglected until recently (Beaulieu 2016; see Chapter 5). I connect *qing* with affect, mainly because the two concepts, examined together, illuminate each other and help us arrive at a better understanding of both. This connection is made possible due to the popularity of Bergson in 1920s China that led to a reinterpretation of the traditional concept of *qing* in Bergsonian terms such as *sympathie diviniatrice* (divining sympathy; see Chapter 3). As a result, *qing* was identified as the central concept of the ancient Confucian text *Yijing* 易經 [The book of changes], while its principle of change governing all things in the universe was easily associated with the Bergsonian concept of change and ceaseless becoming.[4] In other

3. In the 2007 edited book *The Affective Turn: Theorizing the Social*, highlighting the concepts of "pre-individual bodily forces" and "automatic responses of the body," Patricia Clough identifies "the affective turn" in the humanities since the mid-1990s (Clough and Halley 2007, 2). "The body" here includes the technoscientific products with capacities to affect and to be affected. These concepts are derived from Brian Massumi's *Parables for the Virtual: Movement, Affect, Sensation* (2002).
4. Discussions of the *Book of Changes* can be seen throughout this study, except Chapter 2. See especially Chapter 5 for the topic. According to Alfred Huang and John Minford, two translators of *Yijng* into English, the literal meaning of *jing* 經 is *Dao*, or truth. Originally an oracular text, the *Zhouyi* 周易 [The *Yi* of the Zhou dynasty] that we use today teaches the laws of change. It is a systematic book approaching the unity of Heaven, Earth, and humanity. While the legendary ancient saint Fuxi 伏羲 drew the primary eight *gua* 八卦 (eight trigrams), it is said that Fuxi or Wen Wang 文王 (King Wen, 1112–1056 BCE) developed it into the sixty-four *gua* (hexagrams). It is likely that King Wen named and explained the meaning of the *gua* (*guaci* 卦辭, the hexagram judgments), while *yaoci* 爻辭 (line statements), attributed to Zhou Gong 周公 (Duke of Zhou, reigning in 1042–1035

words, modern Chinese intellectuals, inspired by their understanding of Bergson, rediscovered, or, to be more exact, reinvented their tradition. This is what I want to emphasize in this book: transcultural practice often leads to a renewed understanding of the self and the possibility of creative self-transformation.

For concepts to circulate in different cultures, translation is indispensable. Lexical choices then become crucial in the transmission (or modification) of knowledge. In the case of Chinese Counter-Enlightenment discourses, I use the term "the transcultural lexicon" to indicate how translation plays a key role in Chinese intellectuals' propagation of European life philosophy and their reformulation of Confucianism as such. The major events that contributed to the popularity of the huge set of transcultural lexicon related to the Counter-Enlightenment movement include the Chinese translation of Bergson's *L'Évolution créatrice* [Creative evolution] in 1918, the Aesthetic Education movement in the 1910s and 1920s, the famous 1923 Science and Lifeview debate, and the burgeoning of the theory of *weiqinglun* 唯情論 in the 1920s. How to transmit the concept of *weiqinglun* into English was an ordeal for me during the process of writing this book. I eventually decided to use "affectivism" to render the concept since, in its conceptualization, *weiqinglun* was intended to be an alternative to the translated concepts of *weixinlun* 唯心論 (idealism) and *weiwulun* 唯物論 (materialism). My decision to use such a neologism was reinforced by a June 2021 article in *Nature* entitled "The Rise of Affectivism," coauthored by dozens of leading cognitive scientists such as Daniel Dukes, Antonio Damasio, and Joseph E. LeDoux. Tentatively announcing the coming of "the era of affectivism," it underscores "the impact of affective phenomena" on human thought and behavior (Dukes et al. 2021). The dialectic of affect and reason is an ongoing research topic spanning science and the humanities, after all. Since literary theory announced the affective turn in 2007 (Clough and Halley), it has taken fourteen years for science to recognize the rise of affectivism. The Chinese intellectuals who promoted life philosophy in the 1920s likewise invented the concept of affectivism to highlight the synergy of spirit and matter, mind and body. For them, the affects connect thought and action. Although, due to the mainstream Enlightenment ideology established on mainland China in the 1930s, the term *weiqinlun* (together with the Counter-Enlightenment discourses it represented) has been largely forgotten, my study shows that its traces can nonetheless be detected in

BCE), named and explained the meaning of the 384 *yaoxiang* 爻象 (figures or images) although stories vary. Each *gua* is composed of six horizontal lines, which are called *yao* 爻, representing the intersecting of the *yin* (two broken lines) and the *yang* (a solid line). It is generally believed that the *Shiyi* 十翼 [Ten wings], attributed to Confucius (551–479 BCE) or different Confucian scholars in different times, commented and completed the *Yijing*. Of the *Ten Wings*, *Wings* 3 and 4 are called "Xiangzhuan" 象傳 [On the Images of the Hexagrams]. *Wings* 5 and 6 are called "Dazhuan" 大傳 [The great treatise] or "Xici" 繫辭 [Commentary on the appended statements], a cosmological and metaphysical treatise (Huang 2010, 1–6; Minford 2014, xiv–xv).

literary and philosophical texts, both during and after the 1920s. Many transcultural terms of European origin that came to China via Japan at the time, such as *lixing* 理性 (reason), *zhijue* 直覺 (intuition), and *renshengguan* 人生觀 (*Lebensanschuung*; lifeview), have survived and become part of modern Chinese everyday language. Without such translated terms, which are countless, and which Chinese today may think are originally Chinese, daily conversations are hardly possible. The foreign is absorbed unawares as an integral part of the self. Translation is in fact everywhere. Hence the ethical attitude entailed in transcultural studies: to recognize the numerous others in ourselves, so that we realize that the so-called national or racial "purity," "authenticity," and the like, are nothing but illusions.

Furthermore, East and West, rather than defined as marginal/center, or dominated/dominating, should be considered as co-living and co-becoming. Co-living necessitates co-becoming, because only when all the parties involved are willing to effect timely self-change in order to share global resources in peace can co-living and co-becoming, or living and prospering together, be achieved. The essentialist East/West dichotomy has led to numerous wars, resulting in tremendous destruction and human suffering. To avoid confrontation we should realize that, throughout global history, East-West encounters have effected mutual self-transformation (Hobson 2004; Standaert 2002; Phillips 2014; Osterhammel 2018; Heurtebise 2020).[5] Investigations of this book indicate that indeed the European Enlightenment itself had taken inspiration from the *Lixue* 理學 (philosophy of Universal Order) Confucianism transmitted by Christian missionaries to Europe, while Gottfried Wilhelm Leibniz (1646–1716) found the *Book of Changes* resonating with his own idea of binary arithmetic. Likewise, Eucken considered Confucianism akin to his own life philosophy. His interaction with the Chinese Lifeview intellectuals was a process of mutual illumination, while Bergson thought Buddhism and his own theory shared the idea of direct intuition. In the current century, Julia Kristeva acknowledged her indebtedness to the Chinese logic as expounded by Zhang Dongsun in the 1930s. A new understanding of East-West relationships based on two-way transculturation, rather than one-way acculturation of the "dominated" culture as maintained by postcolonialism, is begging for further studies.

Transculturality indicates as well the blurring of boundaries and freedom from prejudices (Epstein and Berry 1999; Peng 2010). As my study indicates, the

5. John M. Hobson defines the West as "a late developer" and the East as "an early developer," that discovered and led the world through "oriental globalization" from 500 to 1800. Nicholas Standaert points out that, in the seventeenth century, "it was the Chinese that occupied the dominant position" when European missionaries were allowed to stay in China. They were demanded to adapt to the native culture and communicate with the natives in the Chinese language (2002, 3–4). Both Jürgen Osterhammel and Kim M. Phillips denounce Eurocentrism while reexamining Said's concept of Orientalism. Jean-Yves Heurtebise reveals that Hegel's relegation of Chinese thought to the "pre-philosophical" stage contributes to the turn from "Sinophilia" to "Sinophobia" in Europe (2020, 94–126).

categorical dichotomies of modern/tradition, center/periphery, East/West are less valid than are the efforts to cross the divide and connect the seeming opposites. Connectivity is the key to transcultural practice. While proponents of the Lifeview school in China have often been dubbed "conservative" and "unscientific" because of their hold onto traditional wisdom, this book shows their informed opinions during the epistemic debate with the Science school and their audacity to challenge the so-called "progressive" mainstream. Interestingly, Confucianism, which had long been denounced since the May Fourth era as responsible for China's backwardness and failure, was revived almost overnight in the late 1980s. Deng Xiaoping's Open Door policy has ushered in a new era of national confidence emboldened by the continuing growth in wealth and power, while the Confucius Institutes recently established worldwide are now flaunting China's soft power. It is high time to reevaluate the Lifeview intellectuals together with their philosophy of life from a transcultural stance.

Acknowledgments

For this book I am indebted to more people than I can ever enumerate. Especially grateful am I to Ying-shih Yü (1930–2021) for his seminal articles debunking mainstream theory of May Fourth Enlightenment rationality. Without his groundbreaking work I would not have had the courage to pursue such a topic as the affects and modern Chinese Counter-Enlightenment, challenging decades-long established views of modern Chinese Enlightenment. The completion of the preliminary draft of this book manuscript happened to mark the demise on August 1 of a great teacher of Chinese intellectual history, for whose contribution we are all deeply obliged. Leo Oufan Lee's *The Romantic Generation of Modern Chinese Writers* (1973), still a must-read today, points to the question: Whence came the modern Chinese Romantic spirit in addition to the Western model? David Der-wei Wang's 2015 book on the lyrical tradition of *qing* (affect) in modern Chinese literature was also a great inspiration when I tried to conceptualize the May Fourth dialectic of affect and reason. Without their encouragement and support I would not have been able to withstand the prolonged labor of deliberation and writing for over ten years.

Gratitude must be due to my colleagues in philosophy at the Institute of Chinese Literature and Philosophy (ICLP), Academia Sinica, including Huang Kuan-min, Lin Wei-chieh, and Fabian Heubel, to name just a few. Sharing thoughts with them for decades has been a sort of transdisciplinary training for me. For more than a dozen years they have engaged in the concept of transcultural studies, a pioneering effort in conjunction with colleagues in Europe and the United States, especially those in the Center for Transcultural Asian Studies at the University of Freiburg. Transcultural theory still has much room for joint endeavor and further development. I thank ICLP for providing the funds necessary for proofreading at the final stage of preparing the manuscript. Peter Chi-fan Lin, who meticulously checked all the chapters, and the two anonymous reviewers made invaluable suggestions for revisions. This book would not have been in its current shape without them. The librarians and assistants of ICLP, coordinated by Bell Ko-ching Tang, were also indispensable for the completion of this book.

The "Transcultural Sino-Island" Project of National Sun Yat-sen University at Kaohsiung, led by Hsi-san Lai and Mark McConaghy, has spurred me on to deliberate the concept of transcultural co-living and co-becoming, a concept inspired by the idea of "shengsheng" in the *Book of Changes* as well as Deleuzean theory. With the Russo-Ukrainian War breaking out on 24 February 2022 and the rising tensions across the Taiwan Strait, such a concept seems all the more urgent. I thank Daniel Hu for his expertise on the translations of the *Book of Changes*. My young colleagues in Hong Kong, including Lik-kwan Cheung, Ouyang Kaibin, and Kevin Ting Kit Yau, have inadvertently constituted a brainstorming team for me. Their erudition and incredible insight are amazing. Text messages with Ari Larissa Heinrich, who has checked on my work from time to time, seem to be progress reports that always earn feedback and encouragements. Last but not least, I shall never thank Daw-hwan Wang enough, my spouse and best friend, for his expertise in evolutionary biology that has transformed my perception of modern Chinese intellectual history.

A note should be given on the translations of passages from other languages into English in this book. The translations are mine unless otherwise indicated. Every new translation, whether of recent or old texts, is a fresh interpretation. When I venture a translation that is unconventional, I am reinterpreting a Chinese or foreign text from an original perspective on modern China in a global context.

Abbreviations

BXQJ	Complete Works of Bing Xin
CYPQJ	Complete Works of Mr. Cai Yuanpei
FDMQJ	Complete Works of Fang Dongmei
LSMQJ	Complete Works of Liang Shuming
LXQJ	Complete Works of Lu Xun
MW	The Middle Works, 1899–1924, by John Dewey
LW	The Later Works, 1925–1953, by John Dewey
NB	The Nameless Book, by Wumigsnhi
NKZS	Complete Works of Nishida Kitarō
SCWQJ	Complete Works of Shen Congwen
YBSHJ	Collected Works of Ice-Drinking Chamber, by Liang Qichao
ZJSJ	Collected Works of Zhang Jingsheng
ZQZWJ	Collected Works of Zhu Qianzhi
ZTYQJ	Complete Works of Zhang Taiyan

Introduction

Lu Xun and Counter-Enlightenment

Moral rectitude originates from *qing* (情 the affects), rather than *hui* (慧 reason, or intellect). When not based on *qing*, even reasoning as perfect as a small vase and rhetoric as smooth as the hot oil lubricating carriage axles would not prevail. When based on *qing*, it inspires either admiration or animadversions.

—Zhang Taiyan, "Si xiangyuan xia" 思鄉原下 [On hypocrisy, Part 2, 1910] (*ZTYQJ* 4:137)[1]

As I have not yet abandoned hope for the promise of the future, I remain eager to hear the voices of the heart-mind of all wise men and earnestly entreat them to share with me their inner light. For this inner light can break through darkness and silence, while the voices of the heart-mind can provide deliverance from falsehood and chicanery.

—Lu Xun, "Po e sheng lun" 破惡聲論 [Toward a refutation of malevolent voices, 1908] (*LXQJ* 8:23; Lu Xun 2011, 40)[2]

Lu Xun and *Qing* (Affect): The Heart-Mind Has Its Reasons

Depicted as "the chief commander of China's cultural revolution" and deified by Mao Zedong as "the Saint of modern China," Lu Xun has gradually been recognized as a more complex figure than a symbol of party ideology (Goldman 1982, 447; Lovell 2009, xxxii; Yau 2023).[3] During his student days in Japan, he was a

1. "Sixiangyuan xia" is collected in *Zhang Taiyan quanji* 章太炎全集 [Complete works of Zhang Taiyan] (*ZTYQJ* 4:133–38). The original sentence for "Moral rectitude originates from *qing*, rather than reason" is *Lide zi qing bu zi hui* 立德自情不自慧. *Qing* 情 is more appropriately translated as "affect" than "feeling," for reasons explained in this chapter.
2. Jon Eugene von Kowallis's translation with minor modifications (Lu Xun 2011). "Po e sheng lun" is collected in *Lu Xun quanji* 魯迅全集 [Complete works of Lu Xun] (*LXQJ* 8:23–37).
3. Merle Goldman's "The Political Use of Lu Xun" discusses how in different periods Lu Xun's life and work were twisted to fit the latest mutation in party policy (Goldman 1982). For a biography of

proponent of ancient Chinese wisdom, denouncing scientific rationality, as can be seen in the five essays he published in *Henan Monthly* 河南月刊 in 1907 and 1908. The journal was the official organ of the Henan Province Branch of the Chinese Revolutionary Confederation (Zhonghua Tongmenghui 中華同盟會) in Tokyo, edited by Liu Shipei 劉師培 (1884–1919), an anti-Manchurian revolutionary who fled to Japan in February 1907 and became an anarchist there under the guidance of Kōtoku Shūshui 幸德秋水 (1871–1911; Wang 2010, 86–87; 2011, 70–72). These early essays written by Lu Xun, in infamously archaic language, have since posed a challenge to many critics. Perplexing as they are, if examined together these texts in fact share the tenet of Counter-Enlightenment thinking, which was prevalent in Japan at the time (Lin Shaoyan 2018, 347–52).[4] The second epigraph above, much more readable in translation, is quoted from the opening paragraph of "Toward a Refutation of Malevolent Voices," published in December 1908.

Before analyzing this essay, it should be noted that Lu Xun's mentor, the late Qing revolutionary Zhang Taiyan in exile in Japan then, consistently critiqued Enlightenment scientism and progressivism. The archaic language Lu Xun uses in these early essays was no doubt due to Zhang Taiyan's influence. An expert on Old Text scholarship, Zhang advocated pre-Qin thinkers and considered Confucius the most significant among them, as opposed to the New Text scholars who maintained the incontestable status of Confucianism as religion. For Zhang, the six Classics (六經 liujing) were historical texts that evidenced Confucius as a historian and an educator. With recourse to Buddhist and Daoist thought to complement Confucianism, Zhang believes that the *Book of Changes* is not some mysterious book of premonitions. Rather, it is a record of ancient society and its daily life experiences, while Confucianism is mainly about human affairs or the way of the world (Zhang 2011, 52–68; Wang 1985, 46–67).[5] All these concepts are integral to the May Fourth life philosophy (*rensheng zhexue* 人生哲學), as this book argues. Distrusting hypocritical doctrinaires and flowery rhetoric, Zhang Taiyan highlights the value of texts (wen 文), or literature in a broad sense, as the indispensable human medium for sincere affective expressions. For him, the origin of morality is by no means reason 慧 (*hui*),

Lu Xun, see David Pollard's *The True Story of Lu Xun* (2002). For translation of Lu Xun's fictional works, see Julia Lovell's *The Real Story of Ah-Q and Other Tales of China: The Complete Fiction of Lu Xun* (2009). Kevin Ting Kit Yau reads Lu Xun, Chen Duxiu, and Cai Yuanpei through the lens of the dialectic of affect and reason.

4. Lin Shaoyang's study is the first to investigate systematically the connection between late Qing intellectuals sojourning in Japan and the Japanese Counter-Enlightenment movement.

5. For Zhang Taiyan's view of the great masters, see "Lun zhuzi xue" 論諸子學 [On the great masters] (*ZTYQJ* 4.1: 48–67); for his view of the six Classics as historical records, see "Lun jingshi shilu buying wugu huaiyi" 論經史實錄不應無故懷疑 [The historical truths recorded in the Classics should not be offhandedly doubted] (4.2:573–81); For his view of *Yijing* as a record of ancient society and daily experiences, see "Yilun" 易論 [On the *Book of changes*] (3:385–92).

but the affects 情 (*qing*), which are stirring in literary texts and reverberating like music (*ZTYQJ* 4:137).[6]

At the turn of the twentieth century, Chinese intellectuals taking refuge from Manchurian persecution or studying in Japan witnessed the Enlightenment and Counter-Enlightenment movements during the Meiji (1868–1912) and Taishō (1912–1926) periods. Reformers and revolutionaries such as Liang Qichao, Cai Yuanpei, and Wu Zhihui 吳稚暉 (1865–1953), prominent May Fourth Counter-Enlightenment and life philosophy leaders, were also sojourning in Tokyo around this time. While Fukusawa Yukichi 福澤諭吉 (1835–1901) was Japan's leading Enlightenment thinker during the Meiji period, the most famous Counter-Enlightenment intellectual was Nakae Chōmin 中江兆民 (1847–1901), who, known for his translation of Jean-Jacques Rousseau's *Social Contract* (1762) between 1882 and 1883, was lauded as the Rousseau of the East (Lin 2018, 388). We will see in Chapter 1, how Nishida Kitarō, founder of the Kyoto school philosophy and advocate of life philosophy (*jinsei tetsugaku* 人生哲學, or *seimei shugi* 生命主義),[7] has recourse to irrational concepts such as *ujō* 有情 (sentient beings) in Buddhism, "Gefühl" (feeling) in German Romanticism, and *qing* in traditional Chinese texts to refute Enlightenment rationality. Central to Lu Xun's early writings published in Tokyo as well, these concepts expressed in traditional Chinese and Buddhist terms are particularly illuminating for this study.

In "Malevolent Voices," Lu Xun's Counter-Enlightenment stance is crystal clear when he writes: "The confessions of Augustine, Tolstoy, and Rousseau embody true greatness; these are the exuberant voices of the heart-mind" (*LXQJ* 8:27; Lu Xun 2011, 48). Through voices of the heart-mind (*xinsheng* 心聲), "the inner light" (*neiyao* 內曜) is able to shine through the suffocating darkness and "silence," which are forced upon the people by the sophistry of "rash doctrines" and "reckless demagogues" (*LXQJ* 8:23; Lu Xun 2011, 40). What doctrines and demagogues is Lu Xun referring to? He takes Ernst Haeckel (1834–1919, German zoologist and philosopher) for an example of those who, endeavoring to eradicate religions as superstitions, worship instead science and build a temple for reason (*lixing* 理性; *risei* in Japanese; *LXQJ* 8:28; Lu Xun 2011, 51). Note the juxtaposition between the sound of the heart-mind, which refers to *qing* in Chinese tradition, and *lixing*, which is a Japanese *kanji* term originating from the West. The sound of the heart-mind,

6. These lines fully disclose Zhang Taiyan's views: "The texts [wen 文] of the six Classics are all elegant and magnificent, the best of which can be attuned to music and sung, while the rest can also be like meandering melodies. As recorded in the six Classics, the language teaching morals is distributed properly in them. When read aloud, it inspires adoration, while its repetition is never tiring."

7. The term "jinsei tetsugaku" 人生哲學, rendering "philosophy of life," appeared in Takahashi Gorō's 高橋五郎 manual of English literary and philosophical terms translated into Japanese (Takahashi 1909, 114–15). Later Japanese critics would use the term *seimei shugi* 生命主義 to discuss Nishida Kitarō's life philosophy (see Chapter 1).

which yearns for the divine, is contrasted with scientific rationality. The former "can provide deliverance from the falsehood and chicanery" of scientism, because it expresses the natural feelings of the people, uncontaminated by theoretical hypocrisy. In other words, the sound of the heart-mind reaches truth without depending on reason. The "inner light" that can break through darkness and silence is the light that comes from the heart-mind; it is the "inner sincerity" that seeks to be expressed in words. "Inner sincerity" (*cheng yu zhong* 誠於中) is a citation from *Daxue* 大學 [*The great learning*],[8] while the inner light refers to intuitive knowledge, or *liangzhi* 良知 in the words of Wang Yangming 王陽明 (1472–1529), a Ming dynasty proponent of *xinxue* 心學 (the Heart-Mind philosophy) as an alternative for *lixue* 理學 (the philosophy of Universal Order). It is also what Nishida Kitarō understands as *la connaissance par coeur* (knowledge of the heart) in modern French philosophy. Chapter 1 discusses this in detail. It is important to bear in mind that the heart-mind in Chinese philosophy refutes the heart/mind dichotomy à la Descartes, or feeling/reason dualism. For the Chinese, the heart-mind is capable of cognitive as well as affective function.[9] The Counter-Enlightenment intellectuals discussed in this study all maintain that, far from being polarized and exclusive to each other, affect and reason are complementary and mutually reinforced, affect encompassing reason.

In "Malevolent Voices" it is emphasized that the heart-mind has its reasons, over which the mind has no control. Lu Xun writes:

> When one returns to the heart-mind, one can keep to his own faith without chiming in on the chorus sung by the world. The sound of the heart-mind is substantial and cannot be self-controlled, because it originates from one's heart-mind and reverberates in one's brain like waves. (*LXQJ* 8:24; Lu Xun 2011, 41)[10]

One's heart must be touched before one's brain begins to respond. The heart, being part of the body as the brain is, is connected to the universal order of affect that stirs the body. For Lu Xun, religions are necessary because they have been created for the need of the human heart-mind to aspire to the divine. A single God or pantheism makes no difference. Pantheism practiced in China since four thousand years ago has expressed rural dwellers' understanding of natural phenomena. Such faith is not to be found with the gentry class, who are only concerned with utilitarianism and petty gains and have no interest at all in the mysteries of life. Lu Xun declares: "Thus

8. It is said in *The Great Learning*: "*Cheng yu zhong xing yu wai*" 誠於中形於外 (Inner sincerity will be expressed outward). James Legge's 1861 translation reads, "What truly is within will be manifested without" (2014, 235).
9. For an analysis of the philosophical significance of the heart-mind in Chinese philosophy, see Yu Ning, "Heart and Cognition in Ancient Chinese Philosophy" (2007).
10. The original for "return[s] to the heart-mind" is *fan qi xi* 反其心, meaning "return to the original self," or "return to one's conscience." The original for "cannot be self-controlled" is *buneng ziyi* 不能自已. Von Kowallis renders it as "[his speech must] not circumscribe or contain them [his own views]."

the most urgent task today is to rid ourselves of this hypocritical gentry; superstition may remain" (*LXQJ* 8:28; Lu Xun 2011, 51).[11] I will explain in Chapter 3 how a decade later "heart-mind" 心 is used to render the French concepts of "*conscience*" and "*l'esprit*" in Zhang Dongsun's 張東蓀 (1886–1973) 1918 translation of Henri Bergson's *Creative Evolution* (1907). Zhang's monumental translated text constituted the theoretical basis for the May Fourth Counter-Enlightenment movement.

It is worthwhile to investigate deeper what Lu Xun calls the "sound of the heart-mind." The concept is derived from the Han dynasty Confucian Yang Xiong's 揚雄 (53 BCE–18 CE) "Wen shen" 問神 [Questions on the divine] in *Fa yan* 法言 [Exemplary words] (Yang 2010). Following the dialogic mode in *The Analects* of Confucius, Yang writes at the outset: "Someone asks about the divine. I answer: 'It is the heart-mind.'" What is then the "sound of the heart-mind"? According to Yang,

> Speech is the sound of the heart-mind, and writing, its graphic depiction. When sound and graphic depiction take form, great and petty persons are revealed. Aren't the speech and writing of the great and the petty where the affects are stirring (*dongqing* 動情)?[12]

I translate *dongqing* as "the affects are stirring," because *qing* in traditional Chinese thought is more than feeling or emotion. It indicates the force-relations constituted by the energies released from celestial, living, and non-living bodies in the universe. This kind of force-relations is also the main concern of Deleuzian affect theory. In fact, "affect" is most often rendered as *qingdong* 情動 in modern Japanese and Chinese. For Gilles Deleuze (1950–1995), while explicating Baruch Spinoza's (1632–1677) affect theory, all forms of matter and life are governed by such force-relations.[13] Chapter 5 discusses how, thanks to the popularity of Spinoza and Bergson in the May Fourth era, the concept of *qing* derived from the *Book of Changes* can be connected with affect theory.

---

11. The original for "the need . . . to aspire to the divine" (*xiangshang zhi xuyao* 向上之需要) means literally "the need to strive upward." In Lu Xun's text, "*xiangshang*" as a rule refers to the aspiration to the divine high above us.
12. The Chinese original reads: *Yan, xin sheng ye; shu, xin hua ye. Sheng hua xing, junzi xiaoren jian yi. Sheng hua zhe, junzi xiaoren zhi suoyi dongqing hu* 言，心聲也；書，心畫也。聲畫形，君子小人見矣。聲畫者，君子小人之所以動情乎。The best rendering of these lines I have read is by Béatrice L'Haridon into French. The last two lines of this quote are rendered by her as follows: "Sons et tracés ne sont-ils pas le lieu où se meuvent les affects de l'homme de bien et l'homme de peu?" (Yang 2010, 43). It is apparent that L'Haridon has the affect theory in mind when she translates Yang Xiong's work.
13. According to Malissa Gregg and Gregory Seigworth, "Affect is in many ways synonymous with force or forces of encounter. . . . Affect can be understood then as a gradient of bodily capacity—a supple incrementalism of ever-modulating force-relations. . . . Hence, affect's always immanent capacity of extending further still: both into and out of the interstices of the inorganic and non-living, the intracellular divulgences of sinew, tissue, and gut economies, and the vaporous evanescences of the incorporeal (events, atmospheres, feeling-tones)" (2010, 2).

Qing: Universal Co-living and Co-becoming

As we can see in "Malevolent Voices," Lu Xun explicates the concept of *qing*, with recourse to a peculiar combination of natural science and traditional thought such as Confucianism and Buddhism. After the lines quoted in the second epigraph, Lu Xun continues to point out how, due to the nature of matter (*wuxing* 物性) and biological principles (*shengli* 生理), all *youqing* 有情, a Buddhist term for "sentient beings," meaning all living creatures[14]—including insects, birds, crawling animals, and humans—are affected by external forces such as wind, sun, moon, the ebbs and flows of tides, and seasons; in the midst of all these external forces they either feel inflicted or blessed, and "changes are bound to occur" (*LXQJ* 8:23; Lu Xun 2011, 41). Here, the sense of the co-living, or co-becoming, of the myriad things in the universe as taught by the concept of *qing* is more than clear. Nevertheless, according to Lu Xun, when it comes to humans, one aspect differentiates them from other sentient beings. Although likewise swayed by natural phenomena, their sentiments inevitably affected by external forces—feeling elated in spring, focused in summer, desolate in autumn, and somber in winter—they are unique among living creatures in that they are able to use speech (*yan* 言) to express their inner light. Perhaps greater than any natural forces (*tianwu* 天物), the power of speech, or the sound of the heart-mind, can reawaken the entire land and shake the human world with a sense of awe, which is the beginning for humans to aspire to the divine (*LXQJ* 8:23–24; Lu Xun 2011, 41).[15] Lu Xun's indebtedness to Yang Xiong is more than clear. Darwinian biology, a major source of inspiration for modern philosophy and a recurrent topic in this book, no doubt plays a role here in Lu Xun's thinking. His interest in biology can also be seen in his first Tokyo essay, "Ren de lishi" 人的歷史 [The history of man, 1907], which is an overview of the history of evolutionary biology (8:8–24).

Let's go back to the opening lines of "Malevolent Voices": "Corroded at the core and wavering spiritually, our once-glorious nation seems destined to wither away of its own devices amid the internecine quarreling among its offspring" (*LXQJ* 8:23; Lu Xun 2011, 41). Throughout the essay the "once-glorious nation" is juxtaposed with twentieth-century China. The latter is beset by foreign military, economic, and cultural invasions that culminate in the hypocritical doctrines of Enlightenment

14. The Tang dynasty monk Huilin 慧琳 points out that *youqing* is originally *sattva* in Sanskrit. *Sa* means *you* 有 (to have), while *ttva* means *qing* 情 (sentiment), hence 'having sentiment.' It is also called *zhongsheng* 眾生 (all beings): "Here we use *zhongsheng* as another term for *youqing*" (Huilin 1983, 54:621). According to a recent study, "In Buddhism *youqing* (*sattva*, transliterated as *saduopo*, *sachueifu*, or *sachuei*, and formerly translated as *zhongsheng*) means 'all living beings with sentiment'" (Ho 2009, 114). *Youqing* in Chinese is pronounced as *ujō* in Japanese.

15. In Lu Xun's original text, *quran* 瞿然 means "a sense of awe" when one faces the supernatural, while *xiangshang zhi quanyu* 向上之權輿 means "the beginning . . . to aspire to the divine," or to strive upward.

scientism, the malevolent voices. They are a contrast to the sound of the heart-mind, which bespeaks *qing*, or affect, as the everlasting universal order of co-living and co-becoming. The "internecine quarreling among its offspring" refers to the late Qing debate on Enlightenment rationality (the faith in science and progressivism) and affective Enlightenment (the faith in the sound of the heart-mind and traditional Chinese values). Of the latter, Zhang Taiyan was a prominent harbinger. Like his mentor, Lu Xun valorizes ancient China and points out the necessity of traditional festivities worshiping gods, because these celebrations are farmers' brief respites from their yearlong labor and commemorate their spiritual connections with the divine. He likens these festivities to the chanting of poets, which depicts the yearning of the heart-mind, and the stretching and bending of dancers, which limber up the body. Myths and fables such as the mythical dragons in ancient China, deemed irrational "in the name of science," were, however, created by the divine imagination (*shensi* 神思) of the ancients. Lu Xun stresses the importance of myths in Western literature, arts, and philosophy (*LXQJ* 8:30; Lu Xun 2011, 54). The refutation of malevolent voices thus indicates a return to the "once-glorious nation," the traditional China uncontaminated by European Enlightenment rationalism, which justifies colonialism and military infiltrations into "backward" and "weak" countries such as China, Poland, and India. Although backward in the eye of the world, the people of Poland are very affectionate (*duo qingsu* 多情愫) and love freedom and peace; India, by contrast, is famous for its philosophies, religions, codes of morality, and arts and literature (*LXQJ* 8:33; Lu Xun 2011, 60). Nevertheless, *qing*, the principle of universal co-living and co-becoming, engenders empathy for the weak among peoples around the globe. At the end of the essay, Lu Xun praises those who fought for the freedom of oppressed peoples: the Polish general Józeph Bem (1794–1850), who participated in the liberation war of the Hungarian people in 1849, and the British Romantic poet Lord Byron (1788–1824), who led the campaign for the Greek war of independence around 1824.

The power of literature and arts is a central theme in Lu Xun's early Tokyo essays. In "Moluo shili shuo" 魔羅詩力說 [On the power of Māra poetry] (*LXQJ* 1:63–115), published in February and March 1908, he maintains that "the most powerful heritage of human civilization is the sound of the heart-mind (63) and that "Poets and bards use their wonderful songs to convey their intuitional instinct (*lingjue* 靈覺) so as to beautify and improve our temperaments and magnify our thinking" (69). A Buddhist term, *lingjue* refers to *bodhi* 菩提[16]—the awakening of "the intuitional instinct that lies dormant in all beings" (Nyanatiloka 1945, 13–14). It is the attainment of true enlightenment, when one, awakening from the slumber or stupor inflicted upon the mind by the defilements of phenomena

16. According to Ding Fubao, *lingjue* refers to the innate, intuitive understanding of *bodhi* (1956, 2:852), which means Buddha's ultimate wisdom (4:2110).

and ego-identity, comprehends the Four Noble Truths.[17] As the "real knowledge gained through intuition by some extraordinary seers or mystics" (*LXQJ* 1:58), and by poets as well, it is also exactly what Lu Xun calls "the inner light," or the innate knowledge in all humans. He constantly juxtaposes literature and science, writing in one instance: "All great literary works in the world are keys to the secrets of life. Literature honestly reflects the facts and laws of life, while science is incapable of doing the same" (1:71–72). He lauds Romantic poets such as Lord Byron, Robert Burns (1759–1796), and Percy Bysshe Shelley (1792–1822) as "great men" who defied hypocrisy and sympathized with the oppressed (1:82–87). Their revolutionary spirit fills both their poetry singing of justice, freedom, truth, and love, and their action aiming to improve life. He calls Shelley "a man of divine imagination," who enjoyed contemplating nature and was infatuated with the secrets of life and death (85). Coming from "palpitations of the heart-mind naturally attuned to sounds of nature" (86),[18] Shelley's lyrical poetry is a divine creation unmatched by none but the works of Shakespeare (1564–1616) and Edmund Spencer (1552–1599; poet of the Medieval romance *The Fairie Queene*). By contrast, when the intellect is devoted solely to science, the aim is to control nature and discover its laws, while the most inferior will never feel their heart-minds stirring when experiencing the magnificent natural phenomena such as the change of seasons.

"Kexueshi jiaopian" 科學史教篇 [Lessons from the history of science], published in June 1908 (*LXQJ* 1:25–43), is a free rendering of Kimura Shūnkiji's 木村駿吉 (1866–1938) "General View of the History of Science," introduction to his 1890 book, *Kagaku no genri* 科學之原理 [The principles of science] (Song Shengquan 2019). It was a physics primer for students of humanities at First Higher School in Tokyo (Kimura 1890, 1–2). While giving an objective overview of the development of science and lauding its stellar achievements, Kimura keeps on reminding the reader that science does not cover everything in human life, that literature and arts are likewise essential, and that throughout Greek and Roman history and the Middle Ages there were repeated shifts from one extreme to the other. What should be maintained, nevertheless, is "the middle course," so that religion, morality, and the arts can prosper along with science (8–9). The conclusion points out the limits of science: it is unable to explain the freedom of will and the wonder of the unknowable (188–89). Lu Xun's essay basically follows this line of thinking. He writes:

> Science is the holy light that shines on the world. . . . However, when the world worships nothing but knowledge, life will completely wither. In the long run, our beautiful, noble feelings will deplete, while our sharp thought will be lost. The so-called science thus also becomes nothing. (*LXQJ* 1:35)

17. The four Noble Truths are "the truths about the universal sway of suffering, about its origin, its extinction, and the path leading to its extinction" (Nyanatiloka 1945, 2).
18. The original sentence is "*xinxian zhi dong, zi yu tianlai hediao*" 心弦之動, 自與天籟合調.

For Lu Xun, just as Isaac Newton (1643–1727), Niels Bohr (1885–1962; Danish physicist), Immanuel Kant (1724–1804), and Charles Darwin (1809–1882) are indispensable to the world, so are writers, musicians, and artists, including Shakespeare, Beethoven, Raphaelllo (1483–1520, Italian painter and architect), and Thomas Carlyle (1795–1881; British historian and satirical writer). Although it seems odd that Kant as a philosopher is listed here with renowned scientists, we will see in this book that his tendency of turning philosophy into a cognitive science made him a target of criticism for all life philosophers in Germany, France, Japan, and China at the turn of the twentieth century.

The critique of science and materialism on the one hand, and absolute idealism and individualism on the other, is the major topic in "Wenhua pianzhi lun" 文化偏至論 [On the extremes of cultural development], published in August 1908 (*LXQJ* 1:44–62). Basically, Lu Xun asks one question in the essay: Should Chinese culture be replaced by Western culture? At the onslaught of foreign invasions on all fronts, many Chinese people have lost faith in their own traditions and believe that the way to wealth and power is to transplant Western culture to China. The problem is that culture is fast changing, and the Western culture in Lu Xun's time had come a long way from Greek and Roman traditions to Catholicism, the Protestant Reformation, and the French Revolution. Lu Xun writes, "All civilizations evolve from previous tracks; they go to extremes in order to correct the past" (49). While the French Revolution, overhauling the despotic regime, resulted in the rule of the masses, the Industrial Revolution brought about unprecedented flourishing of material culture in the nineteenth century. The "extremes of cultural development" thus refers to the overemphasis on matter (*wuzhi* 物質; *busshitsu* ぶっしつ) and the masses (*zhongshu* 眾數 or 重庶): materialism and the tyranny of the majority (46). At the end of the nineteenth century, yet another turn in intellectual history was witnessed: a reaction against materialism (*wuzhi zhuyi* 物質主義; *busshitsu shugi* ぶっしつしゅぎ) and the rise of individualism (*geren zhuyi* 個人主義; *kojin shugi* こじんしゅぎ), which led to "the extreme emphasis on the self" (*jiduan zhi zhuwo* 極端之主我; *kyokutan no shuga* きょくたんのしゅが; 50). Arthur Schopenhauer (1788–1860), Søren Kierkegaard (1813–1855), and Henrik Ibsen (1828–1906) are listed in the essay as leading subjectivists. The most outstanding was Friedrich Nietzsche (1844–1900), whose concept of Superman, valorizing the absolute free will of rare geniuses as a dire contempt for social norms, astounded the whole of Europe (51–52).

For Lu Xun, neither extreme objectivism (*keguan zhuyi* 客觀主義; *kyakkan shugi* きゃっかんしゅぎ), as of materialism, nor extreme subjectivism (*zhuguan zhuyi* 主觀主義; *shukan shugi* しゅかんしゅぎ), as of the idealist philosophy of Georg Wilhelm Friedrich Hegel (1770–1831), is completely plausible (*LXQJ* 1:54). He is aware that idealist philosophy was not exclusive to Hegel's intellectualism that overemphasized reason (*zhuzhi* 主智; *shuchi* しゅち). He points out another line of idealism: the Romanticist and Classicist Earl of Shaftesbury (1671–1713) and

Rousseau, who considered feeling and desire an essential part of human spirit. By contrast, what Nietzsche envisioned was a Superman with the absolute will (*yili* 意力; *iryoku* いりょく) that challenged the will of God (54–55). The best would be Friedrich Schiller (1759–1805), whose concept of "the whole person" (*quanren* 全人; *zenjin* ぜんじん) combines intellect (*zhixing* 知性; *chisei* ちせい) and sensibility in a perfect harmony (54). Lu Xun foresees a new culture emerging in the twentieth century, which awakens people from the hypocrisy and illusion of the objective world and strengthens their inner life while deepening "the meaning of life" (*rensheng zhi yiyi* 人生之意義; *jinsei no igi* じんせいのいぎ) and the dignity of the individual. China in its present predicament should be aware of the cultural trends of the world, avoid their extremes, and learn from their illuminating ideas. He hopes China will become "a nation of human beings" (*renguo* 人國), free from the bondage of materialism and respecting the independent spirit of humans.

In the above two passages, for Western terms rendered into Japanese *kanji* translations and then adopted into Chinese, I deliberately add their *hirakana* pronunciations after the Chinese pronunciations in parenthesis. Numerous terms that we take for granted as Japanese or Chinese in fact are translated from the West, belonging to what I call "the transcultural lexicon" in this book, without which modern Chinese as well as Japanese can hardly express themselves. The texts of Lu Xun's early essays mix archaic Chinese and Buddhist terms with a huge transcultural lexicon, making these essays even more unintelligible. It is indeed astonishing to find that so many Chinese expressions by origin are not Chinese at all. My purpose in pointing out this fact is, however, more than identifying their origins. Take, for instance, the term *quanren*, or the whole person. It is a recurrent theme in this book, meaning a person whose body, mind, heart, and spirit are in perfect harmony (Luserke-Jaqui 2018; Solomon 1983, 53).[19] A term meaning "der ganze Mensch" in German and made famous by Schiller, it is able to connect advocates of Japanese, Chinese, and German Aesthetic Education movements in a transcultural context, as Chapter 2 points out. I call terms like these the transcultural lexicon, while the investigation in this book benefits mainly from the transcultural lexicon as methodology. More will be said about this below.

19. Matthias Luserke-Jaqui considers "the whole person" as the central idea in the aesthetic theory of Schiller. According to Robert C. Solomon, "Schiller did not try to reduce the whole of human experience to a single sphere, whether aesthetic, moral, cognitive, or religious, but argued that all function together as integral parts of the whole person" (1983, 53).

The Lifeview Movement

Lu Xun's early essays published in Tokyo provide excellent entry points into the 1923 Science and Lifeview debate, the main subject matter of this book.[20] Later critics, when revisiting the debate, usually emphasize the essentialist dichotomy of materialism versus spiritualism that divided the two camps and, as a rule, sweepingly call the Lifeview school conservatives who stubbornly opposed modernity and progress. The most prominent example is D. W. Y. Kwok's book *Scientism in Chinese Thought, 1900–1950*, which concentrates on the Science school and pays little attention to the epistemic argument of the Lifeview school (Kwok 1965). Lin Yu-sheng's *The Crisis of Chinese Consciousness: Radical Antitraditionalism in the May Fourth Era* also points out the "total iconoclasm" of the period, without taking into consideration the revival of traditional philosophies that challenged scientism (Lin 1979), not to mention Vera Schwarcz's *The Chinese Enlightenment*. Such a mainstream view is what I intend to refute in this book. My investigation shows that the Chinese Lifeview movement was a well-orchestrated transcultural event aiming to connect tradition with the global Counter-Enlightenment movement. Involving most of the famous intellectuals at the time with a resounding impact on the philosophy, literature, and arts nearly throughout the twentieth century and well into the new millennium, the movement has remained surprisingly underresearched. Although the debate itself did not break out until 1923, the Lifeview movement, led by Liang Qichao and Cai Yuanpei, had in fact begun in the early 1910s and reached its peak in the mid-1920s. Its influences continued throughout the 1940s and lingered on to the turn of the twenty-first century. Postwar writers such as Wumingshi (1917–2002), discussed in the Conclusion, and Mu Xin (1927–2011; Ouyang 2021a, 2021b), were renowned offspring of the Lifeview and Aesthetic Education movements. As this book reveals, even the postwar New Confucianism in Hong Kong and Taiwan, still flourishing, has benefited from its heritage: life philosophy. It is impossible, however, to delve into detailed discussions of the immediate and long-term impact of the Lifeview movement on literature and philosophy without risking overlengthening the book. My overall intention is to direct readers to possible further investigations along this line. This book focuses on the Science and Lifeview debate during the period from the 1910s to the 1920s. The first thing to note is that both the Japanese and the Chinese

20. The debate started with Zhang Junmai's 張君勱 talk titled "Lifeview" at Tsinghua University 清華大學 in Beijing on 14 February 1923 (Zhang 1977, 1:1–13). The text was later published in *Tsinghua zhoukan* 清華週刊 [Tsinghua weekly] no. 272 (9 March 1923): 3–10, and severely criticized by the geologist Ding Wenjiang 丁文江 in a series of articles appearing in *Nuli zhoubao* 努力周報 [Endeavor weekly] from 12 April to 3 June 1923 (1977a, b, c). These articles and other articles of both sides of the debate were collected in a volume edited by Hu Shi (Shizhi 適之) and others in 1923 as *Kexue yu renshengguan* 科學與人生觀 [Science and lifeview], Shanghai: Yadong tushuguan. In this edition all articles start from page one. I quote from Wang Mengzou's edition republished in Taipei; all articles in continuous paging (Wang 1977).

leaders of life philosophy were inspired by Bergson and Eucken, who reacted against Enlightenment rationalism and maintained that philosophy, instead of being a cognitive science, should be based on life. This is the main topic of Chapter 1.

Debunking the commonsense bias that the May Fourth intellectuals' attitude toward Western knowledge was only "grabbism" (*nalai zhuyi* 拿來主義; the unthinking appropriation of the foreign), and that their main concern was all about China's national problems, without any interest in epistemic inquiry (Xu 2011, 12–13),[21] I argue otherwise. My investigation discovers that the Lifeview concept, much more complicated than the essentialist dichotomy of materialism and spiritualism, marked the apex of the May Fourth Counter-Enlightenment. Issues raised in Lu Xun's Tokyo essays are indeed central concerns for the Lifeview intellectuals: the juxtapositions between science and life, matter and spirit, reason and affect, intellect and heart-mind. The main questions then become: Whence comes true knowledge? Is reason, or affect, the path to truth? Is scientific knowledge enough to cover every aspect in the universe? What is the meaning of life, and how can life be improved? Like Lu Xun, those who advocated Lifeview were closely affiliated with anarchists and romantic poets, placing great value on social revolution and romantic literature. Many of their essays were published in anarchist journals, such as *Minduo* 民鐸 [People's tocsin], established in Tokyo in June 1916 and then moving to Shanghai in December 1918. The zenith of the Lifeview movement, the concept of *affectivism*, originally appeared in this journal. Cai Yuanpei's seminal essay, "*Shijieguan yu renshengguan*" 世界觀與人生觀 [Worldview and lifeview], was included in the planned inaugural issue of another anarchist journal, *Minde* 民德 [People's moral], which was scheduled to be published in Paris in winter 1912. It would have marked the 1912 debut of the term *renshengguan* in Chinese. See Chapters 1 and 2 for more of this.

Counter-Enlightenment and Affectivism

This book situates China's Lifeview movement in the global Counter-Enlightenment discourses, which began as early as the European Enlightenment itself. Isaiah Berlin in 1955 first proposed the notion of Counter-Enlightenment, which begins simultaneously with the Enlightenment: "Opposition to the central ideas of the French Enlightenment, and of its allies and disciples in other European countries, is as old as the movement itself" (2013, 1; Pagden 2013, 201). Philosophers across Europe challenged the French *philosophes*' belief that the autonomy of reason and scientific methods could establish the universal truths that govern all human affairs—what

21. Li Zehou points out in 1987 that the Lifeview concept was neither about cognitive inquiry nor about metaphysics. Rather, it reflected the mentality in an era of anxiety and became the guidepost for people in distress, especially young people (2009, 56). Wang Fansen maintains a similar view and holds that Lifeview became a motto in everyday life in the May Fourth era (2017).

the Romans had called *humanitas*. The Italian thinker Giambattista Vico (1668–1744) maintains that each culture, as the expression of its people's feelings and attempts to survive, is unique. He insists on "the plurality of cultures" and the changes ensuing from cultural development as opposed to the Enlightenment idea of universal formula and "a timeless natural law" (Berlin 2013, 5–8). The German theologian and philosopher J. G. Hamann (1730–1788), believing in the power of passion and the inner life of the individual, maintains that passion is what drives human action, that arts and poetry are the expressions of human natural feelings, and that reason is only an instrument "for classifying and arranging data into patterns to which nothing in reality corresponds." He believes in the direct communion of humans with God. Everything in the universe rests on the faith that things, plants, and animals are "symbols with which God communicates with his creatures." We know reality as the truth of God, just as we make acquaintance with reality through our senses. Hamann's theory influenced Johann Gottfried Herder (1744–1803), Johann Wolfgang von Goethe (1749–1832), and the German Romantic movement called *Sturm and Drang* (Storm and stress; 8–21). Modern Chinese Counter-Enlightenment intellectuals were no strangers to the crucial issues raised by their European counterparts. The ideas of the direct communion with the divine through the myriad things in the universe, and of romantic passions propelling human action, were all central to the Lifeview school's affectivist theory as well to Lu Xun's early essays.

We should keep in mind that, while the twenty-eight volumes of *Encyclopedie*, the culmination of the doctrines of Enlightenment rationalism, were published between 1751 and 1772, Rousseau's critique of scientism, *Discours sur les sciences et les arts*, had been published in 1750 (Rousseau 2004). Also well known is that Hume in *A Treatise of Human Nature* (1739–1740) had already emphasized the power of passions by stating that "Reason is, and ought only to be the slave of the passions" (Hume 2001, 2:248). European Enlightenment and Counter-Enlightenment indeed occurred simultaneously. One notion should be emphasized at the outset: "Counter-Enlightenment" does not mean "Anti-Enlightenment." Rather, it is a counter-position to Enlightenment. One should say that Enlightenment and Counter-Enlightenment are in fact the two sides of the same coin. Examining modern Chinese Counter-Enlightenment in its transcultural context—transhistorical and transdisciplinary as well as translingual settings—this book sheds new light on the complexities of Enlightenment. The Lifeview movement in China, seen in the context of the life philosophy and Aesthetic Education movements in Asia and Europe, can serve as a linkage in the global Counter-Enlightenment discourses. My discovery benefits mainly from the concept of transcultural lexicon, as explained in the next section.

The appearance of *weiqinglun* 唯情論, which I render as affectivism, was the acme of Chinese Counter-Enlightenment. It is a concept invented by Zhu Qianzhi 朱謙之 (1899–1972) in 1922, to correct the mistakes of idealism and materialism.

Idealism (or spiritualism) is rendered as *yushinron* 唯心論, a Japanese neologism, and then appropriated by the Chinese as *weixinlun*, whereas materialism is rendered as *yubutsuron* 唯物論, another Japanese neologism, and pronounced *weiwulun* in Chinese. For the Lifeview school, both spiritualism and materialism, overemphasizing reason, easily lapse into rationalism, whereby truth is unattainable. By contrast, affectivism, prioritizing intuition and *qing*, or affect, is the only way to truth. The concept of emotionalism, or sentimentalism, can be traced to Rousseau during the European Enlightenment. In the eighteenth and nineteenth centuries, the Japanese used terms such as *shujōshugi* 主情主義 (emotionalism) and *kanjōshugi* 感情主義 (sentimentalism) to indicate the trend countering rationalism, intellectualism, and voluntarism (Hara 1923, 87–93).[22] I prefer to translate *weiqinglun* as affectivism, which is derived from the Latin term *affectus*, used by Spinoza in *Ethics* (1677), not only because both emotionalism and sentimentalism sound pejorative but because a philosophical reading necessitates a reference to affect. How to translate *affectus* is also problematic for the more than half a dozen English translators of *Ethics* (Spinoza 2000, 40–43).[23] Some of them render it as "affect," while others prefer "emotion."[24] The fact is that *affectus* combines emotions with the Deleuzian concept of affect, as does the Chinese idea of *qing*. If translated as "emotion," both *affectus* and *qing* are limited to human emotions while losing their ontological significance.

The May Fourth: An Enlightenment Movement?

It has almost been common knowledge until recently that the May Fourth was a movement of Enlightenment rationality (Schwarcz 1986; Xu 2011). Ying-shih Yü, at the conference on "The Burdens of the May Fourth Movement," held in Prague in 1994, points out that the New Culture movement was originally for Hu Shi 胡適 (1891–1962) a Renaissance movement, aiming at a "rebirth" of traditional Chinese culture. The biased view that modern Chinese technoscientific narrative had an overwhelming victory over the Counter-Enlightenment discourses has largely been due to the ideological propaganda of the Communist Party since the late 1930s.

22. The Japanese neologism "*kanshōshugi*" 感傷主義 (sentimentalism) was also known in May Fourth China. The author Su Xuelin 蘇雪林 (1897–1999) used it in 1979 to criticize Yu Dafu (1896–1945): "Egotism, sentimentalism 感傷主義, and decadence are elements constituting Yu's works. His stories since *Chenlun* 沈淪 [Sinking, 1921] have been all centered on the 'self'; even though with a few fake names, they are no doubt describing his own experiences" (Su 1980, 300). This quote is from a collection of handouts originally used for Su Xuelin's course on New Literature at Wuhan University from 1932 on.

23. This English version of *Ethics* is translated and edited by G. H. R. Parkinson, who points out the difficulty of translating *affectus* into English.

24. Some translators such as W. H. White (Spinoza 1952) and Edwin Curley (Spinoza 1985) render *affectus* as "affect"; others such as Samuel Shirley (Spinoza 1992) and G. H. R. Parkinson (Spinoza 2000) prefer "emotion."

Those who first interpreted the May Fourth movement in Enlightenment terms were two members of the Communist Party, Chen Boda 陳伯達 (1904–1989) and Ai Siqi 艾思奇 (1910–1966). In order to justify the New Enlightenment movement (also known as the "New Rationalist" movement) they advocated in response to the struggle against Japanese invasions during the 1930s, they claimed in 1936 that it was a "continuation and development of the May Fourth Enlightenment movement" and that it revived the revolutionary spirit of the May Fourth era (Yü 2016, 2:200–201).[25] Because of their Marxist reinterpretation and the establishment of the People's Republic of China (PRC) in 1949 that monumentalized the concept, even most non-Marxist intellectuals today have subscribed to the idea that the May Fourth was an Enlightenment movement, totally wiping out the Counter-Enlightenment movement that likewise engaged numerous intellectuals at the time.

This book argues instead that the May Fourth movement embodied both Enlightenment and Counter-Enlightenment agendas. The Lifeview school's vision of affective Enlightenment challenged the Enlightenment rationality of the Science school, led by New Culture leaders such as Hu Shi and Chen Duxiu 陳獨秀 (1879–1942). While idealism and materialism polarized affect and reason, spirit and matter, subject and object, affectivism maintained their unity. For the Lifeview school, humanity feels the interdependence of self, other, and the universe through affect rather than reason, while affect and reason supplement rather than oppose each other. That's why René Descartes' (1596–1650) mind-body dichotomy is a target of criticism for the Lifeview school in China, just as for Spinoza in *Ethics* (1677) and for Deleuze in *Difference and Repetition* (1968) and later works (Toscano 2010; Smith 2012). Even scientists call into question the validity of Cartesian body-mind dualism, as evidenced by the renowned neuroscientist António Damásio's book, *Descartes' Error: Emotion, Reason, and the Human Brain* (1994). Kant, by contrast, is accused of the separation of subject and object, because his insistence on the self as a thinking subject that gives meaning to the world turns the latter into an object of study. The May Fourth supporters of *affectivism* maintain that affect is the key to the union of subject and object, life and universe, self and non-self, mind and matter, spirit and body. In short, affectivism embraces the ontological method as a

25. Ying-shih Yü's article, titled "Neither Renaissance nor Enlightenment: A Historian's Reflections on the May Fourth Movement," originally published in 2001, is collected in *Chinese History and Culture: Six Century B.C.E to Seventeenth Century* (2016, 2:198–218). A recent study intending to decenter Eurocentrism objects to Hu Shi's concept of "the Chinese Renaissance" that follows the European model (Maissen and Mittler 2018). To my mind, however, transculturality entails the breakaway from essentialist dichotomies such as center/margin and East/West. When one intends to "decentralize" something, one is still thinking in dichotomous terms. The European Enlightenment or European Renaissance are innocent "types" that help understand similar global movements elsewhere, if we manage to get rid of the postcolonial burden of center/margin juxtaposition. For a historical account of the New Enlightenment movement of 1936–1939 that intends to revive the May Fourth legacy, see Schwarcz 1986, 222–30.

refutation of Kant's epistemological method. The Lifeview intellectuals believe that the only way to know noumenon is through ontology rather than epistemology.

Traditional concepts play a key role in the Lifeview intellectuals' relational ontology. Chapter 1 points out that their concept of self and non-self is derived from Eucken's "Ich und Nicht-Ich." However, for the elaborate discussions of self, non-self, false self, true self, big self, small self, selflessness, and so on in Chapter 5, we should be aware that the Daoist concept of the "true self" had had a long tradition and had been a source of inspiration for classical Chinese literature and philosophy (Mun 2013). Take, for an example, "Shejiang fu" 涉江賦 [Rhapsody of river crossing], a prose-poem written in 1552 by the Ming dynasty poet, essayist, and artist Xu Wei 徐渭 (1521–1593), who was a Zen Buddhism practitioner deeply influenced by Wang Yangming's Heart-Mind philosophy. In the prose-poem, Xu describes that, as a thing (*wu* 物) among myriad things, the true self, stemming from the heart-mind (*fangcun* 方寸), roams without any restrictions to everywhere in the universe. For him the true self is distinct from the soul (*jueling* 覺靈), which, inseparable from the body and yet not really attached to it, is subject to change. By contrast, the true self has no confinement and is everlasting (Xu 1983, 1:35–36).[26] That Xu should refer to the soul does not come as a surprise at all. Ying-shih Yü wrote in 1964 and 1987 that the concept of the soul as distinct from, yet dependent on, the body, and the idea of both soul and body as matter, had existed at least since the sixth century BCE, during the Spring and Autumn period (770 BCE–403 BCE). In the Han dynasty

26. Wai-Yee Lee in "Looking for the True Self" translates *jueling* as "awakening numinous," without indicating from which specific religions the original term comes from (2020, 343). I suspect that the term, rather than referring to the presence of an "awakening" spiritual being, indicates a combination of Daoist, Buddhist, Confucian, and even Christian concepts of soul. From Xu's description of *jueling* in the original text, one can see that the term refers to the soul, either the Daoist and Buddhist concept of three souls (*sanhun*) 三魂 or *anima* in Latin. That Xu Wei should contrast the soul with the Chinese concept of true self is no surprise at all, because in 1542 he had lived in Guangdong for two years, where missionary activities were noticeable, since missionaries were stationed nearby, at Macao (Chen 2015). The fact that Xu dedicated two poems in the early 1580s to Michele Ruggieri (1543–1607), the first Western missionary ever allowed to land on the Chinese mainland in 1580, before he ever saw the religious man (Xu 1983, 1:102–3, 144), indicates that he had been interested in Christian concepts much earlier. The introduction of Christianity into China has a long history, starting in the eighth century. Jesuit missionaries began to come to China in the thirteenth century. In the sixteenth century, the Jesuits were still groping for a proper Chinese translation for "anima," and naturally they consulted traditional Daoist and Buddhist texts for equivalents. Ruggieri uses *hunling* 魂靈 in *Tianzhu shengjiao shilu* 天主聖教實錄 [True record of the sacred teaching of the Lord of Heaven, 1584]. Matteo Ricci (1552–1610), also an Italian Jesuit, mentions in *Tianzhu shiyi* 天主實義 [True meaning of the Lord of Heaven, 1595] that there are three souls in the world (*shi you sheng, jue, ling sanhun*) 世有生、覺、靈三魂 and distinguishes *shenghun* 生魂 (soul of plants), *juehun* 覺魂 (soul of animals), and *linghun* 靈魂 (soul of humans) in the world beyond. These terms for rendering *anima* seem alike and apparently had existed in Chinese long before Ricci used them in his book in 1595. Gradually the term *linghun* 靈魂 took hold, and around 1636 Nicholas Longobardi (1559–1654) used it in his book titled *Linghun dao ti shuo* 靈魂道體說 [On human soul and the Ultimate Way] (Song 2019, 210–12; Li 2012, 330).

(206 BCE–220 CE), the concept of soul became a mixture of Confucian ideology and Daoist beliefs, which was "a syncretism of all the indigenous religious beliefs and practices at the popular level" in pre-Buddhist China (Yü 2016, 1:58).[27] By Xu Wei's time, the concept of soul had long been embedded in the Chinese psyche.

For Xu Wei, the true self, distinct from the soul, is the embodiment of *qing*. Xu maintains that "Poetry originates from *qing*," indicating that *qing*, emanating from the true self, is natural and genuine (1983, 2:534).[28] He further says that the true self, rejecting sanctification and lofty aims, engages in altruism in everyday life. This suggests that sagehood or divinity is immanent, manifested in things in the universe rather than above them and transcendent (489).[29] All these concepts from traditional Chinese thought are integral to the May Fourth affectivism, especially the concept of divine immanence, a characteristic of modern Western philosophy and the core of Spinoza's theory. Chapter 5 discusses this in detail. It comes as no surprise that, when modern Chinese intellectuals encounter Western concepts, they tend to search for commensurable ideas in their own traditions. That is, after all, how we make sense of the foreign, while comparison with others only enhances our self-knowledge.

In a manner of speaking, the May Fourth emergence of affectivism could be viewed as a reinvention of traditional Chinese thought in dialogue with Western concepts. Inspired by Bergson and Eucken, the Lifeview intellectuals connected the counter-rationalist thought in their own traditions with its Western counterpart. Having a sound training in both traditional Chinese and Western learning, most of the leading intellectuals, having lived or studied in Japan, also had firsthand knowledge of Japanese philosophy. Their systematic efforts in highlighting the transcultural critique of overemphasis on intellectualism across East and West have been obliterated by the mainstream May Fourth paradigm of Enlightenment rationalism. When examining the Science and Lifeview debate, if one depends solely on the debate materials published in the newspapers and journals at the time, it is indeed hard to debunk the decades-long biased view that never takes into consideration the May Fourth Counter-Enlightenment's idea of *qing* as the principle of co-living

27. Yü's two articles are "Life and Immortality in the Mind of Han China," first published in 1964 (2016; 1:20–57) and "O Soul, Come back! A Study in the Changing Conceptions of the Soul and After Life in Pre-Buddhist China," first published in 1987 (58–84). In the latter, Yü points out that there were two notions of soul since high antiquity, before the arrival of Buddhism in China, *hun* 魂 and *po* 魄, both leaving the body after death (2016; 1:58). While Lu Ji 陸機 (261–303) used the word *ling* 靈 in his poem to indicate the *hun*-souls, his brother Lu Yun 陸雲 (262–303) used *ling-po* 靈魄 instead of *hun-po* 魂魄 (2016; 1:76). There is no doubt that the terms for souls varied over time.

28. Xu Wei's original sentence reads: "Shi ben hu qing" 詩本乎情. For a discussion of the topic, see Jiang 2014, 241–42.

29. Xu Wei's original text says, "*Fan liren zhe, jie shengren ye*" 凡利人者，皆聖人也 (1983, 2:489). For a discussion of the topic, see Xiaobei Li 2016, 113.

and co-becoming. This book, ferreting out publications that have long been forgotten—such as the journal *Meiyu* 美育 [Aesthetic education] and theoretical works on affectivism—intends to reconstruct the May Fourth dialectic of affect and reason, exactly what the Frankfurt school would later call "dialectic of Enlightenment" in the 1940s. As the late Hong Kong philosopher Sze-Kwang Lao 勞思光 (1927–2012) points out,

> One of the characteristics of the Enlightenment movement is its emphasis on rationalist thinking. Those who criticized the Enlightenment included Adorno in the earlier stage and later theorists who did not belong to the Frankfurt school, such as Derrida and Foucault. All of them shared the same mistrust in Reason. (Lao 2002, xviii–xix)

Modern Chinese Counter-Enlightenment, surfacing during the late Qing, became the prominent stance of the Lifeview movement that lasted almost from the early 1910s to the 1940s. It was a missing link in the global Counter-Enlightenment movement that had begun since the European Enlightenment itself.

The Transcultural Lexicon as Methodology

The term "lifeview" was originally "Lebensanschauung," a German word concocted by Rudolf Eucken in 1890. The Japanese rendered the German term into *jinseikan* (じんせいかん人生観) in 1912,[30] and around the same time Chinese intellectuals began to use it as *renshengguan*, which became a widely discussed topic in Republican China. During the two world wars, people in both East and West were questioning the meaning of life in the face of relentless scientific development that had led to wars and unprecedented human disasters. The concept of *Lebensanschauung* triggered a reevaluation of traditional philosophy in Japan and China, including Confucianism, Buddhism, and Daoism: How could traditional Eastern wisdom resolve the dilemma between scientific progress and the ensuing destruction of life? In this book, I call terms such as *renshengguan* "transcultural lexicon." Mostly originating in the West and often first rendered into Japanese *kanji* and then appropriated by the Chinese, they triggered concatenations of sociopolitical as well as intellectual reverberations in Japan and China and eventually became an inseparable part of Japanese and Chinese daily language. The study of transcultural lexicon allows us to rediscover the interconnections of our present selves with the past and with others in crucial moments in global history.

Hinging on the investigation of transcultural lexicon as methodology, this book traces the routes through which Counter-Enlightenment concepts and ideas were

30. The term *jinseikan* has been in use in Japan at least since 1897, in a book written by Inoue Tetsujirō's student. See Chapter 1 for details.

transmitted from Europe to Japan and then to China. Transcultural terms such as "lifeview," bridging the life philosophy movements across Asia and Europe, have led me to previously unknown areas. Suddenly, all the connections are made; all seemingly disconnected fragments fall into place. It is like, following the complex plot of a detective story, one discovers in the end that all mysteries are solved. This experience tells me it is likely that any local occurrence in any place, however insignificant and parochial it may seem, could be connected with other relevant events in the globe. Without looking at a local phenomenon through transcultural lenses, one is likely to lose sight of its global significance. The term *renshengguan*, which most of us in China studies probably think is originally Chinese, in fact belongs to the transcultural lexicon that connects China, Japan, and even Korea in a global context. When asked, Korean scholars may think it is originally a Korean term (*insaeng-gwan*).

During my investigation, other terms such as "aesthetic education" 美育 (*biyiku* in Japanese, or *meiyu* in Chinese), "reason" 理知 (*richi* or *lizhi*), "intuition" 直覚 (*chokkaku* or *zhijue*), "creation" 創造 (*sōzo* or *chuangzao*), and "evolution" 進化 (*shinka* or *jinhua*) prove to belong to the transcultural lexicon as well. Such terms underscore the active role China used to play on the global cultural scene at the turn of the twentieth century (or at any other time in global history, for that matter). Myriad terms like these are everyday Chinese, the origins of which we seldom question. In fact, without the transcultural lexicon, people in China or Japan nowadays would not even be able to communicate with each other. Failing to understand their transcultural nature, a native Chinese may mistake events such as the Lifeview and Aesthetic Education movements as exclusive to China. Investigating how such terms traveled from the West to China via Japan, we are able to map out the human and material networks that connect global flows of concepts and ideas. All who engage in comparative literature, philosophy, sociology, psychology, and even the history of science, cannot overstress the significance of the transcultral lexicon in the development of these disciplines in modern China, Japan, and Korea.

In recent years the concept of transculturality has emerged as a critique of comparative literature, regional studies, and multicultural and postcolonial studies. Comparative literature centers on the comparison of certain national literatures and their influences on others, while traditional boundaries of nations, languages, and identities have been blurred by the global flows of events, people, as well as material and spiritual culture throughout the centuries. How can one categorically divide Asian from non-Asian regions, since human and non-human mobility has never been deterred by continental borders? As distinct from multiculturalism, which focuses on cultural differences, identities, and communications, transculturality as a concept is concerned mainly with the hybridity of cultures and their connectivity. It highlights how the constant infiltrations of cultural others, with the ensuing transcultural practices, result in the creative transformation of the self and constitute its inseparable parts. In contrast to postcolonialism, which emphasizes central hegemony and marginal resistance, the transcultural approach pays attention to how "marginal cultures" find their footholds in the interstices of unbalanced power relations and renew their traditions for the future. The concept of transculturality thus challenges the essentialist dichotomies of hegemony/minority, center/margin, radicalism/conservativism, and so on, while stressing that any marginal place in the globe can be a center.

Nonetheless, as a research paradigm, transculturality faces an unresolvable paradox. In the trend of centuries-old globalization, we have witnessed the undeniable facts of the global flows of material and spiritual cultures; one has to admit that traditional boundaries of national cultures and identities have been relentlessly overhauled. However, deep-rooted ideas about race, blood, nationalism, and essentialism are still tenacious, wars fought in their names becoming nightmares in innumerable regions. While we may think traditional ideas about the local and the native are passé, the frontiers of transculturality are still confronted with the resistance of ingrained localism. As Stephen Greenblatt points out in *Cultural Mobility: A Manifesto*, "There is an urgent need to rethink fundamental assumptions about the fate of culture in an age of global mobility, a need to formulate, both for scholars and for the larger public, new ways to understand the vitally important dialectic of cultural persistence and change" (2010, 1–2). Transcultural co-living and co-becoming versus cultural essentialism is an everlasting paradox; not only do they parallel each other, but they penetrate and contain each other to the extent that traditional and modern, native and foreign, are inseparable.

My conceptualization of the transcultural lexicon is informed by the attention paid to loanwords and neologisms in translation studies in the last few decades (Masini 1993; Liu 1995; Sun and Liu 2013). But, for me the study of lexical invention should not be limited to the transmission and transformation of terms and concepts, or to the formation of new meanings. It should be raised to the level of methodology, as a conduit to new understandings of the global human and cultural movements, to studies of the transcultural practices at crucial moments of global history, and to new discoveries of the truths about ourselves in both Western and non-Western countries. While maintaining the incommensurability of languages and challenging the "hypothetical equivalences" between words and their meanings, Lydia Liu, from a postcolonial stance, argues that "between China, Japan, and the West at the site of translation or wherever the languages happen to meet . . . the confrontations register a meaning-making history" (1995, 32). By contrast, my purpose in advocating the concept of transcultural lexicon is to highlight the connections of languages and cultures despite their confrontations, and the transcultural practices that are made possible because of these differences. A more meaningful question then becomes: Why have East-West contacts continued to grow, notwithstanding sporadic or even systematic local resistances? What I call attention to is the mirror images that are inevitably formed in cultural encounters, as when we face strangers:

how we see other cultures as images in mirrors that reflect our true selves—how we see the reflections of our own images in the mirrored images of others. While the strengths of other cultures may serve as a foil to our own weaknesses, we may as well see our own strengths in others' eyes and thereby reinvent our own tradition. The adoption of transcultural lexicon highlights the immersion of other cultures in our own, which is likely to trigger the reevaluation of our own traditions and status quo and then set off the creative transformation of the self through transcultural practices. As the concept of transcultural modernity I have proposed in a previous study, modernity is possible only on the transcultural site, where languages, concepts, cultural and material products meet and mingle and where transcultural practices and creative transformation are possible (Peng 2010).

Recognizing our connections to a global event through identifying the transcultural lexicon is motivated by the need to avoid the feeling of isolation. It keeps us from the pitfall of self-centrism and urges us to face the hybridity of our own culture. Transcultural practices are made possible due to the infiltrations of others, while the merging of self and others is the key to self-renewal. To really know who and what we are, we have to acknowledge the countless others in ourselves and the crucial historical moments when the self is changed because of our intermixing with others. There is no such thing as a "pure Chinese," a pure European, or a pure American. If one sets out to identify what constitutes a "pure" nationality based on essentialism, one is blind to historical facts. The concept of transculturality, by no means an academic discipline, is thus an ethos as well as a research paradigm: it is an ethical attitude toward self-other relations, possible to shed new lights on suitable subject matter in any field.

In this book, the transcultural lexicon as methodology, blurring language and disciplinary boundaries, allows me to challenge the common notion that the May Fourth movement ushered in a period crowning reason over human passions. In my investigation, modern Chinese Lifeview intellectuals recognized that affect and reason balance out and complement each other, while their ontological inquiry was part of a global event during the military, socio-political, cultural crisis around the two world wars. Their quest for truth knew no bounds: traditional Chinese culture (Confucianism, Buddhism, and Daoism), Western philosophy (from ancient Greece to the twentieth century), life philosophy (in Germany, France, and Japan), Eastern and Western Romantic literature, anarchism, Darwinism, and so on, were all resources from which they drew inspirations. It is only appropriate that an investigation into the topic should likewise be transhistorical, transdisciplinary, and translingual. Using the transcultural lexicon as methodology, this book rewrites the May Fourth movement, proposing a new understanding of the period.

Chapters of the Book

The book contains five chapters and the conclusion. Chapter 1 sets China's Lifeview movement in the context of global Counter-Enlightenment. All the actors who promoted the Lifeview movement in China were either close friends or disciples of Liang Qichao, the principal player that made the connections with Japan, Germany, and France possible. During his exile in Japan, Liang Qichao witnessed the Lifeview movement led by people like Nishida Kitarō, who used the Buddhist concept of sentient beings to critique scientific rationality. Liang actively participated in the Eastern Ethics Renaissance movement headed by Inoue Tetsujirō and Kanie Yoshimaru 蟹江義丸 (1872–1904). In 1918, Liang led a group of burgeoning Chinese intellectuals to Europe and visited Rudolf Eucken, while Zhang Junmai 張君勱 (1887–1969), who was acting as interpreter during the trip, stayed in Jena to study philosophy with the German life philosopher. Zhang's article "Lifeview" triggered the Lifeview and Science debate in China in 1923.

Chapter 2 investigates the Aesthetic Education movement led by Cai Yuanpei. Learning from German and Japanese Aesthetic Education movements, Cai began to advocate the concept in his capacity as the first Education Minister in 1912. Later that year his essay "Worldview and Lifeview" was ready for press. In 1917, he published "Yi meiyu dai zongjiao" 以美育代宗教 [Replacing religion with aesthetic education], which became the bible for the Aesthetic Education movement in China. The journal *Aesthetic Education*, established in 1920, claims that aesthetic education aims to construct a "new lifeview," so that the education overemphasizing intellectualism could be reformed. Cai's blueprint of "an aesthetic life" indicates that theory and praxis are of equal importance to the Lifeview school.

Chapter 3 discusses *Chuanghualun* 創化論, Zhang Dongsun's 1918 translation of Bergson's *Creative Evolution*. Inspired by traditional Heart-Mind philosophy, Zhang turned "consciousness" in French to "heart-mind" in his Chinese rendering. A close ally of Liang Qichao, Zhang Dongsun was serializing *Chuanghualun* in a newspaper established by Liang when the latter embarked on his grand European trip to visit Eucken with his disciples. In February of 1920, Guo Moruo 郭沫若 (1892–1978), while studying in Japan, wrote about his experience of reading Zhang's *Chuanghualun*. The following year, he established the Creation Society with Cheng Fangwu 成仿吾 (1897–1984) and Yu Dafu 郁達夫 (1896–1945), who were then also students in Tokyo.

Dongxi wenhua ji qi zhexue 東西文化及其哲學 [Eastern and Western cultures and their philosophies], published by Liang Shuming in 1921, is the central topic of Chapter 4. He compares Chinese, Indian, and Western philosophies, trying to establish the relevance of traditional Chinese culture in the modern world. Declaring that Confucius was a life philosopher, he connects Confucianism with the life philosophy of Eucken and Bergson. However, while Zhang Dongsun disagrees that Bergson was against science, Liang Shuming believes this to be true. He critiques the concepts of "Easternization" and "Westernization" and wonders if Easternization is possible when all the countries in the world are eager to Westernize themselves. This kind of essentialist dichotomy is, of course, to be questioned.

The central issue of Chapter 5 is affectivism. The Lifeview intellectuals, believing that "all things between Heaven and Earth are sentient," a Buddhist and Confucian teaching, invented the theory of affectivism and intervened in the global dialectic of affect and reason. The theory was proposed in 1922 by Liang Shuming's student Zhu Qianzhi, who maintains that rather than reason, *qing*, or the affects, is the core of ontology. Referring to the *Book of Changes* tradition and resonating with Zhang Dongsun's view of Bergson, Zhu points out that the truth of the universe is *zhenqing zhi liu* 真情之流 (affective flows), which, like life itself, is a holistic force and changes unceasingly. In 1924, Yuan Jiahua 袁家驊 (1903–1980) invented the concept of *qingren* 情人 (*homo sentimentalis*, or sentimental man) to refute Nietzsche's *chaoren* 超人 (Superman).

The Conclusion centers on Fang Dongmei 方東美 (1899–1977), one of the forerunners of New Confucianism in postwar Taiwan and Hong Kong. His 1927 book, *Kexue zhexue yu rensheng* 科學哲學與人生 [Science, philosophy, and life] stands out among the May Fourth life philosophy corpus because it summarizes neatly the Science and Lifeview debate: "The Universe and life are a harmonious unity of affect and reason, which should not be divided." His thought combines Confucian, Buddhist, and Daoist concepts as well as Bergsonism. Fang maintains that the pursuit of knowledge should aim to aid life: "Without you, Life, what's the worth of knowledge?" This statement defines the meaning of life philosophy.

I Feel, Therefore I Am

We are all familiar with Descartes' 1637 maxim "I think, therefore I am" (*Cogito, ergo sum*; *Je pense, donc je suis*), a Latin phrase he invented during the European Enlightenment. What has probably escaped most people's attention is Daniel Mornet's (1878–1954) counter-rationalism maxim in 1929, *Je sens, donc je suis* (I feel, therefore I am), a belated motto that has revived the study of Rousseauesque Counter-Enlightenment (1929, 64). A Rousseau expert, Mornet coined this French phrase to indicate the significance of Rousseauesque sentimentalism vis-à-vis Enlightenment rationality.

According to Mornet, the French Revolution was mainly triggered by Romanticism, which had been inspired by Rousseau's sentimentalism rather than by Enlightenment rationalism. As has been pointed out by quite a few later historians, the work that directly led to the Revolution was not *Encyclopedie*, the monumental collection that immortalized the European Enlightenment, but rather Rousseau's 1762 *Du contrat social* [Social contract] (McDonald 2013). Modern China witnessed a similar case of the interaction between philosophy, literature, and revolution. The establishment of the Creation Society in 1921 ushered in the Romantic generation of modern Chinese literature (Lee 1973). Why the Creation writers declared around 1927 that they would switch from literary revolution to revolutionary literature seems to be a mystery that has puzzled quite a few critics (Zheng 1953; Hou 1974; Xu 2013),[31] but in fact there had been plenty of indicators pointing to that inevitable turnabout. Several chapters in this book point out that life philosophy is a practical philosophy advocating action, as can be evidenced by the idea of "an aesthetic life" maintained by the Aesthetic Education movement (see Chapter 2). Zhu Qianzhi believes that "the universe is an unceasing flux. That is to say, an endless revolution. . . . Revolution means creation simultaneously" (see Chapter 5). That the Creation writers such as Cheng Fangwu and Guo Moruo, having close affinity with the Lifeview school, would call themselves artists and revolutionaries and walk down the path of socialist revolution, was only to be expected (see Chapter 3).

This book argues that modern Chinese Counter-Enlightenment was part and parcel of the global Counter-Enlightenment movement that had begun with the European Enlightenment. "Lifeview," the essay that triggered the May Fourth Science and Lifeview debate, was originally a lecture delivered by Zhang Junmai at Tsinghua University on 14 February 1923. Just ten days earlier, a similar event had occurred in Europe on 4 February. The British geneticist and evolutionary biologist John Burdon Sanderson Haldane (1892–1964) gave a talk at the University of Cambridge titled "Daedalus; or, Science and the Future," lauding science for its capacity to bring about happiness for human beings. The following year Bertrand Russell, who had visited China in 1920, reacted with the publication of a pamphlet titled *Icarus: or, The Future of Science,* in which he warns that the misuse of science would only lead to disasters (see Chapter 4). During the global crisis between the two world wars, the progressive values of the sciences and the self-questioning values of the humanities, seemingly poles apart, were in fact interacting in a dialectic mode. The dialectic of reason and affect has been a recurrent global event since the European Enlightenment. Throughout history it has been impossible for China or any other country to isolate itself from the global interactions of ideas, events, people, and material culture. Such transcultural interactions have transcended the boundaries of time, space, languages, and cultures, linking all that are related in an inseparable connectivity. To avoid war and coexist in harmony, one has to feel the need to reach for others and the indispensability of mutual self-transformation to achieve affective communion and sustainability. This is the significance of transcultural co-living and co-becoming.

---

31. Cheng Fangwu published "Cong wenxue geming dao geming wenxue" 從文學革命到革命文學 [From literary revolution to revolutionary literature] in *Creation Monthly* in 1928, announcing the decision of the Creation writers to embark on a revolutionary agenda. The draft of the essay was finished on 23 November 1927, as is indicated at the end of the essay published in *Creation Monthly.* For more discussion of this, see Chapter 3.

1

The Science and Lifeview Debate

The Transcultural Lexicon

> The sensorial existence (das sinnliche Dasein) exhibits a direct contact with impressions. Thought (das Denken), on the contrary, tends to distinctly divide self (Ich) from non-self (Nicht-Ich); this causes a great problem, afflicting life with an apparent disaccord.
>
> —Rudolf Eucken and Zhang Junmai, *The Problem of Life in China and Europe* (Eucken and Zhang, 1922, 162)

> The center of lifeview is self; complementary to self is non-self.
> (人生觀之中心點，是曰我。與我對待者，則非我也。)
>
> —Zhang Junmai, "Lifeview" (Wang 1977, 1)

The above quotes, respectively from the 1922 co-authored book in German by Eucken and Zhang Junmai, *The Problem of Life in China and Europe*, and from Zhang's 1923 article "Lifeview" that triggered the Science and Lifeview debate in China, speak volumes about the transcultural connections between the German and the Chinese Lifeview movements at the turn of the twentieth century. The relationship between self and non-self was a central issue for the Chinese Lifeview school as for Eucken. Their life philosophy shared the view that life is more about bodily experiences (the sensorial existence) than about thought. Through the five senses that directly contact the world, the self is connected with the non-self, while subject and object are unified. Thought, in contrast, turns the world into an object of study, and the self is thus categorically divided with the non-self, a major problem in Kant's epistemology. Eucken's critique of Kant, shared by the Lifeview school, is clearly laid out in his masterpiece, *Die Lebensanschauungen der Grossen Denker* [The lifeview of the great thinkers, 1890] (Eucken 1907, 405–6), which is discussed in this chapter.

The outbreak of the Chinese Lifeview movement in 1923 was an inevitable outcome of conflicting cultural values and epistemic choices as well as ideologies that had split the Chinese intellectuals for decades since the late Qing. In the May

Fourth era many lamented that the 1911 revolution, though having overthrown the imperial rule, did not bring about a new China with wealth and power. The New Culture movement thus targeted Confucianism and traditional culture as the cause of China's backwardness, calling for Western science and democracy as the panacea for solving China's problems. Yet not all intellectuals subscribed to the Enlightenment apotheosis of science touted by the Science school led by Hu Shi, Chen Duxiu, and Ding Wenjiang 丁文江 (1887–1936). The Lifeview school spearheaded by Liang Qichao and Cai Yuanpei, by contrast, constituted the major Counter-Enlightenment force that endeavored to reinvent the spiritual values of Confucianism, Buddhism, and Daoism in a modern world beset by relentless materialist expansion, the two world wars, and global spiritual crisis. In fact, not a few intellectuals since the late Qing, including Zhang Taiyan and Lu Xun during their sojourn in Japan, had believed that the essence of traditional Chinese culture, far from being backward, was on a par with the Counter-Enlightenment trend in Japan and Europe, as discussed in the Introduction. The May Fourth Lifeview school, the center of this study, both inherited these philosophical tenets from such late Qing intellectuals and were inspired by contemporary European life philosophy advocated by Eucken and Bergson.

How *Lebensanschauung* Became *Renshengguan* (Lifeview)

Before I analyze the roles Eucken and Bergson play in the May Fourth Lifeview movement, some effort to explain the origin and transmission of the transcultural term *renshengguan* is necessary. Meaning "lifeview" or outlook on life, it is originally *jinseikan* in Japanese. This Japanese neologism probably first appeared in *Indo Shūkyōshi* 印度宗教史 [History of Indian religions, 1897], written by Anesaki Masaharu 姉崎正治 (1873–1949), one of the students of Inoue Tetsujirō, a leading Japanese philosopher at the time. The fourth section of the second chapter of this book is titled "Buda no seikaikan oyobi jinseikan" 吠陁の世界觀及人生觀 [Buddha's worldview and lifeview] (Anesaki 1897, 42–48). It is indicated on the title page that the book was proofread by Inoue, who, compiling *Tetsugaku jii* 哲學字彙 [A dictionary of philosophy] in 1881, had helped establish the modern Japanese philosophical lexicon (Inoue et al. 1912).[1] In 1912, when Abe Yoshishige 安倍能成 (1883–1966), another student of Inoue, translated into Japanese Rudolf Eucken's 1890 book, *The Lifeview of the Great Thinkers,* he used the term *jinseikan* to render *Lebensanschauung,* which literally means "lifeview," and rendered the title of

1. Inoue co-compiled *Tetsugaku jii* in 1881 and then revised it in 1884 and 1912. He wrote the prefaces to all three editions. The prefaces to the 1881 and 1884 editions, with the English title *A Dictionary of Philosophy,* are in Japanese. The preface to the 1912 edition, likewise with an English title, *A Dictionary of English, German, and French Philosophical Terms,* is in English.

the book *Dai shisōka no jinseikan* 大思想家の人生觀 (Eucken 1913).[2] It is therefore to Inoue's cohort that we owe the invention of the *kanji* neologism *jinseikan*, or *renshengguan* in Chinese. Abe's Japanese translation was published in October 1912, which in the following year saw the fifth printing (Eucken 1913, i).[3] It was a seminal work that turned "lifeview" into a topic engaging numerous Japanese intellectuals for decades. From then on, terms such as "lifeview," "stateview" (*kokkakan* 國家觀), "worldview" (*seikaikan* 世界觀), and "universeview" (*uchūkan* 宇宙觀) found their way into everyday Japanese, while books centering on these topics were proliferating (Shiraishi 1913; Jinsei Tetsugaku kenkyūkai 1925; Suzuki 1942).

As far as I know, the term *renshengguan* was introduced into China by Cai Yuanpei in his essay titled "Worldview and Lifeview." As explained in the introduction, the essay was planned to be published in the inaugural issue of the anarchist Journal *People's Moral* in winter 1912, but somehow the project fell through, and the essay did not see print until April 1913 in *Eastern Miscellanies* (*CYPQJ*, 459–63).[4] Considering the short interval between October 1912, when Abe's translation of Eucken was first published,[5] and winter 1912, when Cai Yuanpei used the term *renshengguan* in his essay, one cannot help marveling at how closely Chinese intellectuals followed the Japanese lead in intellectual pursuit.[6] In fact, Cai began to study the Japanese language with a private tutor as early as 1897, and it is likely that he had learned about the term before the publication of Abe's translation of Eucken's book. More about this will be discussed in Chapter 2.

Rudolf Eucken on Enlightenment Rationalism: The Division of Self and Non-self

> By its own power reason can neither advance nor hinder anything; it is merely the slave of the affects.

2. For Williston S. Hough and W. R. Boyce Gibson's English translation, see Eucken 1910. Throughout this chapter I quote from the 1907 German edition, unless otherwise indicated. Eucken revised his book with each new edition. The 1922 German edition was drastically revised, very different from previous editions (Eucken 2007). In my study I consult Hough and Gibson's 1910 translation but sometimes slightly revise it.
3. Abe based his translation on the 7th (1911) edition of Eucken's original, while consulting Hough and Gibson's 1910 English translation. See Abe's "Hanlei" 凡例 [Editorial principles] (Eucken 1913, i–ii).
4. In the *Eastern Miscellanies* version, after the title it is noted, "Selected from *People's Moral*" (*xuan Mindebao* 選民德報).
5. On the copyright page of the 1913 edition of Abe's translation it is indicated that the book was first published in October 1912.
6. Thomas Frölich mentions briefly in a footnote the Japanese-German origins of the term *renshengguan* in his book discussing the philosophical ideas in Republican China (2000, 153).

(Aus eigener Kraft kann die Vernunft weder etwas heben noch hemmen, sie ist lediglich eine Dienerin der Affekte.)

—Rudolf Eucken, *Die Lebensanschauunggen der Grossen Denker* (Eucken 1907, 390)

Hume's famous saying in 1739–1740, "Reason is, and ought only to be the slave of the passions" (2001, 2:248), becomes "sie [die Vernunft] ist lediglich eine Dienerin der Affekte" in Eucken's German in *The Lifeview of the Great Thinkers* in 1890. The latter is emphasizing that, for reason to act, the driving force of the passions is indispensable. As will be discussed later, action is a central idea in his *Lebensphilosophie*. A Nobel Prize winner in literature in 1908, Eucken with his life philosophy was often mentioned in the early twentieth century together with Henri Bergson, a 1927 Nobel laureate himself. But unlike the latter, who, thanks to Deleuze, has enjoyed a revival of interest since the 1960s, almost no critic pays attention to Eucken anymore. Yet from the German sociologist and philosopher Georg Simmel's (1858–1918) 1918 book, *Lebensanschauung: Vier metaphysische Kapitel* [Lifeview: Four metaphysical chapters], we know for certain that Eucken's work on lifeview was not unknown during his time (Simmel 1918). With numerous editions of *The Lifeview of the Great Thinkers* between 1890 and 1922 and his *Complete Works* published in 1922 and still republished in 2007, it is remarkable that Eucken should have been obliterated on the German philosophical scene. This is especially unthinkable considering the recently renewed attention given to *Lebensphilosophie* in German and English scholarship, with his student Hans Driesch recognized as one of the leading vitalists and *Lebensphilosophers* (Lebovic 2013).[7] Nonetheless, Eucken was widely known in Japan and China in the early twentieth century and was most welcome for his critique of European Enlightenment rationalism.

In *The Lifeview of the Great Thinkers* Eucken singles out Enlightenment rationalism as the cause of the problems of Western philosophy. For him the Enlightenment, combining individualism with the secularization of life and bourgeois work ethic, marked the decline of the tradition of the holistic lifeview as handed down from Greek philosophy. By contrast, Hume's belief in human emotions and irrationality and Rousseau's advocacy of feeling were reactions against Enlightenment rationalism. In his mind, German Romantic literature culminating in Goethe, with its peculiar world- and lifeview, was also "a powerful rejection and thorough overcoming of the Enlightenment" (Eucken 1907, 42). Eucken points out that Kant's notion of subjectivity—the self that gives order and meaning to the world—is the outcome of traditional German idealism and a breakthrough in the theory of human cognition. Yet Kant's philosophy limits our cognition to the sphere of experience (*Erfahrung*)

7. *Lebensphilosophie* has been stigmatized because of its connection with Nazi biopolitics, as pointed out by Nitzan Lebovic. Nevertheless, while the Nazi connection has not prevented the recent resurgence of interest in *Lebensphilosophie*, Eucken as a *Lebensphilosopher* has been wiped out.

and reason (*Vernunft*). Questions of God, soul, and the universe, questions most vital to human beings, are forever unanswerable in Kant's system of thought. For Eucken, as much as human cognition depends on experience, "it does not constitute the ultimate boundary of our thought" (406). He turns to Goethe's artistic lifeview, which was above all a revival of Platonism "with its union of soul and world" (*mit seiner Verbindung von Seele und Welt*; 429). For Eucken, people through art and fantasy can strive above the utilitarianism and necessities of the bourgeois world and aim "at a new reality, a rich spiritual culture, a world of pure structure and greater beauty" (422). In his mind, the Romantic movement suffers from the pitfalls of the deification of the self, but in its moderate form it has a great contribution: instead of maintaining an outright opposition to things, the subject returns to them and shares with them its deepened spirituality, allowing them to acquire a life of their own (442).[8]

Eucken's belief in continued and gradual modernization as opposed to the Enlightenment idea of progress, his advocacy of spiritual life (*Geistleben*), and his urge for the cultivation of the self, certainly appealed to the generation of Japanese who felt spiritually lost in the pursuit of Western modernization and the turmoil of war and endless colonial expansions. Most noteworthy is that the reception of Eucken's *Lebensphilosophie* in Japan triggered a trend of self-examination; the term "lifeview" gave the Japanese an impetus to search for their own spiritual truth. They reexamined Confucian and Buddhist traditions, to see whether they were sufficient to solve the problems of life in the modern world. Nishida Kitarō, leader of the Kyoto school philosophers, was among the first to discuss related issues.

Nishida Kitarō: *Jō* (*Qing*) as a Critique of Enlightenment Rationalism

Nishida was fully aware of Eucken's kinship with Bergson and always mentioned them together, but he pointed out in 1916 that Eucken, eager to advocate spiritual life, lacks "refined, deep self-reflection" (*NKZS* 1:364). However, Nishida shares with Eucken quite a few basic concepts, which he has formulated mainly through reading, in addition to Bergson, German philosophers such as Schopenhauer, Nietzsche, Schelling, and Hegel as well as American thinkers such as Dewey and William James (1842–1910). In 1887 or 1888, during his Fourth High School years, Nishida talked about the "immortality of the spirit" (*seishin hukyū* 精神不朽) and maintained that "religious sentiment is beyond the power of intellect" (18:3–7).[9]

8. For Eucken, the Romantic movement is marred by "completely unhindered mood" (die freischwebende Stimmung), the "boundless unconstrained subjectivity" (die "unendlich freie Subjektivität"), and the "vain mirroring of the self" (die eitle Selbstbespieglung; 1907, 442).
9. These ideas were expressed in his two letters written in 1887 or 1888 to Yamamoto Ryōkiji 山本良吉 (1871–1942), a classmate in high school.

In the fourth chapter of *Zen no kenkyū* 善の研究 [An inquiry into the good, 1911], he discusses the concept of "*Intellektuelle Anschauung*" (intellectual intuition; 1:339),[10] which, derived from Fichte, indicates for him "the unity of subject and object" (40–41).[11] According to him, this concept refers to intuition (*chokkaku* 直覺), which is above experience in general, and is often found in artists and religious people. Nishida criticizes the European Enlightenment for holding science and reason as the ultimate authority, while "all that pertains to the mystic realm are eliminated" (335).[12] What Eucken calls "eine unmittelbare Berührung der Eindrücke" (a direct contact of impressions; Eucken and Chang 1922, 162), Nishida calls the "Unmittelbare Erfahrung" (direct experience; *NKZS* 16:275). For both of them "direct experience" is the realm where subject and object are fused as one. According to Nishida, "Behind direct experience there are infinite mystic secrets" (275).[13] This statement fully discloses his belief that direct experience is an area beyond the analytical power of reason.

In Nishida's mind, Kant represents the pinnacle of Enlightenment rationalism, and throughout his career he criticizes Kant's rationalism for turning philosophy into a cognitive science. Nishida advocates the return to life and to the homeland of *qing* (*jō no kokyō* 情の故郷), as symbolized by "die blaue Blume" (the blue flower; *aoki hana* 青き花), which the minnesinger in *Heinrich Von Ofterdingen*, Julian Schmidt Novalis's 1802 novel, longs for (*NKZS* 16: 341, 368).[14] For Novalis the blue flower represents Romantic poetry.[15] The Romantic symbolism of the blue flower became a constant motif in modern Chinese literature, including Zhao Jingshen's 趙景深 (1902–1985) "Lanhua" 藍花 [The blue flower] (1923), based on the American

10. For Nishida's discussion of Fichte's concept of "*Intellektuelle Anschauung*" (*Chiteki chokkan* 知的直觀), see "Gendai no tetsugaku" 現代の哲學 [Modern philosophy] (*NKZS* 1:334–68).

11. Here, Nishida writes: "shukan to kyakkan to ga gōyitsu" 主觀と客觀とが合一. For *An Inquiry into the Good*, see *NKZS* 1:1–200.

12. Critiques of reason and science at the expense of humanity were common among the Kyoto school philosophers. Tanabe Hajime's 田邊元 (1885–1962) theory of "the absolute critique of reason" aims to expose "the limits of reason and the force of other-power." Nishitani Keiji 西谷啓治 (1900–1990) points out that "the mindset of technology has led to a rationalization of external society, in its work and in its human relationships, in such a way as to erase the human from the picture" (Nishitani 2001, 157–62, 238–41).

13. Nishida's original reads: "*chokusetsu keiken no haigo niwa mugen no shinpiteki himitsu ga aru*" 直接經驗の背後には無限の神秘的秘密がある. This quote is from "*Junsui keiken ni kansuru danshō*" 純粹經驗に關する斷章 [Fragments concerning pure experience, circa 1905] (*NKZS* 16:267–572).

14. Ofterdingen was a legendary thirteenth-century German minnesinger (minstrel poet), who allegedly won the song contest (Sängerkrieg) around 1260 (Novalis 1876). The legend inspired many European artists with their works, including E. T. A. Hoffmann's novel *Der Kampf der Sänger* [The singers' contest, 1819], Heinrich Heine's sardonic poem "Elementargeister" [Spirits in nature, 1837], and Wagner's opera *Tannhäuser und der Sängerkrieg auf Wartburg* [Tannhauser and the singers' contest in Wartburg, 1843].

15. The preface to the 1876 edition of this novel writes: "Even today the 'blue flower' is still a popular term for Romanic poetry" (Noch heute ist die 'blaue Blume' eine populäre Bezeichnung für die romantische Poesie; Novalis 1876, v–xxiii).

author Henry van Dyke's (1852–1933) 1902 eponymous story; Jinyi's 靳以 (1909–1959) story "Qingde hua" 青的花 (The blue flower, 1933); Ma Boliang's 馬博良 (b. 1933) story "Shiluo de lanhua" 失落的藍花 (The lost blue flower, 1942); and Chen Quan's 陳銓 (1903–1969) article "Qinghua (Lixiang zhuyi yu langman zhuyi)" 青花(理想主義與浪漫主義) [The blue flower: Idealism and Romanticism] (1943).[16] "The blue flower" certainly belongs to the transcultural lexicon that connects Europe, Japan, and China.

Nishida's interpretation gives the blue flower a deeper meaning than mere Romantic symbolism: "All things are fused in poetry, all things are *Gemüt* (feeling; Nishida's own German word). As light shines on all things (*banbutsu* 萬物) and reveals their colors, so does *jō* 情 shine on all things" (*NKZS* 1:340–41).[17] He asks: "Yet when will today's philosophical world discover Heinrich's 'blue flower?'" (368). The longing for returning to the homeland of sentiment can be traced to Rousseau, of course. For Nishida, *jō* is an essential part of Chinese philosophy, as can be witnessed in his diary entry on 1 January 1919: "The truth as revealed in *jō*, or Duns Scotus' [1265–1308; Scottish theologian] *sapientia* [wisdom; Latin word in Nishida's text] is not anti-reason, but above reason. Isn't Chinese philosophy based on sentiment?" (*jōyi* 情意; *NKZS* 17:361).[18]

As I have pointed out at the beginning of the Introduction, for the Chinese, *qing* is more than feeling or sentiment; it is in fact very much what Deleuze calls "affect," the connecting force that unifies life and non-life, human and universe, subjectivity and objectivity, mind and body. From this analysis, it is clear that the *kanji* word for *qing*, pronounced *jō* in Japanese, indicates for Nishida a more profound meaning than mere feeling. For him, the power of *jō*, just like God's existence in Duns Scotus' theory, encompasses all things in the universe and is above rational analysis. In his mind the Buddhist view of the universe is based on sentiment: all beings are sentient (*yissai ujō* 一切有情), meaning "all beings have affective capacity."[19] *Jō* is also for Nishida a kind of *religiouse Anschauung* (*shyūkyōteki chokkan* 宗教的直觀), or "religious sentiment" (*NKZS* 1:340–41), which he relates to Fichte's concept of *intellektuelle Anschauung*, because both denote "the unity of subject and object" (339). His diary from 1901 on discloses repeatedly that, for him, a devout Zen practitioner, Zazen (ざぜん坐禅) meditation is a body-mind exercise, which leads to the forgetfulness of one's body and self so that the fusion with the universe can be

16. Other works using the symbol of the blue flower include Xu Zhimo's 徐志摩 (1897–1931) poem "Zai na shandao pang" 在那山道旁 [On the mountain roadside, 1924], and Shen Congwen's stories "Zhufu" 主婦 [Housewife, 1937] and "Xin zhaixing lu" 新摘星録 [A new record of picking the stars, 1942]. I thank Ouyang Kaibin, who is working on the Romantic symbolism of the blue flower in modern Chinese literature, for sharing the information.
17. "Gemüt" is misspelled as "Gemüth" in Nishida's text.
18. For Nishida's *Nikki* 日記 [Diary] from 1897 to 1945, see *NKZS*, vol. 17.
19. See Introduction, note 14, for the original Sanskrit meaning of *youqing* (*ujō* 有情) and Lu Xun's concept of "sentient beings."

achieved (*NKZS* 17:51, 53, 101, 134).[20] In other words, Zazen results in the unity of subject and object. In the process, if he is unable to achieve the body-mind unity, he is despondent. In the entry of 19 July 1905, he succeeds and chants in jubilation, "Zen is music, Zen is art, Zen is a bodily exercise. There is nothing else that I seek for the consolation of my heart" (148).[21] For Nishida, religion is a matter of heart rather than reason. Due to his own religious sentiment, he finds French philosophers such as Maine de Biran (1766–1824) and Bergson especially appealing. He points out that French philosophy is distinct from its German or English counterparts in that it uses the intuitive method of thinking, and Descartes, though generally thought to be a pioneer of rationalist philosophy, depends on intuitive thinking as well. Derived from *sentir* (feeling), the French word *sens* is different from "sense" in English or *Sinn* in German, according to Nishida. Although the three words may be given the same meaning in a dictionary, *sens* in French in fact refers to *connaissance par coeur* (knowledge of the heart), or *sens intime* (intimate feeling), which is the core of Bergson's *la durée* and de Biran's philosophy (*NKZS* 12:126–30).[22]

In addition to Zen Buddhism, Confucianism and Daoism permeate Nishida's philosophical system.[23] Called the three teachings in China since approximately the third century, they have a long history of development in Japan. For what Nishida owes to Confucianism, one can pay attention to his affinity with the Heart-Mind philosophy of Lu Xiangshan and Wang Yangming. Following Mencius' teachings and maintaining that the "original heart-mind" (*honshin* 本心) is the center of morality and subjectivity (Liu and Shun 1996; Lin 2001), they challenged the philosophy of the Universal Order of Zhuxi 朱熹 (1130–1200), who maintained the distinction between heart and mind. During the late Ming, the Heart-Mind philosophy became

20. The pages cited here refers to the diary entries of 14 February 1901, 23 March 1901, 1 January 1903, and 7 February 1905.

21. For the translation of the whole diary entry, see Yusa 2002, 79. I am quoting from her translation, changing "physical exercise" to "a bodily exercise," since I want to draw attention to the body. She points out that Zazen meditation is a "body-mind engagement" (xix).

22. In "Furansu tetsugaku ni tsuide no kansō" フランス哲學についての感想 "Thoughts on French Philosophy," Nishida uses the katakana term サン to render the French word *sens*, indicating that he considers the final "s" in *sens* to be mute. Although many French words end with an "s" that is not pronounced, *sens* is an exception, of which the correct *katakana* transliteration should be サンス.

23. It is known that the modernization of Japanese philosophy is deeply connected with Confucian and Daoist thought. Modern Japanese philosophers such as Nishi Amane 西周 (1829–1897), Nakae Chōmin 中江兆民 (1847–1901), and Nishida were all indebted to Daoism as well as Confucianism. As early as the mid-sixth century, Daoist texts and Chinese translations of Buddhist scriptures were introduced into Japan. In the mid-seventh century, Prince Shōtoku 聖德太子 (574–622) stipulated the "Seventeen-Bills Constitution" (*Jūnanajō kenpo* 一七條憲法) in Confucian, Daoist, and Buddhist terms. During the Edo period (1603–1867) Daoist thought and Confucianism became extremely popular, with twenty-nine annotated editions of Daoist texts by the Sōrai school 徂徠學派 alone, while a considerable number of popular primers of Daoism were published (Xu 2007). However, most Japanese and English studies of Nishida explore his connections with Zen Buddhism rather than Daoism (Nishitani 2001; Carter 1997; Yusa 2002; Wargo 2005).

closely related to Zen Buddhism (Chen 2002). On the reading lists included in Nishida's diary kept in the late 1880s, *Laozi* and *Zhuangzi* as well as the four Books and Wang Yangming's works can be seen (*NKZS* 17:22–23, 33).

Nishida's affinity with Daoist thought can be witnessed in the essays and poems he wrote in his youth. In an essay he playfully discloses that his penname, Uyokusei 有翼生, meaning "the winged gentleman," is derived from the wings of the butterfly in the Daoist master Zuangzi's dream. He praises the great master's wisdom, which, unbound by his body, gives him the ability to fly: "When he goes no one knows where he goes, when he stops no one knows where he stops" (*NKZS* 16:607–9). In another essay, written in *Kanbun* 漢文 (classical Chinese), he calls Zhuangzi "the immortal" (*shinjin* 眞人, or *tento* 天徒), whose freedom from desire enables him to unite with nature and know the secret of the creation of Heaven and Earth (627). Indeed, it is a recurrent concept in *Zhuangzi* that "Those who have forgotten themselves are those who have become identified with Heaven." Another renowned concept in *Zhuangzi* that finds its way into Nishida's philosophical system is the fusion of subject and object: "All things and I are one" (627–28).[24] In Nishida's term, it is *butsuga yittai* 物我一體, or the unity of the self and things (*NKZS* 1:171–72). The Hegelian dialectical method, which he uses in his theory of "unification of the dialectical self" (*mujunteki jiko dōyitsu* 矛盾的自己同一), is not alien to *Laozi* and *Zhuangzi*, as evidenced by a statement from the former, "The Dao that can be trodden is not the enduring and unchanging Dao" (*Dao ke dao fei changdao* 道可道非常道; Legge 1962, 4), and from the latter, "There is nothing in the world bigger than the tip of an autumn hair, and Mount Tai is little" (*tianxia mo da yu qiuhao zhi mo, er taishan wei xiao* 天下莫大於秋毫之末，而太山為小; Watson 1964, 38). Even his concept of *basho* (場所 topos), the realm of nothingness where all things are created, can be attributed to the Daoist concept marked by oxymoron and dialectics: "Nothingness is the name of the origin of Heaven and Earth; being, the name of the mother of all things."[25] Nishida's indebtedness to Daoism is a topic worth further investigation.

Nishida's preface to the 1929 Chinese translation of *An Inquiry into the Good* fully acknowledges the Chinese origins of his philosophical system:

> The philosophy of us Easterners must be the expression of our life. It has to carry forward the Eastern culture that for thousands of years has nurtured us since the

---

24. The original reads: *wangji zhi ren shi zhi wei ru yu tian* 忘己之人是之謂入於天; *wanwu yu wo wei yi* 萬物與我為一. These quotes are from "Tiandi" 天地 [Heaven and Earth] and "Qiwu" 齊物 [On the equality of things] in *Zhuangzi*. See Legge's 1891 translation (1962, 318, 188). I have changed James Legge's romanization to pinyin for consistency's sake.

25. Here, I read the original sentence in Chapter 1 of *Laozi*, or *Daode jing* 道德經 [Book of moral], as "*Wu, ming tiandi zhi shi, you, ming wanwu zhi mu*" 無, 名天地之始, 有, 名萬物之母. This quote can also be read as "*Wuming, tiandi zhi shi, youming, wanwu zhi mu*," which Legge renders as "Having no name, it is the originator of heaven and earth; having a name, it is the Mother of all things" (1962, 4).

> time of our ancestors. For the form of philosophy as a scholarly discipline, I think we need to learn from the West. As to the content, it has to be our own stuff. And I believe that the foundations of our religion, art, and philosophy, far from being inferior, are much superior to those of the West. (Nishida 1929, 1–2)[26]

At the end of the preface, Nishida says he feels honored to be read by the citizens of Japan's neighboring country, which his own ancestors looked up to as "the Great Tang" (Nishida 1929, 1). Nishida's efforts to connect Eastern thought as manifested in Confucianism, Buddhism, and Daoism with Western philosophy marked a unique milestone in the transcultural history of world philosophy.

Liang Qichao and Japan's Revival of Eastern Ethics

When China's Lifeview movement became prevalent during the 1920s, the three teachings of traditional China were loosely defined as Eastern culture, or metaphysics (*xuanxue* 玄學), as opposed to Western culture, represented by science and materialism. As I will explain shortly, the concept of metaphysics became known in China mainly because of Rudolf Eucken, who associated his own *Lebensphilosophie* with traditional Greek metaphysics. Here it is time to discuss the key figure that bridged the Japanese and Chinese Lifeview movements: the famous scholar-journalist Liang Qichao. It was also Liang who brought Chinese intellectuals and Eucken together.

Although there was yet no evidence of Liang's direct contact with Nishida during his exile in Japan from 1898 to 1911, the two were no doubt connected through mutual friends, the renowned philosopher Inoue Tetsujirō and his disciple Kanie Yoshimaru 蟹江義丸 (1872–1940). The latter, like Nishida, went to Fourth High School and then became Inoue's student at Tokyo Imperial University, as did Nishida later (Nakamura 1999). During his time in Japan, Liang often participated in conferences held by Inoue and Kanie, who were at the time compiling *Nihon rinri ihen* 日本倫理彙編 [Collected works of Japanese ethics, 1903], comprising ten volumes. An effort to promote the "renaissance of Eastern ethics," it includes almost all Japanese schools studying traditional Chinese philosophy, such as the Yangming school, the Ancient Study school, the Zhuxi school, the Eclectic school, and the Laozi and Zhuangzi school (Nakamura 1999, 390–92). The efforts of reviving Confucianism (along with Buddhism and Daoism), which had been systematically suppressed due to the early Meiji all-out policy of Westernization and scientific modernization, became prominent from the late 1880s on because German-educated intellectuals like Inoue argued for the necessity of emulating "German-style models

26. In "Kōki" 後記 [Postscript], Shimomura Toratarō 下村寅太郎 (1902–1995), when mentioning Wei Zhaoji's 魏肇基 Chinese translation of *An Inquiry into the Good*, admits that he has not seen the original text of Nishida's preface (*NKZS* 1:461–70).

of national morality" rooted in Christianity. The result was that Confucianism, touted as a philosophy rather than a religion, became in the 1930s linked with Fascism and functioned as the guiding rationale for the Japanese colonizing mission under the name of the Greater East-Asian Coprosperity Sphere (Paramore 2016, 141–66). It has been pointed out that Inoue's speech on the reformulations of Confucianism given at the Japanese Society for Philosophy in 1906 was attended by Liang Qichao (150), who later would become the leading intellectual of the Chinese Lifeview movement.

Witnessing the revival of Eastern philosophy in Japan as a reaction against the European model of Enlightenment rationalism and modernization, Liang Qichao was certainly reassured of his own belief in traditional Chinese teachings, while a series of projects reinforcing that conviction were undertaken with his allies. Motivated by connecting Confucianism and the life philosophy of Eucken and Bergson, in his mind the two most important contemporary philosophers in the world, and in his capacity as an unofficial observer at the Paris Peace Conference, he led a group of six burgeoning Chinese intellectuals to Europe, including Zhang Junmai. According to Liang's *Ouyou xinyinglu* 歐遊心影錄 [Impressions of European travels, 1920], on 28 December 1908, they boarded *The Yokohama Maru*, a Japanese passenger and cargo vessel, from Shanghai to Europe, traveling together for a year. It was not until 17 January 1920 that they departed from Paris to return to China (*YBSHJ* 7.23:38–43).[27] During the European trip they visited friends, famous people, and historical monuments, went to lectures, and learned English, French, or German, according to each one's need. Their meeting with Rudolph Eucken in Jena on this trip resulted in a noteworthy direct contact between modern Chinese and European philosophers. After the trip, Zhang Junmai stayed in Jena and co-authored in 1922 with Eucken a book in German titled *The Problem of Life in China and in Europe*, in which the German life philosopher lauded Confucianism for its close affinity to his own thought. Also in 1918, Zhang Dongsun, Liang Qichao's close friend, called for a reading of Confucianism as a Bergsonian life philosophy while translating Bergson's *Creative Evolution* into Chinese (see Chapter 2). The 1921 book *Eastern and Western Cultures and Their Philosophies*, by Liang Shuming, Liang Qichao's faithful disciple, expounded on Confucianism as a life philosophy and related it with Euken's and Bergson's theories (*LSMQJ* 1:319–547; see Chapter 4).

On top of everything, thinking that the key to China's problem was cultural rather than political reform, Liang Qichao left politics and established the Lecture Society in September 1920 with friends such as Cai Yuanpei and Zhang Dongsun.

27. The group of young intellectuals traveling with Liang Qichao to Europe included Jiang Baili 蔣百里 (1882–1938), Liu Chongjie 劉崇傑 (1880–1956), Din Wenjiang 丁文江 (1887–1936), Zhang Junmai, Xu Xinliu 徐新六 (1890–1938), and Yang Dingfu 楊鼎甫 (life span unknown). Part of *Impressions of European Travels* is collected in *YBSHJ* 7.23:1–162. For accounts of the European trip, see Liu and Luo 1996, 38–50. Chapter 3 has further discussions of *Impressions of European Travels*.

The purpose was to introduce current Western and Eastern philosophical trends to China. Funded by the Beijing government under the Northern warlords, the society invited famous philosophers such as Dewy (1919–1921), Russell (1920–1921), Tagore (1924 and 1929), as well as Eucken's student Driesch (1922–1923) to China, exerting a great influence on the May Fourth intelligentsia and the New Culture movement (Li Yongqiang 2016).

Last but not least, the journals and newspapers Liang Qichao established along the years were certainly instrumental in promoting his cause. These were the organs of Research Coalition, which was evolved from the Progressive Party led by him. They included *Shishi xinbao* 時事新報 [Current times] (Shanghai, 1911–1949), *Jiefang yu gaizao* 解放與改造 [Liberation and *La Konstruo*] (Shanghai and then Beijing, September 1919–September 1922), and *Chenbao* 晨報 [The Morning post] (Beijing, August 1916–June 1928). From May 1911 on, *Guomin gongbao* 國民公報 [National gazette] (Beijing, July 1910–October 1919) also propagated the ideas of Research Coalition. All these publications introduced socialist theories as part of their agenda (Zhou 2019). Liang Qichao's project of drawing strength from transcultural connections to reinvent the values of traditional culture, fully supported by his coterie, was systematic and meticulously organized.

Bringing the European, Asian, and Anglo-American connections into perspective, I intend to show that the 1923 Science and Lifeview controversy in China was integral to the global dialectic of reason and affect, which in fact had existed since the European Enlightenment. One could say that the May Fourth Science and Lifeview debate was part and parcel of a transcultural phenomenon—transcultural in the sense of transhistorical, transterritorial as well as translingual—and should not be viewed as an event exclusive to China in the 1920s.

Eucken and Zhang Junmai, *The Problem of Life in China and in Europe*

To understand Eucken's connection with the Science and Lifeview debate in China, one should examine his 1922 co-authored book with Zhang Junmai. During his study for a bachelor's degree in economy and politics at Waseda University in Japan in 1906–1910, Zhang became a disciple of Liang Qichao, a leading figure in the Chinese intellectual community in Japan (Yang 1993, 15–51). Beginning in 1913, two years after the establishment of Republican China, Zhang Junmai studied at Humboldt-Universität zu Berlin for three years. Then, after the grand European tour with Liang Qichao, he stayed and studied philosophy with Eucken in Jena. Their association eventually bore fruit, *The Problem of Life in China and in Europe*. It contains a succinct summary of Eucken's philosophy. For him the human soul never tires of the process of unifying the material world. With such a unifying power, all is coherent, while "sensual impressions are subject to a guiding order" (Eucken and

Chang 1922, 162), in which the abstract takes precedence of individual existence. In the end, "a system of terminology," or concepts, is able to structure the whole reality. In such a tendency the most drastic change is the separation of subject and object, of state of things and essence of things (*Zustand und Gegenstand*) as a result of the working of thought, or rational thinking (*das Denken*). Thus, rational thinking leads to the division of self and non-self, the cause of the problems of the world today (162). To overcome such a division, which is the initial chaos, one needs to enlarge and transform life from within; only through this way can life as a whole co-live with an independent self, or a being-by-itself (*Bei-sich-selbst-Sein*; 163), while truth can be reached if the self speaks from within life. Meanwhile, we will be surrounded by a world of simple connections (*eine Welt blosser Beziehungen*), in which the sensorial existence exhibits a direct contact with impressions (162).

Eucken stresses the direct experience of the self in understanding the world. He maintains that only through spiritual life can goodness, truth, and beauty arise from the scattered elements in nature (Eucken and Chang 1922, 164). Most importantly, it is in humans' nature to proceed from the stage of experience to that of creation. The fundamental basis of spiritual life is metaphysics (*Metaphysik*), which is not the product of school learning but what life from its own sources leads to and what creates life anew (167). In metaphysics lies all original creation as well as genuine ethics—not simply social ethics or ethics in human spheres, but ethics that lends a new, spiritual self to human beings against their natural and social existence. Only on this basis can humans become both an "essence of the world" (*Weltwesen*) and an "independent energy of life" (*selbständige Lebesenergie*; 168). Obviously the Lifeview school in China drew strength from Eucken's idea of the creative power of the metaphysics of human existence, and this is why the Science and Lifeview debate in China was also known as the Science and Metaphysics debate (*kexue yu xuanxue lunzhan* 科學與玄學論戰).

Eucken calls his co-authored book with Zhang Junmai "a teaching of life for the Chinese" (*eine Lebenslehre für Chinesen*; Eucken and Chang 1922, iii). In the Preface he admits the book is inspired by "highly esteemed Chinese statesmen and scholars" who, their psychic life undergoing a "strong inner agitation" at the moment, look to a tight connection with German philosophical idealism and his own activism. Since, for various reasons, he is unable to accept their invitation to visit China, he intends to write a book indicating a "spiritual connection between China and Germany." The purpose of the book is

> to undertake a kind of bifocal language (*eine Art Zwiesprache*) between European and Chinese culture, which allows each of them to express themselves independently in each's own way. (Eucken and Chang 1922, iii)

From Eucken's preface, it is clear that, in a time of spiritual crisis in China, Liang and Zhang visited him in Jena with a specific purpose—to connect Chinese traditional culture with his philosophy in order to prove to their own compatriots that Confucianism was valuable and a solution to China's current problem. On the surface it seems Liang and Zhang looked to Eucken for guidance, but I would rather say that, finding Eucken's philosophy akin to Confucian teachings, they particularly sought him out and hoped that he would point out to the Chinese the values of their own tradition. It was an effort to seek the self in the other and to prove one's own value with recourse to the similar in the other.

Eucken himself also recognizes the similarity between Confucianism and his own philosophical system. According to him, The guiding philosophical thinking in China was "the structuring of life as a whole" (*die Gestaltung des Lebens als eines Ganzen*; Eucken and Chang 1922, iii–iv). Even though his co-authored book with Zhang aims mainly for the Chinese intelligentsia, he hopes that it will appeal to readers in Germany as well, readers "who fully appreciate the great significance of a tight connection between East and West and, in so doing, hope for a strong collaboration with the German spirit" (v). For Zhang Junmai, the feeling is certainly mutual: his purpose of co-authoring the book is to attempt "a synthesis of European and Chinese culture" (v). One might as well say that Eucken's understanding of Chinese philosophy is "superficial," or that *The Problem of Life in China and in Europe* reveals serious mutual "misunderstandings" on both sides and that there are in fact more "differences" than the "superficial similarities" between Eucken's and Zhang Junmai's theories of "lifeview" (Song 2015).[28] As a response, I would like to clarify my transcultural position through a critique of such views, which are mainly based on traditional comparative studies. By contrast, the concept of transculturality strives to go beyond the comparative mode that stresses the "differences" or "similarities" between cultures (Berry and Epstein 1999). It goes without saying that all cultures are different, but, if one tries hard enough, it is always possible to find similarities between two distinct cultures. What then do we expect to achieve after determining how one culture is different from or similar to another? Instead of looking for differences and similarities, transculturality as a research paradigm highlights the creative transformation of the self as a result of cultural contacts. Recognizing others in the self, it necessitates an ethical attitude towards others. It is crucial to realize that there is no such thing as a "pure" culture. Second, aren't most, if not all, encounters with

28. Song Ming maintains that, for Eucken, who follows closely the spiritual tradition of Kant and Hegel, spiritual life is transcendental and thus "transcends reality and human cognition." Zhang Junmai, by contrast, totally forsakes the transcendental aspects of spiritual life. But as I demonstrate in the following, Eucken believes that spiritual life is based on materiality (hence his advocacy for philosophy to return to life itself), and that Kant is wrong in asserting that noumenon is beyond human cognition. For Eucken it is through fantasy (or imagination) and art that spiritual life can best transcend reality. The German Romantic tradition is thus of great value for him. In tune with most modern philosophical trends, life philosophy in the late nineteenth and early twentieth centuries was an effort to transition from transcendence, true knowledge that goes beyond human understanding, to immanence, true knowledge that is found in everyday reality.

other cultures marked by "misunderstandings?" Going beyond the comparative mode and the trap of critiquing "correct" or "incorrect" translations, transcultural study endeavors to investigate transcultural events that connect different cultures and to demonstrate how such connections reveal the common concerns that different cultures share. The ultimate goal is to prove that no culture stands alone; all are connected if put in a global context.

In their co-authored book, the opening part on European philosophy is an abridged version of Eucken's masterpiece, *The Lifeview of the Great Thinkers,* and the second part, Zhang's analysis of Chinese philosophy. In the last part of the book, beginning from the chapter titled "Illumination and Appreciation of Chinese Structuring of Life" (Eucken and Chang 1922, 119–200), Eucken engages in a thorough evaluation of Chinese teachings of life as found in Confucius' writings. His analysis proceeds in three steps: first, the unique characteristics of Chinese philosophy of life; second, its similarity with its European counterpart; and third, the goals they share. When Eucken analyzes Confucian teachings, European philosophy, especially the Enlightenment, is always at the back of his mind. It is obvious that the analysis of Confucianism, be it misunderstanding or not, provides him with an opportunity to reexamine Western philosophical tradition as well as his own life philosophy.

For Eucken, the most noteworthy features of Confucian teachings are their emphasis on life here and now and the close connection between present and past, and their rational attitude toward anything beyond human knowledge, such as ghosts and afterlife. By contrast, the West lacks such historical consciousness (*solches geschichtliches Bewußtsein*; Eucken and Chang 1922, 134) and forsakes the present for the restless, meaningless pursuit of an afterlife. He especially praises the Chinese for their way of the "golden mean" (*die "goldene Mitte"*; 136). Under such a guideline, the relationship between nature and humans is harmonious; freedom and fate are not poles apart, while freedom is given more room to play. Unlike in the West, where reason dominates, in China, "rational and positivist [meaning practical] attitudes" (*Rationales und Positives*) toward life work hand in hand, without posing a sharp conflict with each other (140). For Eucken, the Chinese wisdom of the golden mean serves as a mirror that reflects what is currently wrong with Europe, or with the West in general. According to him, the problem of the world stems from Western people's willpower to conquer nature, or their preoccupation "to overcome the chasm between humans and the world" (*die Kluft zwischen Mensch und Welt zu überwinden;* 149).

According to Eucken, while Enlightenment philosophy uses reason (*Vernunft*; Eucken and Chang 1922, 19) to control social and worldly orders, Chinese philosophy is based on the ethical conviction of the *dao* (Tao 道, *Weltvernunft*; 147), which unifies the principles of all things in the universe. It keeps balance between reason and positivism, situates the individual in well-structured social relationships, where each finds his own proper place, while harmony between humans and their environment is maintained. By contrast, Western society pushes individualism and reason to extremes, and as a result, human pettiness (*Kleinmenschliches*) shown in the endless scientific pursuit is divorced from the spiritual (150). For him, the process of cognition, in addition to rational thinking, begins with our direct observation of nature and then is realized through the function and judgment of feeling. In his mind, the increasing dependence on reason, exercised through intelligence and willpower, leads humans to great complications and this creates "sharp conflicts" (*schroffe Gegensätze*) between people and things around them (149–50). However, Eucken is also fully aware of the problem China is going through at the moment. China in the past, with its isolated position and rich resources, was sufficient in itself. But now the meeting and competition of nations forces it to take part in the global movement of progress, while mutual exclusion (*ein gegenseitiges Sichabschließen*) among nations becomes impossible (148). When the old China encounters the outer world, a terrible shock is inevitable; the necessary transformation leads to a soul-searching experience like going through a "purgatory" (*Fegefeuer*; 152), in which not only the problem of truth but the relationship with reality is fundamentally changed. The contradictions dormant in the past now totally awakened, the balance and status quo of China's former life is ripped apart. Although denial or "negation" (*Verneinung*) reigns now, Eucken is sure that the Chinese with their foundation of moral competence will find "the way to the affirmation of life" (*den Zug zu einer Bejahung des Lebens*; 152).

The question then becomes: In China's endeavor to find the affirmation of life, should the West pose as a model? Eucken points out that, because the severe problem of European life is ongoing, the Chinese should by no means take the Western example as "the key to wisdom"; they can think that in the core of their life they are a full match to the West. China lags behind the West only in "form," or in technology, trade, and industry. How should both China and the West, then, solve the problem of life? The only way to do this is to investigate the current status of humans from the basis and thereby find guidelines to solve the present problems in both Europe and China (Eucken and Chang 1922, 152–53).

Eucken bases his view of human life on people's relationship with nature. In the chapter titled "Human Beings of the Present" (Der Mensch der Gegenwart), he proposes to understand the nature of human beings by examining their "historical becoming" (*aus seinem geschichtlichen Werden*; Eucken and Chang 1922, 157). Here it is clear that he is responding to Darwinism. According to him, out of all the organisms that struggle for survival in the natural process, humans distinguish themselves from animals with their capacity for spiritual life, which is fully shown in their use of language and creation of culture, including their aesthetic, religious, and moral performances. But, with "a continual spiritualization of human life" (*eine durchgehend Vergeistigung des Lebens*), humans are more and more detached from their sensorial binding with nature. As a result, human history shows a senseless advancement of material culture, while the material world (*das Sinnliche*) becomes a tool and aid for spiritual life (161). Therefore, the solution for the current problem of the West as well as China is to realize that humans with their material being are part and parcel of the natural world. They should exercise the direct experience of their five senses and return to their sensorial binding with nature, so that spiritual life and nature can co-live without subjecting nature to the service of human beings.

The emphasis on humans as sensorial, or material, beings could very well lead to a theory of the body that unifies spirit and matter. But Eucken did not engage further. In Western philosophy the most pronounced articulation of the body as both material and spiritual would appear two decades later with Maurice Merleau-Ponty's (1908–1961) *Phénoménologie de la Perception* (1945). In mid-1920s China, Zhang Jingsheng (1888–1970), nicknamed Dr. Sex, was probably the first to attempt a discourse of the body, which up to now has never been systematically investigated. This was partly because his theory sounds strange to readers today, since in his time the modern Chinese philosophical lexicon was still in the making, the same transcultural terms often translated into different neologisms, inevitably adding to the confusion. Another reason was that his attempt to combine praxis with his theory of sexuality aroused more suspicion and ridicule than admiration, as I will demonstrate in a separate monograph.

The Science and Lifeview Debate in China: Creation Is Action

To understand further the Lifeview movement in China, we need to look into Zhang Junmai's interpretation of Eucken as well as his article titled "Lifeview." At the time of the debate he was acting as interpreter for Hans Driesch, the German experimental embryologist, on his teaching tour in China from August 1922 to July 1923. Driesch was lecturing on European philosophy and vitalism (*shengjixue* 生機學), at universities such as Southeast University in Nanjing, and Peking University (Liu and Luo 1996). It was upon Eucken's recommendation that the Lecture Society invited Driesch to China as a visiting professor.

Before I discuss "Lifeview," we should be aware that, long before the famous debate broke out, when visiting Paris with Liang Qichao in late 1918, Zhang Junmai gave a talk to his Chinese friends studying in Paris, who longed to hear about his firsthand experience of meeting with Eucken in Jena. The lecture text was later published in 1921 as "Woyikeng jingshen shenghuo zhexue dagai" 倭伊鏗精神生活哲學大概 [Outlines of Eucken's philosophy of spiritual life]. In this superb essay, which has been neglected by critics, he gives a concise account of the context in which Eucken's philosophy emerged in Europe and its main arguments (Zhang

1921a).[29] Here, Zhang Junmai points out that there are two main trends in the history of philosophy, idealism and materialism. To him, Eucken is by no means an ordinary idealist philosopher but a life philosopher. Zhang distinguishes two branches in current idealist philosophy: life philosophy (*shenghuo zhexue* 生活哲學) and speculative philosophy (*sixiang zhexue* 思想哲學). Modern speculative philosophy can be traced to Descartes, Kant, Hegel, advocates of Neo-Kantianism, and others. By contrast, modern life philosophy began with Nietzsche, whose words he quotes in both Chinese and German: "Soll nun das Leben über die Wissenschaft herrschen, oder das Erkennen über das Leben?" (Now should life rule over learning, or knowledge over life?) Nietzsche chooses life over learning, the basic concept being that all thoughts come from situations in life. Zhang also names William James and Henri Bergson as life philosophers (1).

According to Zhang Junmai, while speculative philosophy starts with thought, thus emphasizing reason and concepts (*gainian* 概念), life philosophy starts with life, considering thought to be only part of it. Eucken's life philosophy was a reaction against late nineteenth-century intellectualism (*zhuzhi zhuyi* 主智主義) and naturalism (*ziranzhuyi* 自然主義), the precursor of the former being Auguste Comte's (1798–1857) positivism, and of the latter, Charles Darwin's (1809–1882) evolutionism. These two trends resulted in the flourishing of science and material civilization. Their initial purpose was to control nature through science, but in the end human life itself became enslaved by materialism and mechanism (Zhang 1921a, 5). By contrast, Eucken, along with the British physicist Olivier Joseph Lodge (1851–1941), Hans Driesch, and Henri Bergson, thinks that the purpose of life transcends our immediate reality, a reality fabricated by machines and factories. Here, to clarify his point, Zhang Junmai quotes from Bergson's preface to the 1912 French translation of Eucken's 1908 book, *Sinn und Wert des Lebens* [The meaning and value of life] (Eucken 1912).[30] According to Bergson, intellectualism governs reality by "intelligence" (*zhishi* 智識) and embraces a formulaic conception of life. Zhang points out that in Eucken's philosophy there is never any fixed formula of life and that the meaning of life does not lie in the intellect but in the constant activity (*huodong* 活動) of the spirit:

> In the whole book he only repeatedly encourages people to strive upward. The purpose of this heightening aspiration is to transcend the present self (*chaotuo hu*

29. This article appeared in *Gaizao* 改造 [*La Rekonstruo*, or Reconstruction] in March 1921. *Rekonstruo* is Esperanto, the language invented by anarchists. Here, Zhang Junmai uses mainly the Chinese term "shenghuoguan" 生活觀 and "shenghuo zhexue" 生活哲學 to render Eucken's terms for lifeview and life philosophy although the term "renshengguan" 人生觀 also appears several times. Two years later his famous talk that triggered the debate is titled "Renshengguan," and the terms "shenghuoguan" and "shenghuo zhexue" are no longer used.

30. In the article, Zhang mentions only "Bergson's preface to Eucken's *Sinn und Wert des Lebens*." It is in fact Bergson's preface to the French version of the book.

> *xianzai zhi wo* 超脫乎現在之我), in order to create other forms of noble activities. In essence, human action is guided by an ideal, which only shows the direction. What we are satisfied with today will be abandoned tomorrow. Therefore, all ideals are temporary, rather than everlasting. Day after day things are in a constant flux (*biandong bujü* 變動不居), rather than fixed.
>
> Indeed, this constant activity is the ontology of the spirit. (*jingshen benti* 精神本體; Zhang 1921a, 6)

A comparison of this passage with Bergson's words in the preface to Eucken's *The Meaning and Value of Life* shows that Zhang Junmai here is in fact translating or paraphrasing him, almost verbatim. The term *nuli xiangshang* (to strive upward) is used to render "le sentiment de l'effort et du progrès" (the feeling of effort and progress). The term "to transcend the present self" is the rendering of "la vie cherche . . . à se dépasser elle-même" (life aims . . . to transcend itself; Eucken 1912, iii). As a result, the concept of the self which aspires to transcend itself is highlighted, very much in tune with Eucken's theory. The sentence "human action is guided by an ideal, which only shows the direction" is a free rendering of "l'idéal toujours provisoire qui marque simplement la direction actuelle de son mouvement." The classical Chinese expression "*biandong bujü*," derived from the *Book of Changes* (see Chapter 3, note 30), is used to convey the idea of "provisoire." The statement that "this constant activity is the ontology of the spirit" refers to "Cette activité est l'esprit même" (iv).

Zhang continues to say that, according to Bergson, Eucken knows well that spirit and matter, though seemingly in opposition, need to reinforce each other and that the coordination between the two is the origin of "creative power" (*chuangzao nengli* 創造能力). Bergson's own words in his preface to Eucken's book are: "l'esprit, inséré dans la nature, est véritablement créateur d'energie" (the spirit, inserted in nature, is truly the creator of energy). It is easy to see that Bergson considers Eucken's concept of the creative power of the spirit in flux as in tandem with his own concepts of *élan vital* (生機 vital force) and *le flux continu* (constant flux; *hengbian* 恆變) in *Évolution créatrice* (Zhang 1921a, 2, 7). In addition to connecting Eucken and Bergson, Zhang tries to understand Eucken through traditional Chinese thought. To Zhang, the last sentence in the above quote, "constant action is the ontology of the spirit," is comparable to a motto in *The Book of Changes*: "Heaven proceeds with vitality and persistence. The superior person thus strives without ceasing."[31] He quotes from Eucken's

---

31. My rendering combines the translations of Alfred Huang and Richard Rutt. The former's translation in *The Complete I Ching* reads: "Heaven acts with vitality and persistence. In correspondence with this [t]he superior person keeps himself vital without ceasing (Huang 2010, 24). The latter's translation in *The Book of Changes (Zhouyi): A Bronze Age Document* reads: "Heaven proceeds: Jian. A prince thus strives without ceasing" (Rutt 2002, 384). The original Chinese, "*Tian xing jian junzi yi ziqiang buxi*" 天行健君子以自強不息, comes from the commentary on the first *gua* 卦 (hexagram), called *qian* 乾 (the Initiating, or the Creative), in *Yijing. Xiangzhuan* 易經・象傳 [*Yijing: Commentary on the figures*].

preface to *The Lifeview of the Great Thinkers*: "Creation is action. It constructs the spiritual world." He points out that, to Eucken, spiritual life is the life of the self as well as the world: "Extend the self to the world, so that the world is endowed with a self. The two therefore involves each other" (8–9). Evolution for Eucken is "eine schaffende Arbeit," a creative act (*chuanzao de laozuo* 創造的勞作). Bergson, by contrast, talks about creative evolution (*chuangzao de jinhua* 創造的進化; 16).

Zhang thinks that the task of life is the search for truth, goodness, and beauty. He points out that philosophers differ as to whether ultimate reality is knowable. Both Bergson and Eucken think it is perceivable; the key to truth for Bergson is intuition (*zhijue* 直覺), while for Eucken, direct spiritual experience (*jingshen de zhijie* 精神的直接). Both intuition and direct spiritual experience lead to "the unity of subject and object" (Zhang 1921a, 15). Zhang points out that, for Eucken, through "Lebenskampf" (the struggle of life), the spirit can move "from finiteness to infinity, from part to whole" (17). In Zhang Junmai's reading, both Bergson and Eucken believe that the twentieth century is a time for action, struggle, and creation. In a word, it is a time for revolution (18).

Zhang's reading of Eucken as shown in this essay is complex and comprehensive. In comparison, his essay "Lifeview" categorically polarizes science and life, much of the subtlety and complexity lost. It was originally a talk on 24 February 1923 to a group of science students from Tsinghua University who were about to study in the United States. The outright dichotomy between spiritual and material civilizations might have aimed to clarify a complex issue for science people. He points out that, with science, everything is governed by formulas and the law of cause and effect, while life is marked by its heterogeneous diversity, resisting formulaic restrictions. He juxtaposes self (*wo* 我) with non-self (*feiwo* 非我). Indentifying the self as the center of lifeview, he lays out a set of binary oppositions represented by science and life: science is objective, theoretical, analytical, uniform, and governed by formulas and laws, whereas life is subjective, intuitive, synthetic, unique, and governed by free will (*ziyou yizhi* 自由意志; Zhang 1977, 7). Most misleading of all is that he distinguishes between "spiritual civilization" and "material civilization" by juxtaposing China and Europe:

> However advanced science is, it is by no means capable of solving the problems of life, which hinge on nothing but human beings themselves. The so-called great thinkers since ancient times are those who contribute to our lifeview. . . . From Confucius and Mencius to advocates of the philosophy of Universal Order during the Song, Yuan, and Ming dynasties, all emphasize the cultivation of inner life. This trend leads to a spiritual civilization. Europe for the past three hundred years, on the other hand, emphasizes the domination of nature by human power. That results in a material civilization. (Zhang 1977, 9–10)

Zhang points out that even Europeans nowadays are severely questioning the tendency of overemphasizing materialism: after the European war some Westerners, tired of this outward, endless materialist pursuit, have begun to denounce the overdevelopment of material culture (1977, 11). Clearly denouncing the apotheosis of science in the New Culture movement, he writes:

> At the present the whole nation is talking about New Culture. Yet the key to transforming culture is lifeview. We have our own culture, the West theirs. How we are going to learn the good and avoid the harmful in the West, and how we are going to preserve the good and discard the harmful in our nation, all depend on our viewpoint. (Zhang 1977, 12)

Zhang intends indeed to provoke controversy. He urges people to be aware that, whatever achievements science has accomplished, there are aspects in life which science has no solution for, including human relationships, feeling, the question of self, the need for religious beliefs, and so on.

The 1923 Science and Lifeview debate had a lasting impact on Zhang Junmai. His 1963 essay reminiscing about the debate, written six years before his demise, fully reveals his obsession with it and his understanding of its epistemic depth. He expounds on Alfred North Whitehead's (1861–1947) philosophy of organism (*shengji zhuyi* 生機主義), which is "an ethic based on shared bonds between self and world" and emphasizes the importance of "the development of sympathetic connections with the environment, including fellow human beings" to construct shared values for the social self (Smith 2010, 1, 14). Zhang writes:

> Whitehead thinks these dichotomous theories [theories of the bifurcation of Nature] have led to the separation of the so-called primary qualities of matter [attributes of matter] and secondary qualities of matter [matter as perceived by the mind], and thus to the separation of phenomena and reality. Therefore, in an effort to correct these theories, he invented the organic philosophy, believing that the ultimate substance of the universe is Feeling [English word capitalized in Zhang's original text]. But feeling in English here should be viewed as the ultimate substance rather than mere emotions. It should be translated as "*ganyingzi*" 感應子 (the way Gottfried Leibniz's monad is translated as *danzi* 單子). I call it *ganyingzi* because of a line I have read in the work by Cheng Yichuan 程伊川, "Between Heaven and Earth there is only the principle of being affected (*gan* 感, to feel) and affecting (*ying* 應, to respond), nothing more."[32] Since Yichuan's words emphasize "only" and "nothing more," does it not indicate that it coincides with what Whitehead calls the ultimate substance? (Zhang 1981, 1049)

32. Zhang Junmai quotes from Cheng Yichuan (1033–1107): "Tiandi zhi jian, zhiyou yige gan yu ying eryi, gengyou shenshi" 天地之間，只有一個感與應而已，更有甚事 (*Siku quanshu* 699:11). Cheng Yichuan (also known as Cheng Yi 程頤), and his elder brother Cheng Mingdao 程明道 (1032–1085; or Cheng Hao 程顥), were famous Northern Song Neo-Confucians.

The "dichotomous theories" here allude to the concept established in the seventeenth century that "marks a turning point in the relation between science and philosophy," as pointed out by Whitehead in *The Concept of Nature* in 1919 (Whitehead 1919, 26). They have led to "the bifurcation of nature into two systems of reality." One reality is "the entities such as electrons which are the study of speculative physics," or the reality for knowledge that is never complete. The other reality is "the byplay of the mind." For Whitehead, the former is "the conjecture," and the latter, "the dream" (30). To redress this problem of "Cartesian dualism and scientific materialism" (McHenry 1995, 2),[33] he formulates the "'Theory of Prehensions,' or his doctrine of feeling," which is deliberated in his 1929 work, *Process and Reality*. For Whitehead, "process is the becoming of experience," while the basic view of his theory of prehension is that the subject, or the experiencing organism, "arises out of the world which he feels, and constructs its own nature from the way in which it feels it" (McCreary 1949, 67). In the third chapter, titled "The Transmission of Feelings," he discusses "subjective unity" and "objective identity" according to categories, writing that "Feeling cannot be abstracted from its subject," while at the same time he discusses "conceptual feelings" and "physical feelings," indicating that feeling is both mental and physical (Whitehead 1978, 247–50).[34] Throughout the book, recurrent terms such as "creative advance," "creative process," and "creative urge" clearly resonate with Bergson's *élan vital*. The whole book on the one hand constructs a cosmology that integrates all things in the world in an idealistic bond, and on the other, argues for an autonomous creativity, or becoming, as a critique of Darwinian evolutionism.

Zhang Junmai's reading of Whitehead as shown in the above extensive quote is very much to the point. Forty years after the Science and Lifeview debate, the quest for ultimate truth still haunts him. His understanding of Whitehead's "feeling" as *ganyingzi*, although seemingly strange in Chinese, in fact refers to the definition of *qing* formulated by Zhu Qianzhi in the 1920s, who was likewise inspired by Cheng Yichuan's famous theories of *gantong* 感通 (affective communion) and *shengsheng* 生生 (co-living and co-becoming) derived from "Commentary on the Appended statements."[35] Another source for Zhu Qianzhi's cosmological ontology was Bergson's concept of creative evolution. For Zhu, "The evolution of the universe

33. Leemon B. McHenry points out that Whitehead's concept of prehension, as a concept of panpsychistic idealism, "is undeniably the master principle of his process metaphysics," while prehension refers to "a process of prehensive unification," meaning "the notion of individual perspectives interlocked in a system of internal relations" (McHenry 1995, 1).

34. In *Process and Reality*, Whitehead formulates a system of forty-five categories to explain reality.

35. In the fifth chapter of "Commentary on the Appended Statements, Part 1," it is written, "*Rixin zhi wei sheng de, shengsheng zhi wei yi*" 日新之謂盛德, 生生之謂易, meaning "Daily renewal is the highest virtue; co-living and co-becoming is called change" (my translation). Richard Rutt's translation reads "[I]ts [Dao's] daily renewal is called 'overflowing power.' Products-producing-products is called *Yi*" (Rutt 2002, 412).

is established through such force-relations: to be affected and to affect" (*ZQZWJ* 3:126).[36] To me there is no better word to translate Zhang Junmai's concept of *ganyinzi* than the Latin word *affectus* used in Spinoza's *Ethics*. We should note that the way to render Spinoza's concept of *affectus* into English has also been problematic for translators. While Samuel Shirley's 1992 translation of *The Ethics* (1677) and Parkinson's 2000 version, among nearly ten other translations, render *affectibus* (dative plural of *affectus*) as "emotions," William Hale White's (1831–1913) 1883 version and Edwin Curley's 1985 version, among others, use "the affects."[37] I prefer to follow Curley's translation of *Ethics*, since in the Deleuzian affect theory *affectus* is not merely about emotions. Rather, it implicates the force-relations that connect humans with other humans, other beings, the environment, and the cosmological order. More of this is discussed in detail in Chapter 5.

36. *Yuzhou Jinhua dou chengli yu zhe yigan yiying de guanxi shang le* 宇宙進化都成立於這一感一應的關係上了. See Chapter 5 for further discussions on the topic.
37. Part 3 of *Ethics* is titled "On the Origin and Nature of *Affectibus*." It was Hubbeling Akkerman who in 1980 first suggested that the title should read "On the Nature and Origin of the Affects" (Spinoza 1985, 1:491). W. Hale White's translation in 1883 is probably the first to render "affectibus" into "the Affects." Cf. Spinoza 1985, 1:491; Spinoza 1952, 29th printing (W. H. White), 395; Spinoza 1992, 102; Spinoza 2000, 163.

2

The Aesthetic Education Movement

Affective Enlightenment

> With the outcry from the New Culture movement getting louder and louder every day . . . our colleagues in aesthetic education intend to construct "a new lifeview" through "fine arts education," cure depression in young people, and reverse the trend toward intellectualism in education. In addition, we hope that aesthetics will replace esoteric religions.
>
> —"Benzhi xuanyan" 本志宣言 [The mission statement of the journal, 1920] (*Meiyu* no. 1, 1)

The Aesthetic Education movement in Republican China advocated the significance of affective Enlightenment. While the mainstream of the New Culture movement advocated science and democracy for the intellectual Enlightenment of Chinese people, this mission statement of the journal *Aesthetic Education* declared that only through aesthetic education could the heart-minds of the people be reformed and Chinese society be renovated. Its position of counter-intellectualism is crystal clear. The statement is unmistakably echoing Cai Yuanpei's essays "Worldview and Lifeview" and "Replacing Religion with Aesthetic Education," to be discussed in this chapter. The terms "the fine arts" and "a new lifeview" were key concepts countering the apotheosis of science during the New Culture movement. These terms, in quotation marks in the original text, indicate they are neologisms borrowed from Japanese. For instance, the term *yishu* 藝術, pronounced as *geijutsu* in Japanese, is the translation of "fine arts." The first Meiji book I can find containing this term is Murota Atsumi's 室田充美 1873 work, *Keizai Shinsetsu* 經濟新説 [A new economic theory]. The first section of the book is titled "Ningen kikō geijutsu" 人間奇巧藝術 [The art of human ingenuities], discussing agriculture, commerce, and artifacts (Murota 1873, 5–27). A new concept accompanying the cultural modernization in Japan, art became a central notion in the Chinese Aesthetic Education movement as well.

When the movement was promoted by Cai Yuanpei during the 1910s, it had the support of all teachers and students of arts schools in the country. As other chapters of this book indicate, the movement was embraced by nearly all famous intellectuals as well, among whom was the renowned anarchist leader Li Shicen. An integral part of the New Culture movement, the Aesthetic Education movement has always been a subject of study in educational research. Recently literary critics have also begun to pay sporadic attention to it (Ban Wang 2015). The 1920 publication of the journal *Aesthetic Education* was a monumental event for the movement, and in 1925, Li Shicen and Cai still published books on theory and praxis of aesthetic education. Even though the Science and Lifeview debate was not triggered until 1923, this chapter highlights the burgeoning of the lifeview discourses that had begun in the 1910s and how the Aesthetic Education movement was part and parcel of the Lifeview movement. This chapter also connects the Chinese Aesthetic Education movement with its counterparts in German- and English-speaking countries as well as Japan.

The Chinese term *meiyu* 美育 (aesthetic education), like *renshengguan*, was originally a Japanese *kanji* term for *äesthetische Erziehung*, a German concept. The task of transculturality as methodology is to investigate this kind of transcultural lexicon, tracing how it travels from its origins in Euro-America to other different cultures. Not only did the Japanese terms and concepts about modern education facilitate the development of modern Chinese education and become its integral part, but they connected the West-Japan-China triangular route of their transcultural transmission. The following starts with the way the concept of aesthetic education came to Japan during the Meiji period.

Aesthetic Education in Japan

At the turn of the twentieth century, the growing concern for aesthetic education was by no means an insulated event occurring exclusively within the borders of China. It was a global phenomenon marked by transcultrality. Around that time, European and Japanese intellectuals were also raising awareness about the need of their citizens to achieve affective enlightenment through aesthetic education. The famous Taishō writer Natsume Sōseki 夏目漱石 (1867–1916), while studying in London in 1901, wrote an essay comparing the education of a Japanese gentleman with that of his English counterpart:

> In this nation [England] how magnificent are literature and the arts, which have been continuously cultivating the character of its citizens . . . In English there is no equivalent for *samurai*, but there is the word for gentleman. . . . I am worried that, as far as ethical education (*tokuyiku* 德育), physical education (*taiyiku* 體育), and aesthetic education (*biyiku* 美育) are concerned, the gentlemen in Japan are falling far behind. (Natsume 1977, 9:287)

Natsume was a mentor for many burgeoning intellectuals such as Abe Yoshishige, who was the first to translate Eucken's philosophy of life into Japan, as discussed in Chapter 1. In the above quote, terms such as "ethical education" (*deyu* in Chinese), "physical education" (*tiyu*), and "aesthetic education" (*meiyu*) belong to the transcultural lexicon, widely used in late nineteenth- and early twentieth-century China as well as Japan. They were Japanese neologisms translating Western, especially English and German, concepts of education during the late Meiji period.

In the National Diet Library digital collection of the Meiji era, at least thirty-nine titles contain the term "aesthetic education," indicating that it was already a popular concept during the period. Among the publishers was "The Aesthetic Education Society" (*Biyikusha* 美育社), which owned seven titles. One of the earliest books using this neologism was Takamine Hideo's 高嶺秀夫 (1854–1910) translation of the American educator James Johonnot's (1823–1888) *Principles and Practice of Teaching* (1878), *Kyōyiku shinron* 教育新論 [A new theory of education] (Takamine 1886). The twelfth chapter, titled "Aesthetic Education," begins with these statements: "The aim of intellectual education is truth (*shin* 真) . . . The aim of ethical education is goodness (*zen* 善) . . . The aim of aesthetic education is beauty (*bi* 美)" (Takamine 1886, 3:447). One of the three normal school students sent by the Meiji government to study in the United States, Takamine was educated at State University of New York at Oswego, where he was taught the German-speaking Swiss educator Johann Heinrich Pestalozzi's (1746–1867) doctrines of self-activity proposed in 1781. They include concepts such as direct concrete observation (*Anschauung*) and "the whole person" completed with intellect (head), moral values (heart), and practical skills (hand; Pestalozzi 1804).[1] As pointed out in the Introduction to this book, the concept of the whole person can be traced to Schiller. James Johonnot and Johann Pestalozzi were among the most influential Western educationists during the Meiji and Taishō periods. Kimura Takatarō 木村鷹太郎, in his 1907 work *Shinzenbi. bi no kan* 真善美・美の巻 (Truth, goodness, and beauty: Volume on beauty), called Plato "the ancestor of beauty" (*bi no ganso* 美の元祖; 1907, 2).[2] "Truth, goodness, and beauty" (*zhenshanmei* in Chinese) as a motto denoting objective values and universal ideals was prevalent in the late Qing and Republican China as well as in Meiji and Taishō Japan.

Ōse Jintarō 大瀬甚太郎 (1866–1944), the founder of pedagogy as an academic discipline in Japan, was among the first to use these newly introduced terms. A professor at Tokyo Advanced Normal University 高等師範學校, he had studied

1. For a recent study of Pestalozzi and the concept of "the whole person" translated into English, see Brühlmeier 2010. According to Mike Mitchell's "Preface to the English Edition," since the end of World War II, Pestalozzi's education theory has been put into practice in Asia and Africa by Pestalozzi World, a charity organization based in England, with the motto "fighting poverty with education" to help children in developing countries (Brühlmeier 2010, ix).
2. For a study of Plato's concept of goodness, truth, and beauty, see Evans 2000.

in Germany, France, and England from 1893 to 1897. In his 1891 book, *Kyōjuhō* 教授法 [Pedagogy], he pointed out the danger of directly appropriating Western pedagogy (Ōse 1891, 2). He was lauded for negotiating between Herbartianism (ヘルバルト主義), which dominated the late Meiji period, and the burgeoning theory of sociology of education in Japan. Johann Friedrich Herbart (1776–1841) was a German philosopher, psychologist, and educator, whose most important contribution was *Über die ästhetische Darstellung der Welt als Hauptgeschäft der Erziehung* [On the aesthetic representation of the world as the major concern of education].[3] Herbart believes that education is a process of socialization. His theory of character building based on inner freedom and discipline had many followers in England, the United States, and France (Blyth 1981).[4]

In 1899, Higuchi Kanjirō 樋口勘次郎 (1871–1917), a lecturer at Waseda Univeristy, advocated music as a subject for affective education in *Tōgō shugi shin kyōjuhō* 統合主義新教授法 [Integralism: New pedagogy] (1899, 213–16). In his 1909 book, *Kyōjuhō* 教授法 [Pedagogy], he gives an overview of the Western education theory of direct visual instruction (*chokkan* 直觀; or Anschauung, the German term originally provided) from Plato to the present. Rousseau, Pestalozzi, and Herbart are included in his discussions (3–12). In 1919, Obara Kuniyoshi 小原國芳 (1887–1977) began to propose the concept of "the whole person education" (*zenjin kyōyiku* 全人教育) in *Kyōyiku no konpon mondai toshite no shūkyō* 教育の根本問題としての宗教 [Religion as the basic issue of education]. According to him, "The whole person" refers to one whose developments of intellect (*chi* 智), feeling (*jō* 情), and will (*yi* 意) are in harmony. The German educators he studies include Pestalozzi and his student Friedrich Froebel (1782–1852; 1). Seven years later, in *Haha no tame no kyōyikugaku* 母のための教育學 [Pedagogy for the mother], Obara discusses the necessity of aesthetic education. Modern education, overemphasizing utilitarianism, intellectualism, moralism, imperialism, and mechanism, alienates God mainly because it is hostile toward the arts. He maintains that, for the cultivation of the whole person, both aesthetic education and religious education are indispensable (1926, 141–42). The relationship between aesthetic education and religion was also a central issue in the Chinese Aesthetic Education movement, an issue raised by Cai Yuanpei in 1917, as will be discussed later in this chapter.

3. Charles de Garmo translates the title of Herbart's book as *The Moral or Ethical Revelation of the World: The Chief Function of Education* (1895, 15).

4. According to Alan Blyth, Herbert believes that every child is born with an individuality, which should be transformed by education into character, the perfection of individuality. Blyth points out that "To Herbart, as to Plato or Kant, the man attained fullness only through becoming the citizen, and the means by which he must do so was through education" (1981, 70).

Wang Guowei and Chinese Aesthetic Education

Wang Guowei 王國維 (1877–1927) was one of the most prominent late Qing and early Republican Counter-Enlightenment intellectuals. He believed China's weakness originates from the enervating of Chinese people's heart-mind rather than intellect. As this book discloses, heart-mind versus intellect became the major issue for the May Fourth dialectic of Enlightenment. For people siding with Wang, the way to really transform China was to cultivate the heart-mind of the individual through aesthetic education. This is mainly due to traditional Chinese teachings that highlight intuitive knowledge (*liangzhi* 良知) gained through the heart-mind, as Mencius maintains: "Every man has a heart-mind sensitive to the suffering of others" (*ren jieyou buren ren zhi xin* 人皆有不忍人之心).[5]

A famous philosophy professor at Tsinghua University in Beijing, Wang Guowei was probably the first Chinese intellectual to discuss aesthetic education. In 1927, he drowned himself in the lake of the Beijing Summer Palace when the controversy over Eastern and Western cultures held sway. In the elegy for his death, the historian Chen Yinke 陳寅恪 (1890–1969) lamented his suicide caused by the pain of witnessing the decline of Chinese culture (Chen 2009). Since the late Qing, suicides of intellectuals and youths had become a serious social problem. Newspapers reported how the anxiety and pain experienced during the crisis of national survival and sociocultural transitions took its toll.[6] Wang Guowei studied in Tokyo in 1901 briefly and then from 1911 to 1916. As early as 1903, he began to write systematically about aesthetic education. These essays, written in classical Chinese, were first published in *Jiaoyu shijie* 教育世界 [The world of education], a journal he established with friends in Shanghai to advocate modern education.

In "Lun jiaoyu zhi zongzhi" 論教育之宗旨 [On the goal of education, 1903], Wang Guowei maintains that the purpose of education is to train "the whole person" 完全之人物 (*wanquan zhi renwu*), which Lu Xun calls *quanren* 全人, a concept that traces to Schiller. According to Wang, the so-called "whole person" is one whose physical education and "heart-mind education" (*xinyu* 心育), meaning spiritual education, are in harmony. The human spirit is divided into three aspects: intellect, which pursues truth; feeling, which finds perfection in beauty; and will, which seeks goodness. He defines intellectual education as *zhiyu* 智育, moral education as education of will (*yiyu* 意育), and aesthetic education as affective education (*qingyu* 情育). The spiritual education for the whole person must cover these three aspects, which are interconnected. Aesthetic education, cultivating the affects so that perfection is reached, is the means to moral and intellectual education (Wang 1993a).

5. The original sentence is a quote from "Gongsun Chou zhangjü shang" 公孫丑章句上 [Chapter on Gongsun Chou, Part 1] in *Mencius*. D. C. Lau in his bilingual edition of *Mencius* renders the sentence into "No man is devoid of a heart sensitive to others" (2003, 72–73).
6. *The Morning Post* reported 113 deaths by suicide from May to December in 1921 alone (Hai 2010).

In "Kongzi zhi meiyuzhuyi" 孔子之美育主義 [Confucius' principles of aesthetic education, 1904], Wang Guowei points out that desire (*yu* 欲) is the cause of all human and societal achievements and sufferings, while the only cure for all possible sufferings is beauty. Not only does he refer to the aesthetic theories of Kant and Schopenhauer, but he investigates traditional Chinese concepts on related topics, including the principles of aesthetic education in Confucian teachings and the aesthetic theories of classical thinkers and poets such as Shao Tao Yuanming 陶淵明 (365–427), Xie Lingyun 謝靈運 (385–433), Shao Yong 邵雍 (1012–1077), and Su Shi 蘇軾 (1037–1101). These Chinese aestheticians and Schopenhauer share the notion that the highest achievement of aesthetics is "the realm free from desire" (*wuyu zhi jingjie* 無欲之境界), which Wang Guowei relates to Kant's concept of "Disinterested Pleasure" (English term provided in the essay). He quotes from Schopenhauer, who in *Die Welt als Wille und Vorstellung* [The world as will and idea, 1819] maintains that the self without desire is a person who, when observing the beauty of an external thing, views it as a pure thing without stakes for oneself. For Shao Yong, one who observes the beauty of a thing turns one's self into a thing among many things, until it becomes a thing that observes another thing; the self thus vanishes in the interaction with nature. This is how the sages unify the sentiments of myriad things (*yi wanwu zhi qing* 一萬物之情; Wang 1993b, 254–55). When this is achieved, self and universe are united as one. Wang quotes from Lord Byron's long narrative poem, "Childe Harold's Pilgrimage" (1812–1818), a few lines from Canto iii, Stanza 72 that express a similar idea: "I live not in myself, but I become/Portion of that around me; and to me/High mountains are a feeling" (255). In other words, in contemplating the beauty of nature, the self is unified with its surroundings. Wang declares that both natural beauty and human-made beauty—including splendorous palaces, elegant statues, serene paintings, and poetry and music that speak to the heart—inspire humans to arrive at "the realm free from desire." One who reaches that realm is called a saint. When all people in society reach that realm, the nation becomes the legendary ideal country called *Huaxü zhi guo* 華胥之國. Wang laments that everything in China today has been guided by utilitarianism, getting thus further and further removed from aesthetic cultivation. He cites the traditional concept of "use of uselessness" (*wuyong zhi yong* 無用之用) in a rhetorical question: Who is aware that the use of uselessness is superior to the use of usefulness (*youyong zhi yong* 有用之用; 257)?

Wang Guowei is very much indebted to Schiller. He studies Schiller's *Über die äesthetische Erziehung des Menschen in einer Reihe von Briefen* [On the aesthetic education of men in a series of letters, 1794], in which Schiller, disappointed at the French Revolution and the rational tendencies of Kant's aesthetic theory, maintains that aestheticism should appeal to the heart (*vor einem Herzen*) and feeling (*Gefühl*), rather than to intellect (*Verstand*) and reason (*Vernunft*; Schiller 1982, 1–5). In addition, reason alone cannot accomplish all. A strong will and passion are needed to help it function, as Schiller writes in the eighth letter: "Reason has accomplished all that she can accomplish by discovering the law and establishing it. Its execution demands a resolute will and ardor of feeling" (48–49). Wang points out that, for Schiller, "Art is the birthplace of science and ethics," and that "aesthetic education and moral education cannot be separated." The highest ideal of art is the "Beautiful Soul" (Wang's own English term capitalized; *die schöne Seele* in German), in which the affects and moral powers are in harmony. This can be achieved only through aesthetic education (1993b, 255–56).[7]

Although his early essays on aesthetic education discuss mainly German and Chinese theories, Wang Guowei's language depends a great deal on the transcultural lexicon originating from Europe and then translated into Japanese *kanji*, including neologisms such as aesthetic education, physical education, aestheticism 審美學 (*shenmeixue*; *shinbigaku* in Japanese), arts 美術 (*meishu*; *bishutsu*), science 科學 (*kexue*; *kagaku*), ethics 道德 (*daode*; *dōtoku*), ideal 理想 (*lixiang*; *risō*), and so on. This indicates no doubt that Wang learned about European theories of aesthetic education from Japanese resources. Although the term concocted by him, *xinyu* (heart-mind education or spiritual education), never took on and was later almost completely forgotten, it manifests that, for Chinese intellectuals at the time, the heart-mind encompasses reason (see Chapters 5 and 6). It may be generally believed that the Vernacular movement advocated by Hu Shi in 1919 was the beginning of the modernization of the Chinese language, but in fact long before that the classical language had undergone a protracted process of revolutionary transformation. The archaic language of illustrious late Qing writers such as Yan Fu 嚴復 (1854–1921) and Lin Shu 林紓 (1852–1924), if examined closely, will be found studded with a copious number of translated terms, many of which are undecipherable at first reading.[8] Modern transcultural lexicon introducing foreign concepts was indeed an integral part of the traditional prose during the late Qing, as seen in Lu Xun's early essays, discussed in the Introduction.

For the Aesthetic Education movement that began in the 1910s, the key issue was the dialectic of heart-mind and intellect, or of affect and reason. Later critics, when revisiting the Science and Lifeview debate, usually emphasize the material/spiritual life dichotomy that divided the two camps (Kwok 1965). Such an

7. David Pugh, studying Schiller's philosophical essay *Über Anmut und Würde* [On grace and dignity, 1793], points out that the idea of *die schöne Seele*, which manifests the perfect harmony of sensibility and reason, can be traced to Platonism. Studying Schiller's poem "Die Künstler" [The artists, 1789], Pugh writes, "the trend underlying Schiller's thought is the redefinition of the dignity of man as the dignity of the artist" (1997, 224–35).

8. Take, for an example, Yan Fu's translation of Hubert Spencer's famous definition of evolution: "Evolution is an integration of matter and concomitant dissipation of motion" (Spencer 1870, 396). It becomes *zhi li xiang tui* 質力相推, a bewildering expression in Chinese, in Yan's *Tianyanlun* 天演論 [Evolution and ethics, 1897] (2012, 4]. Here, *zhi* refers to matter, and *li*, motion. Translated back into English, the term means "the mutual propulsion of matter and motion."

essentialist dichotomy does not reflect at all the epistemic controversy that was involved (Peng 2019, 189–217). The debate should be examined together with the Aesthetic Education movement, so that wider perspectives can be taken into view, and the dialectic of affect and reason is unfolded.

Cai Yuanpei and the Chinese Aesthetic Education Movement

The leader of the Aesthetic Education movement in China was Cai Yuanpei, a revolutionary and educator. He visited Japan briefly in the summer of 1902, and studied education, philosophy, and aesthetic theory in Germany in June 1907 for a year. His anarchist friends such as Wu Zhihui and Li Shicen were also active in Germany and Paris then. After serving as education minister for two months in 1912, Cai resigned as a protest against Yuan Shikai's 袁世凱 (1859–1916) despotic rule and went back to Germany, auditing courses at Leipzig University. It was in the winter of that year while still in Europe that he contributed the essay "Worldview and Lifeview" to the planned journal of his anarchist friends. From 1917 to 1927, he served as chancellor of Peking University, and from 1928 to 1940, the first president of Academia Sinica (Tao 2007).

It was in his office as education minister in 1912 that Cai Yuanpei began to advocate aesthetic education. Most leading figures of the Aesthetic Education movement in China, including Li Shutong 李叔同 (1880–1942), Ouyang Yuqian 歐陽予倩 (1889–1962), and Feng Zikai 豐子愷 (1898–1975), like Wang Guowei, had studied in Japan. We will see in the following discussion that, although they used Japanese neologisms for new concepts in their writings, the theorists they referred to were mainly German-language thinkers. This can be testified to by Cai Yuanpei's essay, "Duiyu jiaoyu fangzhen zhi yijian" 對於教育方針之意見 [Views on the policy of education] (*CYPQJ*, 452–59), originally published with a slightly longer title in *Jiaoyu zazhi* 教育雜誌 [Journal of education] in February 1912.[9] This is the first piece of writing I know of in which the transcultural term *shijieguan* 世界觀 (worldview) appeared in the Chinese language.

In this essay, Cai distinguishes between *xianxiang* 現象 (phenomenon) and *shiti* 實體 (noumenon; *CYPQJ*, 455), philosophical terms translated into *kanji* that can be found in Inoue Tetsujirō's *A Dictionary of Philosophy* (1912, 104, 114).[10] The Kantian distinction between phenomenon and noumenon is a well-known concept in philosophy, and Cai connects the two concepts in his theory of education. He writes:

9. In the original version in *Journal of Education* (no. 11, 1912), the title is "jiaoyu zongzhang duiyu xinjiaoyu fangzhen zhi yijian" 教育總長對於新教育方針之意見 [The education minister's views on the policy of new education]. The shorter title is used in *CYPQJ*.

10. Modern Japanese neologisms translating Western concepts gradually evolve over the years. In the 1912 edition of *A Dictionary of Philosophy*, "noumenon" is rendered as *jitsuzai* 實在, *jittai* 實體, and *hontai* 本體 (Inoue 1912, 104) and only as *jittai* 實體 in the first edition (1881, 60).

> The world of phenomena is mainly about politics, with creating happiness in this world as its goal. The preoccupation of the world of noumena is religion, with forsaking worldly happiness as its goal. Education, though established in the world of phenomena, has the world of noumena in its vision. (*CYPQJ*, 455)

The world of phenomena is governed by laws of cause and effect, inseparable from time and space, and dependent on experience. By contrast, the world of noumena is not confined by cause and effect, has no relation to time and space, and depends on intuition. It is therefore impossible to name the world of noumena, but, as a concept, it needs a name. Be it *dao* 道 (The Way), *taiji* 太極 (the Supreme Ultimate), God, dark consciousness, or subconscious will, all philosophical schools and religious denominations aim at such notions of ultimate truth. However, Cai emphasizes that phenomenon and noumenon are two sides of the same world, rather than two conflicting worlds (*CYPQJ*, 455). He advocates aesthetic education, which bridges the phenomenal and noumenal worlds. For him, civic education (based on militarism), intellectual education (based on utilitarianism), and moral education are all politics-oriented education. By contrast, worldview and aesthetic education are above politics (456–57). Citing Kant, he maintains that aesthetic contemplation always brings about a disinterested pleasure, which leads to the sublimation of feelings aroused by the world of phenomena. Through aesthetic sublimation, humans are thus able to approach the noumenal world and befriend the Creator (457). These concepts, although derived from Kant, are also in keeping with the traditional Chinese idea about artistic beauty: as if created by Heaven (*hun ran tiancheng* 渾然天成). Advocating the implementation of theory in education, he maintains that in the school curriculum there should be ten percent of civic education, forty percent of intellectual education, twenty percent of moral education, twenty-five percent of aesthetic education, and five percent of worldview education (458). No doubt behind this design is the idea of the whole person.

At the outset of "Worldview and Lifeview," Cai maintains that worldview is the prerequisite for lifeview, because humans, with their small stature and limited life span, are only a tiny particle of the world, which is limitless and infinite. As a tiny part of the world, how do we arrive at a worldview that is definitely beyond our perceptions? Since all the tiny parts are endowed with the essence of the whole, if the particulars of the parts are eliminated, then we are able to get the general trait that is the essence of the whole (*CYPQJ*, 459–60). What is the general trait, then? He writes: "Will [*yizhi* 意志, *yishi* in Japanese] is the only element that exists beyond the realm of matter and form. We therefore know that will is the general trait that all the parts of the world possess; in other words, will is the essence of the world" (460). Here Cai Yuanpei returns to the concept of phenomenon and noumenon expounded in "Views on the Policy of Education." He maintains that the will of the noumenal world has nothing to do with teleology, which is limited by time and space. Following laws of cause and effect, it is confined by form and the particulars of parts. Theorists call the noumenal world the dark will, or the blind will, in order to distinguish it from the individual will in the phenomenal world, the ultimate goal of which is to return to noumenon. When all parts of the world are closely related, without distinction between one another, then we come to the tangent where the phenomenal world meets the noumenal world—this is the ultimate grand goal, the complete realization of the "big self" (*dawo* 大我) of the noumenal world (460).

From ruminations on phenomena and noumena, Cai Yuanpei moves on to "evolutionary history" to prove the significance of human will to explore the unknown. He cites the Daoist concept on contentment in the present, a characteristic of the traditional Chinese way of life, and then contrasts it with the trend of the human spirit tied with the history of evolution. While traditional Chinese people were content with the simple necessities of life and interested in neither distant places nor even neighboring countries, Western explorers, out of curiosity instead of necessity, thronged to discover new lands and brave the extreme cold to reach the Arctic and Antarctica. Scientific inventions such as spaceships, airplanes, and automobiles were the results of a series of trial and error. Those who did not live long enough to enjoy these modern vehicles they helped to build along the way never regretted that they had experimented and failed. Writers and artists, who might be worshiped only posthumously, would never give up their efforts even though they endured lives without fame. All these instances tell us that sacrificing the present for the future is a general human trait (*CYPQJ*, 460–61). For Cai, if people take evolutionary history to indicate that the ultimate goal of humans is the preservation of their physical being or the species, then they are wrong. The lesson he learns from evolutionary history is otherwise: the ultimate goal and duty of human beings prioritize the multitude rather than the self, future rather than present, spiritual pleasure rather than physical enjoyment. He concludes that the grand goal for the world and the small goal for individuals are in fact in tandem and that life has value only when following the evolutionary law of the world (462–63). Here, we should take into account that lifeview and worldview are more about ideals than facts. It is true that biology as a scientific discipline is primarily concerned with the physical being and the species; spiritual aspects have no place in it. Nonetheless, it is also true that throughout the past two centuries not a few experts in other disciplines, including feminists and socialists in both East and West, have read more into biology. The most famous is probably Karl Marx's letter to Ferdinand Lassalle (1824–1864) on 16 January 1861: "Darwin's book is very important and serves me as a basis in natural science for the class struggle in history" (Paolucci 2007, 98; Ball 1979). For the feminist philosopher of biology Kate Holterhoff, Darwinian sexual selection implies that human females may be capable of subverting male dominance (Holterhoff 2010). Cai was certainly not alone in "misreading" evolution.

Cai Yuanpei was very likely the first Chinese to use the Japanese *kanji* terms for "worldview" and "lifeview," transcultural lexicon that connected modern China to global lifeview discourses. His interest in Japan had started much earlier. In 1898 he began to study Japanese with private tutors. The following year, as headmaster of Zhongxi Xuetang 中西學堂 (School of Chinese and Western Learning) in his hometown of Shaoxing, he invited Japanese lecturers to teach courses (Wang 1998, 33–38; Kawajiri 2013). For years he continued to learn Japanese and obviously kept a keen eye on both Japanese and German cultural scenes. His translations of Japanese works into Chinese during those years testify to that fact. His 1903 work, *Zhexue yaoling* 哲學要領 [Outlines of philosophy], was translated from Shimoda Jirō's 下田次郎 1897 transcription in Japanese of the German philosopher Raphael von Köber's (1848–1923) course notes at Tokyo Imperial University (Cai 1903). It discusses how philosophy distinguishes itself from science, and the relationship between philosophy and religion. In 1906, Cai translated the first volume of Inoue Enryō's eponymous work as *Yaoguaixue jiangyilu zonglun* 妖怪學講義錄總論 [Handouts on demonology: A general view, 1894], a treatise on how various disciplines of modern sciences and philosophy were established in order to eliminate superstitions emerging from fears aroused by environmental phenomena. Then in 1909, he rendered Kanie Yoshimaru's 1900 study of Friedrich Paulsen's (1846–1908) *Grundbegriffe und Prinzipienfragen* [Basic concepts and questions of principles, 1889] into *Lunlixue yuanli* 倫理學原理 [Basic principles of ethics].

In 1917, in his capacity as chancellor of Peking University, Cai published the famous essay titled "Yi meiyu dai zongjiao" 以美育代宗教 [Replacing religion with aesthetic education] (*CYPQJ*, 729–34),[11] a concept derived from Schiller, who maintained that "art is religion," and the German educationist Friedrich Wilhelm Foerster (1869–1966), whose book *Schule und Charakter* [School and character, 1907] went further, by proposing to replace religion with aesthetic education (Foerster 1914). Cai points out that "intellect, feeling, and will" constitute human beings' spiritual functions. In primitive times people subjected knowledge, ethics, and aesthetics to religion. Aesthetic education, when attached to religion, was undermined by it. The only function of art at that time was to stimulate our feelings rather than cultivate our appreciation of beauty. From the eighteenth century on, evolutionary biology gradually proved that the evolution of the universe has nothing to do with God's creation. As a result, knowledge as well as ethics became independent from religion. When the arts, including painting, sculpture, music, dancing, and architecture, also became independent from religion, the working of our feelings—or aesthetic appreciation—was likewise separated from religion (*CYPQJ*, 729–31). The concept of

11. "Replacing Religion with Aesthetic Education" was originally published in *Xinqingnian* 新青年 [New youth] 3, no. 6:1–5. For an English translation of this essay by Julia F. Andrews, see Cai 1996.

"replacing religion with aesthetic education," the bible of the Aesthetic Education movement in China, would reverberate for decades to come.

In 1919, the New Culture movement touted science and democracy as the panacea for curing China's socio-political illnesses. On 1 December, Cai called attention to the role aesthetic education should play in the New Culture movement in "Wenhua yundong buyao wangle meiyu" 文化運動不要忘了美育 [Do not forget aesthetic education during the Culture movement] (*CYPQJ*, 495–96). In the title, in addition to *meiyu*, the two terms *wenhua* (*bunka* in Japanese) and *yundong* (undō) are all Japanese neologisms. Cai points out that, facing the task of the New Culture movement, impulse and reaction on the spur of the moment only lead to frustration and disappointment when there seems to be no hope. Then, extremely pessimistic and world-weary, people may even tend to be suicidal. He writes, "The citizens of a culturally advanced country need aesthetic education as well as science education," because the former, as affective education, is able to cultivate a temperament of equability and a positive attitude toward life (495–96). The artist Zhou Lingsun 周玲蓀 (1893–1950), a regular contributor to the journal *Aesthetic Education*, discloses later that the event triggering Cai's essay was the death of Lin Deyang 林德揚, a Peking University student who had committed suicide on 16 November 1919 (Zhou 1920). In the December issue of *Xinchao* 新潮 [New tide] that year, there were three essays discussing his death. The educator and historian Luo Jialun 羅家倫 (1897–1969) points out that, because of the difficulty of raising funds for his patriotic project of opening up a national products store, Lin killed himself. Luo proposes three solutions to the problem of depression in young people: an artistic life, friendship (especially romantic relationship), and "a new lifeview" (Luo 1919). The educator and writer Jiang Menglin 蔣夢麟 (1886–1964) and Li Dazhao 李大釗 (1889–1927), a leading intellectual in the New Culture movement and later a co-founder of the Communist Party, agree that the key to problem solving is "a new lifeview" that can resist the degeneracy of modern civilization, reform the flawed social system, and create an interesting, ideal new life (Jiang 1919; Li 1919). "A new lifeview," heralded in the mission statement of *Aesthetic Education* established in 1920, to be discussed in the following, was evidently a concept that had already been shared by many contemporary preeminent intellectuals.

The Journal *Aesthetic Education*

Cai Yuanpei's efforts in promoting aesthetic education found full expression in the journal *Aesthetic Education*, which published seven issues between April 1920 and April 1922.[12] Short-lived as it was, it nonetheless provides a glimpse into the

12. Feng Yiyin 豐一吟, Feng Zikai's son, points out that the journal published only seven issues (2014, 98). They appeared monthly from April to August in 1920, and then in July 1921 and April 1922.

fundamental concepts of the Aesthetic Education movement in China since the early 1910s. The editors were members of the Chinese Association of Aesthetic Education, founded by the faculty members of Patriotic Girls' School (Aiguo nüxue 愛國女學), which Cai helped establish in 1902, and Shanghai Normal College of Professional Training (Shanghai zhuanke shifan xuexiao 上海專科師範學校). The association soon rallied a few hundred arts and music teachers and students from other schools all over the country. Members of the editorial board included the painter, musician, and writer Feng Zikai; the actor, playwright, and stage director Ouyang Yuqian; the musicologists Wu Mengfei (吳夢非, 1893–1979) and Liu Zhiping (劉質平, 1894–1978); and the aesthetician and Buddhist scholar Lü Zheng (呂瀓, 1896–1989). Most of them had training in Japan and were disciples of the famous artist-monk Li Shutong 李叔同 (1880–1942), who in 1901 had been a student of Cai Yuanpei at Nanyang Public School 南洋公學校. Persuaded by Cai, Li Shutong went to study Western painting and music at Tokyo Fine Arts School and Tokyo Music School (later merged as Tokyo University of the Arts) in 1905. The following year he established the Spring Willow Society (chunliushe 春柳社) in Tokyo, the first Chinese troupe of spoken drama, with Ouyang Yuqian performing in plays such as *Heinu yutianlu* 黑奴籲天錄 [Uncle Tom's cabin] and *Rexie* 熱血 [Passionate blood]. After returning to China with his Japanese wife, Li taught painting and music in Tianjin, Shanghai, Nanjing, and Hangzhou, becoming a famous calligrapher, seal sculptor, dramatist, poet, painter, and composer. The songs with his music and lyrics, such as "Songbie ge" 送別歌 [Farewell song] and "Yi ershi" 憶兒時 [Childhood reminiscences], were sung in every school and home. In 1914, he pioneered nude sketch teaching in China and was among the first to advocate wood carving, long before Lu Xun got interested in it in the late 1920s. In 1918, Li was ordained as a Buddhist monk with the Dharma name Hongyi 弘一 (Chen 2005). The two characters *Meiyu* (Figure 2.1) on the cover of the inaugural issue of *Aesthetic Education* were calligraphed by him. The same issue also includes a facsimile of his painting titled "Nü" 女 [A woman]. It is said that the half-nude woman in the painting was modeled on his Japanese wife, whom he had met when he was a student in Japan, and who returned home heartbroken after he took vows of celibacy. On the back of the painting is printed his short biography, which lauds him as "the harbinger of Chinese aesthetic education."

In the fourth issue of *Aesthetic Education*, its counter-intellectualism agenda as laid out in "The Mission Statement of the Journal" is reiterated in the essay "Duiyu woguo banxuezhe de yige yiwen" 對於我國辦學者的一個疑問 [One question to the educators of our nation], written by Wu Mengfei, the editor-in-chief. He puts to the fore the significance of affective cultivation in aesthetic education, pointing out that Western educators have realized it is a mistake to overemphasize intellectual education at the expense of "sentimental education" (*qingyi jiaoyu* 情意教育; Wu 1920c, 3). The term *qingyi jiaoyu* (*jōyi kyōiku*) is a Japanese neologism; in

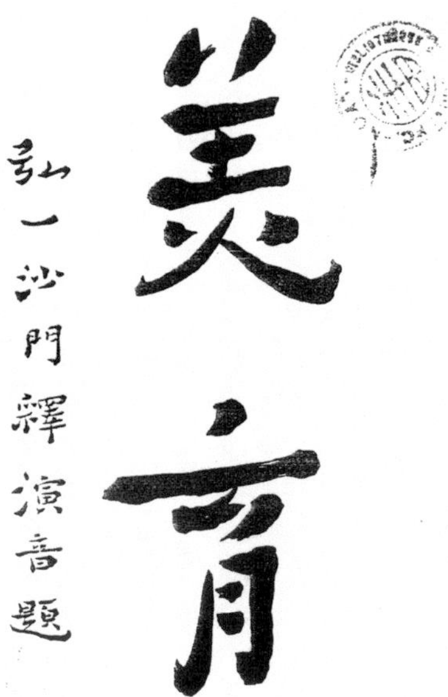

Figure 2.1: Title of the journal *Meiyu* [Aesthetic Education], calligraphy by Li Shutong

Chinese it is usually translated as *qinggan jiaoyu* 情感教育 (sentimental education, or affective education). The concept is derived from Rousseau. In reaction against Enlightenment rationalism, he maintained in *Julie, ou la nouvelle Héloïse* [Julie; or, The New Heloise, 1761] that passions should be given their full due so that one is susceptible to "natural education" (Rousseau 1997). The concept of sentimental education was then made famous by Flaubert's 1869 eponymous novel. Wu hopes that the educators of China will follow "the new global trend" and realize that life does not depend on material culture alone. He maintains that it is now "the age of educational reform" and pleads for aesthetic education, which is "the latest trend fit for the new age" (Wu 1920c, 3).

In an earlier article in the inaugural issue, "Meiyu shi shemo?" 美育是什麼？[What is aesthetic education?], Wu mentions the German Aesthetic Education movement that began a few years before and points out that one of its foremost leaders was Alfred Lichtward (1852–1914), a famous art historian and the first professional curator of Kunsthalle Hamburg (Hamburg Art Museum). Discussing Friedrich Foerster's *School and Character*, Wu writes, "Foerster was the main advocate of the 'Ethical movement' in Europe. His aim was to replace religion with civic moral education" (*xiushen* 修身; 1920a, 4). The term *xiushen*, pronounced *shūshin* in Japanese, refers to a newly established discipline in elementary and high schools in Japan before World War II. For Foerster, aesthetic education is important, because aesthetics is the passageway to ethical education, the aim of both being to cultivate human nobility (1920a, 6). In the second part of the essay, after discussing Kant's three Critiques, Wu cites the German aesthetician Edward von Hartmann's (1842–1906) idea that beauty is not noumenon but false phenomenon (*jiaxiang* 假像) and that the feeling of beauty is not real feeling but false feeling (Wu 1920b, 1). Wu then refers to the German musician and educator Karl Lange's (1849–1893) rebuttal against Hartmann in *Über Apperzeption: eine psychologisch-pädagogische Monographie* [On apperception: A monograph on psychological pedagogy, 1879]. For Lange, beauty is similar to what is called "illusion" (*cuojue* 錯覺) in psychology: "Beauty is between false phenomenon and noumenon . . . It is a kind of illusion, neither the false phenomenon mentioned by Hartmann, nor the real phenomenon" (1). He also believes that "When we learn about the truth of things, it is an intellectual activity; when we are fascinated by what is beyond the truth of things, it is beauty." Wu then refers to Darwinian biology, which indicates that the appreciation of beauty also exists in animals: "The sense of beauty has developed for the necessity of the preservation of animals. What contributes to the preservation of the species is beautiful, while what does not is ugly" (1). Here Wu is referring to Darwin's theory of sexual selection in *The Descent of Man, and the Selection in Relation to Sex* (1871): female animals choose the most beautiful males to ensure that their offspring have the best chance of survival. Wu Mengfei demonstrates here that he is fully aware of the influence of the Darwinian theory of beauty on modern aesthetic theories (Holterhoff 2010).[13]

Wu Mengfei points out the power of aesthetic education over affective education. Using the German philosopher Johannes Volkelt's (1848–1930) term, he says the fundamental nature of beauty is *gande* 感得 or *Einfühlung* (empathy; German original provided by Wu), which means "affectivity" or "affective communion." He explains what he means by the term: "*Gande* is the unity and fusion of the feelings of self and others; it can also be seen as the acme of people's mutual feelings" (1920b, 3). From the perspective of affect theory as expounded by Lisa Blackman and John Cromby, *gande* or *Einfühlung* is similar to "contagious communication" or "affective transmission," and the so-called "ordinary suggestibility" that sociologists and psychologists were concerned with at the turn of the nineteenth century. This kind of theory explains why tradition, affects, faith, and ideas can speedily, actively, and effectively pass on from generation to generation. Bergson was very much interested in mediumship, hypnotic suggestion, and psychological pathology such as fantasy and illusion. This sort of "inter-psychological mechanism" formed the basis of his philosophy (Blackman and Cromby 2007, 9). Wu Mengfei emphasizes Volkelt's idea

13. Kate Holterhoff points out that Darwin's theory of sexual selection implies that women as well as female animals are capable of aesthetics and thus subverts Victorian aesthetic theory that stresses the divine inspiration of the aesthetic experience, which, as maintained by aestheticians such as Edmond Burke (1776–1794) and John Ruskin (1819–1900), addresses the "immortal part of men."

that aesthetic education "is not about solace in life, but about action. It is not passive, but active" (Wu 1920b, 4). In other words, aesthetic education has a practical value. For Wu it aims to cultivate not only the aesthetic knowledge and noble character of the individual but also the unity and fusion of the feelings of the national subjects, as when people gather and sing the national anthem together (although, he points out, a formal national anthem for the Republic of China is still pending; 1920b, 3).

The so-called "unity and fusion of the feelings of self and others" thus indicates what the Lifeview school intellectuals have always maintained: affect functions to unify subject and object. Here, Wu Mengfei assigns to aesthetic education the task of recreating the national subject through affective cultivation. While art creates a disinterested pleasure, as Kant maintains, aesthetic education has a distinct purpose—to establish "a new lifeview." Although the journal *Aesthetic Education* published only seven issues between 1920 and 1922, it provides ample proof of the confluence of the Aesthetic Education and Lifeview movements. Before the Science and Lifeview debate broke out in 1923, the groundwork of the theoretical basis of the Lifeview School had already been paved with the publication of the journal. Its call for affective Enlightenment to redress intellectualism in education highlighted the dialectic of affect and reason, which reached its apex in 1922 and 1924 with the concept of affectivism proposed by Zhu Qianzhi and Yuan Jiahu, who maintained that truth can be reached by affect only, rather than by reason. Chapter 5 discusses this topic in detail. The Lifeview movement was indeed a collective effort of the cohorts of Liang Qichao and Cai Yuanpei to systematically challenge Enlightenment rationalism.

An Aesthetic Life: From Theory to Praxis

The Aesthetic Education movement reached its peak in 1925, the year in which two collections of essays, titled *The Principles of Aesthetic Education* and *The Methods to Implement Aesthetic Education*, were published. The former was edited by the renowned anarchist Li Shicen 李石岑 and the latter, by Cai Yuanpei, as mentioned in the Introduction (Li 1925; Cai 1925). Cai says, "Mr Li Shicen asked me to discuss 'the methods to implement aesthetic education.' I am stating my personal opinions as follows" (1). It was therefore Li Shicen who planned the publication of the two collections, which both continued the discussions of the theories of aesthetic education and embarked on the implementation of theory with a concrete proposal: the purpose of aesthetic education is to create "an aesthetic life" (*meide rensheng* 美的人生; Li 1925, 13).

Li Shicen had studied in Japan in 1913–1919, where he became close friends with Liu Shipei and the Japanese anarchist Ōsugi Sakae. It was he who established the journal *People's Tocsin* in Japan in 1916, as mentioned in the Introduction. Banned by the Japanese government, it resumed publication in Shanghai in 1919, after his return to China. He became the editor of *Journal of Education* in 1926. In 1927–1930 he studied Western philosophy in France, England, and Germany. He published in 1925 a book titled *Rensheng zhexue* 人生哲學 [Philosophy of life], and provides the reader with the English and German terms for *rensheng zhexue*: "Originally *rensheng zhexue* means Philosophy of Life in English, and *Lebensphilosophie* in German" (Li 1972, 1–7). It was a collection of his 1923 lecture series at the Education Department in Shandong. He points out that those who advocate life philosophy include Dewey in England, Liang Qichao and Liang Shuming in China, James Wideman Lee (1829–1919) in the United States and his translator Takahashi Gorō 高橋五郎 (1856–1935) in Japan, and Johannes Volkelt and Eucken in Germany (148–66). Li thinks that, for pragmatists such as Charles Sanders Peirce (1839–1914), William James (1842–1910), Schiller, and Dewey, there is no changeless truth in the constantly changing universe. They believe that "the construction of truth is based on real life," while their utmost contribution is the advocacy for a lifeview that encourages striving to thrive and to create in life. Education and life philosophy were the common concerns of anarchists in China and abroad. The Russian anarchist leader Peter Kropotkin's (1842–1921) 1921 book *Ethics: Origin and Development* was translated in 1928 by the Chinese anarchist and writer Ba Jin 巴金 (1904–2005) as *Rensheng zhexue: qi qiyuan yu fazhan* 人生哲學：其起源與發展 [Life philosophy: Origin and development] (Kropotkin 1928).[14] That Ba Jin changed "ethics" in the original title to "life philosophy" is indicative of the popularity of the concept in China at the time.

In the opening essay of his eponymous collected volume, "The Principles of Aesthetic Education," Li Shicen points out that ethical education, foregrounded in the eighteenth century, was still "within the parameters of traditional thinking." The overemphasis on intellectual and physical education since the nineteenth century has resulted in "the European war marked by militarism," meaning World War I. One should therefore advocate spiritual life and return to human nature, and this is where aesthetic education can help (1925, 2–3). To highlight the function of aesthetic education, he compares it with moral, intellectual, physical, and civic education.

14. The term "life philosophy" is not used in *Ethics: Origin and Development*, translated by Friedland and Piroshnikoff. Most often "morality" or "ethics" are used, as in "the possibility of developing an Ethics based on the natural sciences," or "Darwin's theory of the origin of moral sentiment in man." However, in the English version, the preface written by the two translators points out, "The Russian writer removes ethics from the sphere of the speculative and metaphysical, and brings human conduct and ethical teaching back to its natural environment: the ethical practices of men in their everyday concerns. . . . a subject of special and academic study becomes closely linked to whatever is significant in the life and thought of all men" (Kropotkin 1924, iii–iv). This description certainly fits the aim of life philosophy to bring speculative philosophy back to life itself. There was therefore ample reason for Ba Jin to change "ethics" to "life philosophy" in the title when his translation of *Ethics: Origin and Development* was first published in 1928. Since Ba Jin did not know Russian at the time, he consulted the English, French, Japanese, Spanish, and Esperanto versions (Jiang 1996, 280). In 1941, when Ba Jin's translation was republished, the title became *Lunlixue de qiyuan ji fazhan* 倫理學的起源及發展 [The origin and development of ethics] (Zhou 2011, 64–65).

For him, ethical education highlights discipline (*jiao* 教), while aesthetic education, affectivity (*gan* 感). Affective cultivation is far superior to disciplinary methods, because affects come from within, while discipline comes from without. He writes, "The force of discipline is stored in the brain, while the power of affectivity saturates one's heart-mind" (11). Emphasizing the contrast between "heart" and "brain," he is stating that aesthetic education functions through the heart-mind, which is in charge of affectivity, rather than the brain, which controls reason. For the Lifeview school, the intuition of the heart-mind is prior to and surpasses the function of the brain. Although Li does not elaborate on this, we can push further by saying that, using bodily parts such as heart and brain to indicate the origins of affects and reason, he is already touching on the concept of "the spirituality of matter," or the union of spirit and matter. Citing the neo-humanistic thought represented by Schiller, he writes, "Aesthetic education is ethical education. . . . Not only is aesthetic education the basis for ethical education, but it is the basis of all sciences," because beauty is "the manifestation of truth, the intuitive perception of truth" (7).

For Li Shicen, the appreciation of beauty leads to truth and goodness. He points out that, although aiming to pursue truth, intellectual education may not reach the goal. Neither words, spoken or written, nor natural sciences can reach truth. That is to say, "with all the powers of the intellect, we are still far away from the truth" (1925, 11). By contrast, the essence of aesthetics is "the revelation of truth." Borrowing from Bergson, he writes, "Through a kind of affectivity (*ganying* 感應) the arts can penetrate into the inside of the object and thus grasp its inner life." He maintains that beauty and truth often accompany each other and that "aesthetic education contains more intellectual education than what the latter encompasses by itself" (11). Drawing on William James, Schiller, and Karl Lange, Li maintains that, while containing the functions of ethical, intellectual, and physical education, aesthetic education still has its own unique sphere—the cultivation of the aesthetic sentiment (4). Physical education aims to train "the beauty of the body," but mechanic training is far less effective than what a beautiful environment and serene mood can do to keep a person fit. Aesthetic education contains also the function of civic education, because, according to John Ruskin (1819–1900), beauty is universal and has mediation power. Aesthetic education can thus "reduce social conflicts and class struggles" (12).

As to the relation between aesthetic education and religion, Li points out that while both aim to inspire humans to "the highest level of spiritual life," aesthetic education has an advantage: beauty can be seen in mountains, rivers, and anywhere in the universe, where the magnificence of nature is keenly felt. Aesthetic education can therefore replace religion. For him, the goal of aesthetic education is "the full development of human nature," or "the continuation of life and its advancement," which in Nietzsche is called "the will to life" (*shenghuo yizhi* 生活意志, *der Wille zum Leben* in German), in Bergson, "impulse of life" (*sheng zhi chongdong* 生之衝動, *élan vital* in French; 1925, 12). Li maintains that human beings pursue not only a diligent life that advances itself but "a life of pleasure, which is also called an aesthetic life" (13).

Life philosophy is after all a practical philosophy. With "an aesthetic life" as the highest goal of aesthetic education, those who advocate life philosophy tend to map out a blueprint for the good life they envision. Lü Zheng in "Yishu he meiyu" 藝術和美育 [Art and aesthetic education] points out that not only is art the expression of life, but it is life itself (1925, 15). The core of life is the "love for all forms of life." Based on love, the life of individuals will expand and advance itself and thus naturally transcend itself and proceed toward creation. This he calls "the aesthetic ethos" (*meide taidu* 美的態度; 17). For him, the goal of aesthetic education is more than the appreciation of the arts or creation of artistic works; its primary aim is "an aesthetic life" (*yishu de rensheng* 藝術的人生; 30). In order to achieve this goal, two steps are necessary. First, one has to correct the commonsense idea that art only encompasses the art works created by rare geniuses. We should realize that ordinary people, who pour out their lives to fuse themselves in a harmonious whole with others, are also appreciating and creating beauty. Second, social organizations that privilege a few artists must be reformed, because ordinary people are excluded from aesthetic appreciations in such a society. Here, like Li Shicen, Lü maintains that aesthetic education aims to reform life. The methods include transmitting the correct knowledge of art, carrying out a social reform movement, and cultivating talents who are devoted to aesthetic education. He mentions the British poet William Morris (1834–1896), who envisioned an aesthetic life for his age (31–33).

Hu Renchun 胡人椿 (1905–1992), by contrast, points out that in ancient Greece people maintained that goodness and beauty were inseparable and that morals were most effectively taught through aesthetic education, which centered on music, physical education, and literature, and which balanced the harmonious development of body and mind. After the Dark Ages, since the late eighteenth century to the first three decades of the twentieth century, Neo-Humanism has arisen in Europe, advocating sentimentalism, aestheticism, and the organic lifeview to oppose Enlightenment rationalism, utilitarianism, and the mechanic lifeview. Neo-Humanists maintain that the real life of human beings does not depend entirely on reason as suggested by the Enlightenment philosophers, but on sensitivities and emotions, which can be cultivated by aesthetic education (Hu 1925, 35–36). This trend is also a reaction against naturalism and materialism. Naturalism, which developed from eighteenth-century rationalism, gradually turned into utilitarianism. The lifeview and worldview of rationalism and naturalism were materialistic, with the value of everything in the universe judged by utilitarian yardsticks. As a result, humanitarian values were destroyed, and human life became dull and meaningless. It is only natural that aesthetic education has become the hope for a revival of humanitarian values. Facilitated by the progress of civilization, transportation vehicles, and the circulation of published works, the aesthetic sentiments promoted during the Neo-Humanistic age have become popular knowledge, while people have begun to realize that the trend of intellectualism should be modified by aesthetic education (36–38).

Although advocates of the Aesthetic Education movement were unanimous in their support for aesthetic education, their theories showed diversity and they often argued with each other. Attached as an appendix to *The Principles of Aesthetic Education*, the 1921 correspondences between Lü Zheng and Li Shicen are most revealing in this regard (Li 1925, 83–92).[15] The former refers to the Finnish aestheticist Kaarle Sanfrid Laurila's (1876–1947) aesthetic theory on the affects. Those who opposed him, including the German art theorist Konrad Fiedler (1841–1895), emphasized perception, while the Italian philosopher Benedetto Croce (1866–1952) emphasized direct observation. Both Fiedler and Croce excluded the role of affects in their theories (84). Lü comments that all spiritual activities, including the affects, perception, and direct observation, are connected with the self, and that all experiences are shaped by affects; therefore, without affects there would be no spiritual activities (84–85). Lü does not agree with Cai Yuanpei's idea of replacing religion with aesthetic education, because the priority for religion is eternal life, while for art, the expansion of life. One who engages in artistic activities lives a life guided by the aesthetic ethos, which aims at truth, goodness, and beauty not only for oneself but for others (88–89). For Lü, aesthetic education, with the realization of an aesthetic life as its goal, should be independent from other disciplines (90).

In his answer to Lü's letter, Li Shicen agrees that the core of aesthetic education is to create an aesthetic life but points out that, Lü, preoccupied with theory, has neglected its practical implementation. Li writes:

> An aesthetic life deserves a society of its own, one that is distinguished from the present society. . . . Aesthetic education is a tool to guide the present society to the path to an aesthetic society. (1925, 90–91)

While Lü objects to Cai's concept of "replacing religion with aesthetic education" on grounds that the latter is an independent category of knowledge, Li accepts Cai's concept as true, because the power of aesthetic education in cultivating the heart-mind is far superior to the disciplinary power of religion (Li 1925, 92). Lü's error lies in confounding aesthetic education with art, which, like religion, is also concerned with eternal life. Religion aims at universal spiritual life and is therefore also concerned with life expansion. In addition, what Cai Yuanpei opposes are the religions that unduly arouse people's passions by spreading sinister doctrines while attacking other religions. By contrast, aesthetic education engages in the processes

15. Li's letter is dated "22 December, the tenth year of the Republic," i.e., 1921 (Li 1925, 92).

of affective cultivation. Li concludes: art emphasizes artistic creations, and aesthetic education, the methods to achieve an aesthetic life (91–92). As fellow members of the Lifeview school and supporters of the Aesthetic Education movement, they critique each other's theory.

The focus of the collection *Methods to Implement Aesthetic Education* is exactly on the issue of praxis: the process by which reflection is turned into action in order to transform society. In the opening eponymous essay, originally published in 1922, Cai Yuanpei points out that aesthetic education can be implemented in family, school, and society, while he does not believe that it is possible for home education alone to achieve a perfect result (1925, 1). He maintains that aesthetic education should start as early as possible, at least from the time of pregnancy, since eugenics (*youshenxue* 優生學) seems unlikely. His primary ideal is for the government to establish prenatal education centers and nurseries in appropriate locations, preferably in the countryside. They are to be surrounded by excellent scenery, with gardens and squares in the vicinity fit for walks, light exercise, and moon watching and stargazing. In gardens there is lush greenery, with flowers and trees that take turns to bloom and leaf throughout the four seasons. Animals with beautiful feathers and fur should be allowed to wander in the gardens. Water flows quietly from springs to ponds, which are stocked with colorful fish. The buildings demonstrate a balance between traditional local styles and Greek or Renaissance styles. Inside the buildings the furniture shows a systematic design, with paintings and sculptures displayed. The wallpaper and carpets are in tranquil colors, and the music heard is peaceful and elegant. All the designs are conducive to the serene happiness of pregnant women, so that there would be no bad influences on the fetuses. After birth, the mother and the child are moved into a public nursery; she will take care of the child herself until the child is one year old. The babies of mothers who want to return to the workforce can be entrusted to nurses (2–3). At the age of three, children are ready for kindergarten, and at six, for primary school.

At the stage of elementary education, not only art but all art-related subjects should meet the requirements of aesthetic education. Even mathematics, which seems to be the dullest of all subjects, can be used to explain the concepts of proportion and rhythm in art. The concept of affectivity, or empathy (*ganqing yiru* 感情移入; *kanjō yinyū* in Japanese; *Einfülung* in German), in aesthetics can be illustrated according to physics and chemistry; for instance, power chord in music and colors in optics. In a word, no subject is unrelated to art (Cai 1925, 4–5). At the college level, all subjects directly related to aesthetic education should be taught separately in specialist schools, such as music and art colleges, just as those who are interested in science should study in specific disciplines. Social education for those who have left school should be reinforced by the establishment of art museums, art exhibits centers, music halls, theaters, cinemas, natural museums, and archeological, anthropological, and botanical museums, and so on (6–7).

Social aesthetic education is not complete without the beautification of local constructions such as roads, buildings, parks, sightseeing spots, historical monuments, and, especially in China, public cemeteries. According to Cai, from a rationalist viewpoint, the dead body, autopsied by a forensic doctor, should be preserved if it can be used for pathological references. Otherwise, the blood and flesh can be used for manure, and the bones, for sculpture—a way to put the worthless to use. But, human beings are after all creatures of feeling, and it would be more feasible to give the body a proper burial. In that case, the burial customs of local people, with ugly tombs or lumps of earth anywhere possible for the poor, or the gigantic tombs occupying too much land and using up too much elaborate woodwork and too many stones for the rich, are definitely to be reformed. Following the customs in the West, the body will be buried in a public cemetery in a scenic spot, or cremated. The ashes should be put in an urn to be stored in a beautifully constructed pagoda park (1925, 10–11).

Covering every crucial stage of human life, from prenatal to postmortem, Cai Yuanpei draws up the blueprint of an aesthetic society that his co-members of the Aesthetic Education movement were envisioning. As part of this utopian vision, in 1925, the famous Dr. Sex Zhang Jingsheng proposed an alternative aesthetic society purported to combine affect and reason. This I will investigate in another full-length study.

Resonances in Literature: Shen Congwen, Bing Xin, and Xu Zhimo

As president of Academia Sinica since 1928, Cai Yuanpei took charge of the institution's grand exodus to Sichuan, in southwest China, after the Sino-Japanese War broke out in the north in 1937. In November of that year he came from Shanghai to Hong Kong to prepare for the art exhibits planned to be inaugurated at the church of Saint John's University in May of the following year. Before he had a chance to return to Sichuan, he became severely ill and was detained in Hong Kong for treatment. He passed away there on 3 March 1940 (Tao 2007, 88–89).

A few years after Cai Yuanpei passed away, the renowned writer Shen Congwen published "Ai yu mei" 愛與美 [Love and beauty, circa early 1940s], a story commemorating his theory of replacing religion with aesthetic education. In the story, the narrator laments that nowadays people care about nothing but a mediocre lifestyle, politics and money trumping everything else, and no interest at all in the meaning of life. This kind of life only reflects "a lifeview that has castrated the affects" (*qinggan bei yange de renshengguan* 情感被閹割的人生觀). He points out that eternal life originates from love, be it the reproduction of living creatures or the literary and artistic productions of humans. Human beings are inspired to pursue eternal life because they find beauty, or God, in all that is alive. Beauty is everywhere; through pantheist sentiments (*fanshen qinggan* 汎神情感) we know that life's significance lies in God's existence in every living being (*shen zai shengming zhong* 神在生命中). This refers to the concept of pantheism embraced by Zhu Qianzhi, the first May Fourth intellectual to theorize affectivism (see Chapter 5). At the end of the story Shen writes:

> We indeed need a religion of beauty and love[16] to incite the younger generation's enthusiasm to be a good person, encourage them to pursue the abstract meaning of life, and arouse their noble and earnest passions for all reasonable designs that ensure an improved future. . . . We are reminded of the old gentleman Mr. Cai Yuanpei's theory of "replacing religion with aesthetic education" and his contributions to our national reconstruction. (*SCWQJ* 17:359–62)

Shen was one of the numerous May Fourth intellectuals who supported the Aesthetic Education movement. Due to its advocacy, the ideas of truth, goodness, and beauty became the mottos for May Fourth writers and artists. Bing Xin, among others, believed in these ideals all her life. Between 1919 and 1921 she wrote 164 poems, which were published serially in *Chenbao fukan* 晨報副刊 [Literary supplement to Morning post]. She speaks to youths:

> Young men!
> From the vast expanse of white earth,
> Find empathy!
>
> —*Chunshui* 春水 [Spring waters, poem 34] (*BXQJ* 1:357)

Just as empathy and love are recurrent motifs in these poems, so are truth and beauty:

> Truth
> In the silence of babies
> Not in the sophism of intelligent people
>
> —*Fanxing* 繁星 [Myriad stars, poem 43] (*BXQJ* 1:245–46)

> O poets!
> Be silent
> What you fail to delineate
> Is absolute beauty
>
> —*Myriad Stars*, poem 68 (*BXQJ* 1:252)

In these three poems, sophism and silence are juxtaposed. Truth, existing only "In the silence of babies," cannot be reached by rational arguments. Likewise, the language of poets, however flowery it may be, fails to describe "absolute beauty." In other words, truth and beauty exist only in the true affections of babies uncontaminated by reason and thus are impossible to capture by language and words.

16. "Religion of beauty and love" (Ai yu mei de xinyang 愛與美的信仰) refers to the title of the second chapter in Zhang Jingsheng's 1925 utopian treatise, *The Organization of An Aesthetic Society* (*ZJSJ* 1:154–74).

Bing Xin's poetry was deeply influenced by the Indian poet Tagore, winner of the Nobel Prize in Literature in 1913. He was invited to China in 1924 by the Lecture Society. However, long before his visit, several translations in Chinese of his collection of poems *Feiniaoji* 飛鳥集 [Stray birds, 1916][17] had been circulating in China. The most famous was the 1920 rendering by Zheng Zhenduo 鄭振鐸 (1898–1958), who, like Bing Xin, was a member of the Literary Society (Wenxue yanjiuhui 文學研究會). In September 1920, Bing Xin published an essay dedicated to Tagore, "Yaoji Yindu zheren Taige'er" 遙寄印度哲人泰戈爾 [To the Indian philosopher Tagore from afar], in which she confesses that she first knew about Tagore a year before, while thanking him for his belief in "the harmony between the universe and individual souls," and for the "natural beauty" found in his poetry (*BXQJ* 1:115).

An essay by the future young poet Xu Zhimo 徐志摩 (1897–1931) published in 1923 in *Chuangzao jikan* 創造季刊 [Creation quarterly], the organ of the Creation Society, speaks volumes about the general support for the Lifeview discourses and the Aesthetic Education movement among May Fourth intellectuals. Titled "Art and Life," it was originally written and published in English.[18] According to the editor-in-chief, Cheng Fangwu 成仿吾 (1897–1984), the essay was the text of a lecture delivered at the Tsinghua Literary Society in late December 1922, the first lecture that Xu ever gave in China after his return from studies in England on 15 October that year. Intending to translate it into Chinese but eventually giving up, Cheng decided to publish the essay in the original English.[19] Delivered right before the Science and Lifeview debate broke out in February 1923, this debut lecture fully shows Xu's erudition in Chinese and Western artistic traditions. He points out that China is lagging behind in the development of art despite a wonderful heritage from traditional painters like Wu Daozi 吳道子 (circa 680–759), Wang Wei 王維 (701–761), and Jin Dongxin 金冬心 (1687–1763) and the spectacular dancing of Chinese opera artists such as Mei Lanfang 梅蘭芳 (1894–1961) and Qin Xuefang 琴雪芳 (1905–1931). Quoting extensively from English critics such as Walter Pater (1839–1894) and Coventry Patmore (1823–1896), Xu defines art as "the consciousness of life." All great works of art should "comprehend life as a whole," while Chinese education,

17. Tagore's original work is titled *Sādhanā: The Realization of Life* (1913). According to Wisdom Library online definitions, *Sādhanā* in Hinduism refers to "an intentional act designed to achieve a transformation of one's inner state," and in Buddhism, "psychic exercises in the form of visualization and intense meditation."
18. "Art and Life," first published in *Creation Quarterly* 2.1:1–15, is collected in Kirk A. Denton, ed., *Modern Chinese Literary Thought: Writings on Literature, 1893–1945* (Xu 1996, 169–81). The original publication date of this essay is 1923 rather than 1922, as indicated in Denton's collection (Xu 1996, 169, note 1). For a recent study of "Art and Life," see Ouyang 2022.
19. In Denton's collection, the English translation of Cheng Fangwu's postscript at the end of "Art and Life" indicates that Xu Zhimo himself originally wanted to translate the essay. But Cheng's own words in Chinese reveal that it was he, as the editor-in-chief, who wanted to do so and then gave up the idea (Xu 1996, 181).

stressing practicality and appropriate etiquette, fails to open up our minds and eyes to "the secret and enchanting possibilities of a great life" and thus fails to allow us to interpret life through our faculty of imagination. Xu therefore entreats his fellow Chinese to "enrich, augment, multiply, intensify and, above all, spiritualize your life, and art will come of itself" (1996, 172–75).

Xu refers to Hellenic culture, pointing out that the Greek preoccupation with beauty does not entail that the Greeks were "irresponsible aesthetes." Rather, they valued beauty because it "contributes to the realization of a good life" (Xu 1996, 176). He praises the Greeks for "the discovery of the human body" and the Italian Renaissance for "the discovery and the embodiment of the human spirit," a period when both intellectual and imaginative pursuits were prevalent. Such a "unity of spirit" allowed them to achieve both the subjective self-expression for individuals and "the recognition of the objective reality of the universe" (177–78). As a result, art, as well as science, was flourishing. In his mind, Modern China, like Renaissance Europe, is experiencing a spiritual crisis. Hu Shi, a proponent of the Science school and a close friend of his, later in 1923 also delivered a lecture in English likening the May Fourth Renaissance to its European counterpart (Lee 2013, 235–39).[20] In "Art and Life" Xu criticizes "the cocksure rationalism and bald-headed materialism" originating from the European Enlightenment, along with "a few pseudo-scientists" and "sanguine-colored Bolshevists" who are against "a new idealism" that embraces humanity and "art as its religion" (1996, 178). This is clearly a reference to the development of Neo-Humanism in Europe, while one cannot overlook how it resonates with Cai Yuanpei's famous maxim pronounced in 1913: "replacing religion with aesthetic education." At the end, quoting two passages from Walter Pater's (1839–1894) conclusion to his book titled *The Renaissance* (1873), Xu advocates passions and love that are central to human sensorium and that "give us this quickened sense of life, ecstasy and sorrow of love, the various forms of enthusiastic activity, disinterested or otherwise, which come naturally to many of us" (181). The transcultural practices of May Fourth writers deserve to be investigated.

The impact of the affective Enlightenment advocated by the Lifeview and Aesthetic Education movements on the May Fourth and later generations is yet to be fully assessed. In Chapter 3 we will see more of the interaction between the Creation writers and the Lifeview school intellectuals.

---

20. Lee Kwai Sang points out that Hu Shi discloses in the diary entry on 3 April 1923 that he was writing an essay titled "The Chinese Renaissance" and that the idea originated from Philippe de Vargas' long article "Some Elements in the Chinese Renaissance," which had been serialized in *The New China Review* from April to June 1922. De Vargas was a Swiss, who served as chair of the History Department at Yanjing University (present-day Peking University). The journal *New Tide*, published by students of Peking University from 1919 to 1921, was called *The Renaissance* in English.

3

Zhang Dongsun's *Chuanghualun* [Creative Evolution]

Heart-Mind versus Reason

> I would rather create some new light,
> Than be a goddess in this niche.
>
> —Guo Moruo, *Nüshen* 女神 [The goddesses, 1921]

Thanks to *Chuanghualun* 創化論 (Figure 3.1), Zhang Dongsun's (1886–1973) 1918 translation of Henri Bergson's *Creative Evolution* (1907), May Fourth affectivism reexamined the traditional learning inherited from *The Book of Changes*, connecting the becoming and flows (*bianhua liuxing* 變化流行) of *qing* with the Bergsonian concept of creative evolution (see Chapter 5). Also due to Zhang's monumental translation, the transcultural term *chuangzao* 創造 (creation) became a familiar usage in daily language in the May Fourth era, while the same term, meaning "writing an original piece of work" or "inventing an apparatus," had existed during the Northern and Southern dynasties (420–589 CE).[1] Even though Chen Duxiu and Li Dazhao, prominent founders of the Communist Party in 1921 and proponents of the Science school during the 1923 debate, had published essays on *Creative Evolution* in 1915 (see the conclusion), it was Zhang Dongsun's translation of the book in 1918 and the establishment of the Creation Society in 1921 that precipitated the popularity of the term "creation" among ordinary people as well as intellectuals.

1. In "Ying Shao zhuan" 應紹傳 [Biography of Ying Shao], collected in Fan Ye's 范曄 (398–445 CE) *Hou Han shu* 後漢書 [History of the Later Han, 432–45 CE], Ying Shao (fl. before 207 CE) explained in thirty essays to the emperor his method of tidying up the laws. All of the essays except one were taken from previous historical accounts and revised by him. The term *chuangzao* was used when Ying Shao referred to the twenty-seventh piece originally written by him. The original reads: 其二十七, 臣所創造 (Fan 1973, 6.48:1613). In Shen Yue's 沈約 (441–513 CE) *Song shu* 宋書 [History of the Liu Song dynasty, 487 CE] it is recorded that the compass chariot, believed to have been invented by the legendary ruler Huangdi 黃帝 in antiquity, was not known during the Qin (221–207 BCE) and the Western Han, or Former Han (202 BCE–9 CE). It was not reinvented until the Eastern Han, or Later Han (25–220 CE) by Zhang Heng 張衡 (78–139). The original reads: 至於秦漢，其 [指南車] 制無聞，後漢張衡始復創造 (Shen 1974, 2.18:496).

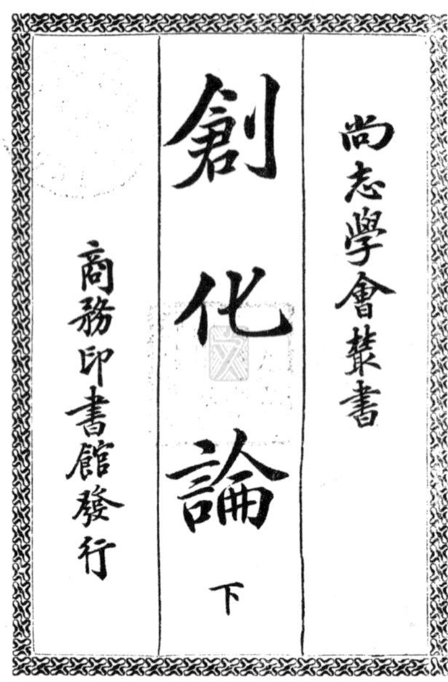

Figure 3.1: Cover of *Chuanghualun* [Creative Evolution], translation by Zhang Dongsun

When Liang Qichao took Zhang Junmai and five other young intellectuals to Europe in late December 1918 to visit Eucken, he had intended to visit Bergson as well, because for him they were the two most important contemporary philosophers in the world. To his disappointment, the latter was not available for an interview. Although he missed the opportunity of meeting the French philosopher in person, Zhang Dongsun, his close ally, had serialized *Chuanghualun* in the newspaper *Current Times*, one of the organs of Liang Qichao's Research Coalition. The serialization of *Chuanghualun* lasted from 1 January to 31 March 1918 (Bergson 1919; Zuo 2013, 81–82). The following year the whole translation was published by Commercial Press in Shanghai, with a preface written by the political commentator Tang Hualong 湯化龍 (fl. 1910s) advocating the complementarity and mutual reinforcement of Eastern and Western philosophies (Bergson 1919, iv), a concept the Lifeview school fully embraced.[2] Unfamiliar with French, Zhang mainly relied on the 1911 English translation by Arthur Mitchell (Bergson 1975) and the 1912 Japanese translation by Kaneko Umaji 金子馬治 (1870–1937) and Katsurai Tōnosuke 桂井當之助 (1870–1915), as he divulges in "The Translator's Preface" (Bergson 1919, i). The Japanese version, titled *Sōzōteki shinka* 創造的進

2. In Zhang Dongsun's text, the preface written by Tang Hualong, "The Translator's Preface," and the main text all start with page one. To distinguish them, I use roman numerals for the page numbers of the prefaces. I do likewise for other similar books published in the same period or earlier.

化 (Bergson 1913), was certainly a significant resource when Zhang deliberated the lexical choices in his own translation. While the Lifeview discourses had been in the making since the early 1910s, the publication of *Chuanghualun* provided the main concepts and transcultural lexicon needed to forward its cause.

On 26 May 1921, Zhang Junmai, arriving from Jena and with a co-member of the Research Coalition Lin Zaiping 林宰平 (1879–1960), who was on a European tour at the time, managed to meet with Bergson and converse with him for an hour at his home in Paris. The report on this visit, discussed later in this chapter, was published in *Gaizao* 改造 [*La Rekonstruo*][3] in August that year (Zhang 1921b) and later included in *People's Tocsin*'s special issue on Bergson in December of the same year.[4] Others who contributed to the special issue include Li Shicen, Zhang Dongsun, Cai Yuanpei, Lü Zheng, and Liang Shuming, all Lifeview intellectuals that are discussed in this study, in addition to Feng Youlan 馮友蘭 (Fung Yu-lan, 1895–1990). Feng, like Liang Shuming, would also be lauded as a first-generation New Confucian trying to revive Confucianism based on modern Western philosophy (Bresciani 2001, 35–36).[5] Both stayed in China after World War II and suffered persecution during the Cultural Revolution.

Zhang Dongsun was sent by the Qing government to Japan to study philosophy from 1905 to 1911. He studied at Tokyo University first, and then at The Private Academy of Philosophy (now Toyo University). In 1906, he established the journal *Jiaoyu* 教育 [Education] with friends like Lan Gonwu 藍公武 (1887–1957), exploring issues of philosophy and ethics. While in Japan, he befriended Zhang Junmai and supported Liang Qichao's constitutional position. After returning to China, he was hired by the provisional government in Nanjing. Although listed as a member

3. The journal, issued twice a month, was originally named *Jiefang yu gaizao* 解放與改造 [Liberation and *La Konstruo*], a bimonthly edited by the Research Coalition under Liang Qichao's aegies. Introducing socialist thought as the dominant theme, it was first published in Shanghai on 15 September 1919. The Research Coalition then moved to Beijing in August 1920, and the name of the journal was changed to *Gaizao* beginning with the issue dated 15 September 1920, but the journal continued to be published in Shanghai. After the issue dated 15 September 1922, it stopped publication due to financial strain.
4. For the interview collected in the special issue on Bergson, see *People's Tocsin* 3, no. 1 (December): 10–14.
5. For the three generations of New Confucians listed in *Reinventing Confucianism: The New Confucian Movement*, see Bresciani 2001, 11–36. According to Bresciani's chart of the members of the "New Confucian movement" (35–36), Liang Shuming, Zhang Junmai, Fang Dongmei, Xiong Shili 熊十力 (1885–1968), and Feng Youlan are the first-generation New Confucians; Tang Junyi 唐君毅 (1909–1978), Mou Zongsan 牟宗三 (1909–1995), and Xu Fuguan 徐復觀 (1904–1982), are among the second generation; Ying-shih Yü 余英時, Tu Wei-ming 杜維明 (b. 1940), Chung-ying Cheng 成中英 (b. 1935), and Liu Shu-hsien 劉述先 (1934–2016) are the third generation. Many of the second and third generations left the People's Republic of China after the war and went into exile in Hong Kong, Taiwan, and the United States. Tang Junyi, Mou Zongsan, and Xu Fuguan were students of Xiong Shili 熊十力 (1885–1968), who was purged during the Cultural Revolution. Zhang Junmai left for the United States and passed away there.

of the Nationalist Party, he was in fact closer to the Progressive Party led by Liang Qichao, who opposed Yuan Shikai's 袁世凱 (1859–1916) plan of restoring the monarchy. Later, Zhang Dongsun became an editorial writer for major newspapers in Shanghai. In 1918, he succeeded Zhang Junmai as the editor-in-chief of *Current Times*. In 1920, the Lecture Society invited Russell to lecture in cities like Hangzhou, Nanjing, and Changsha, Zhang Dongsun escorting him along the way (Wang 1999, 1–22; Zuo 2013). In 1921, his translation of Bergson's *Matter and Memory* was published by Commercial Press in Shanghai. Zhang later taught philosophy at Kwang Hua University 光華大學 (present-day East China Normal University 華東師範) and Zhongguo Gongxue 中國公學 (Chinese Public University) in Shanghai, and National Chengchi University 政治大學 in Nanjing. After the war he stayed in mainland China and passed away in prison during the Cultural Revolution.

Theory of Knowledge and Theory of Life

Zhang Dongsun's *Chuanghualun*, rarely studied so far (Chan 2009),[6] had a lasting impact on the May Fourth generation; it was a tour de force that shaped the Lifeview discourse. Translated into archaic Chinese, the book is not easily accessible to the general reader today. Even for readers at the time it would have been a struggle to read it, the major obstacle being the transcultural lexicon rendering philosophical and scientific concepts unfamiliar to the Chinese. Due to Zhang's antiquated language, the sizable transcultural lexicon in the translation becomes even more problematic. One thing we should bear in mind: both the Japanese version of *Creative Evolution* and Zhang's rendering are interpretive rather than verbatim translations, quite free in their lexical choices and often tending to add explanations or eliminate sentences as necessary. It takes an effort of comparison to see what is behind the choices made by the translators. As we can see in this chapter, Zhang Dongsun is struggling between available Chinese translated terms, Japanese neologisms, and his own invented lexicon. As history proves, either his inventions carried the day, or the Japanese neologisms prevailed.

Bergson's main purpose is to show that "theory of knowledge" and "theory of life" are inseparable and that they should reinforce each other when it comes to questions of life (1975, ix).[7] The former refers to epistemology as well as scientific knowledge. It was Kant who successfully transformed philosophy into epistemology,

6. While Yan Fu's translation of Huxley's *Evolution and Ethics and Other Essays* features two entries in Chan Sin-wai's *A Chronology of Translation in China and the West: From the Legendary Period to 2004*, *Chuanghualun* is not even listed.
7. In the introduction to *L'Évolution créatrice*, Bergson maintains that "la théorie de la connaissance" (theory of knowledge) and "la théorie de la vie" (theory of life) are inseparable. For a study of Bergson's advocacy for philosophy and biological science to "reach a new rapport concerning questions of life," see Ansell-Pearson 2010, 347–48.

combining Cartesian rationalism and Lockean empiricism. "Theory of life" refers to biology, especially Darwinian evolutionary biology, which is mainly a science of life. In Zhang Dungsun's Chinese translation, the two terms become "*quanzhi zhi xue*" 詮知之學 and "*shisheng zhi xue*" 釋生之學 (Bergson 1919, 5), which are his own odd neologisms that would never catch on. When he further explains what they mean, the two terms he uses, "*zhishilun*" 知識論 and "*shengminglun*" 生命論, are easier to understand. The former has been in use as a philosophical term in Chinese, but the meaning of the latter, also used in the Japanese version (Bergson 1913, 8),[8] is still unclear. It is only when one reads through a substantial part of the book, in Chinese, Japanese, English, or French, that one realizes "theory of life" indicates evolutional biology and that Bergson's own concept of creative evolution intends to improve, or supplement, it.

Bergson maintains that "a theory of life" should be accompanied by "a critique of knowledge," meaning a critique of knowledge based mainly on intellect and materialism (1998, ix; 1975, xxiii).[9] In 1920, when Dewey lectured in China, he pointed out that Bergson was critiquing the mechanism of Darwinian evolutionism (2005, 247), but Darwin never discussed mechanism. Although Bergson does criticize Darwin for attributing the cause of evolution to exterior environment, and thus eliminating the possibility of an interior urge of the organism to transform itself, the possibility of "élan vital" (vital impetus; Bergson 1998, 56), here his main target is not Darwin. Rather, it is Herbert Spencer (1820–1903), whose *First Principles* (1862) treats evolutionism as a positive science from a pure materialist view, believing that evolution is mechanic and determined by physical laws (Durant 1953, 351–400). The aim of *Creative Evolution* is to forward a new theory of life based on evolutionary biology—meaning Bergson's own life philosophy centering on the concept of creative evolution. It intends to correct the materialism and intellectualism manifested in both Spencerian evolutionism and Kantian epistemology (Bergson 1998, 223–28), as Bergson declares in the introduction: "the false evolutionism" 偽進化論 of Spencer should be replaced by "a true evolutionism" (1998, x; 1975, xxiv; 1919, 6), meaning creative evolutionism.

Critique of European Enlightenment

While Kant synthesized the rationalist and empiricist traditions inherited from the European Enlightenment, in *Creative Evolution*, Bergson consistently denounces the Enlightenment *philosophes* for their tendency to use the laws of physics to analyze the

8. While Zhang uses the term *zhishilun* 知識論 for "la théorie de connaissance," the Japanese version uses *ninshikiron* 認識論, which has also been widely used in present-day Japanese and Chinese.
9. Bergson criticizes biological theory for lacking a critique of knowledge: "Une théorie de la vie qui ne s'accompagne pas d'une critique de la connaissance."

function of thought (1998, 149–51, 153–54, 156). First, he points out that the *philosophes* "distinguish between the matter of knowledge and its form" (la matière de notre connaissance et sa forme; 1919, 153–54). For them, our perceptive faculties, relying on instinct, perceive the matter of knowledge in its crude, or natural, state. Intelligence, by contrast, pursues the form of knowledge; that is to say, a systematic knowledge that is derived by establishing the interrelationships among the materials perceived (1998, 149–51). But for Bergson, if we trace far enough to the time when life began, we would find that instinct and intelligence were implied in each other and that they were nearer to each other in insects and vertebras than we understand today (1998, 142; 1975, 156; 1919, 145). The separation of instinct and intelligence into two separate directions led to the famous Cartesian body-mind dualism, which Bergson, as well as the May Fourth Lifeview school, objects to. While the Japanese version uses "*chishiki no jisshitsu to keishiki*" 知識の實質と形式 (the matter and form of knowledge) to render Bergson's concepts, here Zhang Dongsun uses *tiyong zhi fen* 體用之分 (the distinction between substance and function), a rendering that is based on the *tiyong* theory in traditional Chinese learning (Bergson 1913, 271; 1919, 153–54).[10] The Neo-Confucian Wang Yangming, when analyzing intuitive knowledge, points out that there should be unity of *dong* 動 (motion) and *jing* 靜 (steadiness), *yong* 用 (the external functioning of the mind) and *ti* 體 (its internal substance; Feng 1953, 619). The concept of *tiyong* is one of the central principles of Chinese philosophy. Whether *tiyong* is an accurate rendering for Bergson's matter and form is less significant than the fact that Zhang clearly finds affinity between Bergsonian and Confucian concepts. In the following we will see that he indeed has ample reason to think so.

Another aspect that Bergson blames the Enlightenment *philosophes* for is the separation of knowledge and action, which for him should be "two sides of one and the same faculty" (1998, 151; 1975, 166; 1919, 156). This concept is not alien to Chinese philosophy. Wang Yangming is known to have maintained in the sixteenth century that "knowledge and action are one" (*zhixing heyi* 知行合一; Frisina 2002).[11] For Bergson, since our action aims at mobility, creation, and freedom, and since the faculty of intelligence is intended for pure speculation, utility, and immobility, it

10. *Ti* is often translated as "substance" or "original reality," and *yong*, "function" or "utility." For Xiong Shili, who often refers to the philosophy of mind in Yogācāra Buddhist idealism, *ti* is productive power, and *yong*, its manifest activity. Most importantly, the two are "non-dual," a concept that is also rooted in traditional Chinese philosophy (Sang 2020, 111–19). For the origins and interpretations of *tiyong* in Chinese and Buddhist philosophy, see Sang 2020, 29–70.

11. Warren G. Frisina, drawing insights from Wang Yangming, John Dewey, and Alfred North Whitehead, maintains that the knowledge-action distinction should be replaced by a "nonrepresentational theory of knowledge." Chapter 5 discusses further "the unity of knowledge and action" as a Neo-Confucian principle of self-cultivation.

is wrong for the *philosophes* to "transport a method of thinking aimed for action into the domain of speculation" (1998, 157; 1975, 171; 1919, 162). Yet human intelligence has another aspect beyond pure speculation: it can enter the frame of action that is "characterized by the unlimited power of decomposing according to any law and of recomposing into any system." In other words, it has a tendency for fabricating things (1998, 158; 1975, 173). The possibility of fabrication is never "perceived" but "conceived." "It is a view taken by mind," according to the English version of Arthur Mitchell. The French original reads: "c'est une vue de l'esprit." In Zhang Dongsun's rendering, the sentence becomes *cun hu xin zhong* 存乎心中 (it exists in the heart-mind; Bergson 1919, 163). What Mitchell takes for "mind" and the Japanese version renders as "sōzō" 想像 (imagination; Bergson 1913, 284),[12] Zhang interprets as "heart-mind," inspired no doubt by the Lu-Wang Heart-Mind philosophy, which Lu Jiuyuan 陸九淵 (1139–1193) of the Southern Song dynasty initiated, and which Wang Yangming in the Ming dynasty integrated into a systematic study, as mentioned in the introduction. I have also pointed out that in Chinese philosophy "heart" possesses both affective capability and the cognitive capability of "mind." In other words, "heart" and "mind" are seen as being one; the heart-mind is "a holistic-comprehensive structure in which all human faculties are unified and integrated," including reasoning, intuitive imagination, moral will, aesthetic feeling (Lin 2001, 202). To me, Zhang Dongsun's *xin* is closer to Bergson's "l'esprit" or "la conscience," since the latter believes that the brain (*le cerveau*; *nao* 腦 for Zhang) and consciousness (*la conscience*; *xin* 心 for Zhang) reinforce each other and that they are interdependent. Most importantly, "the more complicated the brain becomes, thus giving the organism greater choice of possible actions, the more does consciousness outrun its physical concomitant" (Bergson 1998, 181; 1975, 197; 1919, 190). In other words, there is a tendency for the heart-mind (or the brain) to transcend what is circumscribed by the physical condition. While action is the instrument of consciousness, the latter is imprisoned in the body and can only be set free by action. In the Japanese version *la conscience* is rendered into *yishiki* 意識, and *le cerveau*, *nōtsui* 腦髓 (Bergson 1913, 322). In "The Translator's Preface," Zhang Dongsun objects to the Japanese use of *yishiki*, which, pronounced as *yishi* in Chinese, is a Buddhist term and for him inappropriate in this context (Bergson 1919, iv).

Chad Hansen points out that for Mencius, *xin* (heart-mind) is where the *shi-fei* 是非 (right and wrong) capacity is generated, that it has "an entire innate moral grammar," and that it is "an independent route of access to practical wisdom" (1992, 187, 343; see Chapter 4 for further discussion of Mencius' concept of *xin*). For a practical philosophy like Bergson's as well as Confucianism, knowledge provides

12. Here, the Japanese version adds a great deal of explanation as to how space is imagined by intelligence, which animals lack, while Bergson's "c'est une vue de l'esprit" becomes "gojin no mono no mikata dearu" 吾人の物の見かたである (the way we look at things).

choices of actions, as he writes, "all the elementary efforts of intelligence tend to transform matter into instruments for action" (Bergson 1998, 162). What is then the "method of thinking aimed for action" that is beyond the domain of speculation? As we read on, it is clear that this method of thinking refers to instinct and intuition.

Instinct, Intuition, and Reason

Referring to the entomologist Jean-Henri Fabre's *Souvenirs entomologiques* [Entomological memories, 1890], Bergson analyzes how insects catch victims to feed their young. Take, for example, the hunting wasp (*le sphex* in French), which paralyzes its victim by injecting toxin into the exact spot of its complex nerve centers without killing it, so that the young can feed on the paralyzed insect. The hunting wasp is acting on instinct, an inborn knowledge that cannot be explained by science. For metaphysics, instinct works in a direction imbedded in the unconscious. It is an intuition resembling "divining sympathy" (*sympathie divinatrice*), which is "lived rather than represented" (*vécu plutô que representée*; Bergson 1998, 176–77). Following the Japanese version, Zhang Dongsun renders instinct as *benneng* 本能 (*honnō*), and intuition as *zhijue* 直覺 (*chokkaku*). Intuition would become a dominant concept in the Chinese Lifeview discourses (see the following chapters). But while the Japanese version uses *jintzuteki dōkanryoku* 神通的同感力 to render *sympathie divinatrice*, Zhang uses *gantong* 感通 (affective communion), a Confucian concept originating with the *Book of Changes* (Bergson 1913, 315; 1919, 185–86; see Chapter 5). Bergson's original sentence, *L'instinct est sympathie* (instinct is sympathy), becomes in Zhang's version "*benneng zhe gantong er*" 本能者感通耳, while the Japanese version uses *kannō* 感應 (*ganying* in Chinese) instead of *gantong* (Bergson 1998, 177; 1919, 186; 1913, 316). *Gantong*, synonymous with *ganying*, is one of the principal ideas of Confucianism, while *kannō* in Japanese refers more to the communion between humans and Buddhas. As Lin Wei-chieh points out, in addition to energetic affectivity 氣化的感通 (*qihua de gantong*), the concept of *gantong* in Confucianism also implies moral affectivity 道德感通 (*daode gantong*). Such moral affectivity connects the sympathetic divination of the *Book of Changes*, the concept of *ren* 仁 (benevolence) in Confucius, and the affective power of human nature in the two Cheng brothers. *Ren*, the core of subjective affectivity and agent of moral practices, is the manifestation of transcendence in immanence: the self that communes with the non-self and the *dao*, the Heavenly Way. For Tang Junyi, a New Confucian who moved to Hong Kong and Taiwan after World War II, *wuxin* 吾心 (my heart-mind) is the key that connects all the affective capabilities implied in *gantong*, establishing a "Heart-Mind theory of affective communion" that penetrates through metaphysics, theory of human nature, and theory of subjectivity (Lin

Wei-chieh 2018).[13] Bergson's relational ontology, manifested in his idea of instinctual sympathy, is certainly akin to the May Fourth Lifeview intellectuals, who find traditional philosophy resonant with his view.

Just as *xin* in Chinese philosophy is capable of intuitive knowledge, so is *la conscience* in Bergson. He points out that, in order to set consciousness free, organisms proceed in a double evolutionary direction: intelligence molded on the configuration of matter, and instinct and intuition accorded to the forces of life. These two directions seem to oppose each other, but in reality they are derived from a common source—*la conscience,* or *daxin* 大心 in Zhang Dongsun's rendering (Bergson 1998, 186–87; 1919, 198–99). In order to fully understand the evolution of life, we should establish a theory of knowledge (for the study of matter) and a theory of metaphysics (for the study of life) that are reciprocal. While the Japanese version translates metaphysics as *keijijōgaku* 形而上學, in Zhang Dongsun's translation it becomes *xuan'ao zhi zhexue* 玄奧之哲學 or *bentilun* 本體論 (ontology; Bergson 1913, 331; 1919, 197). Later he translates *métaphysique* as *xuanxue* 玄學, which, as he points out in "The Translator's Preface," is originally Cai Yuanpei's translation (Bergson 1919, iv, 200).[14] That is why the 1923 Science and Lifeview debate has also been known as the Science and Metaphysics debate (*Kexue yu Xuanxue lunzhan*). Both *xuanxue* and *xing er shang xue* are commonly used in Chinese philosophy today.

While the Enlightenment *philosophes* represent the unity of nature under an abstract and geometrical form, for Bergson, philosophy should grasp nature and reality by a "direct vision" (*une vision directe*), which is the strength of metaphysics (1998, 191–92). It is a great obstacle for philosophy to rely on reasoning (*le raisonnement*), which is the method of positive science, because reasoning tends to shut us up in the circle of the given, which is but a local solidification in the ocean of life. Only action can break the circle. Bergson uses swimming to illustrate the idea: if one's reason, based on all the experiences of walking, tells one that swimming is impossible, the only way to learn to swim is to plunge into the water, struggle to keep afloat, and gradually get used to moving ahead in it. It is exactly the task of philosophy to rely on instinct and to plunge into life, thereby embracing the whole anew, as humanity always seeks to transcend itself (1998, 193; 1975, 210–11; 1919, 205–6). In *Chuanghualun,* "intelligence," "reason," and "intellect" are all rendered as *zhihui* 智慧. In the Japanese version, however, *richi* 理知 (*lizhi* in Chinese) is used for

13. Lin Wei-chieh's article in Chinese, "Tang Junyi's Theory of *Gantong*: A Hermeneutic Understanding of the *Yi,* the Two Cheng Brothers, and Confucius," sums up the implications of Tang's complex theory of *gantong* in a succinct way. See Chapter 5 for more discussion of the concept of *gantong,* or *ganying.*

14. After the Peking University flag was created, Cai Yuanpei explained in a 1918 article titled "Beijing Daxuexiao xiaoqi tushuo" 北京大學校旗圖說 [On the design of the Peking University flag] that the horizontal red, blue, yellow colors on the right of the flag, the white on the left, and the characters "Beida" 北大 in black, represented science, philosophy, and metaphysics respectively. He pointed out that the theories of Schopenhauer and Bergson belonged to metaphysics (*CYPQJ,* 488–90).

"reason," and both *richi* and *eichi* 叡智 (*ruizhi* in Chinese) are used for intelligence.[15] Yet, from hindsight, we know that Zhang's resistance to the Japanese kanji term *lizhi* did not prevail. May Fourth intellectuals in general used it, and it has become the standard Chinese translation for "reason" or "intellect."

What is intuition, then? This is how Bergson defines it: "[B]y intuition I mean instinct that has become disinterested, self-conscious, capable of reflecting upon its object and of enlarging it indefinitely" (1998, 178; 1975, 194). In other words, as a contrast to instinct, intuition is disinterested and able to go beyond its single object of concentration to create indefinite understanding of life. Most importantly, just as intelligence depends on intuition, so does intuition on intelligence, without which it would have remained at the level of instinct, concentrating only on the specific object of its practical interest. Intuition, transcending intelligence, lets us grasp what it fails to give us, thus supplementing it. Disinterestedness, a major characteristic of intuition in Bergson's definition, links intuition to the aesthetic faculty. The fact that humans have an aesthetic faculty along with normal perception proves that intuition is possible. While sense perceptions fail to capture the intention of life, aesthetic intuition with its power of sympathy, by contrast, breaks down the spatial barrier between the artists and their models. Bergson advocates metaphysics, because it takes life in general as its object, relying on intuition and the "sympathetic communication" that intuition establishes between humans and the rest of living beings (1998, 178–79; 1975, 194–95).[16] Thus intuition brings about the expansion of our consciousness and introduces us into life's domain, the basic feature of which is "reciprocal interpenetration, endlessly continued creation" (1998, 179; 1975, 195).

The Ceaselessly Changing Self: *La durée, élan vital,* and Relational Ontology

For Bergson the intellect, unique to humans and meant to work solely upon inert matter, or solids, is unable to fully grasp whatever is fluid and totally incapable of capturing whatever is living. He criticizes the method of Freudian psychoanalysis, in which the self is *un moi amorphe* ("a formless ego" in the English version), separated into independent entities of psychic states (id, ego, and super-ego) and reunited by "an artificial bond," the science of psychology (1998, 3; 1975, 5). Since "real time" (*le temps réel*) is eliminated from it, psychology obtains at best "an artificial imitation of the internal life," lending itself to logic and language. *Creative Evolution*, by contrast, intends to explore the precise meaning of the concept of "to exist" (*exister*),

15. Take, for example, "*la théorie de la connaissance doit tenir compte de ces deux facultés, intelligence et intuition*" (Bergson 1998, 179); "認識論は理知と直覺との兩能力を併せ考えなければなかならる" (1913, 319); "自昔知識論於智慧與直覺之間, 不置鴻溝" (1919, 188).

16. Zhang Dongsun's rendering reads, "wuren you zhijue yu wo yiwai zhi zhu shengwu xiang gantong" 吾人由直覺與我以外之諸生物相感通 (Bergson 1919, 188).

which the Japanese version translates as *sonzai* 存在, while Zhang, as *you* (有 being), a reference to Laozi's theory of the reciprocality of "being and nothingness" no doubt (1998, 1; 1919, 7; 1913, 12).[17]

To understand why in Bergson's theory "to exist" and "real time" are inseparable, we need to investigate first his definition of the self: I change unceasingly (*Je change donc sans cesse*), always in flux (Bergson 1998, 1). It is impossible to know about the self through psychology, because one's character is determined by "real time" rather than "abstract time." The latter refers to clock time, while the former, *la durée* (duration), refers to the time of life. "Real time," which Zhang Dongsun translates into *zhenshi* 真時, will become the key to the Lifeview school's life theory, which I examine in detail in Chapter 5. Bergson compares *mon état d'âme* ("my mental state" in the English version) to a snowball that continuously conflates itself as it rolls down with the passage of time, collecting *la durée* along the way. Here, *la durée* refers to "memory," which pushes things in the past to the present and gnaws into the future. Bergson calls the memories that manage to cross the threshold of oblivion into consciousness "messengers from the unconscious" (*messagers de l'inconscient*) (1998, 3–4; 1975, 6–7). He maintains that "for a conscious being, to exist is to change, to change is to mature, to mature is to go on creating oneself endlessly" (1998, 7; 1975, 11). The concept of *la durée*, which is constantly flowing like water (*la durée qui coule*; 1998, 4), is a key to Bergson's idea of creative creation. Zhang Dongsun objects to the Japanese version's rendering of *la durée* into *renzoku* 連續, because to him this Japanese *kanji* term means the connection of two things, while the original French term indicates the self-extension of the same thing. To emphasize self-extension, he reinvents the term *mianyan* 綿延, which originally meant "continuous and ceaseless" in classical Chinese and still does (Bergson 1919, iii, 10).[18] The term *mianyan* would then become a defining feature of Bergsonism for the Chinese. This neologism in connection with Bergson has been widely used since the May Fourth era, by the general public as well as intellectuals.

For Bergson, consciousness means the will to life (*vouloir* in French or "will" in English), which prolongs our spontaneous *élan vital*. The main characteristics of *élan vital* and will are creation, freedom, and their interlocking relationship with matter, or the body. He writes:

---

17. The supplementary concept of "being" and "nothingness" (or nonbeing) runs through Laozi's *Daodejing* 道德經 [Book of moral]. It is written in the fortieth chapter: "*Tianxia wanwu sheng yu you, you sheng yu wu*" 天下萬物生於有，有生於無 (All things under Heaven are born of Being; Being is born of Nonbeing; Wu 2016, 92).

18. The term *mianyan*, meaning "continuous and ceaseless," appeared in the Southern and Northern dynasties (420–589), as in "Qili" 七勵 [Seven encouragements], a prose text written by Emperor Jianwen 簡文帝 of Liang 梁 (503–551): *Zhongsu mianyan, changlang zhoumi* 中宿綿延，長廊周密 (The midnight is ceaseless, the long corridors are winding and tightly encircling; *Siku quanshu* 1336:301).

> When we put back our being into our will, and our will itself into the impulsion it prolongs, we understand, we feel, that reality is a perpetual growth, a creation pursued without end. Our will already performs this miracle. Every human work in which there is invention, every voluntary act in which there is freedom, every movement of an organism that manifests spontaneity, brings something new into this world. True, there are only creations of form. How could they be anything else? We are not the vital current itself; we are this current already loaded with matter, that is, with congealed parts of its own substance which it carries along its course. (Bergson 1998, 240; 1975, 261; 1919, 258)

Vital impulse is the primal force for human invention and freedom, and for spontaneity in all organisms. Zhang Dongsun's exposition in "The Translator's Preface" is relevant: for Bergson spirit and matter are two sides of the same motion (Bergson 1919, viii). Although the former follows the law of consciousness and is irrational, and the latter follows that of geometry and is rational (Bergson 1998, 237; 1919, 255), both are propelled by vital impulse. Here in this passage Bergson is saying that matter (the body) is the carrier of vital force, while the vital force propels matter. In other words, spirit and matter are mutually dependent; none can exist alone. He thus criticizes both idealists, who believe that creation is simply an act of the mind, and materialists, who consider the universe is only composed of atoms. Bergson stresses "the universe in its totality": there is a connection between all the worlds in the solar system, heated by the same sun, moving in the same direction. More significant is the solid interdependence of all the parts in the same world. As a living being, we depend on the earth and the sun. As a thinking being, we may apply the laws of physics to our own world and extend them to the whole solar system, and we need to understand that the universe is not made but is renewing itself ceaselessly, without doubt indefinitely due to the new worlds that are added to it (1998, 241–42; 1975, 262–63). Here Bergson is articulating his relational ontology, which the May Fourth Chinese Lifeview school certainly find congenial to the Confucian ontology that emphasizes the relational bonding between Heaven, Earth, and human.

Interview with Bergson in Paris on 26 May 1921

The report on the interview with Bergson at his Paris residence was published in *La Rekonstruo* in Shanghai (Zhang 1921b). Famous Lifeview school leaders such as Zhang Dongsun and Liang Qichao are listed as editorial board members of the journal.

Written by Zhang, the report first lays out his analysis of Bergsonism: (1) the basic principle of Bergson's theory is change (*bian* 變) and motion (*dong* 動); contrary to previous philosophers who maintain that things (*wu* 物) exist first and then change and motion follow, Bergson believes that change and motion lead to the creation of things. (2) Bergson distinguishes between real time (*la durée*, French in

Zhang's text) and arithmetic, spatial time; real time refers to consciousness and real life, which connects past, present, and future as a whole. (3) For Bergson, "There are no things, but only motions; things are only our eventual motions" (English in Zhang's text). (4) The origin of substance is change and motion, while sensual perception, concept, and judgment, leading to the choices of knowledge, are only parts of the whole process of change and motion, which is noumenon itself (Zhang 1921b, 7).[19]

During the one-hour interview with Bergson, at first Zhang, on behalf of Liang Qichao's Lecture Society, wants to confirm when he plans to visit China. Bergson replies that, due to the war going on, he has too much in hand to make himself useful to the nation, while his philosophical work is interrupted. In addition, recently he has felt his energy is declining. What used to take a short while often demands more time to accomplish, and thus he has less and less free time as days go by (Bergson is now sixty-two years old). The visit to China has to wait until he finishes his lecture appointments at the University of Edinburg and a university in Sweden. He asks about Dewey's trips in China, and, after learning about the topic of Russell's lectures there, comments, "Russell is not my friend in philosophy. He is indeed unable to understand the meaning of my philosophy" (Zhang 1921b, 8). Zhang and Lin then ask Bergson to explain concepts that they have found difficult in his writings. What is the distinction between philosophical intuition (*intuition philosophique*), spatial intuition (*institution spatiale*), and sensible intuition (*intuition sensible*)? Bergson replies that philosophical intuition, which is the basic principle of his philosophy, refers to direct knowledge, while sympathy means "one places oneself within an object." Spatial intuition can be understood as the graphs in geometry, which can induce axioms. Bergson's philosophical intuition, not concerned with matter, is applicable to life and consciousness. Sensible intuition refers mainly to Kant's philosophy, which is *infra-intellectuelle*, or a step before intellectualism. Bergson's philosophical intuition, by contrast, is *supra-intellectuelle* and transcends intellectualism (8–9). What is intuition for Bergson, then? He points out that the intuitive method, always used by poets and artists, should be applied to philosophy as well. What we call instinct in animals is intuition in humans. That is not to say that intuition is instinct, but as far as placing oneself within an object, they are similar. Humans are prone to analysis and comparison, seeing all "ready-made ideas" as fixed. The results derived from this method are far from the truth. Intuition, by contrast, is creative. This is not saying that intuition is equal to creation but that everything created is derived from intuition.

19. In Bergson's replies, the French and English phrases in quotation marks are Bergson's own wording recorded in the report. I have corrected some of the grammatical or spelling mistakes printed in the report.

Zhang Junmai then asks, "Is the intuitive method inborn or cultivated?" Bergson thinks that, for those who have already shown its burgeoning, it is inborn and can be further cultivated. If one does not have the ability, however, it cannot be created by a philosopher. But it is in human nature to pursue action, success, and practical things, so all knowledge is tinged with utilitarian purposes (*utilité*). We can say that intuition is "the reverse side of nature" (Zhang 1921b, 9). After we get rid of the habit of pursuing utility, we can reach the absolute, the truth. Should intuition include a kind of spiritual meditation? For Bergson, the meditation in Indian philosophy that aims to transcend the division of knowledge is not what he has in mind. If meditation refers to "concentration of the mind," then no school of European philosophy can do without it (9). What he calls intuition is a means to supplementing knowledge, beyond the division of knowledge. One has to go deep inside an object in order to reach the truth.

Lin Zaiping points out that, according to Bergson's work, intuition is often used in life. Then can one say that color, sound, and fragrance are also applicable to intuition? For Bergson, the knowledge about color and sound does not belong to the domain of intuition. As to color for an artist and sound to a musician, color and sound themselves are certainly applicable to intuition, while fragrance is not. Are there general rules for intuition, the way there are rules for thought? Can intuition do away with thought? For Bergson, intuition means "Intellectual sympathy" and has no general rules (Zhang 1921b, 10). Yet thought, including comparison and analysis, is indispensable when we apply intuition. As much as he knows about Buddhism, *yogācāra* 瑜珈行 (yoga practice) aims to eliminate intellectualism (10). European philosophy and philosophical intuition, however, cannot do away with thought and analysis. Once truth is achieved, language and words are needed to translate it. The reliance on knowledge is therefore indispensable. That is why intuition is supplementary to knowledge rather than objecting it. For Bergson, this is the main difference between European philosophy and Buddhism.

Lin asks: In the book *Spiritual Energy* [L'Énergie spirituelle, 1919], is the so-called "energy" the same as the energy in physics, or how do they differ? Bergson replies that the energy in physics refers to "motion"; it can be deduced from mathematical formulas. Spiritual energy, by contrast, can never be so deduced. The former endeavors to control nature, while the latter aims to control and reform the self, so that our spirit can strive upward. The energy in physics is therefore mechanical and definite, while spiritual energy is free and creative (Zhang 1921b, 10). Lin Zaiping then relays a question from Cai Yuanpei, who, having left for the United States the day before, is not able to join them at the interview: How does one put in practice what Bergson calls intuition? He replies that there are no set rules for intuition. Negatively speaking, it is "non-analysis": neither the "hairsplitting" under a microscope, nor "dialectic." Positively speaking, it is "self-observation" and "introspection" (10).

Bergson is indeed interested in Buddhism, asking Lin Zaiping if he practices *śamatha* meditation (*jingzuo* 靜坐; tranquility meditation), and, if he does, whether he sees another realm before him. Lin replies that he does sit quietly and concentrate his mind for some time daily, but he does not practice the method of meditation for direct intuition (*zuoguan* 坐觀; *Vipassana* meditation).[20] During tranquility meditation does he feel all major problems in life are solved? Lin says he never takes this into consideration when practicing it. Zhang Junmai then comments, "Tranquility meditation in Buddhism and what you call philosophical intuition are absolutely different" (1921b, 11). Bergson, however, does not agree, saying, "To my view there are similarities in differences. In other words, with myriad things returning to the same source, complexity inclines to simplicity." At the end of the interview, Bergson discloses that he is working on *La Methode philosophique* [Philosophical method] and *Les Deux sources de la morale et de la religion* [The two sources of morality and religion] (11). The latter would be published in 1932. Since there is no book titled *La Methode philosophique* in Bergson's corpus, I suspect it was later published in 1934 as the fourth chapter titled "L'intuition philosophique" in the collection *La Pensée et le mouvant* [The creative mind: An introduction to metaphysics] (Bergson 1934, 135–62).

The report on Zhang Junmai's interview with Bergson reveals how diligently the Lifeview school scholars studied his philosophy. Zhang Dongsun's translation of Bergson's *Creative Evolution* was widely read by Chinese intellectuals around the May Fourth period. The impact of his translation on modern Chinese thought is still to be assessed. As we will see in the following and in later chapters of this study, the gradual spread of transcultural terms such as *zhijue* 直覺 (*chokkaku* in Japanese; intuition) and *mianyan* 綿延 (la durée) speak volumes to that effect.

The Creation Society and *Chuanghualun*

The translation of *Chuanghualun* in 1918 directly led to the establishment of the Creation Society. Guo Moruo (1892–1978), leader of the society, was studying at Tokyo Imperial University from 1914 to 1923. On 15 February 1920, he wrote a letter to Zong Baihua 宗白華 (1897–1986), an active member of the Young China Association.[21] Zong was at the time the editor-in-chief of *Xuedeng* 學燈 [Lamps of

20. In the report, Lin is recorded as saying, "*dan weiyong zuohuan fangfa*" 但未用作歡方法. I suspect that *zuohuan* 作歡 is a typo of zuoguan 坐觀 (*Vipassana*), which means "direct intuition of the three marks that characterize all worldly phenomena." The three marks refers to impermanence, suffering, and non-self. *Vipassana* is one of the two meditation methods, the other being *śamatha* (*zhichan* 止禪 or *chanding* 禪定), meaning tranquility (Vipassana meditation). *Śamatha* meditation entails the cultivation of mental concentration (Buswell Jr. 2003, 889–90).
21. The "Young China Association" (Shaonian Zhongguo Xuehui 少年中國學會) was established in Beijing in 1919 by intellectual leaders and students returning from abroad, such as Wang Guangqi 王光祈 (1892–1936), Zhou Taixuan 周太玄 (1895–1968), Chen Yusheng 陳愚生 (d. 1923),

learning], the literary supplement to *Current Times*. In the letter, Guo mentions that he has read Zhang Dongsun's translation: "I have already read *Chuanghualun*. In my view some of Bergson's thought is derived from Goethe. All artists are prone to the 'philosophy of life' that he talks about"[22] (Tian 1982, 57). As a student having spent six years in Japan at this point, Guo should be able to read the Japanese translation, but apparently either he has not read it, or the Chinese version directly stimulates his thought. Zheng Boqi 鄭伯奇 (1895–1979), who would be a co-member of the Creation Society, testifies to this fact in "Memories of the Creation Society": "The *Lamps of Learning*, edited by Comrade Zong Baihua, provided him [Guo Moruo] with a wonderful venue for creative works, continually stimulating his writing activities" (Zheng 1982, 9). Many of Guo Moruo's early poems, first published in *Lamps of Learning* and *People's Tocsin*, were later collected in 1921 as a volume titled *The Goddesses* by Taidong shudian 泰東書店, a bookstore with limited means in Shanghai.[23] In this long poem, the Muses set goals "to create" a new universe:

> Goddess One:
> I would rather create some new light,
> Than be a goddess in this niche.
>
> Goddess Two:
> I want to create some new warmth,
> So that it can connect with the light you create.
>
> Goddess Three:
> Newly made wine pulp
> Should not be held in an old leather wine bag.
> To take in your new warmth and new light,
> I want to create a new sun! (Guo 1921, 4–5)

Zhang Mengjiu 張夢九 (1893–1974), Zeng Muhan 曾慕韓 (1892–1951), Lei Meisheng 雷眉生 (birth and death dates unknown), and Li Dazhao. The idea of the association, inspired by the Young Italy movement in the 1830s, was initiated in 1918, its aim being to rejuvenate China, to study "true theories," to expand social enterprises, and to overhaul backward customs. Promoting the New Village movement briefly in 1919 (see Chapter 5, note 3), the association functioned until 1925 (Chow 1960, 80, 188–89, 251–53, 322–23). Most members of The Young China Party (Zhongguo Qingniandang 中國青年黨), established in Paris in 1923 by Zeng Muhan and others, were members of the Young China Association. The party moved to Taiwan with the Nationalist Party in 1949 and played a significant role in the politics on the island until the early 1990s (Chen 2008).

22. The letters exchanged between Tian Han 田漢, Zong Baihua, and Guo Moruo, who later all joined the Communist Party, were collected in *Sanyeji* 三葉集, a thin volume published by Yadong shudian 亞東書店 in Shanghai in 1920. According to Tian Han's preface, *sanye* is translated from the German word *Kleeblatt* (three-leaved clover), which is *trifolium* in Latin. It is a flowering plant, of which the leaves are often trifoliate. Tian writes: "It usually symbolizes the friendship of three people. The friendship of the three of us is united by this book called *Kleeblatt*" (Tian 1982, 1).

23. The main poem of the collection, originally titled *Nüshen zhi zaisheng* 女神之再生 [The rebirth of the goddesses], was first published in *Minduo* 民鐸 [People's tocsin] 2, no. 5 (15 February 1921): 1–14.

The Goddesses eventually becomes the poem that defines Guo Moruo's reputation as a poet, celebrating the romantic mentality of a new cohort on the literary scene in China.

The Creation Society was established in Tokyo in 1921, by Chinese students in Japan who would later become prominent writers, including Guo Moruo, Yu Dafu 郁達夫 (1896–1945), Cheng Fangwu 成仿吾 (1897–1984), Zheng Boqi, Tian Han, and Zhang Ziping 張資平 (1893–1959). Supported by Taidong Bookstore, they established between 1922 and 1929 several journals, including *Creation Quarterly, Creation Weekly, Creation Day, The Deluge,* and *Creation Monthly*.[24] The inaugural issue of *Creation Quarterly* opens with Guo Moruo's poem *Chuanzaozhe* 創造者 [The creators], which highlights the fated "lonely superiority" (*gugao* 孤高) and "anguish" (*kunao* 苦惱) of poets who set themselves apart from the mainstream, including ancient Chinese lyricists, Indian singers chanting the Vedas, Dante, Milton, and Goethe. But they are also proud of the "revelry" (*kuanghuan* 狂歡) and "glory" (*guangyao* 光耀) they enjoy as creators. Pangu 盤古, the legendary God in Chinese mythology, is lauded as the spirit of creation and noumenon itself (Guo 1922, 2–3). According to Zheng Boqi, members of the Creation Society were never on good terms with the cohorts of *New Youth,* the Literary Research Society established by Zheng Zhenduo and Maodun, and the Crescent Society led by Xu Zhimo and others. Zheng Boqi writes: "For events of long-term impact, the Creation Society was always fighting a lone battle" (1982, 3).

From the serialization of Zhang Dongsun's *Chuanghualun* in 1918 and its subsequent publication as a book in 1919, to the establishment of the Creation Society in 1921, it is clear that there was an unmistakable connection between philosophical thought and literature. Through the examination of a simple transcultural term such as *chuangzao,* we are able to connect events that seem to be happening separately in different disciplines. In Chapter 5 we will see how Guo Moruo's long poem *The Goddesses* inspired in turn Zhu Qianzhi, the young Lifeview school intellectual who first invented the term *weiqinglun* 唯情論 (affectivism) in 1922. There is no coincidence at all that the Creation Society announced in 1928 its transition "from literary revolution to revolutionary literature," or from Romanticism to revolution, since they were closely related to the Lifeview school intellectuals, who were keen on socialist theories and advocated action, turning theory into praxis. As early as May 1923, Guo Moruo's essay "Women de wenxue xin yundong" 我們的文學新運動 [Our new movement in literature] discloses the Creation Society's proclivity for social revolution. Highlighting the contrast between spirit and matter, he maintains

24. *Chuangzao jikan* 創造季刊 [Creation quarterly] was published from May 1922 to February1924; *Chuangzao zhoubao* 創造週報 [Creation weekly], from May 1923 to May 1924; *Chuangzaori* 創造日 [Creation day], or *The Literary Supplement to Zhonghua xinbao* 中華新報 [China news], from July to November 1923; *Chuangzao yuekan* 創造月刊 [Creation monthly], from March 1926 to January 1929; and *Hongshui* 洪水 [The deluge], from August 1924 to December 1927.

that the New Literature movement must eliminate the "deep-rooted Bourgeois bad habits." He writes, "All nations suffering from paucity of material resources must benefit from their spiritual wealth"; "In our literary career . . . . we must break up the old patterns and pursue new expressions of a new life"; "Before light, there is chaos; before creation, there is destruction"; "Our purpose is to use the bomb of life to shatter the macabre palace of this toxic dragon [capitalism]" (1923a, 14–15). In other words, in order to shatter the materialist bondage of the Bourgeoisie and create new visions with new literary expressions, writers should destroy the old and answer the call to life, pursuing spiritual excellence.

While the Aesthetic Education movement maintains that the purpose of aesthetic education is to construct "an aesthetic life," Guo Moruo, in the September 1923 essay "Yishujia yu gemingjia" 藝術家與革命家 [Artists and revolutionaries], points out that, be they supporters of "art for art" or "art for life," all artists are revolutionaries sharing the goal to "aestheticize human society." He writes, "All genuine revolutionary movements are aesthetic movements. All enthusiastic activists are sincere artists, just as all zealous artists are sterling revolutionaries"; "Just as the literary and artistic movements in the twentieth century aim to aestheticize human society, so do the grand global revolutionary movements. We share the same goal. . . . We are revolutionaries as well as artists, intending to be martyrs as much for our own art as for human society" (1923b, 2). The idea of being martyrs for art, as if it were a religion, clearly refers to Cai Yuanpei's 1917 proposal for "Replacing Religion with Aesthetic Education" (see Chapter 2), but here the idea of martyrdom combines social as well as artistic revolutions. In the February 1924 essay "Yishu zhi shehuide yiyi" 藝術之社會的意義 [The social meaning of art], Cheng Fangwu maintains that the social value of art lies in its ability to "awaken sympathy" among humankind and to stimulate life to "strive upward." He believes that both science and art can contribute to society, and writes, "Science enhances our intellectual life, while art enriches our affective life. Art and Science are the most powerful means of human education" (1924, 3). Juxtaposing intellectual life with affective life, he is no doubt reverberating the key arguments of the Science and Lifeview debate. It comes as no surprise at all that Cheng's essay "Cong wenxue geming dao geming wenxue" 從文學革命到革命文學 [From literary revolution to revolutionary literature] appeared in February 1928, criticizing the New Culture movement for being all talk without action, while announcing its death (1928).[25]

25. It should be noted that proletariat literature was also a transcultural genre. During the 1920s, Japanese proletariat literature was on the rise due to the literary magazine *The Sowers* [*Tanemakuhito* 種蒔く人], established by Komaki Ōmi 小牧近江 (1894–1978) and Kaneko Yōbun 金子洋文 (1893–1985). Following the lead of *La Clarté* [Illumination], the antiwar movement in France in 1919–1921, the magazine was published from 1921 to 1923. Aiming to revolt against the old order and expose its oppression of the proletariat class, it stopped publication after the Tokyo earthquake.

Bergson and Eucken, introduced by Lifeview school intellectuals into China, were by no means the only philosophers during the nineteenth and twentieth centuries who critiqued scientific rationalism and advocated the return to philosophical truth. Philosophers who belonged to "worldview philosophy"—including the *Lebensphilosophie* of Bergson and Eucken; the functionalism of Alan Turing (1912–1954), Gilbert Ryle (1900–1976), and Norman Malcolm (1911–1990); the monism of Spinoza, Leibniz, Schopenhauer, and Ernst Haeckel (1834–1899); the voluntarism of Schopenhauer and Nietzsche; the theosophy of Helena Petrovna Blavatsky (1831–1891) and Leo Tolstoy (1828–1910)—all emphasized experienced, relativized, and historicized truth (Bambach 1995, 26). Their effort to dispute scientific rationalism and probe the irrational depths of the human mind reflected a tendency in modern philosophy to thoroughly reexamine Enlightenment rationality.

Chuanghualun and the Lifeview School

Around the time of the 1923 Science and Lifeview debate, the transcultural lexicon and ideas used in *Chuanghualun* guided and reinforced the Lifeview discourses. This can be amply seen in the writings of Liang Qichao, a mentor of the Lifeview school. After visiting Eucken in Jena in late 1918 and witnessing postwar Europe in a state of dilapidation, he composed *Impressions of European travels*, a series of essays first serialized in *Current Times* in Shanghai, from 3 March to 18 July 1920, and then three days later in *Morning Post* in Beijing, from 6 March to 17 August the same year. These essays, according to the fourth-generation New Confucian Liu Shuxian 劉述先 (1934–2016), inspired Liang Shuming's assessments of Eastern and Western cultures in 1921, and triggered the Science and Lifeview debate in 1923 (2010, 7). The episode published on 7 March 1920 in *Current Times* (13 March in *Morning Post*) claims that science is on the verge of bankruptcy and that the Europeans who have pursued science for hundreds of years are like a person lost in the desert while chasing a huge shadow. Scientific progress and the industrial revolution have destroyed our inner life, while the human mind is relegated to "a phenomenon of material motion," becoming the object of psychological studies:

> These schools of materialism have established a pure materialistic, mechanic lifeview under the aegis of science. They have attributed all inner and external lives to the "necessary laws" of the motion of particles (*wuzhi yundong* 物質運動). . . . According to experimental psychology, human spirit is no more than a kind of matter, likewise under the control of those "necessary laws." As a result, human free will is categorically denied. (*YBSHJ* 7.23:11)[26]

26. This episode, titled "Kexu wanneng zhi meng" 科學萬能之夢 [The dream of an omnipotent science], is collected in *YBSHJ* 7.23:10–12.

Here, the outright juxtapositions between materialism and spiritualism, between mechanic laws and human free will, are exactly the key concepts developed in *Creative Evolution*. Later, in a lecture at The First High School of Jinling University in early January 1923, Liang Qichao points out that, according to Hans Driesch's speech at Hangzhou, all material civilization is accumulative rather than evolutionary. Only "the civilization of the heart-mind is creative and evolutionary" (*YBSHJ* 5.40:6).[27] Here the distinction between "material civilization" and "civilization of the heart-mind" certainly indicates that, in commenting on Driesch's lecture, he is taking his cue from the transcultural lexicon used in *Chuanghualun*. Liang criticizes Driesch's definition of culture for being "too narrow," while he himself believes that "historical evolution" depends on two aspects: the truth of humankind as a whole, which keeps us striving upward; and the "collective cultural forces" (*wenhua gongye* 文化共業) developed by the capacity of the human heart-mind (*renlei xinneng* 人類心能) all over the world, which will never disappear. Our accumulated inheritance is thus guaranteed to expand day by day (6–7).

From 1922 to 1923, upon the arrangement of the Lecture Society, Liang Qichao gave a series of lectures with Driesch at Southeast University. Right before the outbreak of the Science and Lifeview debate, at the conclusion of their joined courses on 13 January 1923, Liang Qichao used Confucian and Buddhist concepts to explicate Bergson's ideas of the unceasing creation and becoming of the universe. For him the universe is not complete, while "in the process of being created, it is awaiting humankind's effort. It is therefore in ceaseless flux every day (*tiantian liudong buxi* 天天流動不息; *YBSHJ* 5.40:13)."[28] Referring to the Confucian concept of *wuwo* 毋我 (no egoism), he points out that the "self" is part of the world, impossible to be separated from it. Confucius therefore cautions against a fixed self and egoism. This is a reference to "*Zihan* 4" 子罕四 of Part 9 of the *Analects*: "Confucius is free from four things: no foregone conclusions, no arbitrary predeterminations, no obstinacy, and no egoism" (14).[29] For him the Buddhist idea of *wuwo* 無我 (no self) also opposes the idea of a "self" that is fixed and unchanging.

To see the self as a micro-universe, which is in constant flux like the macro-universe, is the major thesis of *Creative Evolution*. Using Confucian and Buddhist concepts to interpret Bergson, Liang is responding to Tang Hualong's call, in the preface to *Chuanghualun*, to read Bergson in tandem with the *Book of Changes*. Tang believes that Bergson's idea of "the I that is changing unceasingly" is comparable to the teaching in the *Book of Changes*: "Heaven proceeds with vitality and persistence.

27. The text of the lecture, "*yanjiu wenhuashi de jige zhongyao wenti*" 研究文化史的幾個重要問題 [A few key issues concerning the study of cultural history], is collected in *YBSHJ* 5.40:1–7.

28. The text of the talk, "Dongnan Daxue kebi gaobieci" 東南大學課畢告別辭 [Farewell address to the classes at Southeast University), is collected in *YBSHJ* 5.40:7–15.

29. "*Zi jue si: wuyi wubi wugu wuwo*" 子絕四：毋意毋必毋固毋我. For the English translation, see Legge 2014, 83.

The superior person thus strives without ceasing. Everything is ever-changing and moving without rest, the divine is illimitable, and *Yi* has no permanent substance" (Bergson 1919, iv). Here, "ever-changing and moving without rest" is a reference to the eighth chapter of *Commentary on the Appended Statements of the Book of Changes, Part 2*: "*Yi* as a document should not be set away from life. As *Dao* it is ever-transforming, ever-changing and moving without rest" (Huang 2011, 392; Rutt 2002, 428, with modifications).[30] That "the divine is illimitable, and *Yi* has no permanent substance" is derived from the fourth chapter of *Commentary on the Appended Statements, Part 1*:

> *Yi*, modelled on the transformations of Heaven and Earth, never goes beyond them. It follows the intricate courses of the myriad things, without exception. It is in communion with the *Dao* of day and night, with perfect understanding. As the divine is illimitable, *Yi* thus has no permanent substance. (Huang 2011, 215; Rutt 2002, with modifications)[31]

Referencing the teachings of the *Book of Changes* is a common practice for the Lifeview school. Most unsatisfying, however, is that here Liang Qichao nonchalantly dichotomizes Eastern and Western cultures: "Eastern learning proceeds from spirit, while Western learning, from matter. To satiate the hunger for knowledge, one seeks materials in the West. To satiate the hunger for spirit, one seeks materials in the East" (*YBSHJ* 5.40:12). This kind of outright dichotomy is what gives the impression that the Science and Lifeview debate had no epistemic complexity. Nonetheless, after the debate broke out, due to the geologist Ding Wenjiang publishing a series of essays debunking Zhang Junmai's "Lifeview" (Ding 1977a, b, c),[32] Liang gradually revised his thinking and formulated a well-thought-out argument, in which the basic concept of the Lifeview school is made clear. On 29 May 1923, Liang published an essay in the *Literary Supplement to Morning Post*, "Renshenguan yu kexue—duiyu Zhang Ding lunzhan de piping (qiyi)" 人生觀與科學，對於張丁論戰的批評（其一）[Lifeview and science—A critique of the debate between Zhang and Ding, Part 1]. It starts with a critique of both parties, neither of whom has ever given readers a clear definition of "lifeview" and "science." While these two terms may not mean the same for them, Liang thinks a clarification of the two concepts would avoid a lot of unnecessary crossfire. Both Zhang and Ding belonged to the group of seven that he took

30. *Yi zhi wei shu ye, buke yuan. Wei Dao ye lüqian, biandong bujü* 易之為書也，不可遠。為道也屢遷，變動不居。

31. The original Chinese reads: *Fanwei tiandi zhi hua er bu guo, qücheng wanwu er buyi, tonghu zhouye zhi dao er zhi. Gu shen wufang er yi wuti* 範圍天地之化而不過，曲成萬物而不遺，通乎晝夜之道而知. 故神無方而易無體.

32. Ding Wenjiang criticizes Zhang Junmai for misunderstanding science, European civilization, and Chinese spiritual culture, and maintains that scientific method should be applied to solving human problems. His three articles were originally published in *Nuli zhoubao* 努力週報 [Endeavor weekly], nos. 48–49 (12 April–22 April), 54–55 (27 May–3 June), and 56 (10 June).

to Europe in late 1918. Calling them "our two dearest old friends," he proceeds to define the two concepts in question:

> Human beings' existence, which harmonizes and unifies the spiritual world (*xinjie* 心界) and material world (*wujie* 物界), is called "life." Our ideal to fulfill such a life is called "lifeview." . . . Facts based on experiences are analyzed so that general laws (*gongli* 公例) can be synthesized and used to postulate similar things. This kind of learning is called science. (*YBSHJ* 5.40:23)

For Liang, the so-called "material world" includes the body, other human beings, the society one lives in, and so on. As to science, one should not confound it with the things derived from applied science, which are merely "results of science" rather than science itself. Liang points out that Zhang is wrong to say that everything can be partially decided by free will and intuition, because our spiritual life cannot be separated from the material world and exist alone, while the latter is subject to temporal and spatial rules. Liang agrees with Ding that "lifeview cannot be detached from science," maintaining that lifeview and reason must complement each other. Zhang believes that lifeview is subjective, and science, objective. Liang, by contrast, proposes to unify subjectivity and objectivity. This shows that he fully embraces the concept of the unity of mind and body, subject and object, as maintained by Bergson, Eucken, and Nishida Kitarō. As to Ding's proposal to apply the scientific method to life, Liang comments: although a great part of the problems of life can and must be solved by science, a small part, perhaps the most important part, exceeds the control of science. To unify lifeview with science, as Ding proposes, is not only unnecessary but harmful. In this essay, Liang clearly lays out the relationship between reason and affect, maintaining that our affective life transcends the control of science:

> Although human life cannot be separated from reason, it is not to say that reason dominates all aspects of human life. In addition to reason, the most significant part—or, we can say, the original impulse of life—is "the affects" (*qinggan* 情感). The affects are manifested in many ways, of which at least two things are vested with mysteriousness: "love" and "beauty." (*YBSHJ* 5.40:26)

Liang then flaunts his sense of humor: even though "the scientific empire" keeps on expanding its sphere of influence and authority, "Mr. Love" and "Mr. Beauty" are always beyond its rule. Here of course he is parodying the so-called "Mr. Science" and "Mr. Democracy" that are dominating the discourse of the New Culture movement. A scientist trying to analyze "beauty" with concepts of lines, light variations, tonal variants, and so on, definitely misses the point. As to "love," it is no doubt all the more "mysterious and metaphysical." Isn't it hilarious when a young man and a young woman agree on a "scientific love"? (*YBSHJ* 5.40:26). Those familiar with the Science and Lifeview debate should know that here Liang is also in fact mocking Zhang Jingsheng, a Peking University professor of philosophy and psychology, who triggered the "Laws of Love" debate that is simultaneously ongoing in *Morning Post* from 29 April to the end of June 1923 (*ZJSJ* 2:1–175). As a response to the Science and Lifeview debate, he maintains that, even though love seems to be mysterious, there are laws of love, and that these laws, like scientific laws, can be analyzed. When Liang's essay jibing him appeared on 29 May in *Morning Post*, the Laws of Love debate had been going on for a month.[33] Zhang later in 1924 composed a treatise titled *Meide renshengguan* 美的人生觀 [An aesthetic lifeview], highlighting love and beauty as the signposts of his utopian society (*ZJSJ* 1:1–121). Zhang Jingsheng's response to the Lifeview and Aesthetic Education discourses, an interesting topic to pursue, will be treated in a separate monograph of mine as a sequel to this study.

Mao Zedong: My Heart-Mind Is the Universe

The heart-mind concept, a central principle of Confucianism, was very much vibrant around the 1910s and 1920s because of the flourishing of the Lifeview discourses. In 1917, still studying at Hunan First Normal University, the young Mao Zedong 毛澤東 (1893–1976) composed an essay titled "Xin zhi li" 心之力 [The forces of the heart-mind] (Mao 2013, 1:251).[34] It opens with a quote from Lu Jiuyuan, the leader of the Heart-Mind philosophy in the Southern Song dynasty: "The universe is my heart-mind, my heart-mind is the universe" (Lu 1966, 36:4 right page).[35] This statement entails the idea that the world, the universe, and all things in them are driven by the feeling and thinking heart-mind. Mao declares that since ancient times humankind has been called the spirit of all things, because the human heart-mind is the major force that contributes to evolution. Ancient Chinese civilization, centering on the spiritual communion between human beings and the myriad things in

33. After the Laws of Love debate began, the Science and Lifeview debate articles originally published in *Endeavor Weekly* were reserialized in *Morning Post* from the beginning of May to late June, side by side with the ongoing Laws of Love debate. Liang's essay referring to Zhang Jingsheng's Laws of Love theory, apparently a deliberate editorial arrangement, was added to the Science and Lifeview debate articles reserialized in the same newspaper.
34. "The Forces of the Heart-Mind" is collected in *Mao Zedong quanji* 毛澤東全集 [Complete works of Mao Zedong] 1:251–55. Going viral on the internet in recent decades, this essay never saw press until the *Complete works* was published in Hong Kong in 2013. Written when Mao was twenty-four years old, the essay was given a full score by his professor, Yang Changji 楊昌濟 (1871–1920), and widely circulated at Hunan First Normal University (Snow 2001, 27; 1937, 171), as Mao himself testifies to in his autobiography (2001, 1–63), originally published in traditional Chinese in Hankou 漢口 in September 1937 (Snow 1937). Transcribed in English by Edgar Snow (1905–1972) and translated by Li Du 李杜, the 1937 version is more or less the same as what is recorded in Part 4 of Snow's *Red Star Over China* (Snow 1972, 152–210), first published in London in October 1937. While Snow translates "Xin zhi li" into "The Energy of the Mind," I translate it into "The Forces of the Heart-Mind" to connect it with the Heart-Mind philosophy tradition.
35. Lu Jiuyuan's original text, collected in *Xiangshan quanji* 象山全集 [Complete works of Xiangshan), reads, "yuzhou ji wuxin, wuxin ji yuzhou" 宇宙即吾心，吾心即宇宙. In this collected volume, each *juan* 卷 starts with a new pagination on the left page, while the right page has no page numbers.

the world, used to be the model of justice and moral for other nations. China is now, however, under the onslaught of relentless foreign invasions, while Chinese people, readily submitting to the dominance of the viscous invaders, have gradually forgotten their own past glory (Mao 2013, 1:251). This exposition reminds one of Lu Xun's essay nearly a decade ago, "Toward a Refutation of Malevolent Voices," which is discussed in the introduction of this study. While Lu Xun appeals to the "voices of the heart-mind," Mao is calling for the "forces of the heart-mind." He urges education of the people so that the heart-mind forces of the nation can be reborn.

Mao attributes the current moral degradation and insatiable desire for expansion in the West to the materialism brought about by technoscientific modernity. While the wise and brave willing to fight against the mainstream are neglected, the people simply do not care about the truth and the origin of problems. He writes, "In Heaven no force is greater than the sun. On Earth no force is greater than electricity. In a man no force is greater than the heart-mind" (Mao 2013, 1:254). Although not as talented a writer as Lu Xun and certainly not as nuanced in his argument, Mao's youthful enthusiasm to embrace the newly introduced Counter-Enlightenment discourses is nonetheless fully disclosed. Although Mao later would become the leader of the Communist Party and a proponent of Marxist and Leninian theory of historical materialism, as a young student he enjoyed reading Kang Youwei and Liang Qichao, worshiped them, and believed in their reform movement of Constitutional monarchy, as he himself confesses in his autobiography (Snow 2001, 15–16; 1972, 161–62). At Hunan First Normal University, under the influence of his teacher Yang Changji, an idealist who taught ethics, he read *Basic Principles of Ethics* (1909) translated by Cai Yuanpei and was inspired to write the essay "The Forces of the Heart-Mind."[36] Mao discloses, "At that time I was also an idealist" (2001, 27; 1972, 171).

In "The Forces of the Heart-Mind" Mao urges people with lofty ideals to use the spiritual force of the heart-mind to turn the current tide of materialism. In order to save the nation and eliminate the enemies of its ancient glory—including the feudal society, the ignorance and evil ways of bureaucracy, compradors, and slaves of Westerners—the renewal and strengthening of the heart-mind forces is the indispensable first step. New learning based on this principle is the next step (Mao 2013, 1:252). It is crucial to combine the essences of Eastern and Western cultures; while liberating our thought to create a spiritual culture for the new generation, research in science and technology can bring about an industrial culture that surpasses Western achievements (1:255).

36. Here a discrepancy is found between *Mao Zedong zizhuan*, the Chinese version published in 2001, and Mao's own account in the 1937 *Red Star Over China*. According to Snow's English version, Mao wrote "The Forces of the Heart-Mind" because of a book on ethics translated by Cai Yuanpei, but in the 2001 Chinese version it is simply written, "Under his [Yang Jichang's] influence, I wrote an essay titled 'The Forces of the Heart-Mind.'" Cai Yuanpei, highly valued by the Guomindang government, is here eliminated from view.

Always with the juxtaposition of spirit and matter in mind, Mao believes that they are complimentary to each other, while emphasizing the priority of the heart-mind. He comments on the dichotomy of materialism and idealism:

> Human beings live in this world, with blood and body as tools driven by the heart-mind, and our consciousness following the ways of Heaven. While blood and body are matter that lives and dies, the heart-mind is the essence that never changes. This is the law that governs all living beings. From ancient times to the present day, all cultural truths are derived from the heart-mind and result in matter. (Mao 2013, 1:254)

Mao praises the heart-mind as the "origin of all forces" (*xin wei wanly zhi ben* 心為萬力之本). Emanating from inside out, it can generate good and evil, be creative or destructive; absorbing influences from outside inwards, it can pollute, drag us down, and be accepted or rejected. If cultivated with virtue, the heart-mind forces can contribute to the welfare of all beings; if with evil, it can plunge all beings into misery and suffering (2013, 1:254–55). Mao's essay, prioritizing spiritualism over materialism, indicates that the Counter-Enlightenment discourses based on traditional Heart-Mind philosophy were prevalent before *Chuanghualun* was published in 1918. As indicated in the introduction to this study, the publications of Zhang Taiyan and Lu Xun during their sojourn in Japan in the first decade of the twentieth century had paved the way for the Lifeview school to propagate on Chinese soil.

Xu Fuguan: "The Heart-Mind Culture"

Translating Bergson's *la conscience* into "*xin*," Zhang Dongsun was inspired by traditional Heart-Mind philosophy, and in turn the transcultural lexicon used in *Chuanghualun* inspired many of his generation and the generations to come. Originating from such transcultural practice of the Lifeview school during the May Fourth period, postwar New Confucianism has proliferated in Taiwan and Hong Kong. Xu Fuguan's 徐復觀 (1904–1982) publications clearly demonstrate the signature of the heart-mind tradition. Trained at Wuchang First Normal University (modern-day Wuhan University) and Wuchang Academy of Chinese Classics 武昌國學館, he joined the Nationalist Revolutionary Army in 1926. Two years later he went to Japan and studied at Meiji University. In 1930, he entered the Imperial Japanese Army Academy. After being jailed for protesting against the Japanese invasion of China, he was expelled by the academy, and he returned to Shanghai the following year. He fought in the Sino-Japanese War and in 1945 was appointed as a close aide to Chiang Kai-shek, chairman of the Nationalist government in Chongqing as well as of the Central Party of Guomindang. Having met Xiong Shili in 1943, Xu looked upon him as mentor all his life. In 1946, he gave up his army career at the rank of Major General, and moved to Taiwan in 1949, beginning to teach at the newly established Tunghai University in Taichung in 1955. He moved to Hong Kong in January 1967, teaching and giving lectures at New Asia College off and on. He died of stomach cancer in Taipei (Xie 2017). Xu was also known as opinion leader and political commentator. In 1949, with the help of the Guomindang he established *Minzhu pinglun* 民主評論 [The democratic review] in Hong Kong, an influential liberalist journal published until 1966. In 1959, he published *Zhongguo sixiangshi lunji* 中國思想史論集 [Collected essays on Chinese intellectual history]. With the third edition in 1974, a new section, "Xin de wenhua" 心的文化 [The heart-mind culture], was added to the part titled "Kongzi dezhi sixiang fawei" 孔子德治思想發微 [On Confucius' theory of governing by virtue] (Xu 1974, 242–49).

"The Heart-Mind Culture" fully discloses the typical Lifeview school critique of both idealism and materialism. It points out that Chinese culture is basically the heart-mind culture: "For Chinese culture the origin of the value of life lies in one's own 'heart-mind'" (Xu 1974, 242). For Xu, distinct from the "mind" 心 in idealism 唯心論, the heart-mind in Chinese culture belongs to the physiological structure. Though farfetched, the heart-mind might as well be considered as akin to materialism, because physiology is after all about matter. Or one should say that the heart-mind is neither merely metaphysical (*xing er shang* 形而上) nor merely physical (*xing er xia* 形而下) but in-between (*xing yu zhong* 形於中) (243). In other words, the heart-mind connects spirit and matter, or soul and body. The controversy between idealism and materialism—whether spirit surpasses matter or vice versa—has been an ontological debate long existing in the Western philosophical tradition. Xu points out that, for Chinese culture, this is not an issue worth discussing at all.

A crucial transition in Chinese culture is the turn from the illusion of transcendence to the ontology of immanence: for Confucius, the origin of moral does not lie with the gods or Heaven but with human life. The Master therefore says, "Is benevolence far away? If I desire benevolence, hither it comes" (仁遠乎哉？我欲仁，斯仁至矣; Legge 2014, 70). *The Doctrine of the Mean* opens with this saying: "What Heaven confers is nature" (天命之謂性; 254). Though seemingly metaphysical, this proposition must be realized in humans, because nature is rooted in human life. What *The Doctrine of the Mean* emphasizes is not Heaven but human nature. Mencius clearly points out that the origin of moral is the heart-mind: "Benevolence, justice, propriety, and wisdom are rooted in the heart-mind" (Bloom 2009, 148),[37] a statement describing "internal experiences." It is the same with Daoism. The metaphysical concept of Dao in Laozi is realized in the heart-mind for Zhuangzi, who believes that the heart-mind of emptiness, equanimity, and awareness (*xu jing ming* 虛靜明) is Dao. The latter therefore maintains the significance of the practices of "heart-mind fasting" (*xinzhai* 心齋) and "sitting oblivion" (*zuowang* 坐忘), in

37. The original text is found in "Jinxin shang" 盡心上21 [Exploring the heart-mind, Part 1, 21] of *Mencius*: "*Ren yi li zhi genyu xin*" 仁義禮智根於心.

order to fully liberate the human spirit. The practice of "heart-mind fasting" aims to clear the heart-mind of all distracting thoughts so that the spirit can concentrate. The practice of "sitting oblivion" means forgetting one's body and preconceived knowledge while meditating, so that "the communion with Dao" (*datong* 大通) can be achieved.[38] Xu Fuguan writes, "The heart-mind of emptiness, equanimity, and awareness in Zhuangzi indicates in fact the artistic soul; the origin of artistic values lies in such a heart-mind" (1974, 245). Buddhism, by contrast, believes that faith can "transcend *samsāra* [the cycle of birth, death, and rebirth] and attain Buddhahood." In other words, Buddhist faith concerns the ontology of transcendence. Zen Buddhism, which has developed into a distinct school of Chinese Buddhism combined with Daoism since the seventh century, advocates "seeing one's true nature by being aware of the heart-mind" (*mingxin jianxing* 明心見性) and "becoming a Buddha by seeing one's true nature" (*jianxing chengfo* 見性成佛). Zen is therefore called "the Heart-Mind sect" (*xinzong* 心宗; 246). Tu Wei-ming and Ying-shih Yü, renowned representatives of the third generation of New Confucians,[39] have discussed the significance of "transcendence in immanence" or "inward transcendence" in Confucianism (Tu 1989; Yü 2014), a concept that is also a major principle in the affectivist philosophy of Zhu Qianzhi and Yuan Jiahua in the 1920s. See Chapter 5 for details.

At the end of the section, Xu points out that the "heart-mind" in Chinese culture is neither the "heart" in the common sense, nor the "consciousness" in psychology. It is rather the faculty that is responsible for moral and artistic activities as well as objective cognition. To work at full capacity, the heart-mind must be freed from other physiological activities and return to its true nature through self-cultivation, a meditative process that releases it from the bondage of subjectivity. The objective realities, without being distorted by subjective prejudices and desires, can thus enter into the heart-mind in their original appearances, so that they can be united with it. The heart-mind then can make judgments that truly match the objective realities (Xu 1974, 248). The unification of subject and object is exactly what affectivism maintains. Xu emphasizes that the inner experiences of self-cultivation, being an existence in itself rather than derived from reasoning, can therefore be detached

38. In "Renjianshi" 人間世 [Ways of the human world], the fourth chapter of *Neipian* 內篇 [Inner chapters] in *Zhuangzi*, it is recorded how Confucius explains the meaning of *xinzhai*: "*Wei dao ji xu. Xuzhe, xinzhai ye*" 唯道集虛。虛者，心齋也" (The mighty Dao can only gather in emptiness. Emptiness is the fasting of the heart-mind; Wang 1999, 1:54, with modifications). For the concept of *zuowang*, see the sixth chapter of *Inner Chapters*, "Da zongshi" 大宗師 [The most venerable Master]: "*Duo zhiti, chu congming, lixing quzhi, tongyyu datong, ci wei zuowang*" 墮肢體，黜聰明，離形去知，同於大通，此謂坐忘 (Casting off one's limbs and trunk and giving up one's hearing, one is separated from one's physical form and preconceived knowledge. One thus achieves communion with the Dao. This is called sitting oblivion; 1:110, with modifications).

39. For the three generations of New Confucian leaders, see note 5 in this chapter.

from science. He maintains that thought must be predicated on self-cultivation, experience, and praxis; otherwise, it would only be an idle theory (249).

Juxtaposing the heart-mind with scientific rationality, Xu Fuguan is following Zhang Dongsun's lexical choices in translating *Creative Evolution*. The emphasis on the unification of subject and object, values of life and art, and the realization of thought in reality and praxis are all what the May Fourth Lifeview school prioritized. Lifeview discourses and the rise of New Confucianism is a topic worth further examination.

Julia Kristeva and "The Chinese Logic"

In a lecture series given at Fudan University in Shanghai in 2012, the Bulgarian-French literary theorist Julia Kristeva (b. 1941) acknowledges that her 1967 essay on the poetic language of the novel and intertextuality, which earned her instant worldwide fame, was indebted to Zhang Dongsun (Chang Tung-sun) as well as the Russian philosopher Mikhail Bakhtin (1895–1975). She refers to Zhang's 1939 article published in Peking University's *The Yenching Journal of Social Studies*, "A Chinese Philosopher's Theory of Knowledge" (Zhang 1939; Kristeva 2016, 12). Thirty years later, it was translated into French and published in the summer issue of the avant-garde journal *Tel quel* [As Is] (1960–1982), retitled "La logic chinoise" [The Chinese logic] (Zhang 1969).[40] The same issue features articles by Philippe Sollers (b. 1936), the founder of *Tel quel* and Kristeva's husband since 1967; Roman Jakobson (1896–1982), the celebrated Russian-American phonologist and semanticist; Roland Barthes (1915–1980), writer, literary theorist, and semiotician; and Kristeva herself.

In "Le Mot, le dialogue et le roman" [Word, dialogue, and novel], her debut essay, Kristeva points out that a poetic logic based on dialogue and ambiguity is needed when analyzing literary language. The Aristotelian logic, scientific and "censored by grammar and semantics" (Kristeva 1969, 144), is insufficient when applied to literature. Its insufficiencies are pointed out by the Chinese philosopher Chang Dongsun as well as Bakhtin, who tries to go beyond the Russian Formalists by a dynamic theorization. The way she characterizes Zhang is interesting: "one who comes from another linguistic horizon (that of ideograms)," where the monologism

40. The original Chinese version of Zhang's article is titled "Sixiang yuyan yu wenhua" 思想語言與文化 [Thought, language, and culture] (1938). The various English and French versions of this article are more or less slightly different. The 1939 English version is a match with the Chinese original. However, the French version published in *Tel Quel* is based on the English version in Hayakawa's collected volume (Zhang 1959). For an English translation of Kristeva's 1969 essay "Word, Dialogue, and Novel," see Kristeva 1980. For a detailed discussion of the various versions of Zhang Dongsun's essay in Chinese, English, and French, see Cheung Lik-kwan's 張歷君 article in Chinese, "Intertextuality and Correlation Logic: On Kristeva's Reception of Zhang Dongsun's Theory of Knowledge" (2019).

of epic discourse subordinated to God is replaced with the "*Yin-Yang* 'dialogue'" (151). For her, Zhang's Chinese logic stressing the complementarity of obviously contrary forces relates to Bakhtin's theory of polyphony and dialogism.

Zhang's "The Chinese Logic" starts with "two kinds of knowledge," the perceptual and the conceptual. The two, though having different functions—only the conceptual can grasp a Supreme Being, while a real chair can only be touched and perceived by the senses—cannot be separated from each other (1969, 3; 1959, 299). The perceptual and the conceptual contain the elements of each other. While concepts guide and influence perceptions, the interpretations of perceptions lead to the formulation of concepts. In addition to its interpretative nature, according to the Italian philosopher and sociologist Vilfredo Pareto (1848–1923), the conceptual, or theoretical knowledge, is a mixture of various elements: descriptive, axiomatic, concrete, imaginary elements plus those appealing to sentiments and beliefs. He classifies theoretical knowledge into two kinds, "the experimental" and "nonexperimental," which function in conjunction with the nexus between "the logical" and "the nonlogical" (1969, 4; 1959, 300). Underscoring the importance of the logical, Pareto is in fact, according to Zhang, referring to "formal logic," which is an abstract study. What Zhang is treating in the article, however, is "real logic," which "follows the trend of culture" (1969, 4; 1959, 300). People living in different cultures have different types of logic embedded in their traditions. That is why Westerners, Hindus, and the Chinese may think differently. He comments: "Western scholars often mistake their logic for the universal logic of mankind, as we have seen in the case of Kant" (1969, 4; 1959, 300). As much as the idea of universalism is questionable, the way Zhang juxtaposes Western logic and Chinese logic also falls into the trap of essentialist dichotomy. Yet how his thought proceeds in this regard inspires Kristeva's thought on dialogism.

Zhang Dongsun points out the connection between logic and language. The basis of Aristotelian logic lies in the subject-predicate form of the Greek language structure. Latin, French, English, and German belong to the same Indo-European linguistic family, while Western thought is basically confined to "Aristotelian logic and their respective rules of reasoning" (1969, 7; 1959, 304). This logic cannot be applied to Chinese thought, since a Chinese sentence does not always have a subject, which is often understood. "Western logic is essentially based upon the law of identity," which necessitates dichotomous thinking and the rule of exclusiveness (1969, 10; 1959, 308). By contrast,

> Chinese thought puts no emphasis on exclusiveness. Rather, it emphasizes the relational quality between above and below, good and evil, something and nothing. All these relatives are supposed to be interdependent. (Zhang 1969, 11; 1959, 308)

Here "the relational quality" (*la nature de la relation* in French) refers to the relational ontology of Chinese thought, a characteristic the Lifeview school intellectuals highlight in their views of life and the universe. Another view in the article that relates to this study is the relationship between new language and new thought: "Viewing human history as a whole, any creation of new language, e.g., new terminology, represents a development of thought along a new line" (Zhang 1969, 6; 1959, 303). The transcultural lexicon that contributes to the formation of Lifeview discourses discussed so far is exactly a "creation in new language" that leads to a new trend of thought in modern China. Language, if constantly changing by assimilating new concepts from other cultures, certainly does not confine thought in traditional boundaries.

Kristeva's encounter with Zhang Dongsun is a noteworthy event in the transcultural relationship between Eastern and Western cultures. In her famous essay "Word, Dialogue, and Novel," Kristeva's critique of Aristotelian logic in the section on "ambivalence," with her interpretation of the Menippean satire and carnivalesque dialogism in Bakhtin, is clearly inspired by Zhang's analysis of the logic of Chinese language. Zhang points out that "in Chinese there is no verb 'to be' comparable to the English form." Just as the literary Chinese word *wei* 為 (to be) means *cheng* 成 (to become), the colloquial word *shi* 是 (being), rather than conveying the idea of existence, indicates "becoming"—the idea of changing unceasingly. But in English "becoming" is the opposite of "being." That is why for him Western logic may be called "identity logic." In Kristeva's mind, Zhang's Chinese logic emphasizing the concept of "becoming" relates to Bakhtin's dialogism, which implies "the double, language, and another logic." She writes:

> Literary semiotics can accept the word "dialogism": the logic of *distance* and *relationship* between the different units of a sentence of narrative structure, indicating a *becoming*, in opposition to the level of continuity and substance, both of which obey the logic of *being* and are thus monological. (Kristeva 1969, 152–53; 1980, 71–72)

Combining the Bakhtinian juxtaposition of dialogism and monologism with Zhang's idea of becoming and being, Kristeva here formulates her own concept of the "*praxis-poièsis*" separation (1969, 167; 1980, 84). For her, Bakhtin's dialogism, indicating "a logic of relations and analogy, rather than of substance and inference," is a reaction against Aristotelian logic (1969, 168; 1980, 85). Dialogism, emphasizing the social context of language, leads to her concept of intertexuality, which means no text stands alone.[41] While a book is only a discourse within the discursive universe, each text absorbs and transforms other texts. Kristeva announces: "The notion of intertextuality replaces that of intersubjectivity, and poetic language is read as at least *double*" (1969, 146; 1980, 66). In her mind Bakhtin's use of Menippean discourse

41. For an in-depth reading of the differentiation between dialogism and intertexuality, see Lesic-Thomas 2005. The author points out that Kristeva's concept of intertexuality is indebted as much to the Russian Formalists as to Bakhtin.

frees language from presupposed social and political "values," from the distinction between virtue and vice, and bequeaths ambivalence and the carnivalesque to the novel. It celebrates "the eternal joy of becoming," without transmitting any fixed message (1969, 167; 1980, 84). The concept of becoming, which Kristeva, following Zhang Dongsun's logic, prioritizes, was a dominant notion for the Lifeview school in May Fourth China. In 1924, Yuan Jiahua in his *Affectivist Philosophy* elaborated on the subtle distinction between "is" and "to be," very much the way Zhang Dongsun viewed "being" and "becoming." See Chapter 5 for further discussion.

The case of Kristeva acknowledging Zhang Dongsun's influence indicates that, examined from a long-term perspective, East-West encounters cannot be simply described as a process of acculturation, a one-way infiltration of the dominant culture into the dominated as postcolonial theory maintains. By contrast, the Latin-American theorists Fernando Ortiz (1881–1969) and Enrique Dussel (b. 1934) proposed the concept of transculturation, which indicates two-way enculturation, during which both parties of a cultural encounter are transformed (Ortiz 1995; Dussel 1995).[42] Taking age-old East-West encounters into account, one might as well say that mutual processes of influence and assimilation are incontestable. Chapter 5 discusses how Gottfried Wilhelm Leibniz (1646–1716) was fascinated by the *Book of Changes*, which he believed to relate to his own system of binary arithmetic. See also Chapter 5 for Zhu Qianzhi's 1940 study of how Chinese culture influenced the European Renaissance and Enlightenment movement.

Chapter 4 concentrates on Liang Shuming, Liang Qichao's close ally later recognized as a harbinger of New Confucianism that flourished in postwar Hong Kong and Taiwan. Understanding Bergson's concept of becoming as the "*bianhua liuxing*" 變化流行 (becoming and flows) taught in the *Book of Changes*, Liang Shuming was one of the most outspoken advocates of the Lifeview school.

42. Ortiz and Dussel maintain that in the transcultural process of colonialization, both colonizer and colonized undergo self-transformation. Ortiz invented the term "transculturation" in *Cuban Counterpoint: Tobacco and Sugar* (1940) to refute the anthropological concept of "acculturation," which indicates a one-way enculturation: the dominant culture replaces the dominated. Dussel, in *The Invention of the Americas: Eclipse of "the Other" and the Myth of Modernity* (1992), further developed Ortiz's idea of transculturation and the Latin-American tradition of critiquing Eurocentrism.

4

Liang Shuming

Life Is an Unceasing Becoming

> Having explored the ultimate, one realizes that vacuum engenders the illusory appearances of this world. The sudden stir of heart (*huran nianqi* 忽然念起) leads to *karma* and cyclical continuities (*yinguo xiangxu* 因果相續), ceaselessly flowing until this instant. This ceaseless flow means unceasing change for Le Bon, evolution for Darwin and Spenser, will to life for Schopenhauer. It is exactly what Bergson calls life and creative evolution.
>
> —Liang Shuming, "Jiuyuan jueyilun" 究元決疑論 [On the ultimate and casuistry, 1916] (*LSMQJ* 1:13)[1]

> Bergson severely criticizes the concrete and fixed concepts of science. For him, as opposed to science, it is prerequisite for metaphysics to develop flexible, dynamic concepts. Isn't he opening up a road for Chinese thought?
>
> —Liang Shuming, *Eastern and Western Cultures and Their Philosophies* (1921; *LSMQJ* 1:445)

Before the Science and Lifeview debate broke out, Liang Shuming, reputedly a first-generation New Confucian, was invited by the Education Ministry to give two lecture series on the comparison between Eastern and Western cultures. One of these series was delivered at Peking University in 1920, and the other, to the Education Committee of Jinan province in 1921. These lectures were later collected as a book in 1921, *Eastern and Western Cultures and Their Philosophies* (henceforth *Eastern and Western Cultures*; *LSMQJ* 1:319–547). Liang maintains that Western culture, emphasizing science and rational thinking, is a materialistic culture, while Eastern culture, marked by metaphysical thought and intuition, is a spiritual culture.

1. "On the Ultimate and Casuistry" was originally serialized in *Eastern Miscellanies* 13, no. 5: 6–10; 13, no. 6: 5–9; and 13, no. 7: 8–12. *Jiuyuan* 究元 (inquire into the ultimate) means investigating "a final or fundamental fact or principle," and *jueyi* 決疑 (casuistry), "the resolving of moral problems by the application of theoretical rules to particular instances" (*Oxford English Dictionary*).

He points out that "the life of spirit" (Liang's English), which both Rudolf Eucken and Bertrand Russell advocate, is the characteristic of spiritual cultures. Then Liang refers to the Aesthetic Education movement in China: "Those who stand up for an arts-based lifeview or an aesthetic life, or champion replacing religion with aesthetic education (whether this theory is appropriate remains to be seen), are also advocates of 'the life of spirit'" (426). Liang Shuming was a pious Buddhist and studied *Yogācāra* thought 唯識學 almost his entire life (Zeng 2018, 102–11). For him, religion is necessary because its function is much more than mere aesthetic experiences; it is about the meaning of life. Here, Liang Shuming's stark juxtaposition of Eastern and Western cultures as spiritualism versus materialism, a concept that had emerged in the late Qing, became the most obvious talking point during the 1923 Science and Lifeview debate and shaped the biased cultural imaginations of generations of Chinese people to come. By contrast, his life theory is much more sophisticated than that, while *Eastern and Western Cultures* is nonetheless a significant work for the development of modern Chinese Counter-Enlightenment, as this chapter will show.

Liang Shuming's concept of life grew from his life experiences. Throughout his life traditional Chinese culture, at the onslaught of Western materialism, seemed to have lost its stamina. The dismal vision of the death of tradition drove numerous intellectuals and youths to suicide, including Wang Guowei in 1927, as discussed in Chapter 2. Liang Shuming's father, Liang Ji 梁濟 (1858–1918), also drowned himself in a lake in 1918. He left a death note to his children:

> Not only does my death commemorate a nostalgia for the old, but it intends to awaken the new. I call on the citizens of our new nation to prioritize justice over perfidy and treachery, so that the remnants of our national character can survive. If our national character still exists, so can our nation. (Liang and Liang 1968, 195)

From the late Qing to the early Republican period, the anxiety and pain of intellectuals going through the drastic socio-political and cultural transition devastated them. Even Liang Shuming himself made two suicide attempts, and he studied Buddhism in order to alleviate his own pain as well as his father's. As he confesses at the beginning of "On the Ultimate and Casuistry" (*LSMQJ* 1:1–22), centering on the ultimate truth of life and how to solve its problems:

> If our relatives, friends, or even random strangers are tortured by depression and mental illness, we will certainly endeavor to find ways to comfort them and ease their pains. . . . When I face such people and intend to offer my sincere help, the only thing I can do is to teach them Buddha's wisdom. . . . I myself have experienced such depression and lunacy (in winter 1911 and winter 1912 I have attempted suicide trice), which is now mitigated. (*LSMQJ* 1:3)

However, although Buddha's wisdom saved him from suicidal thoughts, it was unable to save his father, who eventually took his own life two years after the essay was published.

As a youth, Liang Shuming looked up to the two great leaders of the Lifeview school, Liang Qichao and Cai Yuanpei, as his mentors (*LSMQJ* 7:548). When he was fifteen, he began to read arduously the six volumes of *Xinmin congbao* 新民叢報 [Journal of the new people], comprising three years of issues of the journal and a huge volume of the journal *Xinxiaoshuo* 新小說 [The new novel], which covered a whole year. Both collections were imported from Japan, and the "new lifeview" and the reform of Chinese society that Liang Qichao advocated in these journals had a great impact on him (*LSMQJ* 2:681–82; Wang 1988, 45). In 1916, at the age of twenty-three, Liang Shuming published an article on the concept of change in *Eastern Miscellanies*, "On the Ultimate and Casuistry." It draws on Buddhist cosmology, the French thinker Gustave Le Bon's (1841–1931) *L'Évolution de la matière* [The evolution of matter, 1905], and *Creative Evolution*. Introduced by a friend, he visited Cai Yuanpei and showed him this essay, which the latter marveled at. At the time he had just resigned as Education Minister and assumed the position of chancellor of Peking University. He immediately asked Chen Duxiu, whom he had appointed as dean of humanities, to hire Liang Shuming to teach Indian philosophy starting in the following year (*LSMQJ* 6:333–34).[2] A 1911 graduate from Shuntian Xuetang 順天學堂 (a modern education high school established in the late Qing) becoming a young lecturer at Peking University, Liang would later inspire Zhu Qianzhi, one of his talented students only six years younger than him, to develop the concept of affectivism in the early 1920s. This is to be discussed in Chapter 5.

The Buddhist Concept of *Karma* (Change) and Evolution

"On the Ultimate and Casuistry" relates the Buddhist concept of *karma* to the scientific concept of evolution. At the outset, Liang Shuming points out that people are usually anxious to find a theory to solve life problems before they get to the bottom of the ultimate principle of life. The life philosophy of Rudolf Eucken, introduced into China by someone using the pen name Minzhi 民質 in *Eastern Miscellanies* earlier in 1916, is just a case in point.[3] Liang maintains that, in order to solve the problems of life, one must enquire into its ultimate truth (*LSMQJ* 1:4). Liang's essay consists thus of two parts, "Investigating the Ultimate Principle

2. See "Jinian Cai Yuanpei xiansheng" 紀念蔡元培先生 [Commemorating Mr. Cai Yuanpei, 1942] (*LSMQJ* 6:330–38). See also the postscript to "On the Ultimate and Casuistry" (1:20–22).
3. According to Minzhi, in England and Japan the life philosophy of Eucken was often studied together with that of Bergson (1916).

of Life: *Ratnagotravibhāga*" 如寶論 [Analysis of the lineage of the Three Jewels][4] and "Solving Life Problems: *Upāya-Kauśalya-Sūtra*" 方便論 [Skillful means sutra].[5] In the first part of the essay Liang confesses that he learned about Le Bon's *The Evolution of Matter* from Huang Shiheng's 黃士恆 interpretive abridged translation of the book published in *Eastern Miscellanies* the year before. According to Huang, in Le Bon's 1905 theory the dematerialization of matter into ether (*yitai* 以太) and its rebirth as other forms of energy—due to the transformation of the equilibrium of the vortex formed in the midst of ether—are repeated every thousand years. Huang compares such cyclic notion of the dematerialization and rebirth of matter to the Buddhist concept of *karma* (*lunhui* 輪迴; Huang 1915a, 1), which, according to the *Cambridge Dictionary*, means "the force produced by a person's actions in one life that influences what happens to them in future lives." Liang comments, "This [Le Bon's] theory, originally intended for examining matter, coincidentally fits Buddha's teachings" (*LSMQJ* 1:4). As rendered in Huang's translation, Le Bon's concept of "evolution of matter" comprises the following propositions: (1) Despite the dogma of the indestructibility of matter, it vanishes slowly because of the continuous dissociation of atoms; (2) Matter dematerializes into products that are "between ponderable bodies and the imponderable ether"; (3) Matter, formerly believed to be inert, is in fact a reservoir of intra-atomic energy, which is within, not without, matter itself; (4) Most of the forces in the universe (such as heat, light, and electricity) are derived from the intra-atomic energy that is released when matter dematerializes; (5) Force and matter are the same thing in different forms; matter represents a stable form of intra-atomic energy, while heat, light, electricity and so on, represent its unstable forms; (6) By the dissociation of atoms, matter is changed into unstable forms of energy; (7) The law of the evolution of living species is applicable to "chemical species" as well; (8) Forces, which originate from matter, are also not indestructible.[6] The most significant propositions that lead both Huang and Liang to compare ether with the concept of *karma* are probably the fifth and the sixth.

4. *Ratna-gotra-vibhāga*, or *Uttara-tantra*, is composed of verses and "a prose commentary which includes substantial quotations from *Tathāgata-garbha* [Buddha embryo, or Buddha essence] oriented *sutras*" (Keown 2003, 234). *Ratnagotravibhāga* in Sanskrit means "Analysis of the Lineage of the Jewels," and *Uttara-tantra* means "Sublime Continuation" (Buswell Jr. and Lopez Jr. 2014, 701–2). The three Jewels refers to *Sangha* (the monastic community of monks and nuns practicing the dharma together), *Dharma* (cosmic law and order and the teachings of Buddha), and Buddha.
5. *Upāya-Kauśalya-Sūtra* means "Skillful Means Sūtra," an early Mahāyāna sutra. *Upāya-Kauśalya* in Sanskrit means "skillful means," "skill-in-means," or "expedient means," referring to the extraordinary pedagogical skills of the Buddhas and advanced Bodhisattvas" (Buswell Jr. and Lopez Jr. 2014, 942–43). A *Dictionary of Buddhism* points out: "At the root of the idea [of Upaya] is the notion that the Buddha's teaching is essentially a provisional means to bring beings to enlightenment (*bodhi*) and that the teachings which he gives may vary: what may be appropriate at one time may not be so at another" (Keown 2003, 318).
6. Huang translates the first seven ideas directly from Le Bon's *The Evolution of Matter*, while adding the eighth, which is systemically expounded throughout *Le Bon*'s text (*LSMQJ*, 1:4–5; Huang 1915a, 4; Le Bon 1907, 8–9).

The "imponderable ether," the concept that stands out throughout *The Evolution of Matter*, is called by Le Bon "the First Cause of things" (1907, 100). It becomes in Huang's Chinese translation and Liang's text "the first noumenon of the myriad things" (*wanwu diyi benti* 萬物第一本體; *LSMQJ* 1:5; Huang 1915b, 3), or "the origin of the myriad things" (*wanwu zhi yuan* 萬物之原; Huang 1915a, 1). Although Huang thinks Le Bon invented the concepts of the vortex and dissipation of atoms, ideas of ether and the vortical forces had in fact long existed since the time of Aristotle. In the philosophy of physics, ether as a metaphysical concept has never been scientifically proved, but even today it has continued to be a thought-provoking concept permeating the history of science. For some, it "forms the foundation of our very formulation and understanding of reality, the concepts of space and time" (Andrade, Faber, and Rosa 2013, 560). Before Liang wrote "On the Ultimate and Casuistry," due to the Western scientific works translated by John Fryer 傅蘭雅 (1839–1928), the concept of ether had repeatedly appeared in late Qing publications.[7] Tan Sitong 譚嗣同 (1865–1898), a co-reformer of Liang Qichao and Kang Youwei 康有為 (1858–1927) and one of the six gentlemen executed after the failed Hundred Days' Reform (1898), published "Yitaishuo" 以太說 [On ether] in 1898. Following Kang's study of the topic in the 1880s,[8] Tan used the traditional Chinese concepts of *qi* 氣 (energy), *ren* 仁 (benevolence), *ganying* 感應 (affect), and *xiangtong* 相通 (mutual communion) to understand how ether fills the universe, transmits forces among the stars, and engenders light and electricity (Tan 1898).[9] Huang Shixiu and Liang Shumin certainly followed the heritage of the late Qing tradition of interpreting scientific notions in ethical terms. Wang Tao 王韜 (1828–1897), another late Qing reformer and director of Gezhi Shuyuan 格致書院 (Shanghai Polytechnic), writes in the preface to *Gezhi Shuyuan keyi* 格致書院課藝 [The Shanghai Polytechnic Prize Essays on Science, 1889]: "Metaphysicists (*xing er shang zhe* 形而上者) call it [science] *Dao*, while physicists (or materialists; *xing er xia zhe* 形而下者) call it *qi* 器 (manufacturing device). *Dao* engenders *qi*,

7. John Fryer was a British sinologist, who from 1861 on taught at missionary schools in Hong Kong, Beijing, and Shanghai. Then he became a newspaper editor and a professional translator. He translated at least seventy-five scientific works in collaboration with Chinese intellectuals for the Translation Department of Jiangnan Arsenal 江南製造局 from 1868 on. He lived in Shanghai for twenty-eight years until 1896, when he was hired as professor of oriental languages and literature at Berkeley.

8. For discussions of Kang Youwei's study on ether and *ren* in the 1880s, see Feng 1953, 2:692–98; Hsiao 1967, 1975.

9. Before "On Ether," Tan Sitong wrote *Renxue* 仁學 [On benevolence] in 1897, maintaining that ether is the conciousness that connects the "physical, mental, and spiritual realms in and through *ren*" (Wright 2000, 372–73). He had read John Fryer's translation of Western scientific works, and he discloses that he met Fryer in 1893 and 1896 to discuss issues concerning science, Buddhism, and traditional Chinese thought and was encouraged by the latter to create a synthetical study thereof. John Fryer's work in China greatly influenced the late Qing reformers (Wright 2000, 124, 373; Wang 2000).

while *qi* conveys *Dao*" (1889, i).[10] In other words, *Dao*, the metaphysical or ethical principle that engenders the myriad things in the universe, is much superior to *qi*, manufactured things that are conveyers, or manifestations, of Dao.

Here it is worthwhile making a little effort to understand ether as a concept in physical science and thereby infer why it fascinated the Chinese imagination. The notion of "something similar to quintessence" had been known before Aristotle, who conceived of ether as the fifth element that is "pure, unchangeable, imperishable, and unfathomable," filling the supralunar or celestial region, and moving in an eternal circular and uniform motion. By contrast, all in the sublunary region is made up of the four elements that are corruptible, changeable, and subject to combination. Aristotle's conceptualization of these two regions shows "the need for a continuous medium or a plenum," because it is difficult to imagine the universe as a void (Andrade et al. 2013, 561–62). This concept lived on in later generations of physicists. Before the mid-seventeenth century, Descartes maintained that ether is the elementary matter—the medium or plenum strictly mechanistic—that fills the space, responsible for the circular motion of planets. In his vision, the universe is filled with this primal and universal matter that organizes itself as large vortices, the motion of which propels the action of one body on another (562). Isaac Newton (1642–1726), near the turn of the seventeenth century, proposed the notion of ether as "an active medium," by the vibrations of which light is refracted and heat transmitted. His concept of gravitation and absolute space indicates that a medium for the interaction of bodies is necessary, but whether this medium is material or immaterial he could not decide (563–64). Around the mid-nineteenth century, the Scottish mathematical physicist James Clerk Maxwell (1831–1879) believed that ether is the indispensable medium that enables the electromagnetic forces to produce waves. However, the lines of these waves are perpendicular to the planes of propagation (566). Although Albert Einstein abolished "the luminiferous ether" in *Special Theory of Relativity* (1905), he often talked about a new type of "ether without substance and without motion" during the 1910s and 1920s. He wrote in his letter to the Dutch physicist Hendrik Lorenz (1853–1928) on 17 June 1916 that "the general theory of relativity (1912) is closer to the ether hypothesis than the special theory." He envisioned "the new relativistic ether" and stated in "Aether und Relativitätstheorie" [Ether and the theory of relativity, 1920] that "According

10. For the English translation of *xing er shang* (*keijijō*) and *xing er xia* (*keijika*), see *Weblio.jp*. The Chinese Prize Essays Contest was designed by Fryer and Wang Tao in 1886 and lasted until the late 1890s. These essay competitions had a great impact on the reformed civil examinations from 1901 to 1904 and the new education schools (*xuetang* 學堂) established after 1905 (Elman 2015, 146–52).

to the general theory of relativity, space without ether is unthinkable" (569–70).[11] Interesting to know is that there has been a revival of ether as plenum in quantum theory. It has been postulated that, instead of vacuum, ether fills the space. The concept of ether has been used to understand the existence of "dark energy," and the University of Oxford has reincarnated ether to solve the puzzle of "dark matter." According to Andrade et al., "[T]he concept of ether is making a strong comeback in physics. It is now an ether that is both substantial and interactive" (570–73).

For late Qing intellectuals such as Kang Youwei, Tan Sitong, and Wang Tao, the concept of ether shed new light on the ultimate truth of life: the transformation of matter from this life to the next and the transconnectivity of things in the universe. Just as the Qing scholars were searching for spiritual meanings in physical science, so was Liang Shuming when he wrote "On the Ultimate and Casuistry" in 1916. Their enthusiasm for the concept centered on its possibility of connecting metaphysical with physical worlds, or the spiritual and the material, a major concern for the Lifeview school during the May Fourth period, as discussed in previous chapters. And these Chinese intellectuals were not alone in this regard. A few British physicists involved in psychical research, such as William Crookes (1832–1919), Joseph John Thomson (1856–1940), and Oliver Lodge (1851–1940), believed that they found in ether "the essential unity of material and spiritual phenomena" (Wright 2000, 376). In his 1916 work, *Raymond, or Life and Death,* Oliver Lodge, whose son was killed in World War I, found consolation in the vision of ether as the region where the myriad existence of this life enters after death and only changes into another state of myriad existence:

> [T]he process called death is a mere severance of soul and body. . . . The body alone dies and decays; but there is no extinction even for it—only a change. For the other part there can hardly be even a change—except a change of surroundings. . . . We change our state at birth, and come into the world of air and sense and myriad existence; we change our state at death and enter a region of—what? Of Ether, I think, and still more myriad existence; a region in which communion is more akin to what we here call telepathy. (Lodge 1916, 298)

As we have seen, for Liang Shuming, the thought of an existence in this life transforming into another existence in another life apparently mitigates the grief over losing his father. Le Bon's idea of matter, transforming into the imponderable ether and then becoming other forms of energy, indicates more than mere science for

11. David Wright maintains that ether was severely attacked in *Special Theory of Relativity* and *General Theory of Relativity* by Einstein, who did not think the theory of relativity requires the existence of an ether (2000, 388). However, Andrade et al. point out that Einstein did not totally denounce the idea of ether and believed that ether is necessary for the concept of space. Jaume Navarro and Massimiliano Badino hold a similar view: "[F]ar from killing the ether off, special and general relativity (and, to a lesser degree, quantum physics) caused an explosion of ether narratives into different directions" (Navarro 2018, 2).

intellectuals like Liang Shuming. It is the ultimate metaphysical truth of reality. He compares ether to *Tathāgatagarbha* 如來藏 (Buddha-nature) or *ālaya* 阿賴耶 (eternal matter)[12]and quotes from the *Śraddhotpāda Śāstra* 起信論 [The awakening of faith śāstra]: "Neither birth nor death, it combines birth and death; neither one nor dissemblance, it can subsume all *dharmas* [aspects of truth or reality] and become every one of them" (*LSMQJ* 1:6).[13] For him, Le Bon's theory that "the elements of matter are in incessant motion" is akin to Buddha's teachings. He quotes from Le Bon's words in *The Evolution of Matter*: "Nature knows no rest. If repose exists anywhere, it is neither in the world we inhabit nor in the beings on its surface; nor is it even existent in death" (Le Bon 1907, 255; *LSMQJ* 1:7).[14] For Liang, just as Buddha's true heart is illuminated by the myriad worlds perceived by us, so is ether the origin of the universe. He compares Le Bon's theory to the the *Śūraṅgama Sūtra* 楞嚴經 [The heroic march sūtra): "Ether vortexes form the world, while the stir of the heart engenders the myriad *dharmas*. . . . the *Śūraṅgama Sūtra* delves into the roots of human nature to reach the true heart-mind 真心" (*zhenxin*; *LSMQJ* 1:6–7).[15]

It is the concept of an unceasing becoming as the ultimate truth of the universe that attracts Liang Shuming to Le Bon's work, so it comes as no surprise that in the second part of "On the Ultimate and Casuistry" he refers to Herbert Wildon Carr's (1857–1931) book *Henri Bergson: The Philosophy of Change* (1911). According to Carr, Bergson himself had read the proofs of the book and suggested the title (1911, viii). From the four passages of the book translated into Chinese in Liang's essay, we can construe that he has read Carr's original English. This quote from Carr's book is one of them:

> [L]ife is the reality for which knowledge is and for which nature receives the order that knowledge discovers. The main task of philosophy is to do what science cannot do, comprehend life. The impetus of life, the springing forward, pushing, insinuating, incessant changing motion of life has evolved the intellect to know the inert world of matter, and has given to matter the appearance of a solid, timeless existence spread out in space. Reality is not solid matter, nor thinking mind, but living, creative creation. (*LSMQJ*, 1:13; Carr 1911, 14)

12. According to the online *Chinese Buddhist Encyclopedia*, *Tathāgatagarbha* means Buddha-nature, or "the potential for becoming a Buddha," which is "possessed equally by all sentient beings," and *ālaya* is "a sort of eternal substance or matter, creative and containing all forms."
13. Liang's Chinese original reads: "不生不滅，與生滅和合，非一非異，能攝一切法，生一切法."
14. Liang's Chinese reads: "宇宙無休息，縱有休息之所，亦非吾人所住之世界，而其間亦必無生物。死非休息也." It is a mildly revised version of Huang Shiheng's translation of Le Bon's original (Huang 1915, 12.4:6).
15. Liang's Chinese reads: "渦動形成世界，心生種種法生……《楞嚴》克就根性，直指真心."

The main message conveyed in the quote is the distinction between science and philosophy. While science, or the intellect, studies the seemingly "inert world of matter," philosophy studies life. The most important is that philosophy, in comprehending the truth of life, accomplishes what science is unable to. A quotable line before this passage by Carr, "Knowledge is for life, and not life for knowledge," can be viewed as the mission statement of life philosophy (1911, 14). Another message conveyed is that it is *élan vital* (the impetus of life, or vital force)—which is understood as the "incessantly changing motion of life"—that has actively evolved the intellect to know the material world. But reality is neither intellect (the thinking mind), nor matter (what the intellect knows). It is rather the vital force, i.e., the incessantly changing motion of life. Our mind, which perceives matter, is only part of the living reality, while its views are "prescribed and limited by the needs of its particular activity" (15). For Bergson, to live means to have consciousness, in which past, present, and future are interconnected as a whole. Carr's words wonderfully capture the gist of the Bergsonian theory of consciousness, which we have discussed in detail in Chapter 3:

> To exist is to be alive, to be borne along in the living stream, as it were on the breast of a wave . . . . The past is gathered into it, exists in it, is carried along in it, as it presses forward into the future, which is continually and without intermission becoming actual. This reality is life. It is an unceasing becoming, which preserves the past and creates the future. (Carr 1911, 15)

From Liang's exposition of Carr's book, it is evident that before Bergson's *Creative Evolution* was serialized in *Current Times* in 1918, Chinese intellectuals had already been attracted to Bergson's life philosophy.

By contrast, unlike other Lifeview school intellectuals, Liang Shuming, though also viewing life philosophy as a practical philosophy, considers Buddha's vision of *nirvāṇa* 涅槃 (the final beatitude that transcends *karma* and suffering) more consoling than life itself. Never mentioning the term *nirvāṇa* in the essay, Liang Shuming states that he longs for *chushijian* 出世間 (*lokottara*), which means the quest for *nirvāṇa* as opposed to the mundane world (*LSMQJ* 1:19). He criticizes Schopenhauer and Bergson for being unaware that the cause of suffering and happiness in life is desire (*yunian* 欲念). For him, suffering is caused by the inability to fulfill one's desires, and happiness, by their fulfillment. The perceptions of our five senses lead to potential, or unconscious, desires (*wunianyu* 無念欲), which, when surfacing to consciousness, become conscious desires (*younianyu* 有念欲). There is therefore no difference between potential and conscious desires. Desires are unceasing, while there are more unfulfilled than fulfilled desires. Utopian visions of the land of happiness in this life, such as the Confucian stateless world (*datongshi* 大同世), socialism, anarchism, Kant's democratic state, and Nietzsche's terrain of the artist-saint,[16] are "not unachievable" in his view. However, all these visionaries, definitely intellectually superior to common people, are ignorant of the fact that the more one desires, the more one suffers. One should therefore heed Buddha's wisdom, which teaches us to forsake desire. For Liang, here it is where Confucianism and Buddhism part ways, and those such as the Song-Ming scholars, who maintain that the two philosophies reach the same goal by different routes, are only talking nonsense. Liang also disagrees with Schopenhauer, for whom, since this world is so undesirable, those who commit suicide have a strong desire to get rid of the pain in this world. But for Liang the correct way to stay away from pain is the Buddhist concept of *lokottara*, which does not mean committing suicide. Rather, it means *guiyi* 皈依 (to convert), or taking refuge in the Three Jewels: Buddha, Dharma, and Sangha. Far surpassing any worldly virtues, *lokottara* enables one to be "free from any doubt or fear, dissolute carnal pleasures, craziness and depression, and suicidal thoughts," and to "obey on one's own the numerous commandments with tranquility and purity" (1:19). In Chapter 5 we will see that, his student Zhu Qianzhi, though acknowledging Liang's influence on his conceptualization of affectivism, criticizes him for maintaining the Buddhist concept of detachment from the world here and now. Living in an imperfect world, how do we cope with the imperfection and the constant disappointments? What is the ethical attitude we should adopt to face the troublesome reality? Liang Shuming found his way out in Buddhism.

One aspect worth noticing is that Liang Shuming was a self-conscious thinker, constantly questioning his own thought. In the Postscript to the essay, dated 1923, he criticizes his own methodology of comparing ether vortexes to "the sudden stir of the heart" in *The Awakening of Faith Śāstra*: "Basically such appropriation of similar discourses to establish one's theory is a way to confounding thought, an unwelcomed barrier to scholarship" (*LSMQJ* 1:21–22). Reflections of this kind repeatedly appear in his writings, as can be seen in the prefaces to *Eastern and Western Cultures* and the appendix (321–29). We in academe today are still asking similar questions: How do we compare? Does the methodology of comparative philosophy, or comparative literature, still hold? (Saussy 2006; Domínguez 2015). For me the thing that matters is not whether comparisons are appropriate or correct—cultural encounters are always likely to breed misunderstanding—but how, juxtaposing elements from different cultures from our own point of view, we thereby understand and assimilate others in order to find new meanings in our own tradition. As Peter Burke says, "Cultural encounters encourage creativity": it is a process of reinterpreting ourselves

16. For a description of the philosopher as an artist-saint, see Thiele 1990, 99–164. For Nietzsche, while the artist is devoted to life, art is also "the great stimulant of life." The saint "transforms his world through love." According to Leslie Paul Thiele, "Love is the saintly equivalent of philosophical wonder and artistic creativity, allowing a third facet to the philosophical-artistic self" (138–39).

and reinventing tradition through "the mixture, interpenetration or hybridization of cultures" (2009, 6–7). This is exactly what transcultural studies are about.

Eastern and Western Cultures: Dewey and Russell

The main purpose of Liang Shuming's *Eastern and Western Cultures* is to compare Chinese, Indian, and Western philosophies so that the significance of Chinese culture in the modern world can be reassessed. The book was a response to Western philosophers such as John Dewey and Bertrand Russell, whose visits to China overlapped, a few years immediately before the Science and Lifeview debate, and who were both deliberating the differences between Eastern and Western cultures and how the two cultures can learn from each other. When visiting Tokyo Imperial University in 1919, Dewey was invited by Peking University and other educational institutions to come to China for one year through the intervention of Hu Shi and Jiang Menglin, his former students at Columbia University. He decided to stay for a second year with the support of the newly established Lecture Society. His total stay in China was from 30 April 1919, just a few days before the May Fourth movement began, to 11 July 1921. He lectured extensively in cities like Shanghai, Nanjing, and Beijing. The experience was also a process of learning for him, exerting a significant impact on his social and political thought (Wang 2008). Chapter 5 will discuss Dewey's middle and later philosophy to show that in the major part of his career he was a believer in life philosophy even though his student Hu Shi thought he was a pragmatist keen on philosophy as a cognitive science. Lecturing in China, Dewey maintained that Eastern and Western cultures should be in "harmony" (*tiaohe* 調和), while Liang Qichao, in *Impressions of European Travels*, and many other Chinese intellectuals echoed the same view (*LSMQJ* 1:331). But is "harmony" between the two cultures possible? As will be seen later, this is the main point Liang Shuming addresses in *Eastern and Western Cultures*. Five of Dewey's lectures, based on the oral interpretation of Hu Shi, were first published in *Chenbao* 晨報 [Morning post] (8–27 March 1920) and then collected in a book. One chapter was entitled "Three Modern Philosophers," discussing William James, Henri Bergson, and Bertrand Russell (Dewey 2005, 228–65). As we have seen in previous chapters, Bergson was consistently hailed as a great modern philosopher by the Lifeview school, and Russell was the first Western thinker invited by the Lecture Society to China (Ding 2016).

On 13 October 1920, Russell arrived in Shanghai. During his stay in China, Yuen Ren Chao 趙元任 (1892–1982), later a world-famous linguist, phonologist, and composer just returning after ten years of study in the United States, acted as his interpreter. As a guest of Peking University, Russell traveled around China for ten months, giving more than sixty lectures. On the afternoon of 11 July 1921, he left China for home (the morning of the same day Dewey had left for the States;

Chao 1972).[17] After returning to England, Russell published in 1922 *The Problem of China*, recounting his experiences of visiting the exotic country. He went to China to teach but thought he learned more in the end (1993, 198). He describes honestly the anarchy and corruption of its politics and the avarice, cowardice, and callousness of its people (209–213), but he predicts that China, if an orderly central government is in place to control its rich mineral resources, large population, and practical approaches to modern education, is likely to become "the greatest power in the world after the United States" (241). He has confidence in the potentials and influence of "Young China," those who have been educated abroad or in modern colleges at home, and the "new ethic" their thoughts have turned to (Chen 2008).[18] They have assimilated Western civilization with a critical attitude and believe that "correct ethical sentiments are more important than detailed scientific knowledge," a view derived from the Confucian tradition (Russell 1993, 77–79). For Russell, the Chinese need Western science and industrialism, but they should not adopt the Western philosophy of life and the vices of the West (251, 260). In addition, disillusioned with Western capitalism and its Christian mission (or the YMCA) and the Russian model of revolutionary socialism (or Bolshevism), he looks for a Chinese style of "international socialism" as an alternative that may be the key to the future prosperity of China as well as the world (184). Russell believes that while Western civilization is built upon "rationalizings of excessive energy" (16), the vision of what constitutes "instinctive happiness" or "human happiness" offered by the time-honored Chinese civilization is superior and can be a corrective to the destruction of Western and Japanese power struggles (11, 167). This is quite a romantic view of traditional China's virtues. His idea about the "harmony" between Eastern and Western cultures, which Liang Shuming deems impossible, is for the Chinese to assimilate the merits of Western civilization while combining them with their own splendid tradition (13). He praises the Chinese "love of compromise" (205) and believes that the Chinese way of life, if adopted, would make all the world happy (17). However, he warns against patriotism, which, though indispensable to China's independence from foreign powers, should be defensive rather than aggressive; otherwise, China may "embark upon a career of imperialism" (241–42). He calls for "enlightened patriotism" for China (245) and cautions against the example of Japan during the two world wars, with its "anti-foreign conservatism as regards everything except armaments" (14). With hindsight, witnessing what has been happening in contemporary global power competitions, one can only marvel at Russell's insight and vision of China becoming the greatest power after the United States. But the

17. Yuen Ren Chao published an essay titled "With Bertrand Russell in China" in 1972, describing his experience of interacting with the British philosopher during his ten-month visit.
18. For the "Young China Association" (Shaonian Zhongguo Xuehui 少年中國學會), see Chapter 3, note 21.

"exquisite sense of beauty" that he believes to make the Chinese nation lovable is sadly disappearing in China's rapid pace of industrial progress; his wishful thinking that "The Chinese have no wish to convert us to Confucianism" (196–97) has been proven untrue by the Confucius Institutes established globally since 2004. China's economic and strategic expansion overseas based on the One Belt One Road Initiative since 2013 has aroused suspicion of exploitation; the parliamentary democracy he thought was best for China has never happened; his belief that for the Chinese "wisdom is more precious than rubies" (225) has been proven wrong; and the polarities between rich and poor still endure, even have worsened, under China's controlled capitalism today.

Equally interesting to this study is Russell's 1924 pamphlet *Icarus: or, The Future of Science*, which uses a tale in Ovid's (43 BCE–17 or 18 CE) *Metamorphoses* as a metaphor for the destructive outcome of relentless scientific advancement (Russell 1924). The architect and inventor Daedalus, in order to flee from the island of Crete, invents two pairs of wings. He attaches one pair with wax on himself and another one on his son, Icarus, telling the latter to keep the middle course when flying. He should fly neither too low, because sea water would dampen his wings, nor too high, because the sun would melt the wax that attaches them. But Icarus gets carried away when he flies happily, totally forgetting his father's warning. The wax melts and he drops dead into the sea. This famous Greek myth has been represented in quite a few European paintings, including the Flemish painter Peter Paul Rubens's (1577–1640) 1636 oil painting *The Fall of Icarus* (Figure 4.1). Russell's pamphlet on Icarus and the dire future of science was a reaction to "Daedalus: or, Science and the Future," a lecture delivered by the British-Indian physiologist, geneticist, and biologist John B. S. Haldane (1892–1964) for the Heretics Society at the University of Cambridge on 4 February 1923. It was later published as a pamphlet (Haldane 1924). Coincidentally, or not, ten days later, the Chinese philosopher and New Confucian Zhang Junmai delivered his talk on "Lifeview" at Tsinghua University in Beijing, which immediately triggered the Science and Lifeview debate in China, as we have seen in Chapter 1. It is apparent that, between the two world wars, the problem concerning science and life was very much a concern for both East and West. Haldane, referring to the marvelous invention of Daedalus, believes that science can bring the utmost happiness for humankind, while Russell, calling attention to the downfall of Icarus, cautions against Haldane's rosy prophecy of a techno-scientific future. It is said that *Brave New World* (1932), the British novelist Aldous Huxley's (1894–1963) famous dystopian story of a technocratic World State, was inspired by Russell's idea of a joyless future population supplied by "vast state incubators," while the family system together with Eros, "beautifully and irresponsibly free," disappear (Nicol 2007, 46). Huxley was sometime friends with both Haldane and Russell, and he certainly shared Russell's mistrust of scientific progress at the expense of human values.

Figure 4.1: *The Fall of Icarus,* oil painting by Peter Paul Rubens. Collected in the Royal Museums of Fine Arts of Belgium (Brussels), inv. 4127, photo by J. Geleyns.

For Liang Shuming, the juxtaposition between science and core life values became that between Western and Eastern cultures as well. There was ample reason for him to think that way. For him, among the countries of Eastern culture, including China, Japan, and India, China has the longest history. Since the West began to force its presence on the East, both Japan and China have begun the process of Westernization. He asks, "Can Eastern culture still exist?" (*LSMQJ* 1:333).[19] In China since the late Qing, in order to pursue military prowess, Western scientific knowledge had been translated into Chinese by state-sponsored translation institutions, while the Fuzhou Naval College (1866) and shipyards such as the Jiangnan Shipyard (1864) and the Fuzhou Arsenal (1867) had been established. But the

19. Liang's original Chinese reads, "*dongfanghua jiujing nengfou cunzai*?" 東方化究竟能否存在? It seems to be saying, "Can Easternization still exist?" But here it simply means "Can Eastern culture still exist?" Sometimes *dongfanghua* does mean Easternization. My translation varies according to context.

navy built up in 1875 was completely wiped out in the 1894 Sino-Japanese War. The Chinese began to realize that there was something fundamental in Western science and that the key to Westernization was the overhaul of the political system. In addition to establishing modern education schools, they thus advocated the Hundred Days' Reform and representative politics. Yet even after the 1911 Revolution overturned the Qing dynasty, the Western political system was still not established in China. Chen Duxiu and Hu Shi therefore advocated the New Culture movement, thinking the crucial thing was the transformation of the Chinese way of thinking, piecemeal transportation was useless, and the Chinese had to bring in Western culture on a whole scale (333–35). For Liang Shuming, the question then becomes: "Will Westernization completely exterminate Eastern culture?" (335). Since science and democracy, quintessential to Western culture, are indispensable to any people in the world and have become a world culture, then can Eastern culture also become a world culture? In other words, is Easternization possible? (338).

Liang Shuming does not believe the two cultures can be in harmony, due to the major differences between them: Western culture is marked by its scientific accomplishments, while Eastern culture, its artistic accomplishments (*LSMQJ* 1:355). It is easy to understand his assessment of Western culture, since science and democracy are generally considered the overarching accomplishments of the West. But why are the accomplishments of Eastern culture deemed artistic? This is where Liang demonstrates his unique insight, and I will explain shortly. First, Liang refutes international scholars' comparative views of the two cultures. Take, for example, Kaneko Umaji, a Waseda University professor and co-translator of Bergson's *Creative Evolution*. When he was invited by a society of overseas Chinese students in Japan to visit China two years before, he pointed out that, as opposed to Eastern civilization that is based on conformity to nature, European civilization endeavors to conquer nature, a binary opposition many contemporary intellectuals subscribe to. But for Liang, democracy has nothing to do with conquering nature, while all cultures, Eastern or Western, have the same need to conquer nature when people engage in farming and building houses (346–47). Rather, it is the distinction between scientific and artistic mentalities that separates West and East. Interestingly enough, Russell in *The Problem of China*, published a year after Liang's *Eastern and Western Cultures*, also maintains that "China may be regarded as an artist nation, with the virtues and vices to be expected of the artist: virtues chiefly useful to others, and vices chiefly harmful to oneself" (1993, 10). His point is that, like an artist who would rather die in poverty than cater to the market, and whose paintings after his death become the collector's treasure, China should keep the peace-loving character of its civilization and not follow the model of progress and aggression set by the West, which is only harmful to others. For Russell, Russia is another artist nation, but, unlike China, it has since the time of Peter the Great endeavored to introduce "all the good and evil of the West" (17). That China will be able to assimilate the good of the West and shun its evil is an idealist (if not romantic or condescending) view, indeed.

Liang's definition of China's artistic mentalities, however, is subtler. He points out that Chinese manufacturing, be it forging iron and gunpowder, woodworking, building houses or bridges, all depends on apprenticeship and artisanship. In the West, by contrast, everything about manufacturing depends on science. Westerners turn fragmented experiences and knowledge into different disciplines of science and separate them completely from artisanry, which concerns only individual wisdom that is handed on from one generation to another. The artistic method of the East is intuitive and metaphysical and arrives at a subjective opinion rather than objective knowledge, which only Western scientific method can achieve. The Eastern outlook is "non-logical" and holistic. In the East, an illness indicates something is wrong with the entire person, body and spirit included. The Western outlook, by contrast, is logical and concentrates on the separate parts. When one is sick, a Western doctor pinpoints a certain organ that is malfunctioning. In the East, things scientific are treated artistically (*yishuhua* 藝術化); in the West, even art is treated in a scientific way (*kexuehua* 科學化; *LSMQJ* 1:355). Science pursues laws and principles that everyone can learn; therefore, new inventions are valued. In art, geniuses and traditional secret formulas are valued; the present is therefore never able to match the past (354–55). In metaphysics, noumenon refers to the one ultimate being that can change into the myriad things. Science, by contrast, studies the multitude of objects that are fixed and unchanging. Defining Eastern spirit as artistic, intuitive, non-logical, and metaphysical, Liang Shuming was reiterating Zhang Dongsun's views disclosed in his 1918 translation of Bergson's *Creative Evolution*. These views would resonate during the Science and Lifeview debate. Liang's theory of the artistic achievements of Eastern civilization was of course also informed by the Aesthetic Education movement, which since the 1910s had maintained "the aesthetic ethos," "an aesthetic life," and "replacing religion with aesthetic education," as we have seen in Chapter 2. The Lifeview school intellectuals were no doubt both sharing and reinforcing the views of one another, while the valorization of art and intuition was central to Rudolph Eucken's life philosophy. Chapter 1 has pointed out that, for Eucken, "art and fantasy" is a means to "a new reality, a rich spiritual culture, a world of pure structure and greater beauty."

Liang Shuming also discusses the question as to why science and democracy first emerged in the West rather than in the East. Kaneko Umaji believes that environmental factors played a key part: Greece, surrounded by mountains with barren lands that produced scarce food, used science to control nature; China, with its vast, fertile land and rich resources, had no need to develop science (*LSMQJ* 1:371). To refute Kaneko's notion, Liang refers to *Kexue fangfalun* 科學方法論 [Scientific methodology, 1920], a book written by the Peking University chemistry professor Wang Xinggong 王星拱 (1887–1949), a Science school proponent (Wang 1920).

According to Wang, Greek science abruptly discontinued because the Greeks were keen on "rational" and "disinterested" (English words in parenthesis in Liang's text) learning that had little to do with human life. What we enjoy as science today was a legacy of the Renaissance, but for centuries science had not concerned itself with practical application (373–74). While both Hu Shi and Li Dazhao, reiterating Marxist materialism, maintain that "All cultural and material systems, thought, and ethical codes transform in accordance with economic change," Liang does not agree, because such a theory presupposes that human beings are passive and that cultural production is only a passive response to the environment. It fails completely to acknowledge the power of human will in creative activities. He cites "Marxism," a 1919 essay written by the Peking University professor of economics Gu Zhaoxiong 顧兆熊 (1888–1972), who points out that "social reform is determined by human opinions; it is neither mechanical nor passive" (Gu 1919, 456; *LSMQJ* 1:373). The critique of the mechanical theory is also the gist of Bergson's *Creative Evolution*. Liang Shuming writes, "What we call culture is in fact the product of geniuses, of their fortuitous fantasy. It is the historical accumulation of strokes of serendipity (*yuan* 緣), rather than of causes and effects" (372). Chapter 1 points out that both Eucken and Bergson believe in human creativity and human beings' will to transcend themselves. This is also Liang Shuming's key concept in *Eastern and Western Cultures*. How should culture be defined, then? From a Buddhist viewpoint, he starts with the concept of life, to which the Lifeview school wants philosophy to return.

Life Is the Continuities of Events

Liang Shuming's definition of life, linking self and universe, best illustrates his transcultural trajectory connecting Buddhism and the life philosophy of Bergson and Eucken. Buddhism teaches that life is *xiangxu* 相續 (continuities), a concept similar to Bergson's *la durée*. For the *Yogācāra* school, all sentient beings are called cyclical continuities. Living beings are life itself, while the universe is the continuities of life: "The universe is founded on life, which is what its existence depends on. As a big life, the universe encompasses the truth of life itself and is its true answer" (*LSMQJ* 1:376). In a narrower, concrete sense, life is the "continuities of events" (*shi de xiangxu* 事的相續), which means the continuities of quests and answers (*yiwen yida* 一問一答). We keep on questing and searching; events therefore flow steadily, while life becomes "endless continuities." What is an event, then? He writes, "A sudden feeling, or a sudden heart stir (*nian* 念), that occurs in a flash of light is an 'event' that generates quest and answer" (377). Interestingly, he emphasizes that the tools to pursue the events of life are bodily organs— eyes, ears, nose, tongue, skin—and desire (*yi* 意), rather than reason. It is the "grand volition" (*dayiyu* 大意欲), the endless conation, that mobilizes these six tools to pursue quests and answers ceaselessly, so that "the past self" or "the accomplished self" can be transcended.

Life in a narrower sense means the "struggle" (*fendou* 奮鬥) that "the present self" is taking to transcend "the past self" (or the accomplished universe). "The past self," or "the accomplished self," is the self that exists in the material world, whereas, "the present self" is immaterial—it is the "heart-mind" or "spirit," the active force that spurs us to move forward. This resonates with the theory of Eucken and Bergson: life is a creative effort. Here, with recourse to Buddhism, Liang Shuming defines life as the ceaseless continuities of quests and answers. His student Zhu Qianzhi's theory of affectivism slightly revises his idea of "quest and answer," replacing it with "the capacity to affect and to be affected" (*yigan yiying* 一感一應; see Chapter 5).

What is the "struggle" of life? Liang Shuming uses the Buddhist concept of "hindrance" (*ai* 礙) to explain it. He gives a few examples to illuminate how "the past self" becomes a hindrance when "the present self" intends to move forward. A stone that gets in the way certainly is a hindrance that needs to be removed. But even when one walks or drinks tea, one's body as well as the teacup are hindrances. The body, while moving itself or bringing the teacup to the mouth, has to make an effort to change the posture of the past self to get what one wants. Such an effort counts for a struggle. One has to make efforts all the time; that is to say, life is a constant struggle. All hindrances become difficulties in life that need to be overcome with struggles. It is the same with all living beings: a fly develops six feet and myriad eyes to counter difficulties it faces in the environment but without being conscious at all. Likewise, a baby drinks milk and sleeps by instinct. Any effort to advance in life, conscious or unconscious, counts for a struggle (*LSMQJ* 1:378). In Liang's exposition of his life ethics, the body, as matter, while being our tool to perceive and interact with the world, is also the hindrance to be overcome when we want to move forward. To do what the past self is incapable of doing, the present self needs to exercise the body constantly to meet the challenges of life. From the survival instinct of babies to the conscious learning of life skills, all efforts in each phase of life are struggles. These life struggles are a result of the interaction between the perceiving body and the spirit, which not only recognizes the need to act but also demands the body to react. In these repetitive life struggles, the spirit-body coordination is indispensable. Any problem that occurs in this cyclical interaction (as when mentally or physically challenged) adds difficulties to these conscious or unconscious life struggles (378–81). As discussed in Chapter 1, for both Bergson and Eucken the coordination between matter and spirit is the origin of creative power. Liang Shuming here is saying that, when spirit and matter fail to coordinate, life struggles will encounter serious problems, be it for individuals, societies, nations, or the entire world (379).

Hindrance is not limited to the material world, or the accomplished self. The other sentient beings, or "other heart-minds" (*taxin* 他心), also constitute hindrances. Are their present selves in agreement with mine? One needs to persuade other heart-minds to accept one's intention. Such efforts are also struggles in life (*LSMQJ* 1:378–790). Natural laws (*ziranlü* 自然律), which cannot be avoided, are hindrances as well; for instance, the law that all humans die. In addition, not all human life is about struggle. All affective activities, such as playing games, music, singing, dancing, painting, and so on, are not motivated by problem solving and are therefore not about struggles in life.

The Three Directions in Life

In *Eastern and Western Cultures*, Liang Shuming compares Western, Chinese, and Indian cultures and points out that cultures differ due to the way they solve life problems. For him, these three cultures take three directions in life, each direction with a different way to handle conation, or desire. The first direction is that of the West. People struggle to change the status quo so that they can move forward to satisfy their desires; this is the direction their life takes. China takes the second direction. When Chinese people encounter problems, for instance, when they have small houses with leaking roofs, they do not make an effort to change houses but modify their own desires and look sideways for whatever else is interesting under the circumstances; they adapt to the situation. The third direction is that of Indian life. People simply negate the problems or give up their desires; they neither change the status quo nor modify their own desires. This is entirely contrary to the nature of life, because they look backward, outright suppressing their desires, while looking for transcendental meanings in life. The basis of life is desire, and culture is nothing but the way people live their lives. In short, cultures differ because people handle their desires differently, depending on whether they are looking forward, sideways, or backward (*LSMQJ* 1:381–82). The West has achieved a flourishing material culture by conquering nature, science and democracy as the pinnacles of accomplishments. But it has not always stayed in the first direction of life. During the Middle Ages when desire was overpowered by religion, Western people looked backward and negated life until the Renaissance rediscovered Greek traditions (383).

Liang Shuming compares the thought of these three cultures. In a broad sense, thought encompasses religion and philosophy, and these three cultures have held different attitudes toward religion. In the West, Christianity was once overwhelmingly powerful but has lost its firm grip on societies and needs to adjust to the changing times. The Chinese have never been enthusiastic about religion; the few religions they have, imitating other cultures', are not tenacious at all. Religions, monopolizing Indian thought, have kept their tenacity since ancient times. Liang points out the three trends of philosophy that each culture may adopt in different times: metaphysics, epistemology (*renshilun* 認識論; Jap. *ninshikiron*), or life philosophy (*LSMQJ* 1:395–96). In the West, metaphysics once prevailed in ancient Greece, but during the Middle Ages the predominance of religion brought in the Dark Ages. Metaphysics was under attack when epistemology became the dominant trend in the eighteenth and nineteenth centuries. Life philosophy, not as powerful and profound as metaphysics and epistemology, has been revived in modern times by people like Eucken and Bergson and is still groping its way forward. In China epistemology has always been neglected, while life philosophy, closely connected with its unique metaphysics (different from Western and Indian metaphysics), is most sophisticated and nuanced in theory and has always been the exclusive trend in philosophy. It is in the nature of living beings to quest for answers to our life problems, and these quests may lead to knowledge and science, but the pursuit of truth in metaphysics, uninterested in progress, leads to a different direction (446). In India, religions occupy the whole of philosophy. Indian metaphysics, as its Western counterpart, has prevailed alongside religions and has remained unchanging. By contrast, Indian epistemology is quite detailed in theory but has never been predominant. Indian life philosophy is attached to religions, religious beliefs trumping life. Indian ethical codes are therefore quite tenuous (395–97). Liang is aware that these three trends of philosophy carry on a complex interaction with religions. He points out the French positivist philosopher Auguste Comte's (1798–1857) mistake of considering religion, metaphysics, and science as three historical stages, one following another in a linear fashion (392). Here Liang is capable of sophisticated thinking and does not mean at all to categorically polarize Eastern and Western cultures into spiritualism versus materialism. It is a pity that, during the Science and Lifeview debate, the polarization stands out, while the nuanced argument is often lost.

Indeed, cultural encounters encourage creation, as Peter Burke points out (2009, 6). The Chinese term *rensheng zhexue* 人生哲學 used in Liang Shuming's discussion of the three trends of philosophy was originally *jinsei tetsugaku*, a Japanese neologism rendering "philosophy of life" in Takahashi Gorō's 高橋五郎 1909 bilingual manual of translated terms (1909, 114–15). Liang Shuming was the first to clearly define Chinese philosophy as a life philosophy, maintaining that Confucian metaphysics is a celebration of "life of the universe" (*yuzhou zhi sheng* 宇宙之生; *LSMQJ* 1:448). Without the Japanese neologism and without the introduction of the life philosophy of Bergson and Eucken into China during the late 1910s, it is unlikely that he would have made such a judgment. Revamping Confucianism as life philosophy, he has brought new perspectives on the traditional wisdom that the New Culture movement vows to eradicate in the name of science and democracy. In his reinterpretation through transcultural perspectives, Confucianism celebrates a creative transformation that would give rise to Zhu Qianzhi's invention of affectivism in 1922.

Chinese Metaphysics: Intuition versus Reason

Agreeing with Bergson that intuition is the only way to the absolute noumenon (or thing-in-itself; *juedui benti* 絕對本體), Liang Shuming uses both *Yogācāra* and Confucian teachings to illuminate the concept of intuition. For the *Yogācāra* school, in order to perceive truth through intuition, one has to give up "attachment to the self" (*wozhi* 我執, *ātma-grāha*) and "attachment to phenomena" (*fazhi* 法執, *dharma-graha*; Muller 2022). Intuition is therefore the combination of subjectivity and objectivity (*LSMQJ* 1:400). In Chinese metaphysics, the *Book of Changes* is concerned with the "becoming and flows" of the universe,[20] of which the abstract meaning and holistic dynamics can be understood only through intuition. Western or Indian metaphysics, by contrast, discusses concrete and fixed concepts developed by reason (442–43). For Liang, "*bianhu*a" (change and transformation) means "from harmony to discord" (*cong tiaohe dao butiaohe* 從調和到不調和) and then from discord to harmony, constituting a cyclical change. Just as the flow of water pursues balance, so all things in the universe are in a relational context of constant adjustment for harmony. He refers to a concept in Paul Carus' 1913 book *Principle of Relativity*, which he read some time before: "Everything is relative" (70, 81).[21] Anything that deserves the name of absoluteness "is after all in a system of relations" (41–42). Because humans are not satisfied with the subjective truth, science provides the ideal of objective truth, but Einstein's new school denies all objectivity and insists upon the truth of relativity. Believing that Chinese metaphysics and Bergson's thought are in sync, Liang writes: "Bergson severely criticizes the concrete and fixed concepts of science. For him, as opposed to science, it is prerequisite for metaphysics to develop flexible, dynamic concepts. Isn't he opening up a road for Chinese thought?" (*LSMQJ* 1:445). In other words, he sees the encounter with Bergson a chance for Chinese thought to renew itself.

Liang Shuming points out that Confucius taught us a crucial attitude: "never hold a fixed idea about anything" (一切不認定 *yiqie bu rending*). The *Book of Changes* is about life. Just as it points out that *Dao*, as life itself, is "ever-transforming, ever-changing and moving without rest" (*LSMQJ* 1:450),[22] so, in the *Analects*, Confucius is said to be free from foregone conclusions, arbitrary predeterminations, obstinacy, and egoism (450; Legge 2014, 83).[23] Confucius did not pursue objective, fixed rationale; those who do so become extremists who are stubborn. Always

20. For a quote demonstrating the concept of change in *Yijing*, see the seventh chapter of *Commentary on the Appended Statements, Part 1*: "*Tiandi she wei, er yi xing hu qi zhong yi*" 天地設位，而易行乎其中矣 (Heaven and Earth both stand in place and change operates between them; Rutt 2002, 413). For another example, see the eleventh chapter of *Commentary on the Appended Statements, Part 1*: "*Fu yi kai wu cheng wu, mao tianxia zhi dao*" 夫易開物成務, 冒天下之道 (Change opens matters up and brings affairs to completion. It embraces the *Dao* of all under Heaven; 417, with modifications).

21. The full title of Paul Carus' book is *Principle of Relativity in the Light of the Philosophy of Science*. While relativity physicists speak of the relativity of time and space, Carus thinks they should talk about "the relativity of things, of the whole actual world in all its parts and interrelations." Discussing Einstein, Lorenz, Heraclitus, and Herbert Spencer, he maintains that reality is a continuous flux; nothing is absolute; the principle of relativity is a matter of course; and time, space, motion, and matter represent relations.

22. For the original Chinese of this concept, see Chapter 3, note 30.

23. For the original Chinese of this concept, see Chapter 3, note 29.

following his intuition and affecting when affected, he had "no predetermined mentality" (*wuchengxin* 無成心; *LSMQJ* 1:451). Here, "affecting when affected" (*suigan er ying* 隨感而應) refers to "changing while maintaining the middle way and seeking harmony," which is the law of the universe, because human life, like a body of water, naturally flows into the middle way and harmony (452). What is intuition, then? Liang Shuming cites Mencius' theory of "the heart-mind of four principles" (*si duan zhi xin* 四端之心), which means conscience and "the intuition to seek the right and the good." The four principles are the heart-mind of commiseration, shame, respect, and right and wrong (452)[24]—respectively connoting benevolence, justice, propriety, and wisdom (*renyilizhi* 仁義禮智). Liang points out that humans are born with this kind of intuition, which is sharp and acute in the beginning but becomes contaminated and obscured later in life. All we need to do is to sharpen our intuition and let it return to the original state, so that whatever we do will be within the right and the good. What Confucius calls "benevolence" (*ren* 仁) refers to this "sharp intuition," or universal human instinct and emotion. For Liang, natural instincts and desires should be allowed to develop freely, as long as they follow the middle way. But when reason intervenes and "divides self from non-self," calculating and weighing advantages and disadvantages, then intuition recedes, as benevolence does (454–55). Chapter 1 has pointed out that for the Lifeview school, scientism is at fault because of its division of self from non-self. According to Liang Shuming, benevolence is about internal life, rather than about ethics and politics. Hu Shi's comment that early Confucians only cared about ritual music and formalities is wrong (456). For Confucius, one who is filled with true affections but not good at reasoning is benevolent, while one who is good at reasoning and rhetoric but lacks true affections is malevolent (455). However, it should be noted that Liang is not saying that reason is unnecessary. Rather, he is saying that the affects and reason should be balanced, or in harmony.

For Liang Shuming, the life philosophy of Confucianism is about living with affections. Its advocacy of filial piety and practice of ritual music constitute the Confucian religion, which, however, is distinct from ordinary religions. Filial piety is the origin of *qing*: children feel the love for their family before they love others. Both the teaching of filial piety and the use of ritual music are intended to cultivate our affective life. Ritual music works on intuition to cultivate our affections, which constitute our true life (*LSMQJ* 1:467). Liang writes:

---

24. Liang Shuming's four original terms are "*ceyin zhi xin*" 惻隱之心 (the heart-mind of commiseration), "*xiuwu zhi xin*" 羞惡之心 (the heart-mind of shame), "*gongjing zhi xin*" 恭敬之心 (the heart-mind of respect), and "*shifei zhi xin*" 是非之心 (the heart-mind of right and wrong). In *Mencius*, however, "*cirang zhi xin*" 辭讓之心 (the heart-mind of courtesy and modesty) is used instead of "the heart-mind of respect." D. C. Lau translates *xin* as "heart," and Irene Bloom, as "mind" (Lau 2003, 82–83; Bloom 2009, 35).

> Sense perceptions (*ganjue* 感覺) have nothing to do with our inner life. What is relevant is intuition, which is attached to sense perceptions. Reason has nothing to do with our inner life. What is relevant is intuition, which is attached to reason. Our inner life and the outer world communicate through intuition, as through a window. (*LSMQJ* 1:468)

This quote highlights Liang Shuming's theory of knowledge: neither sense perception nor reason is relevant to our inner life. What is relevant is intuition, which is attached to both sense perception and reason, while intuition is the window that connects inner life and the outer world. In other words, intuition and reason, though distinct from each other, are closely interrelated.

To illuminate the interrelationship between intuition and reason, Liang spares no words. He defines reason this way: "When one leaves the here and now (*dangxia* 當下) and looks back, it is a conscious activity of reasoning," implying that intuition is a natural, unconscious activity of apperception that occurs at the immediate present. He describes how Confucius often refrained from simply depending on the intuition of the present moment and how he would also rely on intuition when looking back—the intuition that is attached to reason (*LSMQJ* 1:470–71). Depending solely on an immediate intuition, one is likely to deviate from the right path and it may be dangerous. If one also has recourse to the intuition attached to reason, the danger may be avoided. In short, it is crucial to use reason to adjust intuition: in addition to the "natural middle way" (*ziran qiuzhong* 自然求中) of intuition, the "chosen middle way" (*jianze de qiuzhong* 揀擇的求中) of reason functions as a regulating force. For Liang Shuming, the key to the life philosophy of Confucius is the concept of "holding the two ends to find the middle" (*zhi liang yong zhong* 執兩用中; 471). He emphasizes that his aim is to propose an ethos (*taidu* 態度) that is best exemplified by Confucianism: taking forward actions when motivated by the affects (*qinggan* 情感) rather than desire. He believes that the first direction of culture, the one the West is taking to satisfy endless desires, should be modified by combining with the second direction, the one China has always been taking; otherwise, there will be danger. China, passive and inactive in the past while following Laozi's teachings, should take forward actions as taught by Confucius and should not repeat the West's mistakes when doing so (535). Here, Liang's opinion does not seem to be at odds with Russell's idea of the "harmony," or "balance," between Eastern and Western cultures.

The complementarity of intuition and reason is the Lifeview intellectuals' belief. They advocate intuition because reason alone is not enough to make a correct judgment; intuition alone is not devoid of pitfalls either. Reason is therefore needed as a balancing force. The interrelationship between intuition and reason is also the main topic in the concept of affectivism for Zhu Qianzhi and Yuanjiahua, as Chapter 5 discusses.

5

Affectivism

Intuition and Affective Flows

> The truth derived from intuition differs from what reason can construe, because the former is substance (*shizhi* 實質), and the latter, phenomena (*xingse* 形色). Substance is the subjective self-awareness (*zhuguande zijue* 主觀的自覺) relying on affective actions. Phenomena refer to the knowledge and concepts that form ideas relying on thought. Philosophers in general have had different views about this, including Descartes, Spinoza, Leibnitz. . . . Socrates, Plato . . . James, Dewey, and so on. . . . In my view, all of them have committed a serious fault: mistaking knowledge for truth. . . . Life philosophers, in order to correct the mistake of reason (*lizhi* 理知), have recourse to intuition (*zhijue* 直覺) to understand and discover the truth (*zhenli* 真理), . . . which is "absolute living." It is the pure, unified state of life—true affective flows of life (*zhenqing shengming zhi liu* 真情生命之流), which strives to act, and act to create meaning.
>
> —Yuan Jiahua, *Weiqing zhexue* 唯情哲學 [*Affectivist philosophy*] (Yuan 1924, 141–44)

In the above quote Yuan Jiahua is criticizing "formalists" (*xingshizhuyizhe* 形式主義者) such as Descartes, Spinoza, Leibnitz, Socrates, and Plato for maintaining that truth is about concepts and reasoning. It is the same with "experimentalists" (*shiyanzhuyizhe* 實驗主義者) such as James and Dewey, who have inherited the error of intellectualism (*weizhizhuyi* 唯知主義) and believe that knowledge is derived from reason. Although his assessments of these Western philosophers may not be accurate, as will be pointed out in this chapter, the idea is that philosophers are at fault if they mistake knowledge for truth. For Yuan, only life philosophers are able to know the truth. It is derived from intuition rather than reason, and it must be sought in what he calls "life of the true affects," which he believes to be the epitome of creative evolution—a revision of Bergson's theory, apparently.

Here, we see a paragraph of mixed languages typical of the intellectual writing in modern China. The origins of the transcultural lexicon shown in this quote many of us may not be aware of. There are Japanese *kanji* expressions, such as *shizhi* (*jisshitsu*) for the Greek philosophical concept of "substance," *zhuguande zijue* (*shukanteki jikaku*) for the philosophical-psychological term "subjective self-awareness," *lizhi* (*richi*) for "reason," *zhijue* (*chokkaku*) for "intuition," and *zhenli* (*shinri*) for "truth." There are Buddhist expressions, such as "*xingse*" for phenomena, or appearance, Chinese transliterations of Western philosophers' names followed by their names in the Latin alphabet in parentheses, and so on. One can hardly exhaust the transcultural origins of the modern Chinese expressions found in the paragraph. A person trained in either traditional or modern Chinese, without any knowledge of Western philosophy, would be lost in the transcultural labyrinth of neologisms, loanwords, and transliterations. All such expressions are considered everyday Chinese, without which we can hardly talk to each other. Terms such as "absolute living" (*huo de juedui* 活的絕對) and "true affective flows of life," however, were unique to Yuan Jiahua and his friend Zhu Qianzhi in their discussions of affectivism, an epistemic pursuit long obliterated by the mainstream May Fourth Enlightenment discourse. Even these terms that they invented are a transcultural mixture of traditional Chinese learning stemming from the *Book of Changes*, Bergsonism, Spinozism, Nietzscheism, and other trends in Western philosophy.

As China was confronted with its national survival and socio-political problems, epistemic choices became a major concern as well. The invention of affectivism, a theory about the truth of life, was intended to counter Enlightenment rationalism. Two books published consecutively in 1924, Yuan Jiahua's *Affectivist Philosophy* and Zhu Qianzhi's *Yige weiqinglunzhe de yuzhouguan yu renshengguan* 一個唯情論者的宇宙觀與人生觀 [*The Universeview and Lifeview of an Affectivist*, henceforth *An Affectivist*] (*ZQZWJ* 1:455–512), are studied in detail. Both were published by Taidong Bookstore in Shanghai, which for years also published the works and journals of the Creation Society, including Guo Moruo's poetry collection *The Goddesses* and journals with "Creation" in their titles, as pointed out in Chapter 3. The two authors were quite young when they wrote the two books. Zhu was twenty-five years old, and Yuan, twenty-one. Gu Shouchang 顧綬昌 (1904–2002), who wrote the preface to Yuan's book, had just turned twenty.

In 1923, Gu had sent his debut essay criticizing Kant's epistemology and Bergson's theory of intuition, "Ganjue yu renshilun" 感覺與認識論 [Sense perceptions and epistemology], to *Current Times*. Zhang Dongsun, the then-editor-in-chief of the column titled "Lamps of Learning" [*Xuedeng* 學燈], marveled at his originality and immediately published it even though he disagreed with Gu's claim that Bergson fails to distinguish intuition from sense perceptions and that Bergson's theory was only a follow-up of Kang's epistemology. Gu's essay, in six parts, was serialized daily from 15 to 20 May. In the editor's introduction to the essay, Zhang Dongsun points out that for Bergson, intuition is a kind of "affective communion," which concerns memory and life rather than matter, while sense perception is mainly about matter

(Gu 1923, Part 1; 1983, 305; Zhu 1996).[1] Yuan and Gu were close friends, and later both, after graduating from the English Department of Peking University, went to the United Kingdom for further studies. Becoming a renowned linguist, specializing in minority languages and Chinese dialects, Yuan taught at Peking University and National Northwestern Associated University during the Sino-Japanese War. Gu became a professor of English literature, teaching at Sichuan University, Wuhan University, Sun Yat-sen University, and Canton College of Foreign Languages (Wang and Sun 2010).

Zhu Qianzhi was the one who invented the concept of affectivism in 1922. His early life is worth close scrutiny, because it is tightly connected with his thought. At an early age he believed in nihilism, and in his 1923 love letters to his fiancée, Yang Meilei 楊沒累 (1898–1928), he confesses that he attempted suicide in 1916 and then in 1919, when he was a student at Peking University, "due to the influence of the 'world-weary philosophy'" (meaning the Buddhism course) taught by Liang Shuming (*ZQZWJ* 1:9).[2] In October 1920, he distributed anarchist pamphlets alongside a co-member of the Cooperation Society (Huzhushe 互助社). His friend was captured by police while Zhu fled. To save his friend, he turned himself in and was incarcerated for more than a hundred days. While in prison he read books such as Yang Wanli's 楊萬里 (1127–1206) *Chengzhai Yizhuan* 誠齋易傳 [Chengzhai's annotated edition of the *Book of changes*], Tan Sitong's *Renxue* 仁學 [On benevolence] (1897), and *Sunwen xueshuo* 孫文學說 [Sun Yat-sen on knowledge and action, 1919] (8–9). Later, when two of his friends were imprisoned, Zhu became disillusioned with the Communist Party led by Li Dazhao and Chen Duxiu: "I hated Chen Duxiu, because he used the money of the Lenin government to buy over workers, who would then willingly sacrifice themselves for his revolutionary ambitions. I was so disappointed with the historical materialism embraced by such revolutionaries that I decided to fundamentally reform the human heart-mind" (11).

Feeling despondent, Zhu committed himself as a novice to a Buddhist temple by West Lake in Hangzhou in 1921, shortly after graduating from Peking University. He thought about organizing a "religious New Village" but then found the perverse

---

1. For "affective communion," see the section titled "Instinct, intuition, and reason" in Chapter 3. For Gu's criticism of Bergson, see also the section titled "Yuan Jiahua, *Affectivist Philosophy*" in the following.
2. "Hexin" 荷心 [Lotus heart] (*ZQZWJ* 1:1–38), which comprises the letters exchanged between Zhu Qianzhi and Yang Meilei, was originally titled "Xuwu zhuyizhe de zaisheng" 虛無主義者的再生 [The rebirth of a nihilist] and published in *People's Tocsin* 4.4 (June 1923). In one letter it is written: "I attempted to commit suicide in 1909. Three years before, when I was seventeen years old, I had had another suicide attempt" (*ZQZWJ* 1:9). Yet Zhu was seventeen in 1916, when he made his first suicide attempt. His second suicide attempt, taking place three years afterwards, should be in 1919. Apparently 1909 is a typo.

patriarchy of the Buddhist monastery unbearably hypocritical (*ZQZWJ* 1:11).[3] Yuan Jiahua and Creation Society friends such as Guo Moruo and Zheng Zhenduo came to visit him. They roamed the lake resort together, enjoying the natural scenery and the "baptizing by literary fire." Guo Moruo, since the publication of *The Goddesses*, had just emerged as a rising poet. Receiving a galley proof version of the book as a gift, Zhu asks himself, "Isn't the pantheism I am currently ruminating graced by the goddesses?" (13; see discussion of Zhu's pantheism later). His idea of affectivism was therefore closely connected with the burgeoning of the Creation Society. His teacher Liang Shuming and other friends also came to see him. After discussing fervently what each had learned, he finally realized the superiority of order to chaos, while "the cosmic beauty" he witnessed at West Lake inspired his "love for beauty." From then on, he abandoned nihilism and endeavored to promote Confucian teachings (13). His theory of affectivism was conceptualized under these circumstances. It thus expressed an optimistic appreciation of life after severe despair. He went to Japan to study the philosophy of history in 1929. After returning to China in 1932, he taught at Jinan University and Sun Yat-sen University, and then eventually at Peking University (Huang 2005, 1–16).

In March 1922, Zhu Qianzhi published an essay in the anarchist journal *People's Tocsin*, "Weiqing zhexue faduan" 唯情哲學發端 (The origin of affectivism), writing, "The truth of the universe is 'the flow of true affects' (*zhenqing zhi liu* 真情之流), copiously outpouring and naturally changing. It never ceases even if one should attempt to stem it."[4] This was probably the first time the two terms "affectivism" and "true affective flows" were used in Chinese intellectual history. In "Tongxun dai xu" 通訊代序 [Correspondence as a preface] in the same issue, Zhu writes to Li Shicen, the editor-in-chief of *People's Tocsin*:

> At the time of our ancestors, there were the true affects. But since agnosticism became prevalent, everything has been deteriorating and torn apart. Recently your humble brother has therefore taken a turn and advocated faith strongly. . . . When one pursues truth by agnosticism, truth is instead driven away by one's reason. Behind agnosticism there is a huge black curtain, which is human beings' reason that is devouring them. The limitless, absolute truth is manifested only when one

3. The New Village movement (*xincun* 新村運動) was a brief anarchist experiment in the winter of 1919. The project was supported by Cai Yuanpei, Chen Duxiu, Hu Shi, Li Dazhao, and Zhou Zuoren. Imitating its Japanese counterpart and inspired by the work-and-study scheme in France, the villages were organized by the Young China Association in Beijing, Tianjin, Shanghai, and other big cities. The young intellectuals living in the villages worked at least four hours a day to support themselves in addition to studying. Running printing shops, restaurants, laundries, and so on, they contributed their income to the organization, while their expenses, such as tuition, room and board, medicine, and clothes, were paid by the organization (Chow 1960, 190–91).

4. Later, "The Origin of Affectivism" was renamed "The Origin" and included as the beginning part of *Zhouyi Zhexue* 周易哲學 [The Zhou dynasty philosophy of the *Books of changes*, 1923] (*ZQZWJ* 3:101–6).

> has faith in the true affects. . . . Poor humans, the road to agnosticism has come to an end. Why don't you turn about and recognize your God? Why don't you liberate yourself in the midst of the Almighty manifested in the universe? (*ZQZWJ* 3:99–100)

"[T]he Almighty manifested in the universe" here discloses Zhu's pantheism: all things in the universe are seen as the manifestations of an immanent God, whose reality is "the true affects." The "true affects," once ubiquitous in the universe, have been destroyed by humans' agnosticism and rationality. The only way to regain the true affects is to have faith, liberating oneself from rationality so that one can feel the immanence of the Almighty in the universe. Chapter 4 points out Li Shicen as one of the leaders of the Aesthetic Education movement, which was part and parcel of the Lifeview movement. That Zhu's debut essay was published in *People's Tocsin* edited by him bespeaks the close connections between the Lifeview school and the anarchists.

Zhu Qianzhi and Yuan Jiahua share the basic ideas of affectivism: the affects are the truth of the universe, life indicates true affective flows, the true self inhabits the universe, the fusion of self and non-self is crucial, and so on. The two differ in that Zhu announces himself as a pantheist and believes that life of the affects should effect socio-political change. In other words, for him theory should lead to praxis. A close study of their works shows that May Fourth intellectuals like them were well versed in both Western and traditional thought and that they were definitely specific in their choices of thinkers, Western or Chinese, to engage. While drawing inspiration from the West and traditional China, they further establish their own philosophical systems. This chapter studies both how their works illuminate the concept of affectivism and how the concept establishes a systematic lifeview and universeview. Yuan Jiahua's *Affectivist Philosophy* was published in April 1924, and Zhu Qianzhi's *An Affectivist*, in June of the same year. It was apparently a strategic plan for Taidong Bookstore to put on the market two books exploring the same topic so close to each other.

Zhu Qianzhi, "The Origin of Affectivism"

"The Origin of Affectivism" (henceforth "The Origin"), Zhu's 1922 debut essay, interprets the concept of *qing* in the *Book of Changes* while establishing a theoretical basis for affectivism. The transcultural lexicon used in "The Origin," including terms such as "life" (*shengming* 生命), "creation" (*chuangzao* 創造), "evolution" (*jinhua* 進化), "the mystic intuition" (*shenmide zhijue* 神秘的直覺, Zhu's English), "change" or "becoming" (*bianhua* 變化), "*la durée*" (*mianyan* 綿延), "matter" (*wuhzi* 物質), "space" (*kongjian* 空間), "time" (*shijian* 時間), and "real time" (*zhenshi* 真時) indicates that Zhu has surpassed the boundary of traditional parlance. There is no doubt that his choice of diction is inspired by Zhang Dongsun's 1918 translation of *Creative Evolution*. Yet, while Bergson's theory of life centers on the discussions of memory and matter, Zhu's highlights the concept of affective flows. From an aesthetic point of view, emotion plays a crucial role in the cognitive process, as the Aesthetic Education and Lifeview movements have always stressed. Zhu Qianzhi goes further by maintaining that *qing*, permeating all things in the universe, is life itself; it is the cosmological essence (*yuzhou benti* 宇宙本體).[5] Critics have seldom noticed the epistemic theory and ontology developed in his concept of affectivism. The idea of *qing*, or affect, as seen in Zhu's concept of affective flows, is not merely emotion or love. Rather, it is the essence of the universe.

"The Origin" starts with a concept taken from the Northern Song Confucian Cheng Yichuan: "For the benevolent person the myriad things in the universe are unified" (*ZQZWJ* 3:101).[6] Zhu writes:

> Noumenon (*benti* 本體) is derived from what is real, from reality itself. It does not transcend the phenomenal world that I am conscious of; it is the phenomena in my consciousness—it is the here and now. With this understanding, everywhere, above, down, inside, and outside us, is filled with "affective flows," just like an ocean. This is the true life! This is the Almighty! . . . . My theory of affectivism, although derived from the experiences of my heart-mind, has its origin in the *Book of Changes*. It teaches us that all things in the universe are changing at every moment, and that the way to learn the truth is simply to return to the heart-mind of Heaven and Earth . . . My theory comes from the *Book of Changes*—there is no denying that it is the teaching handed down from Confucius. (*ZQZWJ* 3:101)

While the battle cry against Confucianism was raging rampantly during the May Fourth period, Zhu Qianzhi's concept of affectivism countered the current by forcefully advocating Confucian teachings, following his teacher Liang Shuming's theory that Confucianism is a life philosophy. The most crucial idea in the passage is that noumenon does not go beyond the reality that humans are aware of; noumenon is the here and now. In other words, noumenon is not transcendent but immanent. It

5. In Wadagaki's *A Dictionary of Philosophy* (1881), "noumenon" is rendered as *jittai* 實體, which is usually used for translating "substance." We should be aware that the term *benti* 本體 (thing-in-itself) had appeared in the British Protestant medical missionary Benjamin Hobson's (1816–1873) *Bowu xinbian* 博物新編 [Natural philosophy] published in China (Hobson 1855, 2:6, 15). In the Japanese translation of the book, *Hakubutsu shinpen yakkai* 博物新編譯解 [Natural Philosophy translated and annotated], the term "hontai" 本體 was kept (Hobson 1870, 3:21, 36). "Hontai," probably first used by Hobson and his Chinese collaborator, usually indicates "noumenon." See the online dictionary weblio.jp. Joachim Kurtz's essay, titled "Domesticating a Philosophical Fiction: Chinese Translations of Immanuel Kant's 'Things in Themselves,'" includes a useful list of Chinese translations of key terms such as "things in themselves," "essence," and "noumenon" since the turn of the twentieth century. The Chinese term "*benti*" 本體 can refer to any of these three terms (Kurtz 2011, 191–93). My translation of the term *benti* varies following the context.
6. The Chinese original reads: "*Renzhe yi tiandi wanwu wei yiti*" 仁者以天地萬物為一體.

is within the material world in the universe. The Almighty that Zhu refers to here is therefore not a transcendent God, not a God that is above this world, but an immanent God manifested in all things in the universe. What Zhu calls "the true affects" are not merely feeling or emotions but close to the concept of affect that traces to Spinoza and becomes famous because of the worldwide academic attention in recent years on Deleuze's work. It is not far-fetched at all to read affectivism as an affect theory, because Zhu, Yuan, and Deleuze shared an affinity for Spinoza, Nietzsche, and Bergson. The difference is that Zhu and Yuan also had for their inspiration the *Book of Changes*, an essential text for the Confucian philosophical tradition. The transcultural lexicon translated into Japanese *kanji*, as used in Zhang Dongsun's translation of *Creative Evolution*, was an indispensable tool for them to achieve the fusion of traditional wisdom and Bergsonism.

Affective Flows: Ontology of Immanence

Zhu Qianzhi's concept of affective flows, manifesting an immanent God in this world, is not particular at all, if we read it with the counter-rationalist tradition in the modern West. Deleuze's reading of Spinoza and Nietzsche distinguishes ethics, grounded in ontology and practice, from morality, which is about good and evil in the moralistic sense. Their critique of moralistic ontology indicates a transition from "the ontology of transcendence" to "the ontology of immanence" (Bolaños 2007).[7] Nietzsche's idea of "the death of God" is significant not only religiously but epistemologically and ontologically—it is "a defiance of the dominance of Reason" (2007). In Deleuze's reading,

> Nietzsche's philosophy is both a critique and an introduction of a counterculture, that of "nomadism"—a philosophy that does not seek to be bound to abrogated universal essences that are hostile to LIFE (thus, nihilistic), but rather seeks to create, enhance, and celebrate LIFE. (Bolaños 2007)

Nomadism entails the freedom of life, unbound by rational confinements. Nietzsche's concept of *Wille zur Macht* (will to force), a concept widespread in the May Fourth intellectual community, is usually translated as "will to power" in English, and *quanliyu* (will to power 權力欲) in Chinese. In fact, here *Macht* means

7. In *A Thousand Plateaus*, Deleuze and Guattari distinguish between "un plan de transcendence" and "un plan d'immanence" (1980, 325–27). In *Spinoza: Philosophie practique* (1981), Deleuze again refers to the distinction between *le plan de transcendence* and *le plan d'immanence*. The former he defines as *plan théologique* (theological plane), a plane of organization and development that is designed from above. The latter is a plane of composition (similar to musical composition), with neither organization and development, nor any form at all, but movements of rest and dynamic affectivities, slowness and speed. It is the plane of nonsubjectivity where certain writers, poets, musicians, filmmakers, and painters, rather than professional philosophers (such as Goethe and Hegel), find themselves to be Spinozists (Deleuze 1981, 170–75).

"life force" rather than power. Power, force, energy, and potential, all terms derived from thermodynamics, are synonyms.[8] But for life philosophers, there is a distinction between force and power, as clearly explained by Brian Massumi, the translator of Deleuze and Guattari's *A Thousand Plateaus*: "Force is not to be confused with power. Force arrives from outside to break constraints and open new vistas. Power builds walls" (1987, xiii). Fang Dongmei, the New Confucian renowned in postwar Hong Kong and Taiwan and the central figure discussed in the conclusion of this book, knows very well that Nietzsche's concept of "will to force" means "will to life" (*shengmingyu* 生命欲): "Will to life is will to force; the broadening of force is the extension of life" (*FDMQJ* 4:224).[9] The anarchist Wu Zhihui in 1923 also points out that "Force is the will to life": "'The universe is a big life'; matter in it contains force (*li* 力). If we use another term, force can also be called power, since power is the will to life (*shengyizhi* 生意志), which flows unceasingly" (1977b, 517–18). See the conclusion for more about Wu and life philosophy.

Deleuze thinks Spinoza's thought is a "practical philosophy." Spinoza's affects are seen as the forces that can become all the more intense when extended from relations to relations, and the most significant result of this affective connectivity is sociability and community. How does one remain a superior individual while respecting the communal relations and the world (Deleuze 1981, 169)? In *Ethics*, posthumously published in Latin in 1677, Spinoza points out that it is in human nature to strive for happiness for all, which is the goal of an ethical life. People endeavor to bring about joy and avoid sadness for themselves and others, while the mind's power to think and the body's power to act are equal and simultaneous (Spinoza 1985, 1:509–10). According to Seymour Feldman, Spinoza believes that the "intuitive cognition" necessary for human happiness is attainable by people's capacities (Spinoza 1992, 20).[10] Spinoza calls sense perception "knowledge of the first kind"; inference, or reason, "knowledge of the second kind"; and intuitive knowledge, "knowledge of the third kind." He writes: "The greatest striving [conatus] of the Mind and its greatest virtue is to understand things [as God's attributes] by the third kind of knowledge" (1985, 1:477–78).[11] For Deleuze, Spinoza's *Ethics* provides both a systematic reading (propositions, proofs, corollaries, and scholia) and an affective reading (kinetic resolutions, impulses, chance encounter, and love). In the end, concept and life are no

8. Thermodynamics, developed in the nineteenth century, is a branch of physics that studies how heat, work, and temperature are related to energy, radiation, and properties of matter.

9. Fang Dongmei's Chinese original reads: "*shengmingyu jishi quanliyu. Quanli zhi kuoda jishi shengming zhi tuozhan*" 生命欲即是權力欲。權力之擴大即是生命之拓展. See the conclusion for more discussion of "will to life."

10. In the introduction to Samuel Shirley's translation of *Ethics*, the editor Seymour Feldman offers an excellent reading of Spinoza's philosophical system (Spinoza 1992, 1–20).

11. Seymour Feldman points out that, for Spinoza, intuitive knowledge, which is complete and synthetic, is superior to both sense perception, which is fragmentary and partial, and inference, which is discursive and hypothetical (Spinoza 1992, 18).

longer differentiated (1981, 174–75). As we will see shortly, affective connectivity, intuitive knowledge, freedom of life and creation, theory and praxis are all exactly Zhu Qianzhi's major concerns.

Although Zhu Qianzhi was inspired by quite a few Western philosophers, he did not follow them unquestioningly. His pantheism differs from Spinoza's religious view in one major aspect. For Zhu, life itself is the Almighty, while love of beauty is the initial way to reach Him. He writes:

> To understand the Almighty we must first love beauty. Nothing in this world that we encounter lacks beauty. . . . God is unknowable, but we could intuitively recognize His physical attributes (*mozhi ge tiduan* 默識個體段) through His images of beauty. (*ZQZWJ* 3:111)

While Spinoza does not concern himself with aesthetics at all (Morrison 1989),[12] Zhu's preoccupation with beauty is no doubt reflective of the Aesthetic Education movement of his time. He also departs from his mentor Liang Shuming. Believing in the bliss of an affective life, he criticizes Liang: "The here and now is paradise. How can we forsake life to pursue a future nirvana, which transcends humanity?" (*ZQZWJ* 3:100). Although inspired by Liang, he does not agree with his teacher's Buddhist attitude toward life. The thought of the two bifurcates here:

> When it [*Eastern and Western Cultures*] was first published, the book indeed had a great impact on me. Without this book, probably today I would still have stayed on the road to nihilism. Yet, since Professor Liang has always been a Buddhist, he has returned to the negation of life, which I absolutely do not agree to. This is where Professor Liang's thought and mine diverge. (*ZQZWJ* 3:14)

While having the same beliefs in human values, the Lifeview intellectuals nonetheless differ in their own ways and often critique each other, whereby lies the vitality of their theories. Rejecting the transcendence of God, Zhu Qianzhi finds beauty and affects in this world manifesting the magnificence of the Almighty.

12. For Morrison, since Spinoza's doctrine can be called "rationalism" or "intellectualism," he naturally elevates reason and intellect over the imagination and the senses and believes that a free, virtuous, and happy life is possible only when reason dominates passions, and that reality is knowable only by thought. That is why there is no aesthetics in Spinoza's theory. This assessment is at odds with Deleuze's interpretation of Spinoza's counter-rationalism. I think Morrison has neglected Spinoza's valorization of intuitive knowledge and his critique of the Cartesian mind-body dichotomy. Spinoza criticizes Descartes' idea that "the Mind can have absolute dominion" over the passions. Rather, he believes that passions should be "moderated" by reason, as we can see in the preface to the third part of *Ethics*: "no one, to my knowledge, has determined the nature and powers of the Affects, nor what, on the other hand, the Mind can do to moderate them" (Spinoza 1985, 1:491–92). I would go for Will Durant's 1926 analysis of Spinoza's lack of aesthetics: for Spinoza, good and bad, beauty and ugliness, are relative to human and often individual tastes and ends, and are therefore not universal (Durant 1953, 174).

Qing: To Be Affected and to Affect

> The becoming and flows (*bianhua liuxing* 變化流行) of the universe hinge on the capacity to be affected and to affect (*yigan yiying* 一感一應), which continues unceasingly. Affecting and being affected unceasingly, life is thus "everlasting and eternal" . . . This is exactly the truth of co-living and co-becoming! (*shengsheng* 生生; *ZQZWJ* 3:125–26)

In this quote from *An Affectivist*, Zhu Qianzhi is explicating the Northern Song Confucian Cheng Yichuan's concepts of "affective communion" (*gantong* 感通)[13] and "co-living and co-becoming." Zhu points out that *gantong* refers to the dynamic ontology taught in the *Book of Changes*, an ontology that illuminates the truth of co-living and co-becoming of life as manifested in the unceasing force-relations connecting living and non-living bodies, atmospheres, events, and the like in the universe. As recorded in the second chapter of *Commentary on the Appended Statements of the Book of Changes, Part 2*, the legendary saint Fuxi, observing the figures (or phenomena) of Heaven and the laws of Earth (including laws governing birds, animals, and humans), devised the eight trigrams, "in order to be in communion with the virtues of the divine and to be akin to the affects of the myriad things."[14] Most English and modern Chinese versions of the *Book of Changes* translate the word *lei* 類 into "to classify": to classify the myriad things. In my reading, however, here it means "to be akin to," or to feel a kindred spirit in the myriad things. It is synonymous with *tong* 通 ("communion" as a noun, or "to be in communion with" as a verb), which, referring to the unity of Heaven, Earth, and humanity, is a central concept in *Yijing*. As we can see a few lines later in the same chapter, *tong*, as well as *bian* 變 (change), is the key to the laws of change: "*Yi* indicates that a deadlock breeds change; change engenders communion; communion leads to sustainability."[15] The ultimate goal of

13. Chapter 3 has discussed the concept of *gantong* (Wei-chieh Lin, 2018). For another discussion of "gantong" as a concept, see Huang 2018, 18–21.
14. The original reads: "*[Y]i tong shenming zhi de, yi lei wanwu zhi qing*" 以通神明之德，以類萬物之情. Here's Richard Lynn's translation: "[H]e [Fuxi] thereupon made the eight trigrams in order to become thoroughly conversant with the virtues inherent in the numinous and the bright and to classify the myriad things in terms of their true, innate natures" (1994, 77). Richard Rutt's reads: "Hence he [Fuxi] devised the eight trigrams with power to communicate with spirits and classify the natures of the myriad things" (2002, 421). In John Minford's introduction to his translation of *Yijiing* there is a section titled "The I Ching in the West," which names a few early translations of *Yijing* into English and German, including James Legge's *The Yi King* (1882) and Richard Wilhelm's *I Ging: Das Buch der Wandlungen* [Yijing: The book of changes, 1924] (Minford 2014, xxi–xxii). There are innumerable traditional commentaries on *Yijing* throughout Chinese history and countless modern Chinese renderings.
15. The original reads: "*Yi qiong ze bian, bian ze tong, tong ze jiu*" 易窮則變，變則通，通則久." Richard Rutt's translation reads: "When change was effected, there was alteration; alteration gave development; development gave lasting progress" (2002, 421). Richard Lynn's reads: "As for [the Dao of] change, when one process of it reaches its limit, a change from one state to another occurs. As such, change achieves free flow, and with this free flow, it lasts forever" (1994, 78).

change and communion is the sustainability of life, exactly what *shengsheng* refers to. It is interesting to know that the concept of *lei* is indeed interpreted as *bingsheng* 並生 (to co-live) in the eighth chapter of *Liezi* 列子, a Daoist text of around the fifth century: "*Lei* indicates that the myriad things between Heaven and Earth co-live with me."[16] Co-living with the myriad things while considering them as our own kind is an integral part of the meaning of *shengsheng*, the principle of creative transformation. Only when humans understand their affinity with the myriad things in the world, and when they realize that co-living necessitates change on the part of all the parties involved—mutual transformation and co-becoming—can they be in tune with the wisdom conveyed by the Dao of Heaven and Earth.

For Zhu Qianzhi, *gantong*, or affective communion, is the principle of evolution, as he writes: "The evolution of the universe is established through such force-relations: to be affected and to affect" (*ZQZWJ* 3:126). The term *yigan yiying* literally means "to feel and to respond," but it is better understood as "to be affected and to affect" in the Deleuzian sense, since here *gan* means much more than "to feel," which basically implies a human psychological (or animalistic) attribute. As we can see clearly in what follows in Zhu's text, the concept of *yigan yiying* is by no means limited to human and animalistic feelings:

> Yet we should know that in this perpetual creativity of life, nothing is arranged with an effort; everything is affected unconsciously (*wuxin* 無心). When affected, one is bound to respond, again unconsciously. Take for instance motion and steadiness, contraction and extension, coming and going, waxing and waning, summer and winter, day and night, up and down. All these entail a natural process of affecting and being affected. (*ZQZWJ* 3:126)

Here, Zhu Qianzhi defines the affects as the unconscious forces that are part of natural processes, clearly indicating the nonsubjective nature of affect and its cosmological dimension. We know that Deleuze repeatedly stresses that affects, synonymous with forces, are nonsubjective (Deleuze and Guattari 1980, 326).[17] He points out in *Spinoza: philosophie pratique* [Spinoza: Practical philosophy] that on the one hand, Spinoza defines a body as composed of infinite particles, which form connections of rest and movement, speed and slowness. On the other, he defines a body by its capacity to affect and to be affected: to affect other bodies and to be

16. "*Tiandi wanwu yu wo bingsheng, lei ye*" 天地萬物與我並生, 類也 (Yang 1997, 269). *Liezi*, though ascribed to Lie Yukou 列禦寇 (450–375 BCE), was probably composed by scholars during the Weijin 魏晉 period (220–589).

17. Here Deleuze uses terms such as "*des affects, des individuations sans sujet*" (the affects, the individuations without subjectivity) and "affects non subjectivés" (nonsubjective affects) to indicate the nonsubjectivity of the affects. Similar expressions appear recurrently in *Milles plateaux* [A thousand plateaus]. Take, for example, the sentence "*les purs affects impliquent une entreprise de désubjectivation*" (the pure affects implicate an enterprise of desubjectivation; Deleuze and Guattari 1980, 330).

affected by them (Deleuze 1981, 165).[18] In other words, affect is an attribute of matter. We should note that "body" refers to any mass of substance, be it living or non-living, solid or fluid (e.g., a body of seawater), rather than merely a human or an animal body. Deleuze certainly thinks so. In *A Thousand Plateaus,* he uses demonology to illustrate affective capacity. The diabolic art is always associated with natural elements such as wind, rain, hailstorm, and pestilent atmospheres. Such natural elements, favorable to the transports of affects, command the metamorphoses of a devil. Deleuze also mentions the affective capacity of the wind in Charlotte Brontë's novels, and of the different hours of the day and the heat in Lawrence's and Faulkner's works: spatiotemporal relations and determinations affect the multiplicity of individuation (Deleuze and Guattari 1980, 319–21). Deleuze's own cosmological affectivity in connection with the cosmological tradition that can be traced to Plato is an aspect that most critics of affect theory have not yet paid attention to. Alain Beaulieu points out that Deleuze's interest in cosmological ontology can be proved by the facts that he admires Whitehead's *An Essay in Cosmology* (1960), borrows from James Joyce's neologism *chaosmos,* appreciates "an outside which is farther away than any exteriority" experienced by Artaud and Blanchot as a contrast to Nietzsche's invitation "to remain earthly," and inspires Guattari's science-fiction film project "In Search of UIQ" (Beaulieu 2016, 199). For both Spinoza and Deleuze, affect, more than emotion and beyond subjective experiences, is produced by "dispersed and dynamic, not fixed and static, affective flows" between and among bodies rather than from within a body, suggesting that it is produced through "a circulating relationality," and that "it travels through crowds, up mountains, and down spines" (Robinson and Kutner 2019, 112).[19]

Leibniz and the *Book of Changes*

Spinoza's treatise of affect, *The Ethics,* written in a geometrical manner and as axiomatic expositions in a scientific treatise, considers God, mind, as well as human actions and appetites "as if it were an investigation into lines, planes, or bodies" (Spinoza 1992, 103). Zhu Qianzhi's concept of *qing,* or affect, on the other hand, is mainly derived from the *Book of Changes.* It understands life and events in the universe through sixty-four hexagrams (*bagua* 八卦) composed of whole and broken lines encrypting the mysterious mechanisms of dual, complementary forces, *yin* 陰 (feminity) and *yang* 陽 (masculinity), which control the physical world. This classical Chinese philosophical (for some, divinatory) work fascinated Gottfried

18. Deuleuze's French reads: "*un corps affecte d'autres corps, ou est affecté par d'autres corps.*"

19. Bradley Robinson and Mell Kutner's "Spinoza and the Affective Turn: A Return to the Philosophical Origins of Affect" advocate a return to Spinoza's *Ethics* rather than simply citing secondary, tertiary, or even further removed readings of affect theory. They also point out that affect and emotion are concepts that should not be conflated with, or reduced to, one another.

Wilhelm Leibniz (1646–1716) during the European Enlightenment, when "a scientific outlook, typically expressed mathematically, focused scholarly attention on the properties and relationships of number and geometric shape" (Swetz 2003, 276). In 1698, the French Jesuit missionary Joachim Bouvet (1656–1730) in a letter to Leibnitz introduced him to a table of hexagrams in the Flemish Jesuit missionary Philippe Couplet's (1623–1693) *Confucius Sinarum Philosophus* [Confucius the philosopher of China], which had appeared in Paris in 1687. For Leibnitz, the table of Chinese hexagrams, which is ascribed to the ancient ruling prince Fuxi 伏羲 (fl. 2600 BCE), represented "the most ancient monument of science which exists on this earth," and he believed that Fuxi's "consideration of numbers" has a rapport with his own system of the analogy between God and binary arithmetic (287).[20] Both Leibniz and Bouvet, who never met, believed that they had discovered a mystical link binding Confucian China and Europe's Christian civilization and were enthusiastic that they could use this finding to convert the Chinese. While Leibnitz thought he had found the ultimate source of human knowledge and the key to a "universal language," Bouvet believed Fuxi to be "the first prophet" of an ancient theology (288).

The truth is that Leibniz and Bouvet were reading into the classical Chinese text what reflects their own mindset. Fuxi was actually a mythical figure believed to have invented the first humans; the concept of *yin-yang* was established by Boyang Fu 伯陽父 (fl. 780 BCE) and incorporated into the *Yijing* fully developed by Zou Yan 鄒衍 (circa 350–270 BCE). The pre-Heaven hexagrams (*xiantian baguatu* 先天八卦圖) that fascinated Leibnitz was in fact a work by the Northern Song dynasty philosopher Shao Yong 邵雍 (1012–1077), and the ordering of the hexagrams had nothing to do with binary arithmetic (Swetz 2003, 288–89). In their hope to link East and West, Leibnitz and Bouvet saw in the *Book of Changes* what they wanted to see. My purpose is not to say that they misread the *Book of Changes*, since transcultural encounters more often than not lead to misunderstanding. I intend to point out the paradox of transculturality: we reach out to others to confirm the virtues and worth of our own tradition and thus to prove its universality.

Leibniz, and Voltaire (1694–1778) after him, are widely known to have taken special interest in Chinese philosophy in the age of Enlightenment in Europe (Mungello 1977, 13, 79–98).[21] Zhu Qianzhi was fully aware of the transcultural connections between Chinese and European cultures. In 1935, when serving as the

20. Swetz points out that, in 1703, Leibnitz published in *Mémoires*, a journal of the Académie Royale des Sciences in Paris, a communication titled "Explication de l'arithmetique binaire" [Explication of binary arithmetic], in which he explained his binary notation and expounded on its "Chinese connection."

21. In *Leibniz and Confucianism: The Search for Accord*, David E. Mungello points out that Leibniz made an effort to connect the Neo-Confucian concept of *li* 理 (order, or principle) and his own idea of monad as "a simple substance" and "preestablished harmony."

chairperson of the Department of History at Sun Yat-sen University, he gave a series of lectures on "The Influence of Chinese Thought on Western Culture," which were collected as a book in 1940 (*ZQZWJ* 7:15).[22] In both the 1940 and the 2002 *Collected Works* versions (the latter being significantly revised), he points out that, although Eastern and Western cultures have their own specific developments, the Chinese cultural relicts transmitted to the West from the thirteenth to sixteenth centuries by the Mongols and Arabs became the material bases of European Renaissance, while those transmitted by the Jesuits to Europe since the sixteenth century formed the spiritual bases of the European Enlightenment movement (15). Quoting the English version of the German sinologist Adolf Reichwein's *China und Europa* (1923), he writes, "Thus Confucius became the patron saint of eighteenth-century Enlightenment" (39).[23] Many May Fourth intellectuals, erudite in both Chinese and Western learning, knew exactly what they wanted to choose from the great ocean of knowledge to support their own cultural agenda. Their transcultural practice could hardly be swept away under the pejorative term "grabbism" (Xu 2011, 12–13). Later critics using this term to criticize them probably never carefully read their works, or were not even aware of works such as *Affectivist Philosophy* written by Yuan Jiahua.

Yuan Jiahua, *Affectivist Philosophy*

Gu Shouchang's preface to Yuan's book points out at the outset that "The debates between metaphysics and epistemology constitute the central problem of the whole history of philosophy." From Protagoras, Plato, and Aristotle in ancient Greece, to Galileo, Descartes, and Kant, epistemology finally gained sway due to the scientific fervor in the late eighteenth and early nineteenth centuries, Kant as its epitome. Metaphysics, once prevailing in ancient Greece, had been fatally marred by "a few degraded, theological-tempered metaphysicians" since the Middle Ages. The emergence of Bergson has finally reversed the trend and "let the light of metaphysics shine after the overwhelming destruction" (Yuan 1924, i–vi).

22. The book, titled "*Zhongguo sixiang duiyu Ouzhou wenhua zhi yingxiang* 中國思想對於歐洲文化之影響, was published by Commercial Press in Shanghai in 1940, and then by Zhongwen Tushu Gongsi 眾文圖書公司 in Taipei in 1940. The version in the 2002 *Collected Works* (*ZQZWJ* 7:1–250), retitled *Zhongguo zhexue dui Ouzhou de yingxiang* 中國哲學對歐洲的影響 [The influence of Chinese philosophy on Europe], was significantly revised after the establishment of the PRC, during the 1950s and early 1960s. The revisions include references to numerous European and Japanese sinologists' works published after 1940 on the Jesuit missionaries' mediation between China and Europe. Zhu provides an extensive bibliography in the preface dated 1962 (*ZQZWJ* 7:6–14). Another major revision is adding Marxist interpretations to his work, a common practice of intellectuals in mainland China when republishing their pre-PRC works.
23. The complete title of Adolf Reichwein's book is *China und Europa: geistige und künstlerische Beziehungen im 18. Jahrhundert*. The English version is titled *China and Europe—Intellectual and Artistic Contacts in the Eighteenth Century*, translated by J. C. Powell (1925). I have corrected typos of foreign words in Zhu's text.

Gu blames Protagoras for his extreme "sensationalism" (Gu's English) prioritizing sensuous feelings, which led to "perceptions," and then to "concepts." As a result, this became "the only basis of the methodology of later epistemology" (Yuan 1924, ii). The biggest mistake of Kant's epistemology, according to Gu, is his concept of "*a priori* categories" (viii). By contrast, Bergson's contribution to metaphysics is the method of intuition. However, his concept is not free from serious pitfalls. First, he thinks intuition is "intellectual sympathy," failing to acknowledge the distinction between intuition and intellect. Second, searching for a scientific basis for his method of intuition, he makes a major mistake: using the temporality of sense perceptions (*ganjue* 感覺) to prove the existence of intuition. Third, his interpretation of intuition is always clouded by some mysterious hues. Gu believes that "one must eliminate these three mistakes, so that the function of intuition, surpassing sense perceptions, could unceasingly evolve and create in real time" (xiii–xiv). Yuan's affectivist philosophy is a significant achievement in metaphysics, because it gets rid of the bondage of theology and the "mysticism" of Bergson on the one hand, and critiques the delusions of rationalism and voluntarism on the other (xv).

Simply put, affectivism is a life philosophy based on the method of intuition. It maintains that *qing*, or affect, unifies the self and the essence of the universe. Yuan points out at the outset that "The existence of the self is concerned with the meaning and value of life as a whole." To understand the existence of the self, one must discard the bondage and delusion of "the false self" in order to explore the meaning of "the true self." Yet true self and false self, both being part of the self, are not dichotomous. Rather, they are one and the same (1924, 1). The "true" in the term "the true self" refers to both "genuine" and "natural." What is the false self, then? It is the self that is in bondage to reason, which separates the self from all things in the universe and thus undermines the true self—the true self that is unified with the universe (27–28). In a concrete sense, the false self is "the material self," or "the phenomenal self." It is a fixed state confined in a certain time and space. By contrast, life flows incessantly and knows no bounds. The upward striving of life thus endeavors to be aware of the false self and to realize the true self, a process that involves the cultivation of self-awareness (*zijue de gongfu* 自覺的工夫; 4). Since the true self is "the original self" (*benlaide wo* 本來的我), to find the true self all that is needed is self-contemplation. One should return to what is inside the heart-mind that conforms to nature, rather than seek outside the self—the more one searches outward, the more one is degraded (6–7). Yuan writes:

> The substance (*shizai* 實在) of the true self is derived from inner experiences and the activities of the heart-mind; what I call heart-mind and inner experiences are by no means empty names, but rather the essence of the spirit. . . . Following the heart-mind and searching ceaselessly inward, one eventually reaches the purest element: *qing*. From a glimmer of *qing*, everything is extended to infinity to create the life of the true self, which is therefore immanent (*neizai hanyou* 內在含有). . . .

> *Qing* exists by itself forever, unlimited and unbound by anything . . . . Subjectivity, objectivity, time, and space flow from it like water, while it transcends them all. The true self therefore indicates absolute transcendence. (Yuan 1924, 7–8)

This passage conveys the idea that *qing*, or affect, is the ultimate, purest element that exists in the heart-mind as well as the infinite universe. To find the true self, however, one needs to seek inward rather than outward for this purest element. The key idea is that the true self is both immanent and "absolute transcendence," transcending the distinction between subject and object and unbound by time and space. Yuan Jiahua is not alone in seeing the true self and *qing* as both immanent and transcendental. In *Qu'est-ce que la philosophie* [What is philosophy], Deleuze and Guattari maintain that the self (*je*) is not only "the 'I conceive' [*je conçois*] of the brain as philosophy" but also "the 'I feel' [*je sens*] of the brain as art." What is *qing* to Yuan, Deleuze and Guattari here call "la sensation." They write, "Sensation is no less brain than the concept" (Deleuze and Guattari 1991, 199; 1994, 211). It is "pure contemplation," while to contemplate is to create; it is a sort of mysterious, passive creation (1991, 200; 1994, 211). As a contrast to idea, which "acts, but is not," sensation is "a force that is but does not act"; it is therefore "a pure internal awareness [*un pur Sentir interne*]" (1991, 201; 1994, 213). To Yuan Jiahua or Deleuze and Guattari, *qing* or the *pur Sentir interne*, connecting spirit and body, is the purest inner element that is life itself. Guillaume Collett points out that Deuleuze "seeks to relocate the absolute to an impersonal stratum of (equally transcendental and lived) experience." In other words, it is both "pre-personal and pre-subjective" and personal experience in life (Collett 2020, 182–83).

From this point of view, in conceptualizing life as both immanence and "absolute transcendence," and as transcending the subject/object dichotomy, Yuan Jiahua certainly precedes Deleuze. Yuan's concept of life as "the true self" and "the true affects" is derived partly from Bergson, partly from traditional Confucianism. The true self, being the life of the true affects (*zhenqing de rensheng* 真情的人生, or the life of real *qing*), is both "absolute steadiness" and "absolute motion," because *qing* contains both steadiness and motion (Yuan 1924, 9). The true self contains motion because it always endeavors to act, to discard the hypocrisy and sins accumulated in past and present, so that it can create a new life in future. In other words, it is "creative evolution," while its activity conforms to "real time" (*zhenshi* 真時). Certainly "creative evolution" and "real time" are Bergson's concepts, but Yuan Jiahua criticizes the French philosopher for overemphasizing memory and thereby undermining the natural flux of the true self. He writes: "I maintain that the activity of the true self is a natural flux" (9–10). As much as Bergson's influence is unmistakable, Yuan's concept of the true self comes from traditional learning as well. According to Mun Kin Chok, as traditional Confucianism believed that "the true self" is "the creator of immanence," the study of the true self becomes the core issue for postwar

New Confucianism in Hong Kong and Taiwan. The New Confucian leader Mou Zongsan 牟宗三 (1909–1995) maintains that, by way of the spiritual realization of the self, humans will discover the true self, or the original self. Benevolence (*ren* 仁), sincerity (*cheng* 誠), and conscience (*liangzhi* 良知) in Confucianism, natural inaction (*ziranwuwei* 自然無為) in Daoism, as well as the purity of self (*prakṛti-prabhāsvara-citta* 自性清淨心) in Buddhism, are all variations of the true self (Mun 2013, 385).

For Yuan Jiahua, since the true self is both absolute immanence and absolute transcendence, there is neither distinction nor dichotomy between self and other but difference (*chabie* 差別), while the true self is both "the big self" (*dawo* 大我) and "selflessness" (*wuwo* 無我; Yuan 1924, 8). The true self is the self of the true affects and the ontological self, while the universe is the phenomena, or appearances, of the true self-cum-*qing*, or noumenon, on its evolutionary path. The universe is the result of the flowing activities, duration, and creative evolution of the true self, which can therefore also be called the self of the universe. The true self, being the key to the motion of the universe, is both steadiness and motion and non-steadiness and non-motion and has therefore neither beginning nor end. By contrast, the universe, being part of the phenomenon that is motion only, is finite and limited.

Yuan Jiahua's way of thought amply exemplifies transcultural practice, blurring the boundaries between East and West, classical and modern. When discussing the interaction between knowledge and action, although agreeing with Eucken's idea of the active power of life, he also criticizes him. Yuan maintains that truth leads to action, while action allows truth to come to pass. He criticizes Aristotle, and Kant after him, for depending entirely on thought to find truth. Socrates and Plato were also at fault for maintaining that action follows knowledge. Just like James and Dewey, Eucken, believing that thought is prerequisite for action, has neglected the fact that truth is contained in action. By contrast, Yuan maintains "the unity of knowledge and action" (*zhixing heyi* 知行合一), a concept advocated by Song-Ming Neo-Confucians such as Cheng Yichuan and Wang Yangming. While the latter maintains that "Action with illuminating awareness and minute observations is knowledge; knowledge, if genuine and practical, is action" (Yuan 1924, 130–32),[24] for Yuan thought is the hidden potential of the true affective life, and action, its manifestation. The so-called "cultivation" (*gongfu* 工夫) in Confucianism refers to turning life into the affective life. Just as knowledge is derived from rectifying the heart-mind (*zhengxin* 正心), so is action derived from cultivating the body (*xiushen*

24. Wang Yangming's original reads, "Zhi zhi zhenqie dushi chu bianshi xing, xing zhi mingjue jingcha chu bianshi zhi" 知之真切篤實處便是行, 行之明覺精察處便是知. Yuan Jiahua here has reversed the order of the two statements (1927, 108). In *Instructions for Practical Living and other Neo-Confucian Writings*, translated by Chan Wing-tsit, these two statements are rendered as follows: "Knowledge in its genuine and earnest aspect is action, and action in its intelligent and discriminating aspect is knowledge" (Wang 1963, 93).

修身; 133–34).[25] When the affective life is achieved, matter becomes spirit, and body becomes heart-mind, while the absolute essence and truth is thereby achieved (134). Truth must thus be understood from life itself, from action, and by way of intuition. Yuan calls it "the intuitive truth" (141).

Yuan Jiahua accepts Bergson's theory of *élan vital,* believing that "the impetus of life is only another name for *qing,*" and that "Bergson's so-called '*la durée*' is also formed by affective flows" (Yuan 1924, 98). Criticizing the French philosopher for his religiosity, he proposes to replace God with affects and the true self. Yuan writes:

> According to Bergson, the impetus of life is the origin of all things, and is thus God. In fact, the impetus of life, being the origin of the true affects, constitutes a superior ideal. If this is understood, then the hypothesis of God is totally unnecessary. In addition, how can the existence of this God, separated from and unreachable by the true self, be proved? As for me, I use the intuitive method that looks inward to recognize and prove the self-sufficient, unceasingly evolving true "self" . . . . The evolution of the self needs no help from God or other external forces. . . . The impetus of life is thus the self rather than God. The self, with activities of the immanent true affects, . . . evolves into the history of evolution. (Yuan 1924, 271)

Yuan also maintains that his own concept of duration is distinct from Bergson's. While Bergson's duration is "the accumulation of memories," his own concept emphasizes "the natural flows of affect, which," like the ceaseless flow of water, "mysteriously trigger flows of life" (Yuan 1924, 67, 183).[26] Bergson's concept of intuition is suspect as well: as much as he maintains spiritual monism, or the unity of matter and spirit, he still believes that intuition cannot replace reason, that the law of cause and effect, though not applicable to spiritual life, can be applied to matter, and that reason is independent and everlasting. Bergson's so-called "intellectual sympathy" (Yuan's English), indicating a confusion of intellect and affect, is a rational intuition and unable to eliminate the mistake of reason. It is at best a relativist vision marked by dualism (*eryuan* 二元論). By contrast, believing that the true affects exist even in matter, Yuan advocates "the intuition of pure affect" (*chunqing de zhijue* 純情的直覺), to which no deterministic cause and effect can be applied. Through intuition, there is no distinction between observer and observed, self and object; this is the absolute vision marked by monism (*yiyuanlun* 一元論; 179, 267, 281–84). Yuan writes: "Space and matter are physical, and time and spirit, metaphysical. When intuition is in use, physical and metaphysical become one" (284). Metaphysical

25. Yuan Jiahua is referring to the teaching of *The Great Learning*: *gewu zhizhi* 格物致知, *chengyi zhengxin* 誠意正心, *xiushen qijia* 修身齊家, *zhiguo pingtianxia* 治國平天下. James Legge's 1861 translation reads: "Things being investigated, knowledge became complete. Their knowledge being complete, their thoughts were sincere. Their thoughts being sincere, their hearts were then rectified. Their hearts being rectified, their persons were cultivated," and so on (2014, 226–27).

26. Yuan Jiahua adds a note in parenthesis: "See *Creative Evolution* and *Introduction to Metaphysics*" (1924, 183).

refers to the inner heart-mind, and physical, the external phenomena. By way of intuition, internal and external are unified. When true affect fills both, there is no longer distinction between internal and external. This is the true meaning of spiritual life (285). Yuan calls spiritual life "life of the heart-mind" (*xin shenghuo* 心生活; 120).

Yuan Jiahua feels especially akin to the Ming dynasty Confucian Chen Baisha 陳白沙 (1428–1500), who first followed, and then challenged, the Song dynasty philosophy of Universal Order represented by the two Cheng brothers (Cheng Yichuan and Cheng Mingdao, 1032–1085) and Zhu Xi (1130–1200). Chen, combining Confucianism with Buddhism and Daoism and reverenced as a living saint by commoners as well as the emperor, has been assessed to be the pioneer who initiated the Heart-Mind philosophy before Wang Yangming (Jiang 1980; 2007).[27] Chen's method of proceeding from "doubt" (*huaiyi* 懷疑)—which questions common sense ideas—to the "sudden awareness of truth" (*wuru* 悟入), indicates for Yuan a purely intuitive method based on the true affects rather than rational mechanism (Yuan 1924, 117). He maintains that "the true affects" is another name for intuitive knowledge, or conscience (*liangzhi* 良知), a concept advocated by both Chen Baisha and Wang Yangming. For the Heart-Mind philosophy, the knowledge derived from the heart-mind, or *qing*, is true knowledge. In comparison, Bertrand Russell, who in the tenth chapter of *The Problem of Philosophy* equates truth to reason, is wrong, because truth, derived from the combination of intellect, feeling, and will, cannot be reached by reason alone. The true affects is exactly the combination of these three aspects (136–37).

Homo sentimentalis versus Superman

The most interesting concept invented by Yuan Jiahua is *qingren* 情人 (*homo sentimentalis*, or sentimental person), a critique of Nietzsche's Superman. As he writes in *Affectivist Philosophy*:

> Superman is the result of evolution, while *homo sentimentalis* is able to create evolution. . . . *Homo sentimentalis* embraces the life of all beings, dancing forever in the bright world, never falling into the dark abyss of reality. Therefore, the transcendence of *homo sentimentalis* is different from that of Superman. The former's transcendence is inborn and immanent, while the latter's, bred of will and false. (Yuan 1924, 228)

27. Paul Yun-ming Jiang calls attention to the connection between Chen Baisha and Wang Yangming. Jiang maintains that Chen functioned as a bridge linking Lu Jiuyuan's Heart-Mind theory (1139–1193) and Wang's. Although Chen and Wang never met, Chen's close friend Zhan Ganquan 湛甘泉 (1466–1560) was Wang's devoted disciple.

Here, Yuan is criticizing German voluntarists, especially Schopenhauer and Nietzsche, who equate will to the entirety of spiritual life. The latter's Superman, "existing for the will to power, for the opening up of life," overwhelms the internal affective life with selfishness and therefore is unable to achieve pure truth (1924, 226–27). By contrast, Yuan advocates *homo sentimentalis*, whose affectivity strives toward noumenon (*xiang benti huodong de qinggan* 向本體活動的情感). My translation of Yuan's "*qingren*" is inspired by the Czech writer Milan Kundera (b. 1929), who invented the concept of *homo sentimentalis* in his 1990 novel *Immortality*. He writes:

> Europe has the reputation of a civilization based on reason. But one can say equally well that it is a civilization of sentiment; it created a human type whom I call sentimental man: *Homo sentimentalis*. (Kundera 1991, 196)

Here, *homo sentimentalis* is contrasted with *homo rationalis*, the rational person emerging since the European Enlightenment. The list of the so-called *homos sentimentalis* in Europe can hardly be exhausted, including Rousseau (1712–1778), Goethe (1749–1832), Gustave Flaubert (1821–1880), Alexandre Dumas fils (1824–1895, author of *La Dame aux Camélias*), and Boris Pasternak (1890–1960, author of *Dr. Zhivago*). These were household names for the May Fourth generation. In China there has been a long tradition of valorizing *qing* since the *Book of Changes*. During the Western Jin (266–316) dynasty, the literati-official Wang Rong 王戎 (234–305), suffering from the loss of a child, was recorded to have said: "Saints are unruffled by *qing*, while the lowest are below it. Ordinary people like us are the most affected by it."[28] The discourse of *qing* was prevalent during the late Ming, the type of people called *youqingren* 有情人, or *qingren*, highly reverenced in the literary world (Xia 1994). The writer Feng Menglong 馮夢龍 (1574–1646), who created numerous *homo sentimentalis* in his stories, was also known to have theorized *qing*. He wrote in his preface to *Qingshi* 情史 [A history of *qing*], composed before 1620: "If *qing* did not exist between Heaven and Earth, all things would not have existed. If *qing* did not exist in the myriad things, there would have been no cycles of life" (1984, 1).[29] From the late Qing to the May Fourth period, renowned

---

28. The original Chinese reads: "*Shengren wangqing, zuixia buji qing, qing zhi suo zhong, zhengzai wobei*" 聖人忘情，最下不及情，情之所鍾，正在我輩. For the original Chinese text, see Liu Yiqing's 劉義慶 (403–444) literary sketchbook stories, *Shishuo xinyu* 世說新語 [A new account of tales of the world] (2003, 587). The English translation by Richard B. Mather reads: "A sage forgets his feelings; the lowest beings aren't even capable of having feelings. But the place where feelings are most concentrated is precisely among people like ourselves" (Liu 1967, 347).

29. Feng's original reads: "Tiandi ruo wuqing, busheng yiqie wu. Yiqie wu wuqing, buneng huan xiangsheng" 天地若無情，不生一切物.一切物無情，不能環相生. When *Qingshi, or Qingshi leilue* 情史類略 [A history of the various kinds of *qing*] was first republished in PRC in 1984, the twenty-second chapter, explicating homosexual love, or "extraordinary love" (*qingwailei* 情外類), was not included. In most of the later editions, this chapter has been reinstated.

homo sentimentalis abounded in literary circles, such as the poet-monk Su Manshu 蘇曼殊 (1884–1918), the artist-monk Li Shutong, Creation writers Yu Dafu and Guo Moruo, and the poets Xu Zhimo and Bingxin. It comes as no surprise that the Lifeview school should pay so much attention to the concept of *qing*.

Yuan's *homo sentimentalis*, a critique of Nietzsche's claim that life is art, promotes art of life and art in life, because there is no art away from life, while the exuberance of life leads to the production of art, which combines beauty, affect, and creation (1924, 248–52). Yuan criticizes the Nietzschean master-slave morality in *Beyond Good and Evil*, the master valuing pride and power, and the slave, kindness, empathy, and sympathy. He opposes the concept, because what is considered moral by the master is bound to be considered immoral by the slave, and vice versa. In addition, the master no doubt has a master who controls him; the master's master also has his own master, and so on. By the same token, the slave no doubt has a slave who serves him; the slave's slave has his own slave, and so on. The concepts of Master and Superman are therefore only illusional. *Homo sentimentalis*, by contrast, views creation and freedom as the only moral, because moral is constantly in flux, changing with the process of life. Most importantly, it is "Super-moral" (*chaode dexing* 超的德性); it transcends ordinary value judgments and is against habit and obedience (239–47). Referring to the first chapter of Tagore's *Sādhanā:* The *Realization of Life*, Yuan points out that the moral of *homo sentimentalis* is a "moral of affectivity" (*ganqing daode* 感情道德):

> Thus to attain our world-consciousness, we have to unite our affects with the infinite affects that pervade the myriad things. In fact, the only true human progress is consistent with this widening of the range of affects. (Yuan 1924, 247; Tagore 1913, 18)[30]

For Yuan, the moral of *homo sentimentalis* is what is called "unconscious affects" (*wuyishi de ganqing* 無意識的感情) or "unconscious love" (*wuyishide aiqing* 無意識的愛情) in psychology (1924, 247). Such unconscious affects unite humans with the myriad things in the universe in a relational ontology.

Qing: Connecting the Heart-Mind and Matter

Criticizing the dichotomy between idealism and materialism, Yuan Jiahua maintains that *qing*, as the link between mind and matter, connects them and thus unifies self

30. Tagore's original reads: "Thus to attain our world-consciousness, we have to unite our feeling with this all-pervasive infinite feeling. In fact, the only true human progress is consistent with this widening of the range of feeling." Although Tagore uses "feeling" rather than "affects" throughout his text, what he calls "feeling" is best understood as *affectus*, or the capacity to affect and to be affected, in order to indicate its cosmological and epistemological implications, as explained near the end of Chapter 1.

and non-self. He comments on Zhu Qianzhi's pantheism: pantheists imagine that there is a God, because they fail to unite the self with the myriad things in the universe, which they falsely relegate to the category of non-self. Since *homo sentimentalis* intuitively realizes that the self and all things are one and the same, there is no need for God (1924, 222). Yuan maintains that life of the true self and *qing* are one and the same, its nature being "pure oneness" (*chunyi* 純一) and "holism" (*zhengti* 整體), exactly the concept of "concentration in the spirit and oneness of *dao*" (*weijing weiyi* 唯精唯一) taught by Wang Yangming. Yuan writes: "All individual lives are in essence mixed, this mixture-cum-one being holism. The self, as pure oneness, is therefore holism at the same time" (18). He points out that "in an affective life the object of desire is fused with the self"; in other words, in affective relations, subject and object become one, no longer being distinguished (189). He also maintains "the unity of spirit and body" (*lingrou hehua* 靈肉合化; 250–51). Criticizing dichotomous thinking and the concept of relativity, he writes:

> Affectivism, upholding the metaphysical ethos, believes that for true life or noumenon, there is neither distinction between self and things, nor any oppositional or relative relationships. The true, noumenal relationship between life and universe, true self and noumenon, is not dualistic or relative, but holistic and essentially unified. (Yuan 1924, 264)

Defying the distinction between self and things indicates the negation of the mind/matter, or self/non-self dichotomy. Yuan also consistently develops the concepts of "nothingness" and "the absolute," as Zhu Qianzhi does. "Nothingness" refers to "infinity" (*wuxian* 無限), which defines "the essence of the true affects, the reality of life" (Yuan 1924, 18–21). For Yuan, since *qing* is infinite, it is also absolute. Life of the true affects is the absolute truth, the absolute essence (*juedui benti* 絕對本體), and the absolute activity, transcending the dichotomy between steadiness and motion. Bergson is wrong because he only maintains the dynamics of life, neglecting the fact that in life steadiness and motion are inseparable (152).

The concepts of nothingness and the absolute were by no means invented by Yuan. Nishida Kitarō at the turn of the twentieth century had developed the idea of "absolute nothingness," which originates from the idea of "nothingness" in Daoist thought. *Kanji* neologisms for Western philosophical concepts such as "absolute" and "noumenon" (or "essence," *hontai*) had been used by Nishida's predecessors such as Inoue Tetsujirō (Wadagaki 1881, 1, 60). Not only did such neologisms as transcultural lexicon enable Nishida to establish the leadership of the Tokyo school in modern Japanese philosophy, but they contributed to the transcultural modernity of Chinese philosophy. The first generation of Chinese students who studied European philosophy in Japan, such as Wang Guowei, Lan Gongwu 藍公武 (1887–1957), and Zhang Dongsun, began to translate lecture notes, textbooks, and histories of philosophy into Chinese almost immediately after arrival (Kurtz

2011, 171). Even though later, He Lin 賀麟 (1902–1992) and Zhang Dongsun, and Yan Fu before them, thought Japanese philosophical terms were not elegant enough and tried to "Sinicize" or "Confucianize" them, successful cases against Japanese terminology were few (182–85). As seen in Chapter 2, Zhang Dongsun's *xin* 心 and *mianyan* 綿延 rendering Bergson's *conscience* and *la durée*, widely known since the May Fourth period, were among the few Chinese terms that could prevail over Japanese translations. The study of the transcultural lexicon is the key to understanding the interactions between modern Chinese, Japanese, and Western philosophies.

Zhu Qianzhi, *The Universeview and Lifeview of an Affectivist*

Originally a lecture delivered at Jinan First Normal College in 1924, *An Affectivist* opens with a statement of two sentences that summarize neatly its overall purpose: "This lecture is based on how I find truth through the true affects. Knowing how to search for truth, one then knows how to live one's life" (*ZQZQJ* 1:457). They also bring to the fore the central belief of the Lifeview school led by Liang Qichao and Cai Yuanpei: life philosophy is a practical philosophy that searches for truth in life through affect, rather than through reason. In 1921, Zhu's mentor Liang Shuming had equated life with the search for truth, as discussed in Chapter 4. *An Affectivist* inherits Liang's preoccupation with life on the one hand, and theorizes the interconnection between affect and reason on the one other. It emphasizes that the true affects and science are pursuing the same goal: truth. In 1927, Fang Dongmei's *Science, Philosophy, and Life* would reiterate the concept: "The universe and life are a harmonious, well-proportioned conglomeration of affect and reason" (*FDMQJ* 4:4; see the conclusion). Before Fang, Zhu's *An Affectivist* in 1924 had launched the idea of the union of affect and reason. The relationship between affect and reason became the core issue that both the Science and Lifeview schools repeatedly concerned themselves with.

Appearing in the wake of his own previous treatise "The origin of Affectivism" and Yuan Jiahua's *Affectivist Philosophy*, *An Affectivist* continues to advocate the true affects while elaborating on what his previous essay has implied but left undiscussed: theory and praxis. He maintains that, even though humans are all different and what is considered true in different time and space may vary, *qing* is the unchanging truth that connects all human beings whenever and wherever they are (*ZQZQJ* 1:458). For Zhu, suppositions are not always true. The experimentalism advocated by Hu Shi is just a supposition, which may not be considered true fifty years later. By contrast, the truth that corresponds to reality (*shizai* 實在)—the real existence, or the natural, everlasting principle of Heaven and Earth—is life itself (461–62).

Zhu Qianzhi maintains that, to pursue truth, one must follow the teaching of *The Great Learning*, and start with investigating the order of things (*gewu* 格物). George Berkeley's (1685–1753) theory of "subjective idealism" (Zhu's English) was also embraced by Wang Yangming. The theory denotes that "Beyond the heart-mind there is neither order, nor things. The order of the myriad things is nothing but the concepts of our heart-mind." However, one ought to know further that "In the universe, between Heaven and Earth, in past and present, there is only a common truth, that is to say, a common heart-mind" (*ZQZQJ* 1:462).[31] If one thinks the self is larger than the universe, and sees the self as the creator of the universe rather than its product, then such an infinite expansion of the self only leads to a nihilist ontology (463). For Zhu, the order of the universe is also the order of the heart-mind, and "noumenon is nothing but the internal life of all things in the universe" (462).[32] The investigation of things and the acquirement of knowledge (*zhizhi* 致知) are one and the same, and the search for the common truth should be applied to the search for the self. If one only takes the subjective view for truth, then the truth that is vast and infinite is relegated to personal opinions. Believing that what is most significant about truth is its origins in the universe, he agrees with Lu Jiuyuan's teaching: "The universe is my heart-mind, my heart-mind is the universe" (464; see Chapter 3, note 35).

A Monistic Theory of Culture

Zhu Qianzhi, maintaining that the universe is holistic, advocates a monistic theory of culture: cultures, whether Eastern or Western, "share the same heart-mind, tread the same path, the only path that is available" (*ZQZQJ* 1:465). He is referring to his own theory of life: life indicates affective flows, the purest kind of motion that transcends desire, and the only path possible for both East and West. Here he criticizes his teacher Liang Shuming, who, as we have seen in Chapter 4, maintains that the spirit of Western culture is the pursuit of desire. While Chinese culture is the modification of desire in order to adapt to the circumstances, Indian culture is the negation of desire for a future bliss. Zhu thinks Liang overemphasizes the role of desire in life and neglects the fact that in every culture different philosophical schools may hold distinct beliefs. Take, for instance, Greek philosophy: "Socrates emphasizes life, Aristotle maintains the middle way, while the pantheism of Plato is in a way similar to the Chinese ethos." In Chinese culture, should those Confucians who believe in objective knowledge, such as Xunzi 荀子 (circa 298–238 BCE), Zhu Xi, and Luo Zheng'an 羅整菴 (1465–1547), be considered to embrace Western ethos? (465). Liang Shuming is also wrong in saying that the Buddhist negation of life represents Indian culture. The fact is that Brahmanism, which praises life and

31. Zhu's original reads, "*quebuzhi tiandi gujin yuzhou nei, zhi tongci yige zhenli, ji tongci yige xin*" 卻不知天地古今宇宙內，只同此一個真理，即同此一個心.

32. Zhu's original reads, "*Chongsai yuzhou doushi li, jishi xin ye*" 充塞宇宙都是理，即是心也, and "*Benti bushi biede, jiushi yuzhou wanwu de neide shenghuo*" 本體不是別的，就是宇宙萬物的內的生活.

sexual love, is much more popular in India (467). As a counter-proposition, Zhu Qianzhi maintains that all cultures, be they Western, Chinese, or Indian, have three schools of thought: the first is materialism, including British and American materialism, Mozi's 墨子 (circa 490–403 BCE) utilitarianism, and Lokāyata 順世外道; the second, life philosophy (ancient Greek philosophy, Confucianism, Brahmanism); and the third, idealism (Judaism, Daoism, Buddhism). Life philosophy is certainly what he believes to be superior.

The Lifeview school during the 1920s generally maintained that Confucianism, specializing in metaphysical thinking, is a life philosophy. Zhu, however, emphasizes its systemic structure as a life philosophy and especially its systemic approaches to socio-political and economic problems. He believes that the central aspect of Confucianism is "the study of the life of the heart-mind." Theories on the universe, life, and the heart-mind grew perfected from Confucius, Mencius, Cheng Yichuan, Zhu Xi, Cheng Mingdao, Chen Baisha, and Zhan Ganquan, to Wang Longxi 王龍溪 (1498–1583), Nie Shuangjiang 聶雙江 (1487–1563), and the Donglin 東林 school during the late Ming.[33] The Qing Confucians, by contrast, began to inject new thought into socio-political theories, as evidenced by Kang Youwei's *Datongshu* 大同書 [The great unity, 1901], derived from *Liji* 禮記 [Book of rites, 475–221 BCE], and Liang Qichao's *Xianqin zhengzhi sixiangshi* 先秦政治思想史 [History of pre-Qin political thought, 1922]. The "evolution" of Confucian thought thus progresses from universeview in the Song dynasty, to lifeview in the Ming, and then to political philosophy in the Qing, and the present moment is "the synthetic era," or "the era of the holistic life philosophy" for Confucianism (*ZQZQJ* 1:469–70). Zhu Qianzhi's later works would elaborate on traditional Confucian political views revised by modern ideas: *Datong gongchanzhuyi* 大同共產主義 [The communist Great Unity, 1927], *Guomin geming yu shijie datong* 國民革命與世界大同 [National revolution and the global Great Unity, 1927], and *Dao datong de lu* 到大同的路 [The path to the Great Unity, 1929]. For him, the spirit of traditional Confucian politics lies in the concept of the Great Unity, a global polity that transcends any single nation-state:

> I believe that with the expansion of common human communities, there will be no doubt an organization for all human beings that transcends nation-stations. The so-called 'the world community shared by all' in the Great Unity is our ideal organization. (*ZQZQJ* 1:522)

33. Both Wang Longxi and Nie Shuangjiang were Wang Yangming's disciples. The Donglin school was led by Gu Xiancheng 顧憲成 (1550–1612), who lectured at Donglin Shuyuan 東林書院 (Donglin Academy). "*Shuyuan*" refers to a private teaching institute established by individual scholars, as opposed to *guanxue* 官學, a public teaching institute in the capital, established by the court, or in local areas, established by the local governments in provinces or counties. Because of its political clout and oppositional stance, Donglin Shuyuan was destroyed in 1626 by the eunuch-prime minister Wei Zhongxian 魏忠賢 (1568–1627).

For Zhu, "The universe is an unceasing flux. That is to say, an endless revolution—revolution is the necessary path to evolution. . . . Revolution means creation simultaneously" (*ZQZQJ* 3:127–28). Here the influence of Bergson's idea of creative evolution is beyond doubt. It should be noted that there is also a "utopian dimension of thought" in Deleuze and Guattari. Although in *Anti-Oedipus* they decline proposing any political program, in *What Is Philosophy* they proposed "utopianism as a process," as opposed to utopia as a "fixed 'product'" (Holland 2006, 218).

Zhu's concept of endless evolution is closely related to his belief in the endless potential of *qing*. He asks: "Do affective flows indicate a sudden change? Or a gradual change?" (*ZQZQJ* 3:127). Quoting from the *Book of Changes*, he points out that gradual changes are more normal even though sudden changes cannot be ruled out. In addition, even sudden changes are accumulated gradually: "The cause of motion (*dongyin* 動因) therein, which is nurtured secretly and growing unnoticedly, must wait for its permeation and ripeness to result in a sudden change" (127).[34] When the body is affected by external stimuli, its force is accumulating while being passive. In this passive state *qing* is not yet released (*weifa* 未發), a central concept derived from *Zhongyong* 中庸 [The doctrine of the mean] (104).[35] When the body has accumulated so much force that it has to be released, *qing* is released (*yifa* 已發) and becomes active. Zhu believes that the unceasing power of *qing* to affect and to be affected (*yigan yiying*) is based on the principle of "harmony" (*tiaohe* 調和), or "the mean" (*zhong* 中). As seen in Chapter 4, his teacher Liang Shuming also believes that the harmony, or moderation, of desire is the principle that governs the transformation and becoming of the universe. Zhu writes, "Evolution is derived from harmony to discord, and then from discord to harmony, without a moment of rest" (127). Spinoza's famous statement, "No one has yet determined what the body can do," a war cry against rationality, indicates exactly a similar concept of the potentiality of affects (1985, 1:495). The conclusion discusses this in detail in connection with Fang Dongmei's theory.

When discussing universeview, Zhu Qianzhi points out that, in Western philosophy for thousands of years, whether the essence of the universe is spirit or matter has been an unsolved problem. British and American experimentalists such as James and Dewey therefore avoid the discussion of metaphysics (which is not true; see the section "Did Hu Shi understand Dewey?"). By contrast, trailblazers such as

34. Zhu's original reads: "*bixu nali qianzi anzhang de dongyin, zhidao xunxi chengshou le, cai huran tubian qilai*" 必須那裏潛滋暗長的動因，直到薰習成熟了，才忽然突變起來.

35. For the original in *The Doctrine of the Mean* and James Legge's 1861 translation, see Legge 2014, 255: "*xi, nu, ai, le, zhi weifa, wei zhi zhong, fa er jie zhong jie, wei zhi he, zhong ye zhe, tianxia zhi daben ye*" 喜, 怒, 哀, 樂, 之未發，謂之中，發而皆中節, 謂之和, 中也者, 天下之大本也 (While there are no stirrings of pleasure, anger, sorrow, or joy, the mind may be said to be in the state of EQUILIBRIUM. When these feelings have been stirred, and they act in their due degree, there ensues what may be called the state of HARMONY."

Eucken and Bergson in Europe discuss the flux of life in order to find a new path for metaphysics. The tradition of Chinese metaphysics, however, includes *Commentary on the Appended Statements of the Book of Changes*, which is ascribed to Confucius, Zhou Dunyi's 周敦頤 (1017–1073) *Taiji tushuo* 太極圖說 [The Great Ultimate illustrated], and Zhang Zai's 張載 (1020–1077) *Zhengmeng* 正蒙 [Correcting the ignorant]. Zhu criticizes contemporary Chinese philosophers such as Hu Shi and Liang Shuming, who maintain that metaphysics should be discarded. In the West, Spenser and the experimentalists are also erroneous for downplaying metaphysics, since they believe that the essence of the universe is unknowable by human intellect and that what can be studied is only the phenomenal world. Referring to Eucken and Bergson, Zhu maintains that human spirit always tries to transcend the limits of knowledge, and the quest for noumenon is necessary and inevitable. It is natural for a true philosopher to take it as his duty to challenge the theory of "the inconceivable" (*ZQZQJ* 1:471–72).

Critiques of Psychology and the Dialectic Method

Referring to his own past work *Xiandai sichao pinglun* 現代思潮評論 [On modern trends of thought, 1920] (Sakai and Saga 1994, 10:1–198),[36] Zhu Qianzhi points out that psychologists maintain that spirit has three main elements: intellect, emotions, and will. For Schopenhauer, intellect is designed to serve will, while emotions are expressions of will. Emotion, or *qing* in Zhu's term, is therefore the ultimate essence of spirit. Similar to Yuan Jiahua, Zhu emphasizes that, as the essence of the universe, *qing* is absolute, unanalyzable, and undialectical. He criticizes, very much the way Bergson does (as seen in Chapter 3), how psychology analyzes the heart-mind ("consciousness" in Bergson): with its analytical method psychology divides the holistic heart-mind into pieces, while the conclusion of its analyses is only the fragmented states of the heart-mind. This is by no means noumenon but exactly what noumenon negates. Since noumenon is continuously flowing and life is always in motion, how can one analyze it with an immobile tool? If one considers *qing* as noumenon, and the universe as phenomena, then one misses the truth that *qing*—the whole heart-mind, the true life, and noumenon—is the universe itself (*ZQZQJ* 1:474).

36. The work was originally published by Xinzhongguo zazhishe 新中國雜誌社 (Society of New China Magazine) in 1920, and then collected in *Genten chūgoku anakizumu shiryō shūsei* 原典中国アナキズム史料集成 [Chinese anarchism: Collection of original texts] by Japanese scholars. It collects three Chinese texts in facsimile, the first of which is Liu Shifu's 劉師復 (1884–1915) *Wuzhengfuzhuyi taolunji* 無政府主義討論集 [Essays on anarchism], and the second and third are Zhu's *On Modern Trends of Thought* and *Fendou niannian* 奮鬥廿年 [Twenty years of striving]. Each text has its own pagination.

Using the dialectic method to discuss noumenon is also wrong. Dialectics, juxtaposing being and nothingness, good and evil, can only arrive at the dialectical vision, which is by no means the true vision. The dichotomy between good and evil will lead to the conclusion that there is neither good nor evil, and the vision of goodness is never achieved. If being and nothingness are oppositional, then nothingness will be pushed to nihilism (*ZQZQJ* 1:474). Laozi's ontology is wrong, and his idea that "all things in the world are engendered by being, and being is engendered by nothingness" is an erroneous universeview derived from dialectic reasoning.[37] While criticizing nothingness and nihilism, Zhu points out the absolute truth: noumenon is life here and now. Nihilism is dangerous because it may lead to negation of life, for instance, the Buddhist negation of life, while the absolute, "with neither beginning nor end, is the unceasing cycle of co-living and co-becoming (*shengsheng buxi* 生生不息). Lively and energetic, everywhere it is visible in things in the world" (477–78). He believes that all beings are in flux and transformation, forever becoming (*shenghua* 生化) and striving toward infinitude; their constant creative transformation is unceasing. For him, "life" itself represents the Chinese wisdom: where there is life there are manifestations of truth. He believes in "this world," the world here and now (478–49).

The critique of Hegelian dialectic reasoning is a prominent trend in modern philosophy. Deleuze points out in *Nietzsche and Philosophy* (1962) that Nietzsche's Superman is directed against the dialectical concept of a human being, while his concept of transvaluation is against the dialectic of appropriation and suppression of alienation (Deleuze 2005, 9). Here Deleuze refers to Marx's dialectical concept of a human being between an essential being and a socio-historical being, or between essence and existence. When people are unable to experience the world as active agents and feel disconnected from the product of their labor, they become like machines and are alienated from the world as well as themselves. The aim of Communism is to eliminate people's alienation felt in a capitalist mode of production (Fromm 1980, 33–60). For Deleuze, while the dialectic method depends on the role of negation, Nietzsche substitutes difference for negation, never negating difference but enjoying it. The life force that he celebrates engages in a relation with different kinds of force (Communism and Christianity) and is even at war with them, but the objective is to affirm and enjoy the difference rather than negate them. The Nietzschean "Yes" is thus opposed to the dialectical "No" (Deleuze 2005, 10). From this perspective, the significance of Yuan Jiahua's valorization of difference (*chabie* 差別) as a critique of dichotomy (1924, 8), as pointed out earlier in this chapter, becomes clear. The purpose of Zhu Qianzhi's engagement with, and struggle against, nihilism is to promote the affirmation and celebration of life. For him, nature and

37. The quote from *Laozi* reads, "Tianxia wanwu shengyu you, you shengyu wu" 天下萬物生於有，有生於無.

the universe are filled with forces of life, while the "constant singing, dancing, chanting, and howling" emitting from our affective nature are all intuitive, manifesting noumenon, confluent with the becoming and flows of Heaven and Earth (*ZQZQJ* 1:475). This celebrative mode is exactly what Deleuze sees in the Nietzschean anti-dialectic practice: it is joy, enjoyment against the dialectic toil, lightness and dance against the dialectic cumbersomeness (Deleuze 2005, 10). For Yuan Jiahua, the greatness of *homo sentimentalis* lies in his constant motion, striving, and creativity that contribute to the unceasing evolution of life and the universe. His adulation of this ideal human type equates to the commendation of life:

> The enthusiasm of *homo sentimentalis*, when burning, is hotter than the heat of the volcano; his hot blood, when surging like a deluge, is stronger than ocean waves. (Yuan 1924, 231–32)

From Nietzsche, to Zhu and Yuan, and then to Deleuze, the purpose of critiquing the dialectical "nihilism" or "No" is to affirm the absolute value of life.

Immediate Responses to Affectivism: Zhang Jingsheng and An Ruoding

The renowned Dr. Sex Zhang Jingsheng was one of the prominent intellectuals who directly responded to the concept of affectivism. As a contrast to affectivism, he called his own theory "aestheticism" (*weimeizhuyi* 唯美主義). He writes in his utopian treatise *Meide renshengguan* 美的人生觀 [An aesthetic lifeview, 1924]:

> Beauty can unify goodness and truth, while goodness and truth must be based on beauty. Beauty is thus the origin of all behaviors in life. That is why I advocate aestheticism when I talk about an aesthetic life. (Zhang 2021, 1:121–22)

As pointed out in Chapter 2, during the Aesthetic Education movement the anarchist leader Li Shicen in his letter to Lü Zheng in 1921 envisions "an aesthetic life" distinguished from the present society, and believes that aesthetic education can guide the present society to the path to "an aesthetic society." Zhang certainly has the movement in mind when he writes his utopian treatise. The preface reveals that he is venturing a third position that unifies science and philosophy, which become polarized during the Science and Lifeview debate:

> What I propose is neither a pure scientific method, nor a pure philosophical method, but the 'artistic method' that combines the methods of science and philosophy. (Zhang 2021, 1:10)

The title of Zhang's second utopian treatise, *Meide shehui zuzhifa* 美的社會組織法 [The organization of an aesthetic society, 1925], is clearly echoing Cai Yuanpei's 1922 blueprint for "an aesthetic society" intent on regulating life from the prenatal stage to death, as discussed in Chapter 2. For Zhang, aesthetic education includes both affective and sex education. Sharing the Lifeview school's goal for cultivating the heart-mind, he advocates body cultivation as well. Since I am preparing a full-length study of Zhang Jingsheng as a utopian thinker and sexologist, there is no need to go further here.

Another interesting response to affectivism was An Ruoding's 安若定 (An Jianping 安劍平, 1900–1978) call for "true affectivism" (*zhenqing zhuyi* 真情主義) in the late 1920s and 1930s. A follower of Sun Yat-sen, An joined the anti-Manchurian revolution when he was a child. Studying in the Department of Sociology at Shanghai University, he established Guxingshe 孤星社 (Lone Star Society) in 1923 and the eponymous quarterly in 1924 with the support of Sun Yat-sen, Wu Zhihui, Wang Jingwei 汪精衛 (1883–1944), Dai Jitao 戴季陶 (1891–1949; the lyricist of the Republic of China flag anthem), Yu Youren 于右任 (1879–1964, a founder of the Nationalist Party and president of Shanghai University), and so on. It is interesting to know that the Journal *Lone Star* and the society were also supported by early Communist leaders. Shanghai University was a stronghold of the Communist Party, Qu Qiubai 瞿秋白 (1899–1936), an early leader of the Communist Party, serving as dean of studies and head of the Department of Sociology. An Ruoding was thus a believer of Marxism as well as Sun's Three Principles of the People. To support the Nanjing government's anti-Japanese efforts, An established Zhuhun xueshe 鑄魂學社 (Spirit Molding Society) in 1932, which managed to recruit 1,200 strong members around the time the eight-year Sino-Japanese War broke out in 1937. After the war ended, the society became Zhongguo shaonian laodongdang 中國少年勞動黨 (Chinese Youth Labor Party) in 1945. Although the party faded away after the 1949 establishment of the PRC, An remained active until the late 1950s and early 1960s (Wu 2006; Zhu 2013; Hu 2015). From the days of Lone Star Society, An began to advocate *Daxiahun zhuyi* 大俠魂主義 (Great Warrior spiritualism), which in his own definition is synonymous with "true affectivism." A graph in his 1928 book titled *Great Warrior Spiritualism* (Figure 5.1) indicates that the philosophical bases of Great Warrior spiritualism are life, upward endeavor, and creation, all of which are marked by activism (*xingdongxing* 行動性), while the principle of life is true affectivism (An 1928, 10).[38]

In the "Juantouci" 卷頭辭 [Preface] to *Great Warrior Spiritualism,* An lauds the affective flows in the universe as the music and love of life, mitigating suicidal thoughts and bringing about new birth. The song of the Great Warrior at the end of the preface praises the unceasing flows of revolution and evolution as the law of the universe, pursuing freedom, truth, light, health, and happiness. The creation of the world, the endless duration of the universe, and the sustainability of the endeavor

38. The graph was originally published in *Great Warrior Spirit* 3, no. 1.

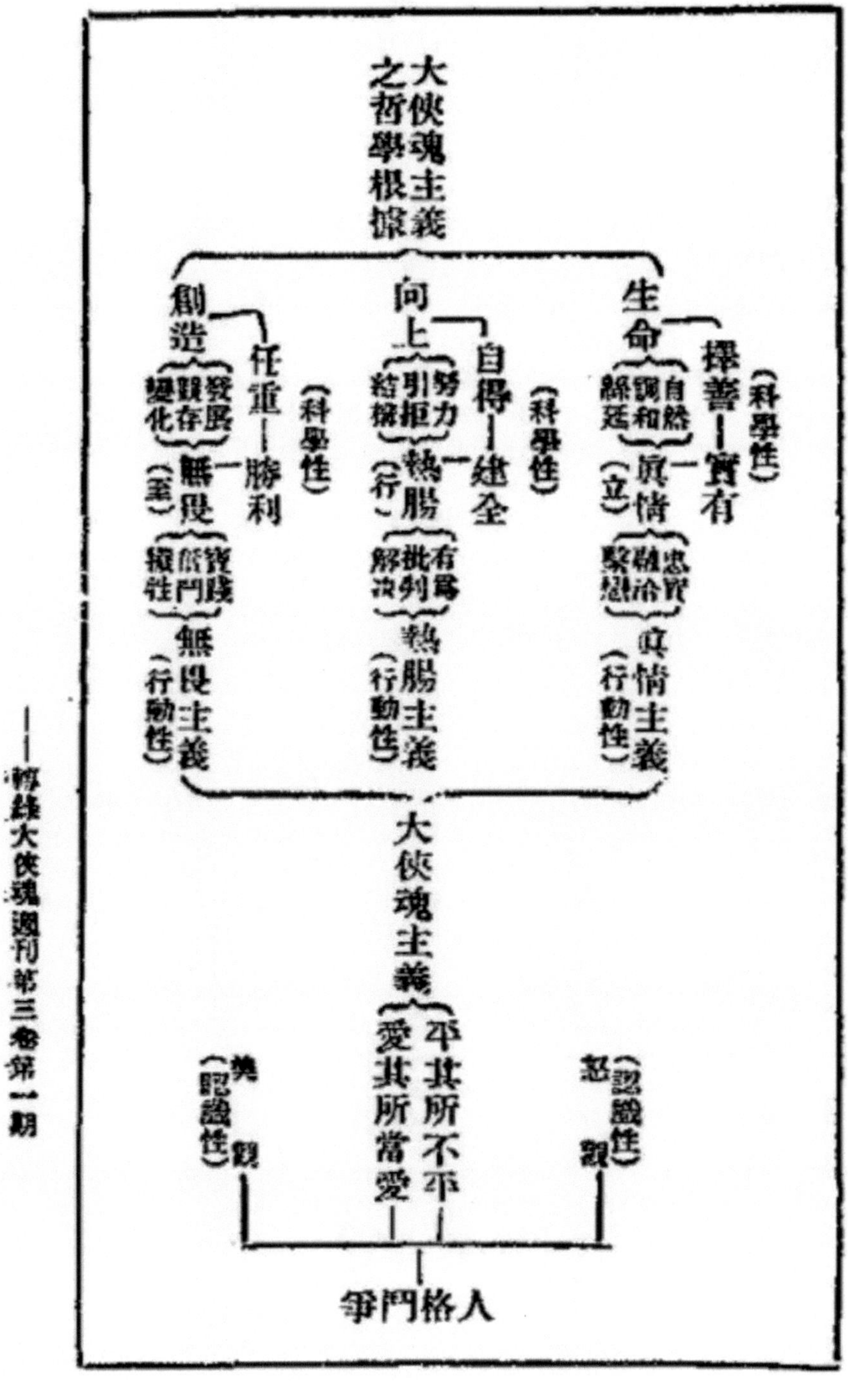

Figure 5.1: A graph in *Great Warrior*, journal established by An Ruoding

of life (*rensheng shiye de buxiu* 人生事業的不朽) are the goals of *homo sentimentalis* (*qingren* 情人 or *weiqingren* 唯情人; An 1928, 1–10):

> Only the great warrior spirit equals the true *homo sentimentalis* of the universe!
>
> Only the true *homo sentimentalis* matches the great warrior spirit of the universe!
>
> Only the great warrior spirit constitutes the unceasing life of the universe!
>
> Only the true *homo sentimentalis* creates the everlasting duration of the universe! (An 1928, 9)

The whole preface is no doubt paying tribute to the affectivist theory invented by Yuan Jiahua and Zhu Qianzhi. In 1932, the latter contributed a short essay titled "Reqing zhansheng yiqie" 熱情戰勝一切 [Passions conquer all] to *Daxiahun* 大俠魂 [Great Warrior spirit], a weekly established by An Ruoding. Zhu writes: "Human history does not develop from absolute rationalism as Hegel maintains. Rather, it is the fervent expression of passions" (1932, 4). For Zhu, although reason opens our eyes, nothing is accomplished without passions. An's concept of Grand Warrior spiritualism, following Zhu's affectivism, was the celebration of the passions for life.

Latter-Day Affectivists: Sima Changfeng and Huang Jianzhong

Zhu Qianzhi believes that the concept of *qing* connects the tradition of Confucianism; both Confucius and Mencius as well as Zhu himself are affectivists. The term "affectivism," even though obscured by the mainstream May Fourth Enlightenment discourse and long neglected by scholars in intellectual history, philosophy, and literature, appeared in a 1976 collection of essays written by Sima Changfeng 司馬長風 (1920–1980), a writer who moved to Hong Kong from mainland China after World War II. The collection is entitled *Weiqinglunzhe de duyu* 唯情論者的獨語 [Monologues of an affectivist]. He writes:

> In the history of ideas, all trends of thought whose name begins with the word *wei* 唯, be it idealism (*weixinlun*), materialism (*weiwulun*), or vitalism (*weishenglun*) 唯生論, are flaunting their egotism and hegemonic aspirations. . . . Affectivism (*weiqinglun*), however, does not promote any political ideas; it is just an attitude of life. (Sima 1976, 1–8)

Sima, a faithful follower of Liang Qichao, believes that "benevolence" in Confucianism teaches the concept of "*buren zhi qing*" 不忍之情 (feelings of empathy). He points out that New Confucians, having braved the May Fourth storm of "down with Confucianism" and still seeing themselves as Confucians, are tasked with putting that concept into practice. He writes, "Our great affectivists must ascend the peaks of goodness and beauty" (1976, 7). To commemorate him, Sima's disciple and a literary critic from Hong Kong, Leonard Kwok Kou Chan, published an essay in

2003, titled "Shiyi yu weiqing de zhengzhi: Sima Changfeng wenxueshi lunshu de zhuiqiu yu huanmie" 詩意與唯情的政治：司馬長風文學史論述的追求與幻滅 [The politics of poetics and affectivism: Sima Changfeng's pursuit of literary history and disillusion] (2003). Inspired by Sima, Chan since the 1980s has been promoting the lyrical tradition in literature. In so doing he has nonetheless preserved the spirit of affectivism even though he has never mentioned Zhu Qianzhi or Yuan Jiahua. Recently in mainland China, however, the concept of affectivism has gradually spread. In 2013, a study of Sima Changfeng's *Zhongguo xinwenxueshi* 中國新文學史 [A history of modern Chinese new literature] points out its "affectivism" (Shi 2013). Scholars of the Yuan dynasty dramatist Tang Xianzu 湯顯祖 (1550–1616) have begun to use the concept of affectivism to study his theory of *qing* (Zuo 2001; Xiao 2013).

As far as I know, the one scholar in philosophy who referred to the concept of affectivism was Huang Jianzhong 黃建中 (1889–1959). After graduating from Peking University in 1917, he taught ethics at Chaoyang University and China University. In 1921, he studied philosophy first at Edinburgh University and then at the University of Cambridge. Returning to China, he taught consecutively at National Central University, Central Cheng-chi University, and Sichuan University. In 1925, he was appointed by Cai Yuanpei to participate in the First Global Conference on Education held in Edinburgh, maintaining that human beings should "replace struggle for life with a harmonious communal life," apparently a critique of evolutionary theory (1962, iii). In 1944, Sichuan University published his *Bijiao lunlixue* 比較倫理學 [Comparative ethics], which he had written and revised for years. Huang writes in the preface to the 1944 edition: "This book traces the origin of moral behavior through the study of biology" (ii). After moving to Taiwan in 1949, he taught at Provincial Normal University (now Taiwan Normal University) while continuing to revise the book. In 1960, it was approved as a university textbook by the Ministry of Education and republished posthumously by Guoli Bianyiguan 國立編譯館 (National Institute of Translation and Compilation) in the following year. In the editor's preface to the third edition published in 1962, it is pointed out that the book is inspired by "a harmonious universeview," "a balanced lifeview," theory of relativity, mutual aid theory, and creative evolution (ii). Huang writes in the thirteenth chapter titled "Self-Realization and Unity of Myriad Things and Self":

> There are rationalism (*weilizong* 唯理) and affectivism in ethics, just as there are conceptualism and sensualism in epistemology. . . . The fusion of rationalism and affectivism is called the 'theory of self-realization.' (Huang's English; Huang 1962, 270)

For Huang Jianzhong, "sentimental self" should be combined with "rational self" to be "the total self," while the "social self" is what distinguishes human beings from animals (Huang's English; 1962, 271). While Peking University as a breeding ground for May Fourth Enlightenment discourses is common knowledge, it is not well known that the inventors of affectivism, Zhu Qianzhi and Yuan Jiahua, were also bred there. One may as well say that Huang Jianzhong, as a Peking University graduate, was transmitting the tradition of affectivism to Taiwan.

Did Hu Shi Understand Dewey?

The May Fourth lifeview discourses led by Cai Yuanpei and Liang Qichao found an afterlife in the New Confucians who took refuge in Hong Kong and Taiwan after World War II. Mou Zongsan (1909–1995), one of the most prominent leaders of postwar New Confucianism, studied philosophy at Peking University. As this section shows, his famous unpleasant interaction with Hu Shi, one of his teachers there, was emblematic of the contentions between the Lifeview and Science schools. After the war, Mou moved to Taiwan, teaching at Taiwan Normal University and Tunghai University. In 1960, he was hired by the University of Hong Kong and in 1968 became the director of the Department of Philosophy at New Asia College, Chinese University of Hong Kong. After his retirement in 1974, he returned to Taiwan and taught at Taiwan University and Taiwan Normal University. Due to organ failure, he passed away on the island in 1995.

The Lifeview discourses have an unmistakable impact on Mou Zongshan's thought. In his essay titled "Guanyu shengming de xuewen" 關於「生命」的學問 [On the knowledge of "life," 1950] (1970, 33–39), he points out that the essence of Confucianism is "the knowledge of life," but since the establishment of the republic, people upholding "scientific rationality" have been preoccupied with Western science and democracy, despising traditional life philosophy. He worries that philosophy has been relegated to a "reasoning game" (*lizhi de youxi* 理智的遊戲). He emphasizes that in Confucianism, subjective virtues such as benevolence and justice must be objectified in the human world (34). His close connection with the Lifeview school can be clearly seen in his 1959 autobiography, *Wushi zishu* 五十自述 [Self-account at age fifty]. While studying at Peking University, Mou Zongsan deeply admired his teacher Xiong Shili 熊十力 (1885–1968), a renowned New Confucian harbinger, and, even though "never feeling in sync" with Liang Shuming, he respected the latter as "a self-disciplined gentleman" (1986, 101–2). Believing that the New Culture movement was motivated by "good intentions for China," he laments that it later, however, deteriorated into either "a shallow, dry rationalism," or "a romantic sentiment separated from reason" (94). In other words, neither rationalism nor irrational Romanticism is recommendable. He writes, "Western learning prioritizes 'nature' and uses 'reason' to control it; Chinese learning valorizes 'life' and anoints it with 'morality'" (89). This is exactly the Lifeview school's viewpoint. Even though he values reason, Mou also believes that life is "irrational" and "beyond logical reasoning" and points out that the "continuity of life" in fact is connected with the life of our ancestors, our nation, and the universe: "Life is an unceasing continuity, marked by duration and affective communion" (*lianmianxing yu gantongxing* 連綿性與感通性; 154–55).

Mou Zongsan's estrangement from Hu Shi, his teacher at Peking University and a leading figure of the Science school, was especially indicative of the bifurcation of their philosophical leanings. Mou criticizes "some doctrinaire professors" at the university who only stuck to "the experimental level" and the level of "knowledge," just like the Qing intellectuals who had dominated the Chinese scholarly scene for three centuries (1986, 88). This no doubt refers to Hu's experimentalism and textual criticism, which he denounces in the 1988 preface to his 1936 work, *Zhouyi de ziran zhexue yu daode hanyi* 周易的自然哲學與道德函義 [The natural philosophy and moral meaning in the *Book of changes*]. Mou studied the *Book of Changes* on his own when he was a Peking University student and finished the draft of the book even before graduation. In his junior year in 1931, he showed part of the draft to Hu Shi, who commented: "You are a diligent student, but your method is dangerous." Mou contested, saying, "I study the *Book of Changes* as Chinese metaphysics." He describes how his teacher answered: "Hearing me saying that, he replied humorously, 'Oh, you are studying metaphysics!,' implying that there is nothing more to discuss" (1988, 1). That Hu Shi, as a leader of the Science school, was suspicious of metaphysics is understandable. He probably never foresaw that Mou Zongsan would become one of the foremost harbingers of New Confucianism in Hong Kong and Taiwan during the 1950s and 1960s and, eventually, a spiritual mentor for later generations of New Confucians in Greater China.

Hu Shi went to study agriculture at Cornell University in 1910, and became a student of John Dewey at Columbia University from 1915 to 1917. When Dewey was lecturing in China in 1919–1920, Hu acted as interpreter, as discussed in Chapter 3. In his 1919 essay "Shiyan zhuyi" 實驗主義 [Experimentalism], Hu writes:

> Dewey has eliminated the essential problems in modern European philosophical tradition since Hume and Kant, believing that there is no value in discussing them. All debates on rationalism and empiricism, idealism and materialism, and the epistemology since Kant, are meaningless and "can be left unsettled." (Hu 1981, 67)

This overview of Dewey is, unfortunately, inaccurate. A careful examination of Dewey's work reveals that throughout his career he was fully engaging in these problems. In *Reconstruction in Philosophy* (1920), based on his lectures at Tokyo Imperial University in 1919, he attempts to reexamine rationalism in modern philosophy. Explaining the significant roles played by feeling, desire, and imagination in philosophy, he points out how they functioned in the socio-historical conditions of traditional Western philosophy, spiritual culture, and scientific development (*MW* 12:77–201). As is well known, Dewey's experimentalism applies the empirical method of science to philosophy, but he does not approve of scientism and rationalism. He points out that the origin of philosophy has nothing to do with science or explanation; it is "figurative, symbolic of fears and hopes, made of imaginations and suggestions, not significant of a world of objective facts intellectually confronted" (83). The conclusion of the book states his vision that "science and emotion will interpenetrate, practice and imagination will embrace" (201).

Dewey probably would not have approved of Hu Shi's negation of metaphysics. The truth is that Hu did not really understand his teacher's thought. In "The Metaphysics of John Dewey" (2002), Richard M. Gale points out that Dewey is opposed to traditional metaphysics, because it cannot be proved by "effective inquiry." For him the ontology of traditional metaphysics—e.g., Plato's forms, Aristotle's essences, Plotinus' the eternal one, Hegel's the Absolute, and God in traditional theology—situates true being in a "timelessly immutable, super-sensible reality," while downgrading "the world of becoming." It has thus deterred the verification of these ultimate concepts (2002, 479). Dewey's 1904 essay "Philosophy and American Life" amply testifies to this view: the problem of traditional metaphysics lies in the Cartesian mind-matter dualism, a concept that separates want and appetite from reason and the ideal. This dualism is also reflected in non-democratic societies, "in which the 'higher' and spiritual life of the few was built upon and conditioned by the 'lower' and economic life of the many" (*MW* 3:76). His 1928 essay "Body and Mind," likewise a critique of mind-matter dualism, maintains the union of philosophical theory and praxis. He points out that the purpose of contemporary American pragmatism is to return to the time of ancient Greece, when science and philosophy were not separated and when both were closely connected with art. At that time, the word *techne* was used for art as well as science, in order to unite reason and praxis. The school of Hippocrates (460–370 BCE) maintained a holistic view of philosophy, believing that philosophy, science, and medicine are inseparable; to understand the body, a holistic view of things is indispensable (*LW* 3:26). Nowadays, the problems challenging education and religion, e.g., the attack of fundamentalists on evolutionary theory, are caused by mind-body dualism and the despisement of life by commercial materialism and intellectuals. To solve these problems originating from the separation of knowledge and praxis, it is crucial to view mind and body as a whole. In the conclusion he writes: "The full realization of the integration of mind and body in action waits upon the reunion of philosophy and science in art, above all in the supreme art, the art of education" (40). Dewey's critique of mind-body dualism, aiming to return to the ancient Greek union of science, philosophy, and art on the one hand, and maintaining the union of theory and praxis on the other, does not seem to jar with the May Fourth Lifeview school's views. From this perspective, Yuan Jiahua's criticism of experimentalists such as James and Dewey for coming into line with "intellectualism," as discussed at the beginning of this chapter, is incorrect. It is a biased view based on insufficient understanding of pragmatism and experimentalism.

Richard Rorty's study "Dewey's Metaphysics" points out that Dewey's masterpiece, *Nature and Experience* (1925), is in fact "a metaphysical system" that many have failed to identify (1982, 72). Or one should say, Dewey's metaphysics is a "naturalistic metaphysics," to use George Santayana's (1863–1952) term (1925, 673). Although naturalistic and metaphysical seem to be "contradictory," they are justifiably put together, since all transcendental insights can be traced to the natural surroundings and passions that have bred them; immediacy of experiences can thus "be thought to be absolute or a criterion of reality" (673, 687–88). The first chapter of *Nature and Experience* points out that the most serious problem of traditional philosophy is that it neglects "the true nature of experience" and becomes "a purely theoretical security and certainty," while its traditional notion of "fixed substances" has been refuted by modern physics (*LW* 1:1–9). We should also note that at the same time Dewey criticizes modern science for replacing the traditional notion of fixed substances with "similar properties," a practice that is likewise a shallow empiricism (5). What is "the true nature of experience" that he refers to, then? The second chapter points out that nature and daily experiences are "messy," while philosophers, through a series of empirical "trial and error," try to find ordering in the messy facts so that it can be the guiding principle for the future. According to David Hildebrand, Dewey opposes traditional metaphysics exactly because of its prioritization of theory and its "top down" method; rather, he maintains the "bottom up" method, searching in daily life experiences for the "Absolute Experience" that can direct future events (2008, 4–5). From this perspective, there is no doubt that, using empiricism and experimentalism in science to establish his own philosophical system and unable to free himself from the Hegelian pursuit of the Absolute, Dewey is one of the partisans of immanence in modern philosophy.

The end of the first chapter of *Nature and Experience* clearly states Dewey's ontology of immanence. He points out that, even though philosophy should use the method of empiricism, it does not deter its pursuit of "the larger liberal humane value" (*LW* 1:40). Philosophers must realize that there are "inherent standards of judgment and value" in ordinary, common, concrete experiences; in other words, in life itself. He criticizes "the transcendental philosophers" for neglecting the deep-rooted humane values in daily experiences (41). Dewey's pragmatism, seen in this light, is in tune with what Zhu Qianzhi and Yuan Jiahua's affectism vouches to do: discovering immanence in life as a critique of traditional Western ontology of transcendence. Immamence, a feature of modern Western philosophy, is the central characteristic of traditional Confucian ontology, which the May Fourth Lifeview school and the postwar New Confucians share, as discussed in Chapter 2.

Dewey's philosophy underscores "from bottom up" and "from transcendence to immanence" mainly because of the influence of Darwinism. As Jerome A. Popp points out, Dewey is "evolution's first philosopher" (2007). From Dewey's 1907 essay "The Influence of Darwinism on Philosophy," we know that Darwinism was key to his philosophical thinking. For him the appearance of Darwinism was "the twilight of intellectual transition" (*MW* 4:8). While the design theory maintained that there was a spiritual power that dominated the world of matter, and that this spiritual power could only be understood through reason, it achieved a double effect: both nature and science had the same purposefulness, allowing the same principle to uphold morality and science at the same time. Theology and idealistic philosophy could thus be in harmony. Darwin's theory of natural selection, however, shattered traditional epistemology. In the struggle for existence, constant variation is the norm, while in the process what is advantageous for survival is kept, and what is harmful is eliminated. Chance therefore becomes the cause of the universe, leaving no more room for the design theory (8–9). Yet, those who opposed Darwinism called it materialism. Bergson and Eucken's life philosophy emerged in this transitional period for epistemology, as we have seen in Chapter 2.

Life Is Both "To Be" and "Is"

The debate on affect and reason that involved almost all famous Chinese intellectuals during the 1920s was in fact a recurrent event in traditional philosophy. Take, for example, the controversy between the Cheng-Zhu philosophy of Universal Order (Cheng-Zhu *lixue* 程朱理學) and the Lu-Wang Heart-Mind philosophy (Lu-Wang *xinxue* 陸王心學) during the Song and the Ming dynasties. While working on the theory of affectivism, Zhu Qianzhi and Yuan Jiahua blur the boundaries between traditional and modern, East and West. The extensive sources copiously referenced in their writings testify to their transcultural awareness and practice. The transcultural connections between Eastern and Western philosophies, as exemplified by the May Fourth affectivism and the Deleuzean affect theory discussed in this book, are an area worth further exploring. This can be fully disclosed in the two following quotes from Yuan Jiahua's *Affectivist Philosophy*:

> Life, or personality, is both "To be" and "Is." In other words, life is mature when it is creative. Since it is forever creative, it is forever mature. (Yuan 1924, 214)
>
> When "To be" and "Is" are unified, "Being" is put in motion. Just to be clear, life evolves unceasingly, exactly the way morality evolves unceasingly. This unceasing evolution is "To be," and becomes infinitely closer to, and mixed with, "Is," while "Being" is contained in this infinite life, infinite morality. Such a life, such a morality, is the life and morality advocated by *homo sentimentalis*. (Yuan 1924, 237)

The English terms in quotation marks are provided by Yuan Jiahua himself in the original Chinese text. What Yuan calls "To be" expresses the same idea as Deleuze's "becoming" (*devenir*) in *A Thousand Plateaus*. Aristotle's (384–322 BCE) ontology using the concept of "becoming" to explain "being" had been developed in *Metaphysics*. For Yuan, both Bergson's creative evolution and the traditional

Confucian concept of *shengsheng* indicate the concept of co-living, co-becoming, and the unceasing flows of life. While Zhu Qianzhi and Yuan Jiahua's concept of affectivism is based on the *Book of Changes,* the traditional understanding of this book of ancient wisdom is certainly transformed by modern-day reinterpretations derived from their transcultural lens.

The celebration of passions by the May Fourth romanticists like the Creation writers is common knowledge, and Leo Ou-fan Lee has rightly dubbed the May Fourth generation "the romantic generation" (Lee 1973). David Derwei Wang's theory of the lyrical tradition in modern China has contested the prejudiced concept that modern Chinese literature was mainly revolutionary (David Wang, 2015). However, affectivism, which the Lifeview school connected with the power of poetry and love that propelled revolution, and which serves as the philosophical basis for modern Chinese lyrical tradition, has largely been neglected by critics. If we delve deeper into the May Fourth dialectic of affect and reason, a new understanding of the complex ramifications of the May Fourth Enlightenment movement is possible. Modern Chinese intellectual history deserves to be rewritten.

Conclusion

Alice Searching for the Key to the Garden of Life—Affect or Reason?

> The Universe and life are a harmonious union of affect and reason (*qingli jituan* 情理集團), which should not be divided.
>
> —Fang Dongmei, *Science, Philosophy, and Life* (*FDMQJ* 4:5)

In *Science, Philosophy, and Life* (1927), Fang Dongmei (1899–1977), a philosophy professor at National Central University in Nanjing, borrows from Lewis Carroll's (1832–1898) *Alice's Adventures in Wonderland* (1865) and deftly makes clear his observation of the contention between science and philosophy throughout European history. Known to be a first-generation New Confucian, in this book he adroitly sums up, in a manner of speaking, the Science and Lifeview debate. At the outset he refers to the traditional concept of *qingli*, or *renqing shili* 人情事理, literally "human affective relations and the order of things." Here "the order of things" includes the systematic understanding of the relational connections between humans, living and non-living things, and the universe. Fang maintains that in life neither affect nor reason is dispensable. They are in a symbiotic relationship and should complement each other and co-live in harmony, but modern intellectuals in Europe were unable to grasp this truth. Spending hundreds of years from the Middle Ages to modern times searching for the secret of life, they are like the little girl Alice, who is eager to open the door to the mysterious garden she is peeping at, but, after several futile attempts, fails to grasp the key to the door.

As everyone may know, in Lewis Carroll's work, at first, Alice discovers on a glass table a tiny golden key that enables her to open the little door leading to the garden. But she is too big to get through the door. Then, on the glass table again, she discovers a bottle labeled with the words "DRINK ME." She drinks the bottle and finds herself shrunk to ten inches tall. To her dismay, she finds the key to the garden lying on the glass table, too high for her to reach. Disappointed, she cries her heart out. She tries to comfort herself, talking to herself as if there were two people debating. Then, suddenly, she makes another discovery: under the table is a glass box, in which there is a small cake marked with the words "EAT ME." She eats the cake, thinking that if she dwindles further, she will be able to get into the garden by creeping under the door. If she becomes bigger, she will be able to get the key. The result is that she becomes nine feet tall, and even though she manages to get the key to open the door, she is again unable to get through. When she is desperate and crying, she sees the White Rabbit running by in a hurry, dropping on the ground a pair of white kid gloves and a fan. While she picks up the fan and is fanning herself, she discovers that she has absentmindedly put on one of the gloves when she was talking to herself. She suddenly dwindles rapidly to two feet and is continually shrinking until she drops the fan she is holding. She is glad that she is still in existence and quickly runs to the little door leading to the garden. But the door is shut again, while the key is again left on the table. Dejected, Alice finds she has fallen into the pool of tears that she has wept (Carroll 1992, 5–16; *FDMQJ* 4:134–36).

Fang Dongmei, after recounting this episode in Lewis Carroll's work, continues to make it a parable of the debate on affect and reason, one that crystalizes Chinese intellectuals' self-evaluation vis-à-vis decades of encounter with Western science and philosophy:

> If this lovely garden is a metaphor of the connection between *qing* and *li* (affect and reason), or of the continuities between the rational aspect of the universe and the affective aspect of life, then in the past three or four hundred years the story of European intellectual history is nothing but these three interesting episodes: drinking the bottle, eating the cake, and putting on a glove. As much as the Europeans, with their green eyes, curly hair, aquiline noses, and white faces, pride themselves on being the best race under Heaven, they are not better off than the poor Alice. (*FDMQJ* 4:134–36)

The "three interesting episodes" in European history Fang refers to are: (1) After the Europeans were emancipated from the religious and patriarchal societies of the Middle Ages, they proudly took out a golden key—scientific materialism—to unlock the secret of the universe. Yet with the development of science and its dazzling achievements, the place of humans in the universe has dwindled. (2) They took out the second golden key—spiritualism in philosophy, advocated by Kant—to magnify the spirit so that it becomes a gigantic colossus, dwarfing material existence into almost nothing. Yet this arrogant attitude, asserting spiritual life while negating the material world, resulted in promoting spiritual nihilism. (3) To rectify these two dogmatic trends, the development of modern physics and Einstein's theory of relativity spurred the recent trends of new understandings of both the universe and life, trends that are ongoing. Their outcomes are therefore hard to predict, but at least it is to be expected that the rational visions of the universe (*yüzhou lijing* 宇宙理境) and the affective nuances of life (*rensheng qingqu* 人生情趣) are bound to undergo significant changes (*FDMQJ* 4:137). One statement earlier in the book summarizes succinctly the key concept of *Science, Philosophy, and Life*: "The fine arts are the representation of the affective nuances of life, whereas science represents the rational aspects of the world" (107). Using this conceptual framework to delineate the development of Western intellectual history, Fang is in fact also summing up the complex debates on science, philosophy, and aesthetics that involved almost all renowned intellectuals during the 1920s, when the New Culture movement in China was at its peak.

Probably the first philosopher to use the adventures of Alice as a metaphor to discuss philosophy, Fang was certainly not the last. Deleuze, in *Logiques du sens* [The logic of sense] (1969), develops the famous concept of "becoming," inspired by how Alice becomes bigger and smaller repeatedly in the novel (7–8). Carroll's story of Alice was translated into Chinese by the renowned linguist Yuen Ren Chao in 1922 (Chao 1947). Shen Congwen in 1928 transformed the story by having Alice visiting China and thereby ridiculed the many flaws of the traditional customs and westernized behaviors of modern Chinese intellectuals (*SCWQJ* 3:1–270). Apparently, by the late 1920s, *Alice's Adventures in Wonderland* was already widely known in China. The reference to Alice in *Science, Philosophy, and Life* testifies to Fang Dongwei's erudition in nonphilosophical disciplines. As we will see in this chapter, Fang's work is brilliantly transcultural, constantly transreferencing philosophy and nonphilosophical disciplines, including art, literature, religion, natural and social sciences such as astronomy, physics, biology, and psychology, while the boundaries between China and West, traditional and modern are blurred.

Fang Dongmei on Science, Philosophy, and Art

In *Science, Philosophy, and Life,* Fang Dongmei is concerned with the transdisciplinary relationships between science, philosophy, and art. He is in a way offering his concluding remarks on the Science and Lifeview debate and the Aesthetic Education movement in his time. It is illuminating if we call into mind Deleuze and Guattari's idea in *What Is Philosophy* that these three disciplines "slip in" on one another's plane although each discipline utilizes its own particular elements. For the two authors, the brain is the junction of three planes (Deleuze and Guattari 1991, 196; 1994, 208): the plane of immanence of philosophy (form of concept), the plane of composition or creation of art (force of sensation), and the plane of reference or coordination of science (function of knowledge; 1991, 204; 1994, 216). For them, philosophy needs a nonphilosophy to comprehend it, just as art needs nonart, science needs nonscience (1991, 205–6; 1994, 217–18). Fang's capability to carry on such a transdisciplinary task was due to his home-based and self-directed learning as well as school education, which prepared him well for transcultural practices—in translingual, transnational, transdisciplinary, and transhistorical dimensions.

A sixteenth-generation descendant of the Qing-dynasty Tongcheng school leader Fang Bao 方苞 (1668–1749), Fang Dongmei had solid training in Neo-Confucianism at home. His love for literature was well known when he was a student of philosophy at Jinling University, Nanjing. Since it was a Christian university, all students had to attend Sunday services. Fang was almost expelled from school because during the services he often read novels instead of the Bible. In 1918, he joined the Young China Association. The following year, when Dewey came to Nanjing to give lectures, Fang delivered the welcome address in fluent English for the Nanjing Branch of the association. Dewey's lectures were on Western philosophy of antiquity, which Fang quite enjoyed, but he was not keen on Dewey's pragmatism. In 1919, Fang published under the pen name Fang Xun 方珣 an article titled "Bogesen 'sheng zhi zhexue'" 伯格森「生之哲學」 [Bergson's "philosophy of life"] in *The Journal of the Young China Association* (Fang 1919).

After graduating from college he was recommended by the university to study at the University of Wisconsin–Madison and later temporarily transferred to Ohio State University to study Hegel's philosophy. At Wisconsin–Madison his essay titled "A Critical Exposition of the Bergsonian Philosophy of Life" was so well argued and written in such beautiful English that Evander Bradley McGilvary (1864–1953), an expert on Bergson and Whitehead, distributed it among the students and teachers of the department. Other May Fourth intellectuals were probably no match for Fang in the study of Bergson. He learned to read German and French by himself and studied Buddhism on his own. Graduating from Wisconsin–Madison in 1924, he returned to China to teach at Wuhan University and Central University. A polyglot engaging in transcultural practice, Fang refers to Nietzsche's *Also Sprach Zarathustra* and *Faust* in the German original, and cites the English version of Bergson's *Creative Evolution*, another notable philosophical work influenced by Darwinian biology. Apparently Fang's German proficiency is better than his French proficiency. His Chinese fully demonstrates the influence of Zhang Dongsun's translation of Bergson's text. Expressions such as *mianyan* 綿延 (duration), *shengming xianxiang, xixi chuangzao* 生命現象, 息息創造 (the unceasing creation of the phenomena of life), and *chuangjin buxi* 創進不息 (unceasing creative evolution) appear constantly in Fang's book. He also relies heavily on traditional Chinese and Buddhist expressions, especially when he discusses the concept of *qing*, or affect. After World War II he moved to Taiwan and taught at Taiwan University, Tunghai University, and Fu Jen Catholic University. In 1957, his monograph *The Chinese View of Life: The Philosophy of Comprehensive Harmony* was published by Union Press in Hong Kong. It originates from six broadcast lectures he gave in Nanjing addressing the nation in moments of national crisis, just two months before the Japanese invasion. When the Chinese version was going through the press, the Sino-Japanese War broke out. The English version aimed to appeal to "the English-speaking world for a sympathetic understanding of Chinese mentality" (Fang 1957, iii–iv). He died of lung cancer in Taipei in 1977 (Sun 1982). Most of his works were lectures recorded and transcribed by his students and published posthumously.

The third-generation New Confucian Liu Shu-hsien 劉述先 (1934–2016) points out that Fang Dongmei, his teacher at Taiwan University, belonged to the first generation of New Confucians (2010, 3–18) and lauds him for the richness and creativity of his thought (Liu 1989), which to a great extent can be attributed to his literary savvy. Fang points out in *The Chinese View of Life* the difficulty of translating Chinese philosophy and its poetic intuition into English: "Philosophy, like poetry—there is a good deal of poetic insight in Chinese philosophical meditations—can never be adequately rendered into a foreign language" (1957, iv). Admitting that the translation of philosophy and literature is a daunting task, he does it anyway. Take, for example, the way he explains how ancient Greeks and modern Europeans differ in their universeviews. Using the British romantic poet Samuel Taylor Coleridge's (1772–1834) two poems, "Dejection, an Ode" and "The Destiny of Nations: A Vision," he illustrates the major difference between the two systems. The first poem, reflecting the materialism of ancient Greeks' universeview, reveals the limited universe perceived by them. In line with this limited view of the universe, mathemetics and Euclidean geometry both stuck to "the size, form, wideness, position, and structure of objects." This universeview was thus unable to inspire the brilliance of the human mind and lacked "abstract, superb ideals." The speaker in "Dejection, an Ode" therefore laments, "I see, not feel, how beautiful they [the stars] are!" (Section II, line 18; 4:139). By contrast, "The Destiny of Nations: A Vision" reflects how for modern Europeans the universe is "a vast, infinite system." What the five senses can perceive is only "a drop in the ocean"; one ought to use "intellectual fantasy and emotional epiphanies" to grasp the infinity of the universe. The reason is that sense impressions are only facile signs that symbolize the infinite order of things in the universe, as the speaker in the poem declares, "For all that meets the bodily sense I deem/Symbolical" (Stanza 3, lines 6–7; 4:139). Fang refers to Faust's praise of the greatness of the universe in Goethe's eponymous play, quoting the original German, "*Welch Schauspiel! aber ach! ein Schauspiel nur!/Wo faß' ich dich, unendliche Natur*?" (Scene I, lines 454–55; Such a spectacle! Ah, alas! Merely a spectacle!/How then can I grasp you, endless Nature?; *FDMQJ* 4:140). Fang quotes two lines from Book 13 of William Wordsworth's (1770–1850) "Prelude," describing how a road disappearing on the top of a faraway hill "Was like an invitation into space/Boundless, or guide into eternity" (Stanza 6, lines 9–10; 4:142).

All the English and German poems Fang uses to illuminate Western philosophy are translated into the format of classical Chinese poems by him, and I have to admit that the original poems are much easier to understand than are his archaic Chinese lyrics, which are, however, exceptionally elegant for adepts. Fang Dongmei is certainly not alone in discussing the development of European philosophy as evidenced by romantic poetry. As pointed out in Chapter 1, Eucken holds Romanticism in high esteem for allowing things in nature to acquire a life of their own, while Nishida values the romantic spirit represented by Novalis's "die blaue Blume." In Chapters 2 and 5 we have seen the Creation writers' enthusiasm for *Creative Evolution* and how their poetry inspires Zhu Qianzhi's affectivism. The mutual appreciation between the Lifeview school and romantic poets is more than obvious.

In the following we will see how Fang Dongmei opposes Cartesian mind-matter, or philosophy-science, dualism, and how he demonstrates that it is through art that such dualism can be resolved. As Will Durant wrote in 1926, "Every science begins as philosophy and ends as art; it arises in hypothesis and flows into achievement" (1953, xxvi), Fang Dongmei believes that art combines the essence of both science and philosophy and that in art affect and reason are in perfect harmony.

Mind-Matter Dualism in the Modern Age

For Fang Dongmei, the invention of function mathematics was a modern scientific revolution. As opposed to Euclidean geometry, function is keen on the abstract analysis of the "infinite." In other words, a new spirit and a new sign appeared during a cultural transition in Europe. He sums up: "The fundamental sign of the Greek people was matter with its individual forms, while the spiritual sign of modern Europeans was the infinite space." Because of the concept of the infinite universe, modern Europe produced great scientific systems, including the astronomy discoveries of Copernicus, Galileo, and Johannes Kepler (1571–1630); Isaac Newton's (1642–1726) laws of motion in physics; and the chemical inventions of Robert Boyle (1627–1691) and Antoine Lavoisier (1743–1794). All these were epoch-making achievements (*FDMQJ* 4:94–95).

Yet, despite their splendid scientific accomplishments, modern Westerners were unfortunate, because their emphasis on natural sciences led to the undermining of human nature. They were like the poor Alice, "Once the sweet dew of science is drunken, their own beautiful image is shrunken" (*FDMQJ* 4:178). Citing Whitehead's *The Concept of Nature* (1919), Fang Dongmei points out that modern scientists, in order to realize the ideal of mathematic simplicity, divided the whole universe into matter and mind, the former being its primary qualities, and the latter, its secondary qualities (178–79),[1] as discussed at the end of Chapter 1. This mind-matter division has led to the stark bifurcation of science and philosophy, which were once "a harmonious unity" before the seventeenth century, a unity that Fang hopes would return to our own age. He writes:

1. For Whitehead's concept of nature's primary and secondary qualities, see the second chapter titled "Theories of the Bifurcation of Nature" in *The Concept of Nature* (Whitehead 1919, 26–48).

> Before the seventeenth century, there was no obvious need for the division of knowledege, while philosophy almost became the suzerain that dominated all knowledge systems. The so-called materialist sciences, biology, psychology, and various social and cultural sciences in modern times were nearly all included in its domain. (*FDMQJ* 4:38)

It was during the Renaissance that the knowledge systems began to diverge, the ascendancy of science confirmed and philosophy losing its traditional clout (*FDMQJ* 4:39).

Modern philosophy, centering on epistemology, intends to correct the mistake of scientific materialism (*FDMQJ* 4:126). Leibniz opposed Cartesian materialism and mechanism; George Berkeley's (1685–1753) theory of consciousness challenged the alleged fixed qualities of matter; and Hume pointed out that the connection between cause and effect was no more than constant conjunction. It was Kant who, reconfirming the basis of the law of cause and effect, resolved the scientific crisis (183–84). Yet at the same time, he maintained that all knowledge is based on the mind, while time and space and all categories of knowledge are a priori (*xiantian qiyong* 先天起用; experience-independent), or "born from the heart-mind" (*yu xin jülai* 與心俱來), in Fang Dongmei's own term (185). Kant's idealism, although never negating matter and science, was a stark contrast to materialism in one major aspect: in science the determining factors to the order of things are the law of cause and effect and the law of nature inherent in matter, while in Kant's philosophy, the law of the mind and the law of consciousness of self. Fang writes, "In scientific theories human dignity was completely lost. In Kant's philosophy, man's stature became sublime" (186). This was the great victory of modern philosophy over science. In a way, Kant's law of the mind created the world and conquered nature. Hegel further used spiritualism to subjugate the material world: social awareness and national consciousness were believed to be inferior to the permanent, ideal order of the transcendental, spiritual realm, which is "the absolute spiritual and religious realm, self-satisfactory, without a single flaw" (186–90). Fang comments, "Modern philosophers of spiritualism were like Alice who is hungry for the cake." Although the human image was enlarged to an unprecedented size, the Europeans were still unable to wander in the garden, or "the universe of tender affectivity and marvelous intellect" (191).

Quoting from Nietzsche's comment on nihilism in *The Will to Power* with his own analysis of and quotes from Greek tragedies such as Sophocles' *King Oedipus*, Aeschylus' *Prometheus Bound*, and Euripides' poem "Bacchus," Fang points out that the wisdom of Greek tragedy united the reason of Apollo—symbolizing matter, and the passions of Dionysus—symbolizing life (*FDMQJ* 4:271–82). Greek views of art and the universe were therefore expressions of "affect and reason in perfect harmony" and "the unanimity of self and other" (298). Yet during the later period of the Renaissance, the disappointed passions of the Europeans led to nihilism. Fang uses *Don Quixote* and Shakespearian sonnets as examples to describe their disillusionment, as these famous lines from Act 5, Scene 5 in *Macbeth* indicate:

> Life's but a walking shadow; a poor player,
> That struts and frets his hour upon the stage,
> And then is heard no more. It is a tale
> Told by an idiot, full of sound and fury,
> Signifying nothing. (*FDMQJ* 4:303)

In addition to poetry, Fang refers to baroque art to illustrate the relationships between rationalism on the one hand, and art and life on the other. He cites Henry Osborn Taylor's (1856–1941) words in *Thought and Expression in the Sixteenth Century* (1920) on Leonardo DaVinci's (1452–1519) faith in mathematics as a science: "No human inquiry can be called true science, unless it proceeds through mathematical demonstrations" (*FDMQJ* 4:310; Taylor 1920, 2:296). Rationalism was the core of baroque culture, which used bizarre and gaudy appearances to gloss over the nihilism at heart, and the final stage of the Enlightenment movement in the late eighteenth century marked the end of the baroque (*FDMQJ* 4:311–24).

It does not come as a surprise that both Fang Dongmei, in 1927, and Deleuze, in 1988, used the baroque to illustrate "the affinity of matter with life and organism" (Deleuze 1988, 9; 1993, 6). While the former refers to Taylor's 1920 book and the like for his insight, the latter's study of Leibniz refers to, among many others, the French version (1967) of Heinrich Wölfflin's (1864–1945) *Renaissance und Barock* [Renaissance and the Baroque, 1888]. The interconnections between art and philosophy is a topic that has engaged quite a few art historians and philosophers. In *Le Pli: Leibniz et le baroque* [The Fold: Leibniz and the Baroque, 1988], Deleuze describes how the folds in the baroque house, divided into two parts, unfurl to two infinities: the lower level is composed of the pleats of matter, or marble curvature, waves, and flares; and the upper level, the folds in the soul, which sings the glory of God. While the upper level has no windows and is blind and closed, the lower level is pierced with windows and has "several small openings" (representing the five senses). The two levels, though separated, are connected through these small openings. For Deleuze, only matter on the lower level can activate spirit on the upper level (1993, 4–13). Using the whole book to analyze the baroque and Leibniz's monadism, he revises the Cartesian mind-body dichotomy. One can tell the interconnection between art and philosophy in European intellectual tradition, while it is more than clear that the mind-body dichotomy has remained a problem to address since Descartes.

For Fang Dongmei, neither scientific materialism, nor philosophical idealism—both derived from reasoning—was satisfactory. A trend of "counter-intellectualism" therefore grew in modern philosophy, advocating the philosophy of life. Philosophers such as Schopenhauer, Nietzsche, and Bergson believed that the will to life, or life force, is the truth that philosophy should pursue. Fang cites Arthur Kenyon Rogers's (1868–1936) words on Nietzsche in *A Student's History of Philosophy* (1925): "Intelligence is only a surface phenomenon—a form which existence assumes for the attainment of its hungry striving, but a form quite foreign to its real nature" (*FDMQJ* 4:193; Rogers 1925, 471). In other words, reason is only used to satisfy humans' desire, while the real nature of life is its insatiable desire that eggs it on eternally. The significance of life is therefore not to "think how to live" but rather to "live and let live!" (Fang's own English in quotation marks; *FDMQJ* 4:193). Fang writes, "Life is the origin of thought, thought is the sign of life" (193). The development of evolutionary biology was a major factor that encouraged this new trend of life philosophy.

The Impact of Evolutionary Biology on Philosophy

Fang Dongmei points out that, before the eighteenth century, mathematics was the primary influence on philosophy: "Natural sciences, using the formulaic method of quantification, eliminated the differences of the myriad things in the world" (*FDMQJ* 4:203). This "mechanical universeview," as the theoretical basis for human beings to pursue equality and freedom, was a great achievement indeed. Philosophers whose methods were highly influenced by mathematics included Descartes and Spinoza (202). By contrast, the development of biology from the eighteenth to the nineteenth century, Darwinian evolution as its epitome, highlighted that, as much as the body is composed of matter, the duration of life has its own device: "Whether the phenomena of life could be explained by the laws of physical sciences alone became a primary issue in modern biology" (209). The British mathematician Ernest William Hobson (1856–1933) had to admit in his book, *The Domain of Natural Science* (1923), that what Jean-Baptiste Lamarck (1744–1829) called the *sentiment intérieur* (inner sentiment) of living organisms could not be understood through physical sciences, and biology was a science combining the physical and psychical sides of life (209). That is to say, even a physical scientist like Hobson was fully aware that biology could not be explained away by the laws of matter alone, and it was a discipline connecting physical sciences and the study of humanities, or *Naturwissenshaften* and *Geisteswissenschaften* in German classification.

Biology, especially evolutionary biology, is highly valued by Fang. While giving an account of the history of biology from Georges-Louis Leclerc Buffon (1707–1788) to Lamarck and Darwin, Fang points out the four characteristics of the phenomena of life: (1) the living organisms are so varied and numerous that, without natural selection, the lands and oceans could in no time be overpopulated with them; (2) as innumerable as they are, living things in nature can be orderly and logically classified into species, genus, family, and so on; (3) all living organisms, thriving prosperously while following their own desires and sentiments, are governed by the laws of "struggle for existence" and "survival of the fittest," as pointed out by Spencer and Darwin; (4) all living things are interconnected and interdependent, forming a complex network of correlations (*FDMQJ* 4:206–8). Fang's conclusion is that it is impossible to use the formulaic laws of physical science to understand the multifarious phenomena of life.

For Fang Dongmei, the delight of life lies in "the desire to make progress, the impulse to move forward" (*FDMQJ* 4:216). Among the life philosophers inspired by biological science, he is especially drawn to Nietzsche, whose philosophy is an outright "celebration of life" (223). Nitzsche's valuation of life force is reflected in his love for modern music, Greek tragedy, and Greek sculpture, since all these art forms highlight the spirit of free creation and the possibility of realizing infinity. The massive sonic grandeur of modern music expresses the rhythm of heartbeat, the magnificent language of Greek tragedy shows the noble elegance of life, while the shapes and forms of Greek sculpture represent pure beauty. Nietzsche's concept of "Wille zum Macht" (will to power or will to force) is exactly Schopenhauer's "Wille zum Leben" (will to life), as Fang Dongmei writes: "Will to life is will to force; the broadening of force is the extension of life" (224). A synonym of "Kraft," a standard German word used in thermodynamics, "Macht" in German denotes potency and capacity as well as authority. "Wille zum Macht" therefore refers to the will to fulfil the potential of life. Nietzschean scholars have recently turned to the influence of thermodynamics on his idea of "eternal recurrence." The transition in physical science that Nietzsche found "from a mechanistic atomism to an energeticist model of Becoming" inspired him to eliminate the "ontology of normative time" and to propose the concept of *Perpetuum Mobile* (perpetual motion; Ulfers and Cohen 2008). Nietzsche, among many others like Spencer, misinterpreted the law of energy dissipation, the second law of thermodynamics, but that is not our concern here. My purpose is to highlight how physical science and philosophy interacted in the nineteenth century.

A Critique of Psychology as a Science

The fifth chapter of *Science, Philosophy, and Life,* titled "The Analysis of Human Nature," distinguishes "psychology in literature" from "psychology as a science." Chapters 3 and 5 of this study have discussed the critiques of psychology by both Bergson and Zhu Qianzhi: it divides the self into separate, stagnant states of consciousness, analyzing the living heart-mind as a motionless object of study. Fang has the same view and refers to Oswald Spengler's mistrust of psychology in *Decline of the West* (1918). For Fang, our psychological life relates to the whole person; psychology, using a scientific method to analyze human nature, only reduces the holistic, lively human nature to "a logical theory without flesh and bone, an abstract, abstruse scientific system" (*FDMQJ* 4:233). Psychology as a science is therefore only "fake psychology," while psychology in literature is called "real psychology," since, when describing human nature, writers and poets immerse themselves in other people's lives by way of *Einfühlung* (empathy; Fang's German), "communing, fusing, and becoming one with them" (235). This is exactly what this book has highlighted all along: co-living and co-becoming with others through affective communion. Citing extensive passages from Bergson's "Introduction to Metaphysics" (1903) and Nietzsche's *Ecce Homo* [Behold the Man, 1888], Fang explains how writers and poets use "intuition" to experience the joy, anger, sorrow, pleasure, and magical wonders of the lives they describe (231–32).

Quoting from "Materialism, Past and Present," Bertrand Russell's introduction to the English translation of Friedrich Albert Lange's *Geschichte des Materialismus and Kritik seiner Bedeutung in der Gegenwart* [History of materialism and criticism of its present importance, 1865], Fang points out that the problem of materialism and modern psychology is to regard human beings as "automatons" (*zidongji* 自動機) or *L'homme machine* (machine man, Fang's French), thus leading to the mind-body dualism, "dismembering the whole person, killing the self" (*FDMQJ* 4:237–39).[2] As is well known, the idea traces to Descartes, who believes animals to be automatons, as can be seen in "Traité de L'homme" [A treatise on man, 1648] (Descartes 1897–1913, 11:119–215) or "La description du corps humain et de toutes ses fonctions" [Description of the human body and all its functions, 1648] (223–90). For him the human body, controlled by the mind, is just an automaton consisting of muscles, tendons, blood vessels, nerves, skin, and so on. The Cartesian image of *animeaux-machines* (machine animals) or *machines mouvantes* (moving machines) became an ultimate symbol of materialism. During the European Enlightenment following the intellectual movement that declared to "anthropologize the machine in order to machinize man," Julien Offray de la Mettrie (1709–1751), a medical doctor and renowned *philosophe*, published *L'Homme-machine* in 1747 (La Mettrie 1981, 12).[3] The central issue this movement engaged in was the question of the soul, which was the major concern of theology. Since it was impossible to explain the soul

2. Fang's original Chinese reads "*canxiao quanren, shalu ziwo*" 殘削全人，殺戮自我. For Russell's introduction to the third edition of Lange's *History of Materialism*, see Lange 1957, v–xix. The terms "automaton" and *L'homme machine* are found in Russell's introduction (ix), as indicated in note 13 of the fifth chapter of Fang's *Science, Philosophy, and Life*. The notes at the end of each chapter of Fang's text, though not as strict in referencing as current scholarship is, are of tremendous help when we study where he gets his ideas.

3. Paul-Laurent Assoun points out in his introduction to *L'Homme-Machine*, "Lire La Mettrie" [Reading La Mettrie], that the text of La Mettrie was part of the European movement to "machinize man," which manifested the triumph and irresistible ambiguity of a "man deciphered by the mechanical logic" (La Mettrie 1981, 13). For a brief account of the discourse of *animeaux-machines* promoted by the Italian theologian Hieronymus Rorarius (1486–1556), the Spanish doctor, naturalist, and philosopher Gomès Pereira (1500–1567), and French *philosophes* such as Michel de Montaigne (1535–1592), Pierre Charron (1541–1603), and Descartes, see La Mettrie 1981, 50–51.

with materialism, the convenient topos was to establish the soul as the one element that controls the materialistic body. The result was the separation of the physical world and the world of the mind, "each subject to its own laws, and neither influencing the other," as Russell puts it in his introduction to Lange's book (Lange 1957, x). According to Russell, this assumption is false, because our minds are affected by our sense perceptions, and our bodies, by our will to make any movements. While the mind-body dualism does not sustain, the fallacy of psychology is exactly using materialism to explain the human psyche. Even the traditional notion of matter as permanent substance has been challenged by the theory of relativity, and it is established in science that "even within the pure physics of inorganic matter the reign of law cannot be asserted to be indubitably universal" (xv). If one regards materialism as "definitely true," then it would be as dogmatic as theology is (xix).

Throughout global intellectual history, the Chinese Lifeview school as well as countless global thinkers and historians of science, including Eucken, Bergson, Whitehead, Dewey, Nishida, and Damásio, have targeted the Cartesian mind-body dualism for criticism, as discussed in previous chapters. Spinoza was one of the precursors of this trend. His famous statement in the Third Part of *Ethics*, "No one has yet determined what the body can do" (1985, 1:495), has become a perennial cheer for affect scholars. For Spinoza, affect refers to affections of the body, by which the body's acting power is increased or diminished, aided or restrained. Using the lower animals and sleepwalkers as examples, he points out that if the body acts simply from the laws of its own nature, rather than only from the dictates of the mind, it can do many things that surprise the mind. This fully indicates the nonsubjective nature of affect. Spinoza objects to Descartes' belief that the mind has "absolute dominion over its affects," maintaining that the mind has only the power to "moderate" them (491–92). Indeed, the French *philosophe*, although believing that the mind controls the body, discloses that it is probably unable to completely control passions. There are two famous anatomical sketches of the brain (Figures 6.1 and 6.2) attached to the end his 1647 work, *Les passions de l'âme* [Passions of the soul] (Descartes, 11:291–497). The pineal gland (H), where he believes passions are seated, is found in the middle the brain. For Rei Terada, this gland

> symbolizes the possibility of an autonomous province, a Vatican City within the brain. . . . Kicked upstairs within the thinking soul, passions are both circumscribed and dangerous. (Terada 2001, 8–9)

The Cartesian notion of passions enclosed in "the innermost part of the brain" but uncontrolled by it thus demonstrates that "nonsubjective engines drive the protocols of emotion and sentimentality" (Terada 2001, 8–9). This is exactly because the capacity to affect and to be affected resides in the body. Seemingly manipulated by the brain, the body has its own volitions. For the May Fourth discourse of the body

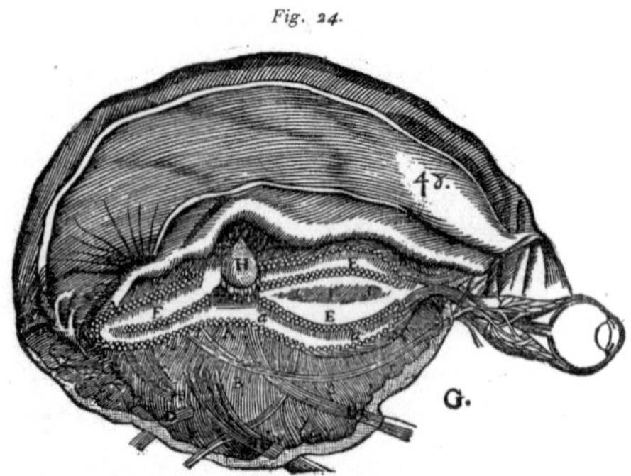

Figure 6.1: Anatomical sketch of the brain with the penial gland (H), by René Descartes

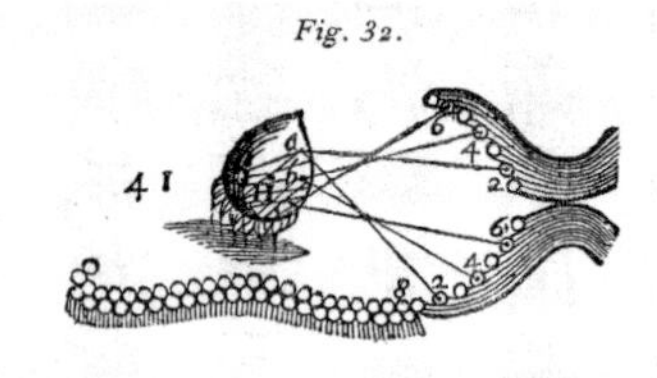

Figure 6.2: The penial gland receiving external stimuli and triggering action

to come into full view, a separate book-length study is needed on Zhang Jingsheng, the utopian thinker with the sobriquet of Dr. Sex.

Qing, Shengsheng, and Deleuze: "Creative Creativity" and "the Force to Love"

> Theoretically speaking, philosophy originates from recognizing the environment. Practically speaking, it originates from the accumulation and release of *qing*. (*qing de yunfa* 情的蘊發; *FDMQJ* 4:50)

Here, the word *yun* 蘊 in *yunfa* is a Buddhist term (*skandha* in Sanskrit), meaning the "accumulation of different 'conditioned phenomena'" in the universe (Liu 2019, 52). The compound term *yunfa* (accumulation and release) indicates that *qing* is a force both passive and active; it accumulates when the body is affected by external stimuli, and the accumulated force is released when it can no longer be held inside, thereby affecting other bodies. This is exactly what Zhu Qianzhi's concept of "*yifa*" or "*weifa*" (already released, or not yet)—derived from the *Doctrine of the Mean*—indicates. The chains of affective concatenations in the universe form a web of force-relations just as complex as the diversified beings in the universe.

Citing extensively the University of Wisconsin–Madison professor Max Carl Otto's (1876–1968) *Natural Laws and Human Hopes* (1926), Fang Dongmei explains how human recognition of the environment proceeded from sensuous experiences to rational inferences, which aimed to establish the order of things (*FDMQJ* 4:50–52). We human beings need "a little order to protect us from chaos" (*un peu d'ordre pour nous protéger du chaos*), as Deleuze and Guattari put it in *What Is Philosophy* (1991, 189; 1994, 201). But this alone did not constitute the origin of philosophy; any epistemological system, however devoted to scientific analysis, could not overlook the creative advancement of the universe and life. After we understand the order of things (*shili* 事理), we pursue the order of *qing* (*qingli* 情理), or the principles of affective relations (*FDMQJ* 4:53). Therefore, both reason and *qing* contributed to the origin of philosophy.

What is *qing*, then? First of all, *qing* is seen as what separates living organisms from matter. In contrast to matter, which moves mechanistically and purposelessly, living organisms are endowed with sentiments, choices, and freedom to act (*FDMQJ* 4:208). In other words, *qing*, or sentiment, is what defines life. How can *qing* be defined? Fang Dongmei writes, "In a broad sense, everything except rational activities is *qing*" (53). If rational activities and matter are the main occupation of science, then the activities of *qing* and life belong to the realms of philosophy and art. Secondly, *qing* is not exclusive to humans and animals; flowers, trees, rocks, mountains—in fact, everything in the universe—are also reverberating with *qing*. When wandering in a garden, a botanist pays attention to the families, genera, and species the flowers and plants belong to; he sees them only as objects of study. The same garden for a poet or an artist, however, is where these objects come alive, resonating with each other, with humans, and with the environment (53–54). In *What Is Philosophy*, Deleuze and Guattari also maintain that plants and rocks, though without a nervous system and a brain as those of living organisms, possess "a faculty of feeling" (*une faculté de sentir*), and that, with "chemical affinities" and "physical causalities," some primary forces and ultimate elements constitute the "micro brains" that are capable of preserving their long chains by contracting and resonating. These ultimate elements and forces thus "constitute a single plane of composition bearing all the varieties of the universe" (1991, 200–201; 1994, 212–13). In Fang Dongmei's cosmological sensibility, the origin of the universe is *qing*, and in that of Deleuze and Guattari, it is a faculty of feeling, or "the force to love" (*la force d'aimer*). It is the capacity of "passing through the wall" (*passer le mur*), or "piercing the wall of the signifier" (percer le mur du signifiant), and becoming others: becoming Chinese, becoming-animal, becoming-flower or rock, becoming-hard just to be one with loving (1980, 229; 1987, 187). Becoming the Chinese that the French philosophers envision, certainly. While the force to love "break constraints and open new vistas," power can only build walls, as Massumi points out (Deleuze and Guattari 1987, xiii).

Fang Dongmei's understanding of *qing* benefits from traditional learning. He interlaces his text with Buddhist as well as classical Chinese expressions, especially when discussing the meaning of *qing*, or sentiment. In the preface to *Science, Philosophy, and Life*, he uses the Qing literatus Shi Zhenlin's 史震林 (1692–1778) work *Xiqing sanji* 西青散記 [West-Green random notes] to illustrate his point:

> Since times of yore, there has been a world of things and phenomena (a world of *dharma* 有法) and a world of sentient beings (a world of *sattva* 有情).[4] Whence came sentient beings? From the multifarious colors and shapes (*rūpa* 色) of the perceived world. Why was the perceived world created? For sentiments. Sentiments and the perceived world have been interwoven for eternity, while even the most gorgeous paintings cannot reproduce their intertwined splendor. (*FDMQJ* 4:62)[5]

Here, *youfa* 有法, *youqing* 有情, and *se* 色 belong to the Buddhist lexicon. *Fa* refers to the laws that govern all things and phenomena in the world; *youqing* means sentient beings, as we have discussed in the introduction. In a broad send, *se* includes all the various colors and shapes in the external environment that are taken in by sense perceptions. In a narrow sense, *se* is what the eye sees. *Qing* could be what is described in the *Book of Rites*: "Affected by external things, man becomes active, pursuing the desires motivated by his nature" (*FDMQJ* 4:62).[6] For Fang Dongmei himself, "*Qing* is the desire of life, the impulse of life, the demand of life" (62). This concept, inspired by Nietzsche's *Wille zum Macht* and Bergson's *élan vital*, is upheld by all the Lifeview school intellectuals, including Liang Shuming, Zhu Qianzhi, and Yuan Jiahua.

Qing that permeates and connects the myriad things in the universe is what makes the concept of *shengsheng* in the *Book of Changes* possible. How does Fang Dongmei define the concept that I render as "co-living and co-becoming" in this study? He writes in *Chinese Philosophy: Its Spirit and its Development*, a book in English published in Taipei in 1981:

> In the *Book of Change*, the expression "sheng-sheng" (生生) means literally in Chinese to beget and to beget or to create and to create. So all along I have taken the Whiteheadian idiom 'Creative Creativity' for its [English] equivalent. (Fang 1981, 111)[7]

---

4. The original Chinese reads: "*zigu yilai, you youfa zhi tianxia, you youqing zhi tianxia*" 自古以來，有有法之天下，有有情之天下.
5. The original reads: "*he zi youqing yin se you, he yuan zao se wei qing sheng. Ru huan qing se cheng qiangu, yanyan yingying hua bucheng*" 何自有情因色有，何緣造色為情生。如環情色成千古，豔豔熒熒畫不成.
6. The quote from the *Book of Rites* reads: "*gan yu wu er dong, xing zhi yu ye*" 感於物而動, 性之欲也. For an English translation of the quote, see An 1999, 171–73: "In response to external things, man becomes active, for activity is the expression of his desires motivated by his nature."
7. In Fang's text, it is written: "So all along I have taken the Whiteheadian idiom 'Creative Creativity' for its Chinese equivalent." Here, "Chinese" should be "English."

For Fang Dongmei, *shengsheng* means literally "to beget and to beget or to create and to create." I would rather say, while "to beget and to beget" is indeed the literal meaning of the Chinese original, there is no doubt that "to create and to create" is inspired by Bergson's *Creative Evolution* as well as by Whitehead. The latter, developing around the same time concepts such as change, creation, and intuition as the French philosopher did, was also quite well known among the May Fourth intelligentsia. Fang Dongmei's work *Shengsheng zhi de* 生生之德 (*FDMQJ* 3:1–479) is known as *The Virtue of Creative Creativity* in English. Each new rendering of a concept is reflective of the concerns of the translators' times and their epistemic as well as lexical choices.

Life Philosophy: The May Fourth Period and After

Life philosophy had a considerable impact on May Fourth intellectuals, far beyond the Lifeview school. Before the outbreak of the Science and Lifeview debate in 1923, quite a few intellectuals had written on Eucken and Bergson, including Chen Duxiu and Li Dazhao, top-notch players of the Science school and eminent co-founders of the Chinese Communist Party. Both commented on life philosophy in 1915. Li published an essay titled "Yanshi xin yu zijue xin" 厭世心與自覺心 [World weariness and self-awareness] in August, stating that Bergson's "theory of free will" (Li's English) and *Creative Evolution* have laid out the general principles of social evolution, inspiring Chinese youths to be self-aware to strive for the best in life and to get rid of their world-weariness and suicidal pessimism (Li 1984).[8] Chen's "Jinggao qingnian" 敬告青年 [An appeal to the young], an homage to the Russian anarchist leader Kropotkin's 1880 eponymous pamphlet, was the forward to the inaugural issue of *Qingnian zazhi* 青年雜誌 [Journal of youth].[9] Here he points out that Eucken and Bergson, raising the flag of life philosophy to fight against the devastating world war, are "progressive rather than conservative," and that Bergson's *L'Évolution créatrice* (Chen's French) therefore "has enjoyed worldwide popularity" (1915, 3–5).

In the May Fourth era, Bergson was read by people of all persuasions, including leftists such as Qu Qiubai and liberalists such as Hu Shi. Hu's *Wushinian lai zhi shijie zhexue* 五十年來之世界哲學 [Fifty years of world philosophy, 1923] points out Bergson's advocacy of intuition, anti-intellectualism, and his theory of *élan vital*. Hu agrees to his criticism of mechanism but thinks that his life impulse is "blind impulse" and his anti-intellectualism "missing the point," because "modern science has already recognized the significance of the role of 'intuition' in thought"

8. Li Dazhao's "World Weariness and Self-Awareness" was originally published in Jiayin 甲寅 [51st year of the 6-year cycle] 1, no. 8 (August 10), 1935.
9. *Journal of Youth* was renamed *Xinqingnian* 新青年 [New youth] on 1 September 1916.

(Hu 1924, 45–46).[10] In his recent book, *Qu Qiubai yu kuawenhua xiandaixing* 瞿秋白與跨文化現代性 [Qu Qiuba and transcultural modernity] (2020), Lik-kwan Cheung, quoting Qu's close friend Ding Ling 丁玲, lays bare the symbolism of the War God Weihu 韋護 (one of Qu's pen names), or the Boddhisatva Skanda, in her 1929 eponymous novella. The image of the War God (Figure 6.3) illustrates how Communism, life philosophy, and Buddhism were precariously co-living in him (2019, 2–3).[11] As can be seen in all temples, while the smiling Maitreya (Milefo

Figure 6.3: The War God Weihu 韋護, symbol of the paradoxical co-living of differing ideologies

10. Hu Shi's *Fifty Years of World Philosophy* was originally published as "Address for The Fiftieth Anniversary of *Shenbao* 申報 [Shanghai news]" in 1923. The newspaper, published from 1872 to 1929, was founded by Ernest Major (1841–1908), a British entrepreneur.
11. Ding Ling, in an article titled "Weihu jingshen" 韋護精神 [The spirit of Weihu, 1980], points out the symbolism of the War God Weihu, disclosing that the male protagonist of her story "Weihu" is in fact based on Qu Qiubai (Ding 2001, 8:91–92). For the novella "Weihu," see Ding 2001, 1:1–111.

彌勒佛) in the outer chamber always faces the gate, Weihu, facing Buddha in the inner chamber, as a rule turns his back to the gate and life in the mundane world, because facing Buddha's mercy would keep in control his killing rage against the evil in the unjust world. The War God symbolizes the contradictory unity of Qu Qiubai as a person: as a Communist he follows the revolutionary cause, as a follower of life philosophy he believes in moderate reform, and as a devout Buddhist, in mercy. For this paradoxical combination, Qu was severely criticized by his comrades in the Communist Party and still is today. Such a phenomenon of precarious co-living is called "the paradox of transculturality" in my next monograph on Dr. Sex.

As pointed out, anarchists were also believers in life philosophy, including Wu Zhihui and Li Shicen. The collection *The Science and Lifeview Debate* published in 1923 contains two essays by Wu. One of them, titled "Zhen yang baguhua de lixue" 箴洋八股化的理學 [Critiquing the westernized eight-legged philosophy of Universal Order], rebukes Zhang Junmai for attacking science, pointing out that neither science nor material culture is dispensable. This, however, does not mean that Wu downplays spiritual culture. He writes, "Spirit and matter are supplementary to each other. Why would one blame matter for causing whatever war there is?" (Wu 1977a, 443–44). The other essay, "Yige xin xinyang de yuzhouguan yu renshengguan" 一個新信仰的宇宙觀與人生觀 [The universeview and lifeview of a new faith], clearly takes sides with the Lifeview school. He emphasizes that his lifeview is not a philosopher's, but a country gaffer's faith in "woodpiles and the shining sun"; it is a "new faith," faith in everyday life, rather than religious faith. He does not believe in a single God, but God's immanence in

> every you and me, every stone in the latrine, the breeze and moon that you love, all material culture and spiritual culture, the hateful dirt and worthless chaff, all snakes, wolves, tigers, panthers, politicians, and solders! (Wu 1977b, 502)

In other words, he believes in the myriad things in the universe, no matter good, evil, ugly, or beautiful. Wu humorously admits that he himself is a *xuanxuegui* 玄學鬼 (haunted metaphysician), a type the geologist and leader of the Science school Ding Wenjiang mockingly repudiates. Yet Wu is confident that his kind of "haunted metaphysician" has been "baptized by science" and will exist until the end of the world, whom even the French founder of positivism Augustus Comte (1798–1857) would not disapprove (Wu 1977b, 497).

As a typical anarchist, Wu believes in both scientific achievements and values of life. He criticizes Zhang Junmai, because the latter maintains that science fails to explain the unknown; only metaphysics is capable of doing so. An advocate of immanence like his young friend Zhu Qianzhi, Wu does not believe in the unknown, or a God that transcends this world. When Zhu and his fiancée, Yang Meilei, decided to keep a platonic relationship, which caused a sensation upon the publication of their love letters in 1923, Wu wrote to him:

> (Just like the shining moon and the green grass, you, Mr. Zhu, are also a material being in nature.) . . . If you and Ms. Yang decide that this should be your life goal, you two are using reason to confine affections, depriving your natural feelings of freedom. (*ZQZQJ* 1:37–38)

Believing that love means the unification of spirit and body, Li is clearly saying here that the body, as matter and part of the natural world, is the motor powered and triggered by the affects.

Li Shicen, another renowned anarchist leader, published a book titled *Philosophy of Life* in 1925, as discussed in Chapter 2. In the May Fourth era there were countless publications that used the term as their titles, including the New Confucian Feng Youlan, the renowned journalist Du Yaquan 杜亞泉 (1873–1933), and the anarchist writer Ba Jin 巴金 (1904–2005). The trend continued in the following decades on both sides of the Taiwan Strait after World War II. Even in the new millennium we still witness such works, the transcultural term *rensheng zhexue* becoming part of everyday Chinese despite the fact that the majority of people who use the term may not be aware of its epistemic implications. The impact of life philosophy is perhaps more profound than we are aware of. Especially since the revival of Confucianism accompanying the rise of China's global influence in the past two decades, life philosophy has been recast as *shenghuo ruxue* 生活儒學 (life Confucianism) in mainland China by Huang Yushun 黃玉順 (2006a; 2017). For a mainstream May Fourth Enlightenment critic like Chen Pingyuan 陳平原, throughout whose life the May Fourth slogan of "Down with Confucianism" 打倒孔家店 (*Dadao Kongjiadian*) was the incontestable signpost, it has been embarrassing to witness the sudden national revalorization of Confucianism. He laments that in some disciplines, "the May Fourth" has even become the target of criticism (Chen 2018, 22). Should literary scholars like Chen have been aware of the May Fourth dialectic of affect and reason, or of Counter-Enlightenment and Enlightenment, they would not have found themselves in such a conundrum. Huang, a philosophy professor skillful at navigating shifting political winds, has been quick to renovate the study of Confucianism while referring to the New Confucian Liang Shuming without naming the May Fourth. Citing his idea of life as the "endless continuities of events," or "the continuities of quests and answers," Huang writes, "We quest ceaselessly—that is to say, we are searching endlessly. Quests are about thought; questing ceaselessly means therefore thinking ceaselessly" (2006b, 352). Yet as pointed out in Chapter 4, for Liang Shuming the "quest" for life is not about rational thinking. Rather, it is about intuition, as he maintains that the tools to pursue quests and answers are the five organs of sense perception, which receive external stimuli, and desire, which is stimulated by them. It indicates the direct, bodily experience of life, before thought is formulated by logic. For Zhu Qianzhi's affectivism, the co-living and co-becoming of life in the *Book of Changes* equates to the capacity of the myriad things in the universe to be affected by and to affect each other, constituting the force-relations Deleuze envisions in his affect theory. The counter-intellectualism of the Lifeview school is unmistakable.

In literature the most prominent case that resonated with life philosophy was probably the six-volume novel, *Wumingshu* 無名書 [The nameless book, abbreviated as *NB*], written by Wumingshi 無名氏 (literally "a nameless person"; 1917–2002), who resurfaced in the 1980s in Hong Kong and Taiwan, after years of oblivion.[12] A self-made writer, he audited classes at Peking University around the mid-1930s, before he finished high school. He began to write and enjoyed almost overnight fame during the Sino-Japanese War with the publications of two novels: *Beiji fengqinghua* 北極風情畫 [North Pole landscape painting, 1943] and *Tali de nüren* 塔裡的女人 [The woman in the tower, 1944]. *The Nameless Book* was an ambitious project written between 1945 and 1960, spanning the tumultuous years from the Chinese Civil War (1945–1949) to the Mingfang yundong 鳴放運動 (Anti-Rightist movement, 1957–1959). Seven volumes were originally planned, but the manuscript of one of them, titled *Huangmo li de ren* 荒漠裡的人 [The man in the desert], went missing. Besides the first two volumes, which saw print in Shanghai before the Communist takeover, the manuscripts of four of them were worked on clandestinely over fifteen years. They were confiscated during the Cultural Revolution (1966–1976) when he was persecuted, then fortunately returned to him after 1978, and eventually sent to Hong Kong and Taiwan and published there. He moved to Hong Kong in 1982, and then to Taiwan the following year, where he passed away nineteen years later (*NB* 6:3–6; Li 1996).

In a 1982 article titled "Luelun renlei weilai lixiang yu xinyang" 略論人類未來理想與信仰 [On future human ideals and faiths] published in *United Daily* in Taiwan, Wumingshi writes:

> The belief in scientific materialism fails to construct our spiritual faith. . . . If we want to establish a faith for future human beings, it must be rooted in a new affective basis, which I call a highly synthetic sense of balance: it will be a profound synthesis of wisdom, moral, beauty, and social reality of human beings. . . . My ideal dualism of life philosophy is in fact a multi-dualism. I will never agree to a pure monism for monism's sake. . . . A great spiritual vision, or epiphany, is by no means the thing-in-itself in nature. Rather, it is a creation of human beings . . . The future epiphany is not merely the extremely cold vision of pure reason, but a vision that is both rational and poetic—it involves human affections. (Wumingshi 1982)

12. The six volumes include *Yeshou, yeshou, yeshou* 野獸，野獸，野獸 [Beast, beast, beast] (vol. 1); *Haiyan* 海豔 [Ocean splendor] (vol. 2); *Jinse de Sheye* 金色的蛇夜 [Golden snake nights](vol. 3); *Si de yanceng* 死的巖層 [Dead rock formations] (vol. 4); *Kaihua zai xingyun yiwai* 開花在星雲以外 [Blossoming beyond the stars] (vol. 5); and *Chuangshiji daputi* 創世紀大菩提 [The great Bodhi of genesis] (vol. 6). For a recent study of Wumingshi in English, see Rosenmeier 2017, 89–112.

This could well be viewed as a latter-day reiteration of the mission statement of the May Fourth Lifeview school. The whole article, serialized in *United Daily* for three days in December 1982, criticizes science and democracy for lacking "affective basis" and proposes a "new faith" that finds balance between reason and affect. In this new faith, Kant's epistemology based on the thing-in-itself and pure reason should be replaced with a new vision that combines reason and (poetic) art synthesized in human affections. Worthy of attention is his idea of "multi-dualism" (*duoyuan de eryuanlun* 多元的二元論), which corrects the monism that Yuan Jiahua proposed to repudiate Cartesian dualism, as seen in Chapter 5.

The Nameless Book is an epic novel that explicates Wumingshi's concept of life philosophy, and what he means by "multi-dualism." The male protagonist Yindi 印蒂, in a spiritual crisis before graduating from high school, leaves home with a note to his father indicating that he is looking for "'something' that is more important than life itself." In the course of reading, we gradually realize that he is looking for the truth of life. During his random journey, he is swayed in turn by the Northern Expedition, the Guomindang Party purge and its conflict with the Chinese Communist Party, and the Sino-Japanese War of Resistance (*Beast, Beast, Beast*). He indulges in carnal desire (*Ocean Splendor* and *Golden Snake Nights*), and eventually, just like Faust, falls into the nihilistic abyss of the negation of the soul. He then begins to ruminate on the meaning of God and religion (*Dead Rock Formations*). At the age of forty-one, Yindi practices Zen Buddhism in a temple on top of Huashan 華山 (Mount Flower), envisioning by and by a worldview that unifies Confucianism, Buddhism, Daoism, and other religions in the world. He becomes concerned with the fate not only of his own nation but also of human beings as a whole (*Blossoming beyond the Stars*). Finally, at the conclusion of the eight-year Sino-Japanese War, Yindi takes an arduous journey, climbing steep mountains and crossing dangerous rivers, back to Sichuan to find his sweetheart, Quying 瞿縈, whom he has not seen in fourteen years. The end of the journey brings him back to the beginning of his quest—the quest for truth. He finds the holistic wisdom of life imbedded in love and the prospect of a new life, their first son (*The Great Bodhi of Genesis*). He says to Quying:

> On top of five thousand *ren* 仞[13] [meaning Mount Flower], I resonated joyfully with the great Nature. But this was not enough. I needed to synthesize the reverberations of mankind—you, our future child. . . . Only through you and him, can I be whole in soul and body, in flesh and blood, to walk to them—mankind. The beginning is me, the mid-phase comprises the great Nature and the universe together with you and him, but the goal is them. The real, final destination, however, is the whole interstellar space. (*NB* 6:141)

13. One *ren* equals roughly 1.6 to 1.8 meters. Five thousand *ren* would make Huashan 8,000 to 9,000 meters in height, but Huashan is only 2,160 meters high. "Five thousand *ren*," or "ten thousand *ren*," is therefore poetic licence for an extremely high mountain.

At the end, Yindi believes in neither divine transcendence nor pantheism as embraced by Zhu Qianzhi, but immanence, the holistic wisdom of life itself. From the self to non-self, including Nature, universe, the sentient beings, and other humans, Yindi extends his concern to all humanity and the "whole interstellar space." To see the self as co-living and co-becoming with the myriad things in the whole universe is what the Lifeview school emphasized decades before. For him the essence of Eastern philosophy, especially ancient Chinese metaphysics, comprises this "noble quality" (*NB* 6:139). For Yuan Jiahua, "The self and noumenon, life and universe, as if connected by blood, are inseparable" (1924, 257).[14] As pointed out in Chapter 5, Zhu Qianzhi also maintains that the present moment is "the synthetic era," or "the era of the holistic life philosophy" for Confucianism (*ZQZQJ* 469–70).

Crucial to Wumingshi's life philosophy is its ethical attitude, as Yindi says: "I can be detached from everything, including the universe, the myriad phenomena, life, death, mankind, and love. The only thing I can't forgo is ethical responsibility" (*NB* 6:141). After getting married, Yindi starts a publication career, aiming to issue three series critiquing Euro-American, traditional Chinese, and Soviet Russian cultures, and another series on the construction of future Chinese culture. In addition, to create a new social praxis that facilitates the realization of a good life, he designs with the help of his wife, artists, thinkers, and industrialists an "earth farm" (*diqiu nongchang* 地球農場), in which "a new relationship between human beings" is experimented on. The idea is that "Unconditionally contributing human and material resources to the community, we do at least our minimum duty as residents of earth" (*diqiuren* 地球人; 569). Yindi maintains that all intellectuals should spare some energy to "enter into real life and do something for the masses." The artists pool revenues from their art exhibits into a startup funding. All take turns to act as the preparatory committee chair, while everyone spares some time for farming—growing plants such as castor beans, raising honeybees and livestock such as chickens, rabbits, and goats (572–74). Twenty young men and women are recruited to work the farm. In addition to farming, they spend two hours every day attending courses designed by the intellectuals, including literature, art, economics, and history (610–14). The ownership of the earth farm will be transferred to the workers after the farm produces a steady income (621). Given autonomy to manage all things around the farm, they will engage in beautifying the farm as the goal of their aesthetic education. Probably the earliest fictional work of modern Chinese nature writing, *The Nameless Book* resonates with its current worldwide booming trend.

The coordination between theory and praxis was a prominent feature for the life philosophy of the May Fourth Lifeview school. If we have in mind the blueprint

14. Yuan's original reads: "*wo he benti, rensheng yu yuzhou, ye xiemai xianglian, buneng fenkai*" 我和本體，人生與宇宙，也血脈相連，不能分開。

of Cai Yuanpei and Li Shicen for an "aesthetic society," there is no doubt where Wumingshi's idea of an aesthetic earth farm comes from. He writes in *Beast, Beast, Beast*:

> Action is the only witness to thought, or at least for socialist ideas and the philosophy of life. . . . Language, words, and thought comprise one half of praxis, while action, the other half. . . . Thought without action is only half-truth. . . . Life itself is a series of motion, a series of action. (*NB* 1:308)

Furthermore, in *The Nameless Book* science is consistently criticized for its materialism and destructive potential. For Yindi, science, although providing us with material enjoyment and sensual pleasures, is also horrifying, like the monster in the bottle in *One Thousand and One Nights*: the atomic bombs may one day destroy the earth (*NB* 6:435–36). Between the extreme mentalities of "I desire" (*woyao* 我要) and "I don't desire" (*wo buyao* 我不要), or between absolute romanticism (e.g., Faust) and religious renunciation of life (e.g., Buddhism and Liang Shuming), he maintains that "a philosophy of life both mythical and scientific" is necessary. A new ethical principle should be formed with a scientific future balanced by philosophical harmony. Only such a "mythical reality" can guarantee the spiritual stability and happiness of humankind and "the duration of life" (*NB* 1:68). The term *mianyan* 綿延, constantly used in *The Nameless Book*, is the standard Chinese translation of the Bergsonian "duration." In the novel the character that best exemplifies Wumingshi's life philosophy is the artist Lansuzi 蘭素子, who "unifies artistic and philosophical visions." Using traditional ink painting, he creates "new tableaus illustrating the transfusion of Eastern and Western cultures" (*NB* 6:410–15). *The Nameless Book* no doubt inherits the idea of the concord of literature, philosophy, and art from the May Fourth Lifeview school.

Before writing *The Nameless Book*, Wumingshi had ruminated on the relationships between reason, affect, and intuition. In a 1943 essay he writes:

> Until now human attributes such as "affects" (*ganjue* 感覺) and "intuition" (*zhijue* 直覺) far surpass the attribute of thought (*sibian* 思辯). Nowadays the elements that make us happy belong more to the category of affects than to the category of thought.
>
> In a strict sense, rational analysis should belong to the duration of affects. The difference between reason and intuition is that the latter is in a state of motion (*dongtai* 動態), while the former, in a steady state. (*jingtai* 靜態; Wumingshi 1972, 1)

The prioritization of intuition and the affects over thought, the idea that reason is part of affect, the emphasis on the motion of intuition and the steadiness of reason, were all maintained by the Lifeview school. In *Science, Philosophy, and Life*, Fang Dongmei points out that Descartes' mistake lies in the fact that he "considers thought as the whole function of the heart-mind" (*xin zhi quanti dayong* 把思想看作心之全體大用; *FDMQJ* 4:317). In order to "correct that mistake and find truth, the only way is for the forces of the heart-mind to be liberated from thought (*xinneng jietuo sixiang* 心能解脫思想) and to trigger other functions," meaning the functions of intuition and affect (318). Affect and reason ought to be complimentary to each other. Today when we talk about modern Chinese Enlightenment, the affective Enlightenment advocated by generations of modern Chinese intellectuals should be remembered. Enlightenment always entails Counter-Enlightenment, be it in China, Asia, Europe, the United States, or other parts of the globe. It advocates the co-living and co-becoming with others. Live and prosper together, rather than live in conflict and escalate into war. Yet, while the Lifeview intellectuals as well as Deleuze believe in *qing* and the force to love, the power of hate and destruction is looming large in the world. The paradox of transculturality persists.

Works Cited

An, Ruoding 安若定. 1928. *Daxiahun zhuyi* 大侠魂主義 [Great warrior spiritualism]. Shanghai: Zhuhun xueshe.

An, Zengcai 安增才, trans. 1999. *Liji* 禮記 [The book of rites (selections)], a bilingual edition plus modern Chinese translation by Xu Chao 徐超. Jinan: Shangdong youyi chubanshe.

Andrade, Elaine Maria Paiva de, Jean Faber, and Luiz Pinguelli Rosa. 2013. "A Spontaneous Physics Philosophy on the Concept of Ether Throughout the History of Science: Birth, Death and Revival." *Foundations of Science* 18, no. 3: 559–77.

Anesaki, Masaharu 姉崎正治. 1897. *Yindō Shūkyōshi* 印度宗教史 [History of Indian religions]. Tokyo: Kinkōdō.

Ansell-Pearson, Keith, Paul-Antoine Miquel, and Michael Vaughan. 2010. "Responses to Evolution: Spencer's Evolutionism, Bergsonism, and Contemporary Biology." In *The New Century: Bersonism, Phenomenology and Responses to Modern Science*. Edited by Keith Ansell-Person and Alan D. Schrift, 347–79. Chicago: University of Chicago Press.

Ball, Terence. 1979. "Marx and Darwin: A Reconsideration." *Political Theory* 7, no. 4 (November): 469–83.

Bambach, Charles R. 1995. *Heidegger, Dilthey, and the Crisis of Historicism*. Ithaca, NY: Cornell University Press.

Beaulieu, Alain. 2016. "Introduction to Deleuze's Cosmological Sensibility." *Philosophy and Cosmology* 16: 199–210.

"Benzhi xuanyan" 本志宣言 [The mission statement of the journal]. 1920. *Meiyu* no. 1 (20 April): 1–2.

Bergson, Henri. 1913. *Sōzoteki shinka* 創造的進化 [Creative evolution, 1912]. Translated by Kaneko Umaji and Katsurai Tōnosuke. Tokyo: Waseda daigaku shuppanbu.

Bergson, Henri. 1919. *Chuanghualun* 創化論 [Creative evolution, 1918]. Translated by Zhang Dongsun 張東蓀. Shanghai: Shanghai shangwu chubanshe.

Bergson, Henri. 1934. *La Pensée et le mouvant: Essais et conférences* [The creative mind: An introduction to metaphysics]. Paris: Librairie Félix Alcan.

Bergson, Henri. 1975. *Creative Evolution* (1911). Translated by Arthur Michell. Westport, CT: Greenwood Press.

Bergson, Henri. 1998. *L'Évolution créatrice* [Creative evolution, 1907]. Paris: Presses Universitaires de France.

Berlin, Isaiah. 2013. "The Counter-Enlightenment" (1955). In *Against the Current: Essays in the History of Ideas*, 1–32. Princeton, NJ: Princeton University Press.

Berry, Ellen E., and Mikhail Epstein. 1999. *Transcultural Experiments: Russian and American Models of Creative Communication*. New York: St. Martin's Press.

Bing Xin 冰心. 1994. *Bing Xin quanji* 冰心全集 [Complete works of Bing Xin]. Abbreviated as *BXQJ*. Fuzhou: Haixia wenyi chubanshe.

Blackman, Lisa, and John Cromby. 2007. "Affect and Feeling." *International Journal of Critical Psychology* 21: 5–22.

Bloom, Irene, trans. 2009. *Mencius*. New York: Columbia University Press.

Blyth, Alan. 1981. "From Individuality to Character: The Herbartian Sociology Applied to Education." *British Journal of Educational Studies* 29, no. 1 (February): 69–79.

Bolaños, Paolo. 2007. "Nietzsche, Spinoza, and the Ethological Conception of Ethics." *Minerva: An Internet Journal of Philosophy*, vol. 11. https://philpapers.org/rec/BOLNSA-3.

Bowler, Peter J. 1983. *The Eclipse of Darwinism: Anti-Darwinian Evolution Theories in the Decades around 1900*. Baltimore, MD: The Johns Hopkins University Press.

Bresciani, Umberto. 2001. *Reinventing Confucianism: The New Confucian Movement*. Taipei: Taipei Ricci Institute for Chinese Studies.

Brühlmeier, Arthur. 2010. *Head, Heart and Hand: Education in the Spirit of Pestalozzi*. Translated by Mike Mitchell. Cambridge, UK: Lightening Source for Sophia Books.

Burke, Peter. 2009. *Cultural Hybridity*. Cambridge, UK: Polity Press.

Buswell, Robert E. Jr., ed. 2004. *Encyclopedia of Buddhism*. New York: Macmillan.

Buswell, Robert E. Jr., and Donald S. Lopez Jr., eds. 2014. *The Princeton Dictionary of Buddhism*. Princeton, NJ: Princeton University Press.

Cai, Yuanpei 蔡元培, trans. 1903. *Zhexue yaoling* 哲學要領 [Outlines of philosophy]. Shanghai: Shangwu chubanshe.

Cai, Yuanpei, trans. 1906. *Yaoguaixue jiangyilu zonglun* 妖怪學講義錄總論 [Handouts on demonology: A general view]. Shanghai: Yaquan xueguan.

Cai, Yuanpei, trans. 1909. *Lunlixue yuanli* 倫理學原理. Shanghai: Shangwu chubanshe.

Cai, Yuanpei, ed. 1925. *Meiyu shishi zhi fangfa* 美育實施之方法 [Methods to implement aesthetic education]. Shanghai: Shangwu chubanshe.

Cai, Yuanpei 蔡元培. 1968. *Cai Yuanpei xiansheng quanji* 蔡元培先生全集 [Complete works of Mr. Cai Yuanpei]. Abbreviated as *CYPQJ*. Taipei: Taiwan shangwu chubanshe.

Cai, Yuanpei. 1996. "Replacing Religion with Aesthetic Education." Translated by Julia F. Andrews. In *Modern Chinese Literary Thought: Writings on Literature, 1893–1945*. Edited by Kirk A. Denton, 182–89. Stanford, CA: Stanford University Press.

Carr, Herbert Wildon. 1911. *Henri Bergson: The Philosophy of Change*. London: T. C. & E. C. Jack.

Carroll, Lewis. 1992. *Alice's Adventures in Wonderland and Through the Looking Glass* (1865). New York: Grosset & Dunlap.

Carter, Robert E. 1997. *The Nothingness beyond God: An Introduction to the Philosophy of Nishida Kitarō*. St. Paul, MN: Paragon House.

Carus, Paul. 1913. *Principle of Relativity in the Light of the Philosophy of Science*. Chicago: The Open Court Publishing Company.

Chan, Albert S. J. 1996. "Two Chinese Poems Written by Hsü Wei 徐渭 (1521–1593) on Michele Ruggieri, S. J. (1543–1607)." *Monumenta Serica* 44, no. 1: 317–37.

Chan, Kwok Kou Leonard 陳國球. 2003. "Shiyi yu weiqing de zhengzhi: Sima Changfeng wenxueshi lunshu de zhuiqiu yu huanmie" 詩意與唯情的政治：司馬長風文學史論述的追求與幻滅 [The politics of poetics and affectivism: Sima Changfeng's pursuit of literary history and disillusion]. In *Ganshang de lücheng: zai Xianggang du wenxue* 感傷的旅程：在香港讀文學 [A sentimental journey: Reading literature in Hong Kong], 95–170. Taipei: Taiwan xuesheng shuju.

Chan, Sin-wai. 2009. *A Chronology of Translation in China and the West: From the Legendary Period to 2004*. Hong Kong: The Chinese University of Hong Kong Press.

Chao, Yuen Ren 趙元任, trans. 1947. *Alisi mengyou qijing ji* 阿麗斯夢遊奇境記 [Alice's adventures in wonderland, 1922]. Shanghai: Shangwu chubanshe.

Chao, Yuen Ren. 1972. "With Bertrand Russell in China." *Russell* no. 7 (Autumn): 14–17.

Chen, Duxiu 陳獨秀. 1915. "Jinggao qingnian" 敬告青年 [An appeal to the young]. *Qingnian zazhi* no. 1 (15 September): 1–6.

Chen, Pingyuan 陳平原. 2018. *Zuowei yizhong sixiang caolian de Wusi* 作為一種思想操練的五四 [The May Fourth as an exercise in thought]. Beijing: Beijing daxue chubanshe.

Chen, Ruilin 陳瑞林. 2015. "Xu Wei yu Ouzhou chuanjiaoshi: Zhongguo huajia yu xifang de zaoqi jiechu" 徐渭與歐洲傳教士：中國畫家與西方的早期接觸 [Xu Wei and European missionaries: The early encounter between Chinese artists and the West]. In *Qiankun qingqi: Xu Wei, Chen Chun shuhua xueshu yantaohui lunwenji* 乾坤清氣：徐渭、陳淳書畫學術研討會論文集 [A fresh breath of air between Heaven and Earth: Proceedings of the conference on the calligraphy and paintings of Xu Wei and Chen Chun], 222–27. Macao: Macao Arts Museum.

Chen, Xing 陳星. 2005. *Li Shutong shenbian de wenhua mingren* 李叔同身邊的文化名人 [The cultural celebrities surrounding Li Shutong]. Beijing: Zhonghua shuju.

Chen, Yinke 陳寅恪. 2009. "Wang Guantang xiansheng wanci" 王觀堂先生輓詞 [Elegy for Mr. Wang Guantang, 1927]. In *Chen Yinke ji* 陳寅恪集 [Collection of Chen Yinke], 12–17. Beijing: Sanlian shudian.

Chen, Zhengmao 陳正茂. 2008. *Xingshi jingshen: Qingniandang renwu qunxiang* 醒獅精神：青年黨人物群像 [The spirit of the awaking lion: Portraits of members of the Young China Party]. Taipei: Xiuwei zixun keji.

Cheng, Fangwu 成仿吾. 1924. "Yishu zhi shehuide yiyi" 藝術之社會的意義 [The social meaning of art]. *Chuangzao zhoubao* no. 41 (24 February): 1–5.

Cheng, Fangwu. 1928. "Cong wenxue geming dao geming wenxue" 從文學革命到革命文學 [From literary revolution to revolutionary literature. *Chuangzao yuekan* 1, no. 9 (1 February): 1–7.

Cheung, Lik-kwan 張歷君. 2019. "Wenben hushe yu xiangguanlü mingxue: lun Kelisidiwa dui Zhang Dongsun zhishilun de jieshou" 文本互涉與相關律名學：論克里斯蒂娃對張東蓀知識論的接受 [Intertextuality and correlation logic: On Kristeva's reception of Zhang Dongsun's theory of knowledge]. *Fangyuan* no. 2 (Autumn): 159–76.

Cheung, Lik-kwan. 2020. *Qu Qiubai yu kuawenhua xiandaixing* 瞿秋白與跨文化現代性 [Qu Qiuba and transcultural modernity]. Hong Kong: Chinese University of Hong Kong Press.

Chow, Tse-tsung. 1960. *The May Fourth Movement: Intellectual Revolution in Modern China*. Cambridge, MA: Harvard University Press.

Clough, Patricia T. 2010. "The Affective Turn: Political Economy, Biomedia, and Bodies." In *The Affect Theory Reader*. Edited by Melissa Greg and Gregory J. Seigworth, 206–25. Durham, NC: Duke University Press.

Clough, Patricia T., and Jean Halley, eds. 2007. *The Affective Turn: Theorizing the Social*. Durham, NC: Duke University Press.

Collett, Guillaume. 2020. "Deleuze, Practical Philosophy: The Trans/disciplinary Basis of the Deleuzian Conception of Immanence." In *Deleuze, Guattari, and the Problem of Transdisciplinarity*. Edited by Guillaume Collett, 182–213. London: Bloomsbury.

Conrad, Sebastian. 2012. "Enlightenment in Global History: A Historiographical Critique." *The American Historical Review* 117, no. 4: 999–1027.

Damásio, Antonio R. 1994. *Descartes' Error: Emotion, Reason, and the Human Brain*. New York: Avon Books.

De Garmo, Charles. 1895. *Herbart and the Herbartians*. New York: Charles Scribner's Sons.

Deleuze, Gilles. 1969. *Logique du sens* [The logic of sense]. Paris: Editions de Minuit.

Deleuze, Gilles. 1981. *Spinoza: Philosophie pratique* [Spinoza: Practical philosophy]. Paris: Les Éditions de Minuit.

Deleuze, Gilles. 1988. *Le pli: Leibnitz et le baroque* [The fold: Leibnitz and the baroque]. Paris: Les Éditions de Minuit.

Deleuze, Gilles. 1993. *The Fold: Leibnitz and the Baroque*. Translated by Tom Conley. Minneapolis: University of Minnesota Press.

Deleuze, Gilles. 2005. *Nietzsche et la philosophie* [Nietzsche and philosophy, 1962]. Paris: Presses Universitaires de France.

Deleuze, Gilles, and Félix Guattari. 1980. *Mille plateaux: capitalisme et schizophrénie* [*A thousand plateaus: Capitalism and schizophrenia*]. Paris: Les Éditions de Minuit.

Deleuze, Gilles, and Félix Guattari. 1987. *A Thousand Plateaus: Capitalism and Schizophrenia*. Translated by Brian Massumi. Minneapolis: The University of Minnesota Press.

Deleuze, Gilles, and Félix Guattari. 1991. *Qu'est-ce que la philosophie?* [What is philosophy?]. Paris: Les Éditions de Minuit.

Deleuze, Gilles, and Félix Guattari. 1994. *What Is Philosophy*? Translated by Hugh Tomlinson and Grahm Burchell. New York: Columbia University Press.

Descartes, René. 1897–1913. *Oeuvres de Descartes* [Works of Descartes]. Paris: Lépold Cerf.

Dewey, John. 1983a. *The Middle Works, 1899–1924* (1977). Abbreviated as *MW*. Carbondale: Southern Illinois University Press.

Dewey, John. 1983b. *The Later Works, 1925–1953* (1977). Abbreviated as *LW*. Carbondale: Southern Illinois University Press.

Dewey, John 杜威. 2005. "Xiandai de sange zhexuejia" 現代的三個哲學家 [Three modern philosophers, 1920]. In *Duwei wu da yanjiang* 杜威五大演講 [Dewey's five great lectures]. Orally interpreted by Hu Shi and transcribed by Fu Lu 伏廬, 228–65. Hefei: Anhui Jiaoyu chubanshe.

Ding, Fubao 丁福保, ed. 1956. *Foxue da cidian* 佛學大辭典 [Glossaries of Buddhist studies]. Taipei: Huayan lianshe.

Ding, Ling 丁玲. 2001. *Ding Ling quanji* 丁玲全集 [Complete works of Ding Ling]. Shijiazhuang: Hebei renmin chubanshe.

Ding, Wenjiang 丁文江. 1977a. "Xuanxue yu kexue—Ping Zhang Junmai de renshenguan" 玄學與科學—評張君勱的人生觀 [Science and metaphysics: On Zhang Junmai's "lifeview," 1923]. In *Science and Lifeview*. Edited by Wang Mengzou, 1: 15–30. Taipei: Wenxue chubanshe.

Ding, Wenjiang. 1977b. "Xuanxue yu kexue—da Zhang Junmai" 玄學與科學—答張君勱 [Metaphysics and science: In response to Zhang Junmai, 1923]. In *Science and Lifeview*. Edited by Wang Mengzou, 1: 241–89. Taipei: Wenxue chubanshe.

Ding, Wenjiang. 1977c. "Xuanxue yu kexue de taolun de yuxing" 玄學與科學的討論的餘興 [The aftermath of the metaphysics and science debate, 1923]. In *Science and Lifeview*. Edited by Wang Mengzou, 2: 361–71. Taipei: Wenxue chubanshe.

Ding, Zijiang 丁子江. 2016. *Luosu yu zhongxi sixiang duihua* 羅素與中西思想對話 [Russell and the dialogue between Chinese and Western thought]. Taipei: Xiuwei zixun keji.

Domínguez, César, ed. 2015. *Introducing Comparative Literature: New Trends and Applications*. New York: Routledge.

Du, Weiming 杜維明. 1989. "Chaoyue er neizai—Rujia jingshen fangxiang de tese" 超越而內在—儒家精神方向的特色 [Transcendence in immanence: The characteristic of the spiritual direction of Confucianism]. In *Ruxue disanqi fazhan de qianjing wenti* 儒學第三期發展的前景問題 [The prospects of the development of the third generation of New Confucianism], 165–211. Taipei: Lianjing.

Dukes, D., K. Abrams, R. Adolphs et al. 2021. "The Rise of Affectivism." *Nature: Human Behavior* 5: 816–20.

Durant, Will. 1953. *The Story of Philosophy: The Lives and Opinions of the Greater Philosophers* (1926). New York: Pocket Books.

Dussel, Enrique. 1995. *The Invention of the Americas: Eclipse of "the Other" and the Myth of Modernity*. Translated by Michael D. Barber. New York: Continuum.

Elman, Benjamin A. 2015. *Science in China, 1600–1900: Essays by Benjamin A. Elman*. Edited by Ho Yi Kai. Hackensack, NJ: World Century and World Scientific.

Epstein, Mikhail, and Ellen E. Berry, eds. 1999. *Transcultural Experiments: Russian and American Models of Creative Communication*. New York: St. Martin's Press.

Eucken, Rudolf. 1907. *Die Lebensanschauungen der Grossen Denker: Eine Entwicklungsgeschichte des Lebensproblems der Menschheit von Plato bis zur Gegenwart* [The lifeview of the great thinkers: A history of the development of the problem of human life from Plato to the present, 1890]. Leipzig: Verlag von Veit & Co.

Eucken, Rudolf. 1910. *The Problem of Human Life: As Viewed by the Great Thinkers from Plato to the Present Time*. Translated by Williston S. Hough and W. R. Boyce Gibson. London: T. Fisher Unwin.

Eucken, Rudolph. 1912. *Le sens et la valeur de la vie* [Sinn und Wert des Lebens; The meaning and value of life, 1908]. Translated by Marie-Anna Hullet and Alfred Leicht. Paris: Librairie Félix Alcan.

Eucken, Rudolf. 1913. *Dai shisōka no jinseikan* 大思想家の人生觀 [The lifeview of the great thinkers, 1912]. Translated by Abe Yoshishige 安倍能成. Tokyo: Tōadō shobō.

Eucken, Rudolf. 2007. *Die Lebesanschauungen der Grossen Denker: Eine Entwicklungsgeschichte des Lebensproblems der Menschheit von Plato bis zur Gegenwart* (1907). In *Gesammelte Werke* [Complete Works], vol. 12. Hildesheim: Georg Olms Verlag AG.

Eucken, Rudolf, and Carsun Chang (Junmai Zhang). 1922. *Das Lebensproblem in China und in Europa* [The problem of life in China and in Europe]. Leipzig: Quelle & Meyer.

Evans, David. 2000. "'Beyond Reality': Plato's Good Revisited." In *Philosophy, the Good, the True and the Beautiful*, 105–18. Cambridge: Cambridge University Press.

Fan, Yeh 范曄. 1973. *Hou Han shu* 後漢書 [History of the later Han, 432–445 CE]. Beijing: Zhonghua shuju.

Fang, Dongmei 方東美 (Fang Xun 方珣). 1919. "Bogesen 'sheng zhi zhexue'" 伯格森「生之哲學」[Bergson's philosophy of life]. *Shaonian Zhongguo* 少年中國 [Journal of the Young China Association] 1, no. 7: 5–7.

Fang, Dongmei (Thomé H. Fang). 1957. *The Chinese View of Life: The Philosophy of Comprehensive Harmony*. Hong Kong: Union Press.

Fang, Dongmei (Thomé H. Fang). 1981. *Chinese Philosophy: Its Spirit and its Development*. Taipei: Linking Publishing Co.

Fang, Dongmei. 2005. *Fang Dongmei quanji* 方東美全集 [Complete works of Fang Dongmei]. Abbreviated as *FDMQJ*. Taipei: Liming wenhua.

Feng, Menlong 馮夢龍. 1984. *Qingshi, or Qingshi leilue* 情史類略 [A history of the various kinds of *qing*, before 1620]. Changsha: Yuelu shushe.

Feng, Yiyin 豐一吟. 2014. *Wode fuqin Feng Zikai* 我的父親豐子愷 [My father Feng Zikai]. Hong Kong: Zhonghe chuban gongsi.

Feng, Youlan. 1953. *A History of Chinese Philosophy*, vol. 2. Translated by Derk Bodde. Princeton, NJ: Princeton University Press.

Foerster, Friedrich Wilhelm. 1914. *Schule und Charakter: Beiträge zur Pädagogik des Gehorsams und zur Reform der Schuldisziplin* [School and character: On the pedagogy of obedience and the reform of school discipline, 1907]. Zürich: Schulthess & Co.

Frisina, Warren G. 2002. *The Unity of Knowledge and Action: Toward a Nonrepresentational Theory of Knowledge*. Albany: State University of New York Press.

Frölich, Thomas. 2000. *Staatsdenken im China der Republikzeit (1912–1949): Die Instrumentalisierung philosophischer Ideen bei chinesischen Intellektuellen* [Ideas of the state in Republican China (1912–1949): Chinese intellectuals' instrumentalization of philosophical ideas]. Frankfurt: Campus Verlag.

Fromm, Erich. 1980. *Das Menschenbild bei Marx: Mit den wichtisten Teilen der Frühschriften von Karl Marx* [Marx's concept of man: With the most important parts of Karl Marx's early writings, 1963]. Frankfurt am Main: Europäische Verlagsanstalt.

Gale, Richard M. 2002. "The Metaphysics of John Dewey." *Transactions of the Charles S. Peirce Society* 38, no. 4 (Fall): 477–518.

Goldman, Merle. 1982. "The Political Use of Lu Xun." *The China Quarterly* no. 91: 446–61.

Gottlieb, Anthony. 2016. *The Dream of Enlightenment: The Rise of Modern Philosophy*. New York: Liveright Publishing Co.

Greenblatt, Stephen. 2010. *Cultural Mobility: A Manifesto*. Cambridge: Cambridge University Press.

Gregg, Malissa, and Gregory J. Seigworth, eds. 2010. *The Affect Theory Reader*. Durham, NC: Duke University Press.

Gu, Shouchang 顧綬昌. 1923. "Ganjue yu renshilun" 感覺與認識論 [Sense perceptions and epistemology]. *Shishi xinbao. Xuedeng* 5, no. 15–20 (May): 4.

Gu, Shouchang. 1983. "Wangshi huiyi yuanwang" 往事 回憶 願望 [The past, reminiscences, wishes]. In *Zhongguo dangdai shehui kexuejia diliuji* 中國當代社會科學家第6

輯 [Contemporary Chinese social scientists, vol. 6]. Edited by Beijing Library and Jilin Provincial Library Editorial Board 6: 304–17. Beijing: Shumu wenxian chubanshe.

Gu, Zhaoxiong 顧兆熊 (Gu Mengyu 顧孟餘). 1919. "Makesi zhuyi" 馬克思主義 [Marxism]. *Xin qingnian* 6, no. 5: 450–65.

Guo, Moruo 郭沫若. 1921. *Nüshen* 女神 [The goddesses], 1–17. Shanghai: Taidong shudian.

Guo, Moruo. 1922. "Chuangzaozhe" 創造者 [The creators]. *Chuangzao jikan* 1, no. 1 (1 May): 1–4.

Guo, Moruo. 1923a. "Women de wenxue xin yundong" 我們的文學新運動 [Our new movement in literature]. *Chuangzao zhoubao* no. 3 (27 May): 13–15.

Guo Moruo. 1923b. "Yishujia yu gemingjia" 藝術家與革命家 [Artists and revolutionaries]. *Chuangzao zhoubao* no. 18 (9 September): 1–2.

Hai Qing 海青. 2010. *"Zisha shidai" de lailin? Ershi shiji zaoqi Zhongguo zhishi qunti de jilie xingwei he jiazhi xuanze* 「自殺時代」的來臨？二十世紀早期中國知識群體的激烈行為和價值選擇 [The coming of a suicide era?: The drastic behavior and value choices of early twentieth-century Chinese intelligentia]. Beijing: Zhongguo renmin daxue chubanshe.

Haldane, John Burdon Sanderson. 1924. *Daedalus; or, Science and the Future*. London: E. P. Dutton and Co.

Hansen, Chad. 1992. *A Daoist Theory of Chinese Thought: A Philosophical Interpretation*. New York: Oxford University Press.

Hara, Zuien 原隨園. 1923. *Seiyōshi gairon* 西洋史概論 [A general view of Western history]. Tokyo: Tōmondō shoten.

Heurtebise, Jean-Yves. 2020. *Orientalisme, occidentalisme et universalisme: Histoire et méthode des représentaions croisées entre mondes européens et chinois* [Orientalism, occidentalism, and universalism: History and method of the interwoven representations between European and Chinese worlds]. Marseille: MA Éditions-ESKA.

Higuchi, Kanjirō 樋口勘次郎. 1899. *Tōgō shugi shin kyōjuhō* 統合主義新教授法 [Integralism: New pedagogy]. Tokyo: Dōbunkan.

Higuchi, Kanjirō 樋口勘次郎. 1909. Kyōjuhō 教授法 [Pedagogy]. Tokyo: Waseda daigaku shuppanbu.

Hildebrand, David L. 2008. *Dewey: A Beginner's Guide*. Oxford: Oneworld Publications.

Ho, Shibin 何石彬. 2009. *Apidamojushelun yanjiu: yi yuanqi, youqing yu jietuo wei zhongxin* 《阿毗達磨俱舍論》研究：以緣起、有情與解脫為中心 [An inquiry into *Abhidharmakosabhasyam*: on pratītya-samutpāda (arising from conditional causation), sattva (sentient), and vi-mokṣa (liberation)]. Beijing: Zhongjiao wenhua chubanshe.

Hobson, Benjamin (He Xin 合信) et al., eds. 1855. *Bowu xinbian* 博物新編 [Natural philosophy]. Guangzhou: Guangzhou chubanshe.

Hobson, Benjamin et al., eds. 1870. *Hakubutsu shinpen yakkai* 博物新編譯解 [Natural philosophy translated and annotated]. Translated by Ōmori Yichū 大森惟中. Tokyo: Aoyama seikichi.

Hobson, E. W. 1923. *The Domain of Natural Science*. Cambridge: Cambridge University Press.

Hobson, John M. 2004. *The Eastern Origins of Western Civilisation*. Cambridge: Cambridge University Press.

Holland, Eugene W. 2006. "The Utopian Dimension of Thought in Deleuze and Guattari." *Arena Journal* no. 25/26: 217–42.

Holterhoff, Kate. 2010. "Beauty as a Terministic Screen in Charles Darwin's *The Descent of Man*." *Victorian Network* 2, no. 1 (Summer): 49–69.

Hou, Jian 侯健. 1974. *Cong wenxue geming dao geming wenxue* 從文學革命到革命文學 [From literary revolution to revolutionary literature]. Taipei: Zhongwai wenxue yuekanshe.

Hsiao, kung-chuan. 1967. "K'ang Yu-wei's Excursion into Science: Lectures on the Heavens." In *K'ang Yu-wei: A Biography and a Symposium*. Edited by Jung-Pang Lo, 375–407. Tuscon: University of Arizona Press.

Hsiao, kung-chuan. 1975. *A Modern China and a New World: K'ang Yu-wei, Reformer and Utopian, 1858–1927*. Seattle: University of Washington Press.

Hu, Ketao 胡可濤. 2015. "Fuxing Zhonghua chongzhu huang hun—An Ruoding de 'Daxiahun zhuyi' shulue" 復興中華 重鑄黃魂—安若定的'大俠魂主義'述略 [Chinese Renaissance and the remolding of the Yellow Spirit—An outline of An Ruoding's "Great Warrior spiritualism"]. *Zhongguo kuangye daxue xuebao* no. 2: 42–49.

Hu, Renchun 胡人椿. 1925. "Yishu jiaoyu gailun" 藝術教育概論 [Outline of arts education]. In *The Principles of Aesthetic Education*. Edited by Li Shicen, 35–56. Shanghai: Shangwu yinshuguan.

Hu, Shi 胡適. 1924. *Wushinian lai zhi shijie zhexue* 五十年來之世界哲學 [Fifty years of world philosophy]. Shanghai: Shenbaoguan.

Hu, Shi. 1981. "Shiyan zhuyi" 實驗主義 [Experimentalism, 1919]. In *Hu Shi zhexue sixiang ziliaoxuan* 胡適哲學思想資料選 [Hu Shi: Selected philosophical texts]. Edited by Ge Maochun 葛懋春 and Li Xingzhi 李興芝, 45–90. Shanghai: Huadong shifan daxue chubanshe.

Huang, Alfred. 2010. *The Complete I Ching: The Definitive Translation* (1998). Rochester, VT: Inner Traditions.

Huang, Hanli 黃漢立. 2011. *Yijing jiangtang san—Xici Shangzhuan fahui* 易經講堂三—《繫辭上傳》發揮 [Lectures on *Yijing* 3—Explicating *Commentary on the appended statements, Part 1*]. Hong Kong: Sanlian shudian.

Huang, Jianzhong 黃建中. 1962. *Bijiao lunlixue* 比較倫理學 [Comparative ethics, 1944]. Taipei: Guoli bianyiguan.

Huang, Kuan-min 黃冠閔. 2018. *Gantong yu huidang: Tang Junyi zhexue luntan* 感通與迴盪：唐君毅哲學論探 [Affective communion and reverberances: On Tang Junyi's philosophy]. Taipei: Lianjing.

Huang, Shiheng 黃士恆, trans. 1915a. "Faguo Lupang boshi wuzhi shengmielun" 法國魯滂博士物質生滅論 [The French philosopher Dr. Le Bon's theory of the life and death of matter, Part 1]. *Dongfang zazhi* 12, no. 4: 1–8.

Huang, Shiheng. 1915b. "The French Philosopher Dr. Le Bon's Theory of the Life and Death of Matter, Part 2." *Dongfang zazhi* 12, no. 5: 1–5.

Huang, Xianian 黃夏年. 2005. "Qianyan: Zhu Qianzhi xiansheng de xueshu chengjiu yu fengfan" 前言—朱謙之先生的學術成就與風範 [Preface: The academic achievements and ethos of Mr. Zhu Qianzhi]. In *Zhu Qianzhi xuanji* 朱謙之選集 [Selected works of Zhu Qianzhi]. Edited by Huang Xianian, 1–16. Changchun: Jilin renmin chubanshe.

Huang, Yushun 黃玉順. 2006a. *Ai yu si: Shenghuo Ruxue de guannian* 愛與思—生活儒學的觀念 [Life Confucianism as a new philosophy: Love and thought]. Chengdu: Sichuan daxue chubanshe.

Huang, Yushun. 2006b. *Mianxiang shenghuo benshen de Ruxue: Huang Yushun "Shenghuo Ruxue" zixuanji* 面向生活本身的儒學：黃玉順「生活儒學」自選集 [Confucianism as life itself: Huang Yushun's "Life Confucianism," a self-collection]. Chengdu: Sichuan daxue chubanshe.

Huang, Yushun. 2017. *Life Confucianism as a New Philosophy: Love and Thought*. Translated by Li Xuening and Meirong Yan. Los Angeles: Bridge21 Publications.

Huilin 慧琳. 1983. *Yissaikyō ongi* 一切經音義 [The pronunciation and meaning of the *All Beings Sutra*, 1924–1934]. In *Taishō shinshu Taizōkyō* 大正新修大藏經 [Taishō tripitaka]. Taipei: Xinwenfeng.

Hume, David. 2001. *A Treatise of Human Nature* (1739–1740). Bristol, UK: Thoemmes Press.

Inoue, Tetsujirō et al., eds. 1912. *Tetsugaku jii* 哲學字彙 [A dictionary of philosophy, 1881]. Tokyo: Maruzen.

Jiang, Deming 姜德明, ed. 1996. *Ba Jin shuhua* 巴金書話 [Ba Jin on books]. Beijing: Beijing chubanshe.

Jiang, Fei 姜飛. 2014. *Zhongguo wenxue de zhenshi guannian* 中國文學的真實觀念 [The idea of reality in Chinese literature]. Taipei: Xiuwei zixun keji.

Jiang, Menglin 蔣夢麟 (Menglin). 1919. "Beida xuesheng Lin Deyang jun de zisha—jiaoyu shang shengsi guantou de dawenti" 北大學生林德揚君的自殺—教育上生死關頭的大問題 [The suicide of Beijing University student Mr. Lin Deyang: The severe problem of life and death in education]. *Xinchao* 2, no. 2 (December): 349–50.

Jiang, Paul Yun-ming 姜允明. 1980. *The Search for Mind: Ch'en Pai-sha, Philosopher, Poet*. Kent Ridge: Singapore University Press.

Jiang, Paul Yun-ming. 2007. *Wang Yangming yu Chen Baisha* 王陽明與陳白沙 [Wang Yangming and Chen Baisha]. Taipei: Wunan tushu chuban gongsi.

Jinsei Tetsugaku kenkyūkai 人生哲學研究会 [Research Society on Life Philosophy], ed. 1925. *Kindaijin no jinseikan* 近代人の人生觀 [Modern man's lifeview]. Tokyo: Etsuzandō.

Kawajiri, Fumihiko 川尻文彥. 2013. "'Zhexue' zai jindai Zhongguo—yi Cai Yuanpei de 'zhexue' wei zhongxin" 「哲學」在近代中國—以蔡元培的「哲學」為中心 ["Philosophy" in modern China: On Cai Yuanpei's "philosophy"]. In *Yazhou gainianshi yanjiu* 亞洲概念史研究 [Studies of Asian history of ideas]. Edited by Sun Jiang 孫江 and Liu Jianhui 劉建輝, 66–83. Beijing: Sanlian shudian.

Keown, Damien, ed. 2003. "Ratnagotravibhāga." *A Dictionary of Buddhism*. Oxford: Oxford University Press.

Kimura, Shūnkiji 木村駿吉. 1890. *Kagaku no genri* 科學之原理 [The principles of science]. Tokyo: Kinkōdo.

Kimura, Takatarō 木村鷹太郎. 1907. *Shinzenbi.bi no kan* 真善美.美の巻 [Truth, goodness, and beauty: Volume on beauty]. Tokyo: Shinzenbi kyōkai.

Kristeva, Julia. 1969. "Le Mot, le dialogue et le roman" [Word, dialogue, and novel]. In *Sèméiotikè: Recherches pour une sémanalyse* [Semiotics: Essays on semantic analysis, 1967], 143–73. Paris: Éditions du Seuil.

Kristeva, Julia. 1980. "Word, Dialogue, and Novel." In *Desire in Language: A Semiotic Approach to Literature and Art*. Edited by Leon Roudiez. Translated by Thomas Gora, Alice Jardine, and Leon Roudiez, 64–91. New York: Columbia University Press.

Kristeva, Julia (克里斯蒂娃). 2016. *Zhuti, huwen, jingshen fenxi* 主體 · 互文· 精神分析：克莉斯蒂娃復旦大學演講集 [Subject, intertexuality, and psychoanalysis: Kristeva's lectures at Fudan University]. Translated and edited by Zhu Keyi 祝克懿 and Huang Bei 黃蓓. Beijing: Sanlian shudian.

Kropotkin, Peter. 1924. *Ethics: Origin and Development* (1921). Translated by Louis S. Friedland and Joseph R. Piroshnikoff. New York: Tudor Publishing Co.

Kropotkin, Peter. 1928. *Rensheng zhexue: qi qiyuan yu fazhan* 人生哲學：其起源與發展 [Ethics: Origin and development]. Translated by Ba Jin (Li Feigan 李芾甘). Shanghai: Ziyou Shudian.

Kundera, Milan. 1991. *Immortality* (1990). Translated by Peter Kussi. New York: HarperCollins.

Kurtz, Joachim. 2011. "Domesticating a Philosophical Fiction: Chinese Translations of Immanuel Kant's 'Things in Themselves.'" *Concept and Communication* 7: 165–202.

Kwok, D. W. Y. 1965. *Scientism in Chinese Thought, 1900–1950*. New Haven, CT: Yale University Press.

La Mettrie, Julien Offray. 1981. *L'Homme-Machine* [Man-Machine, 1747]. Paris: Éditions Denoël/Gonthier.

Lange, Frederick Albert. 1957. *The History of Materialism and Criticism of Its Present Importance* (1865). Translated by Ernest Chester Thomas with an introduction by Bertrand Russell. London: Routledge & Kegan Paul.

Lao, Sze-Kwang 勞思光. 2002. *Wenhua zhexue jiangyanlu* 文化哲學講演錄 [Lectures on cultural philosophy]. Hong Kong: Chinese University of Hong Kong Press.

Lau, D. C. 2003. *Mencius* (1970). London: Penguin Books.

Le Bon, Gustave. 1907. *The Evolution of Matter* (1905). Translated by F. Legge. London: Charles Scribner's Sons.

Lebovic, Nitzan. 2013. *The Philosophy of Life and Death: Ludwig Klages and the Rise of a Nazi Biopolitics*. New York: Palgrave Macmillan.

Lee, Kwai Sang 李貴生. 2013. "Lun Hu Shi Zhongguo wenyifuxing lunshu de laiyuan ji qi zuoyong" 論胡適中國文藝復興論述的來源及其作用 [On the origin and function of Hu Shi's discourse of the Chinese renaissance]. *Hanxue yanjiu* 31, no. 1 (March), 219–54.

Lee, Leo Ou-fan. 1973. *The Romantic Generation of Modern Chinese Writers*. Cambridge, MA: Harvard University Press.

Lee, Wai-yee. 2020. "Looking for the True Self." In *Keywords in Chinese Culture*. Edited by Yuri Pines and Wai-yee Lee, 335–79. Hong Kong: Chinese University of Hong Kong Press.

Legge, James, trans. 1962. *The Sacred Books of China: The Texts of Taoism* (1891). New York: Dover Publications.

Legge, James, trans. 2014. *Confucian Analects, The Great Learning, The Doctrine of the Mean* (1861), a bilingual edition. Shanghai: Sanlian shudian.

Lesic-Thomas, Andrea. 2005. "Behind Bakhtin: Russian Formalism and Kristeva's Intertetuality." *Paragragh* 28, no. 3 (November): 1–20.

Li, Dazhao (Shouchang 守常). 1919. "Qingnian yanshi zisha wenti" 青年厭世自殺問題 [The problem of pessimism and suicide in youths]. *Xinchao* 2, no. 2 (December): 351–56.

Li, Dazhao 李大釗. 1984. "Yanshi xin yu zijue xin" 厭世心與自覺心 [World weariness and self-awareness]. In *Li Dazhao wenji* 李大釗文集 [Collected works of Li Dazhao, 1915], 145–52. Beijing: Renmin chubanshe.

Li, Sher-shiueh 李奭學. 2012. *Yishu: Mingmo Yesuhui fanyi wenxue lun* 譯述：明末耶穌會翻譯文學論 [Transwriting: Translated literature and late-Ming Jesuits]. Hong Kong: Chinese University of Hong Kong Press.

Li, Shicen 李石岑, ed. 1925. *Meiyu zhi yuanli* 美育之原理 [The principles of aesthetic education]. Shanghai: Shangwu chubanshe.

Li, Shicen. 1972. *Rensheng zhexue* 人生哲學 [Philosophy of life, 1925]. Taipei: Dipingxian chubanshe.

Li, Wei 李偉. 1996. "Wumingshi—Bu Naifu chuanqi" 無名氏—卜乃夫傳奇 [Wumingshi: The legend of Bu Naifu]. *Wenshi chunqiu* no. 5: 36–39.

Li, Xiaobei 李小貝. 2016. *Mingdai "Xingling" shi qingguan yanjiu* 明代『性靈』詩情觀研究 [On the views of *qing* in Ming dynasty spiritual poetry]. Beijing: Zhongguo shehui kexue chubanshe.

Li, Yongqiang 李永強. 2016. "Liang Qichao yu Jiangxueshe" 梁啟超與講學社 [Liang Qichao and the Lecture Society]. *Heze xueyuan xuebao* 28, no. 6 (December): 97–100.

Li, Zehou 李澤厚. 2009. *Zhongguo xiandai sixiangshi lun* 中國現代思想史論 [On modern Chinese history of ideas, 1987]. Taipei: Sanmin shudian.

Liang, Qichao. 1989. *Yinbingshi heji* 飲冰室合集 [Collected works of Ice-Drinking Chamber]. Edited by Lin Zhijun 林志鈞. Abbreviated as *YBSHJ*. Beijing: Zhonghua Shuju.

Liang, Shuming. 1989. *Liang Shuming quanji* 梁漱溟全集 [Complete works of Liang Shuming]. Abbreviated as *LSMQJ*. Jinan: Shandong renmin chubanshe.

Liang, Shuming 梁漱溟 (Liang Huanding 梁煥鼎) and Liang Huannai 梁煥鼐, eds. 1968. *Guilin Liang xiansheng yizhu* 桂林梁先生遺著 [Collected Works of the late Mr. Liang from Guilin]. Taipei: Huanwen shuju.

Lin, Min. 2001. *Certainty as a Social Metaphor: The Social and Historical Production of Certainty in China and the West*. Westport, CT: Greenwood Press.

Lin, Shaoyang 林少陽. 2018. *Dingge yi wen: Qingji geming yu Zhang Taiyan "fugu" de Xin wenhua yundong* 鼎革以文：清季革命與章太炎「復古」的新文化運動 [Literary revolution: The Qing revolution and Zhang Taiyan's New Culture movement of revitalizing ancient culture]. Shanghai: Shanghai renmin chubanshe.

Lin, Wei-chieh 林維杰. 2018. "Tang Junyi de gantong lunshu: Dui *Yi*, er Cheng yu Kongzi de quanshixing lijie" 唐君毅的感通論述：對《易》、二程與孔子的詮釋性理解 [Tang Junyi's theory of *gantong*: A hermeneutic understanding of the *Book of Changes*, the two Cheng brothers, and Confucius]. *Zhongyang daxue renwen xuebao* no. 66 (December): 57–95.

Lin, Yu-sheng. 1979. *The Crisis of Chinese Consciousness: Radical Antitraditionalism in the May Fourth Era*. Madison: University of Wisconsin Press.

Liu, Jin-song 劉勁松. 2019. "'Yun' yi bianxi: bupai fojiao zhi bijiao yanjiu" 「蘊」義辨析：部派佛教之比較研究 [An analysis of "Skandha": A comparative study of the Buddhist sects]. *Yuan kuang fojiao xuebao*, no. 33 (June): 49–82.

Liu, Lydia. 1995. *Translingual Practice: Literature, National Culture, and Translated Modernity*. Stanford, CA: Stanford University Press.

Liu, Shu-hsien. 1989. "Fang Dongmei xiansheng zhexue sixiang gaishu" 方東美先生哲學思想概述 [A general view of the philosophy of Fang Dongmei]. In *Ping Xinrujia* 評新儒家 [On New Confucianism]. Edited by Luo Yijun 羅義俊, 458–90. Shanghai: Shanghai renmin chubanshe.

Liu, Shu-hsien. 2010. *Rujia zhexue de dianfan chonggou yu quanshi* 儒家哲學的典範重構與詮釋 [Confucian philosophy: Paradigm shift and hermeneutics]. Taipei: Wanjuanlou.

Liu, Shu-hsien 劉述先 and Shun Kwong-loi 信廣來. 1996. "Some Reflections on Mencius' Views of Mind-Heart and Human Nature." *Philosophy East and West* 46, no. 2: 143–64.

Liu, Yiqing 劉義慶. 1967. *A New Account of Tales of the World*. Translated by Richard B. Mather. Ann Arbor: The University of Michigan Press.

Liu, Yiqing 劉義慶. 2003. *Shishuo xinyu* 世說新語 [A new acount of tales of the world, 5th century]. Taipei: Sanmin shuju.

Liu, Yilin 劉義林, and Luo Qingfeng 羅慶豐. 1996. *Zhang Junmai pingzhuan* 張君勱評傳 [Zhang Junmai: A critical biography]. Nanchang: Baihuazhou wenyi chubanshe.

Lodge, Sir Oliver. 1916. *Raymond, or Life and Death: With Evidence for Survival of Memory and Affection After Death*. Edinburgh: Morrison & Gibb Limited.

Lok, Matthijs, and Joris van Eijnatten. 2019. "Global Counter-Enlightenment: Introductory Remarks." *International Journal for History, Culture and Modernity* 7: 406–22.

Lovell, Julia, trans. 2009. *The Real Story of Ah-Q and Other Tales of China: Lu Xun's Complete Fiction*. New York: Penguin Group.

Lu, Jiuyuan (Xiangshan) 陸九淵 (象山). 1966. *Xiangshan quanji* 象山全集 [Complete works of Xiangshan, Song dynasty]. Taipei: Taiwan zhonghua shuju.

Lu Xun 魯迅. 1989. *Lu Xun quanji* 魯迅全集 [Complete works of Lu Xun]. Abbreviated as *LXQJ*. Beijing: Renmin wenxue chubanshe.

Lu Xun. 2010. "Lessons from the History of Science" 科學史教篇 [Kexueshi jiaopian, 1908]. Translated by Nathaniel Isaacson. *Renditions* (Autumn): 80–99.

Lu Xun. 2011. "Toward a Refutation of Malevolent Voices" 破惡聲論 [Po esheng lun, 1908]. Translated by Jon Eugene von Kowallis. *Boundary 2* 38, no. 2: 39–62.

Lü, Zheng 呂瀓. 1925. "Yishu he meiyu" 藝術和美育 [Art and aesthetic education]. In *The Principles of Aesthetic Education*. Edited by Li Shicen, 15–33. Shanghai: Shangwu yinshuguan.

Lü, Zheng, and Li Shicen. "Fulu: Lun meiyu shu" 附錄：論美育書 [Appendix: Letters on aesthetic education]. In *The Principles of Aesthetic Education*. Edited by Li Shicen, 83–92. Shanghai: Shangwu yinshuguan.

Luo, Jialun 羅家倫 (zhixi 志希). 1919. "Shi qingnian zisha haishi shehui sha qingnian—Beida xuesheng Lin Deyang jun de zisha, jiaoyu shang zhuanbian de dawenti" 是青年自殺還是社會殺青年—北大學生林德揚君的自殺，教育上轉變的大問題 [Was it the youth who killed himself or society that killed him?: The suicide of Beijing University Student Mr. Lin Deyang, a severe problem that calls for a change in education]. *Xinchao* 2, no. 2 (December): 346–48.

Luserke-Jaqui, Matthias. 2018. *Schiller-Studien: Der ganze Mensch und die Ästhetik der Freiheit* [A study on Schiller: The whole person and the aesthetic of freedom]. Tübingen: Narr Francke Attempto Verlag.

Lynn, Richard John, trans. 1994. *The Classic of Changes: A New Translation of the I Ching as Interpreted by Wang Bi*. New York: Columbia University Press.

Maissen, Thomas, and Barbara Mittler. 2018. *Why China Did not Have a Renaissance—And Why That Matters*. Berlin: Walter de Gruyter GmbH.

Mao, Zedong 毛澤東. 2013. "Xin zhi li" 心之力 [The forces of the heart-mind, 1917]. In *Mao Zedong quanji* 毛澤東全集 [Complete works of Mao Zedong] 1: 251–55. Hong Kong: Rundong chubanshe.

Masini, Federico. 1993. *The Formation of Modern Chinese Lexicon and its Evolution toward a National Language: The Period from 1840 to 1898*. Berkeley: Project on Linguistic Analysis, University of California.

Massumi, Brian. 2002. *Parables for the Virtual: Movement, Affect, Sensation*. Durham, NC: Duke University Press.

McCreary, John K. 1949. "A. N. Whitehead's Theory of Feeling." *The Journal of General Psychology* 41: 67–78.

McDonald, Joan. 2013. *Rousseau and the French Revolution 1762–1791* (1965). London: Bloomsbury Academic.

McHenry, Leemon B. 1995. "Whitehead's Panpsychism as the subjectivity of Prehension." *Process Studies* 24: 1–14.

Minford, John, trans. 2014. *I Ching: The Book of Change*. New York: Viking Penguin.

Minzhi 民質. 1916. "Wokeng renshengxue dayi" 倭鏗人生學大意 [A general review of Eucken's life philosophy]. *Dongfang zazhi* 13, no. 1: 1–8.

Mornet, Daniel. 1929. "Le Romantisme avant les romantiques" [Romanticism before the romanticists]. In *Le Romantisme et les lettres* [Romanticism and literature]. Edited by Société des amis de l'Université de Paris, 43–68. Paris: Édition Montaigne.

Morrison, James C. 1989. "Why Spinoza Had No Aesthetics." *The Journal of Aesthetics and Art Criticism* 47, no. 4: 359–65.

Mou, Zongsan 牟宗三. 1970. *Shengming de xuewen* 生命的學問 [The knowledge of life, 1950]. Taipei: Sanmin shuju.

Mou, Zongsan. 1986. *Wushi zishu* 五十自述 [Self-account at age fifty, 1959]. Taipei: Ehu chubanshe.

Mou, Zongsan. 1988. *Zhouyi de ziran zhexue yu daode hanyi* 周易的自然哲學與道德函義 [The natural philosophy and moral meaning in the *Book of Changes*, 1936]. Taipei: Wenjin chuban.

Muller, Charles et al., eds. 2022. *Digital Dictionary of Buddhism*. www.buddhism-dict.net.

Mun, Kin Chok 閔建蜀. 2013. *Chuantong zhihui zhong de zhenwo* 傳統智慧中的真我 [The true self in traditional wisdom]. Hong Kong: Chinese University of Hong Kong Press.

Mungello, David E. 1977. *Leibniz and Confucianism: The Search for Accord*. Honolulu: The University Press of Hawaiʻi.

Murota, Atsumi 室田充美. 1873. *Keizai shinsetsu* 經濟新說 [A new economic theory]. Tokyo: Kinokuniya.

Nakamura, Tetsuo 中村哲夫. 1999. "Ryō Keichō to kindai no chōkokuron" 梁啟超と近代の超克論 [Liang Qichao and the 'overcoming the modern' discourse]. In *Ryō Keichō: seiyo kindai shisō juyō to Meiji Nihon* 梁啟超：西洋近代思想受容と明治日本 [Liang Qichao: The reception of modern Western thought and Meiji Japan]. Edited by Hazama Naoki 狹間直樹, 387–413. Tokyo: Misuzu shobō.

Natsume, Sōseki. 1977. "London shōsoku" 倫敦消息 [News from London, 1901]. In *Natsume Sōseki zenshū* 夏目漱石全集 [Complete works of Natsume Sōseki] 9: 287–302. Tokyo: Chikuma shobō.

Navarro, Jaume, ed. 2018. *Ether and Modernity: The Recalcitrance of an Epistemic Object in the Early Twentieth Century*. Oxford: Oxford University Press.

Nicol, Caitrin. 2007. "Brave New World at 75." *The New Atlantis: A Journal of Technology & Society* (Spring): 41–54.

Nishida, Kitarō. 1929. *Shan zhi yanjiu* 善之研究 [An inquiry into the good]. Translated into Chinese by Wei Zhaoji 魏肇基. Shanghai: Kaiming shudian.

Nishida, Kitarō. 1978. *Nishida Kitarō zenshū* 西田幾多郎全集 [Complete works of Nishida Kitarō, 1947]. Abbrievated as *NKZS*. Tokyo: Iwanami shoten.

Nishitani, Keiji. 2001. *Nishida Kitarō* (1991). Translated by Yamamoto Seisaku and James W. Heisig. Berkeley: University of California Press.

Novalis, Julian Schmidt. 1876. *Heinrich von Ofterdinggen*. Leipzig: Brockhaus.

Nyanatiloka, Mahathera. 1945. *Fundamentals of Buddhism, Four Lectures*. Kandy, Sri Lanka: Buddhist Publication Society.

Obara, Kuniyoshi 小原國芳 (Ajisaka Kuniyoshi 鰺坂國芳). 1919. *Kyōyiku no konpon mondai toshite no shūkyō* 教育の根本問題としての宗教 [Religion as the basic problem of education]. Tokyo: Shūseisha.

Obara, Kuniyoshi. 1926. *Haha no tame no kyōyikugaku* 母のための教育學 [Pedagogy for the mother]. Tokyo: Idea shoyin.

Ortiz, Fernando. 1995. *Cuban Counterpoint: Tobacco and Sugar*. Translated by Harriet de Onnís. Durham, NC: Duke University Press.

Ōse, Jintarō 大瀬甚太郎. 1891. *Kyōjuhō* 教授法 [Pedagogy]. Tokyo: Kinkōdō.

Osterhammel, Jügen. 2018. *Unfabling the West: The Enlightenment's Encounter with Asia* (2013). Translated by Robert Savage. Princeton, NJ: Princeton University Press.

Ouyang, Kaibin 歐陽開斌. 2021a. "Langman yingxiong: Chuanyue Wenge de Mu Xin yu Beiduofen" 浪漫英雄：穿越文革的木心與貝多芬 [The romantic hero: Mu Xin and Beethoven through the Cultural Revolution]. *Dongfang wenhua* no. 1 (June): 163–200.

Ouyang, Kaibin. 2021b. "Wenhua yishu de 'zhiwuxing zhanlue': Mu Xin yingdui xiandaixing weiji de langman xinzhi" 文化藝術的"植物性戰略"：木心應對現代性危機的浪漫心智 ["The vegetal strategy" of culture and art: Mu Xin's romantic mind towards the crisis of modernity]. *Zhongguo xiandai wenxue* no. 39: 91–126.

Ouyang, Kaibin. 2022. "'Yige chongxin faxian de guohun': Xu Zhimo guiguo shoujiang "Art and Life" zaitan 「一個重新發現的國魂」：徐志摩歸國首講 "Art and Life" 再探 ["A re-discovered national soul": Xu Zhimo's homecoming speech revisited]. *Tsinghua xuebao* 52, no. 3 (September): 593–630.

Pagden, Anthony. 2013. *The Enlightenment and Why It still Matters*. Oxford: Oxford University Press.

Paolucci, Paul. 2007. *Marx's Scientific Dialectics: A Methodological Treatise for a New Century*. Leiden: Brill.

Paramore, Kiri. 2016. *Japanese Confucianism: A Cultural History*. Cambridge: Cambridge University Press.

Peng, Hsiao-yen. 2010. *Dandyism and Transcultural Modernity: The Dandy, the Flâneur, and the Translator in 1930s Shanghai, Tokyo, and Paris*. London: Routledge.

Peng, Hsiao-yen. 2014. "Yi mei wei zun: Zhang Jingsheng 'Xinnüxing zhongxin' lun yu daerwen 'xingze' shuo" 以美為尊：張競生「新女性中心」論與達爾文「性擇」說 [Beauty rules: Zhang Jingsheng's gynocentrism and Darwin's sexual selection]. *Zhongguo wenzhe yanjiu jikan* no. 44 (March): 57–77.

Peng, Hsiao-yen. 2019. *Weiqing yu lixing de bianzheng: Wusi de fanqimeng* 唯情與理性的辯證：五四的反啟蒙 [The dialectic of affect and reason: The May Fourth Counter-Enlightenment]. Taipei: Lianjing.

Pestalozzi, Johann Heinrich. 1804. *Lienhard und Gertrud: Ein Buch für das Volk* [Leonard and Gertrude: A book for the people, 1781]. Zürich: Bei Heinrich Gessner.

Phillips, Kim M. 2014. *Before Orientalism: Asian Peoples and Cultures in European Travel Writing, 1245–1510*. Philadelphia: University of Pennsylvania Press.

Pollard, David. 2002. *The True Story of Lu Xun*. Hong Kong: The Chinese University of Hong Kong Press.

Popp, Jerome A. 2007. *Evolution's First Philosopher: John Dewey and the Continuity of Nature*. Albany: State University of New York Press.

Pugh, David. 1997. *Dialectic of Love: Platonism in Schiller's Aesthetics*. Montreal, QC: McGill-Queen's University Press.

Reichwein, Adolf. 1923. *China und Europa: geistige und künstlerische Beziehungen im 18. Jahrhundert* [China and Europe: Spiritual and artistic contacts in the eighteenth century]. Berlin: Oesterheld.

Reichwein, Adolf. 1925. *China and Europe—Intellectual and Artistic Contacts in the Eighteenth Century*. Translated by J. C. Powell. London: Kegan Paul, Trench, Trubner.

Robinson, Bradley, and Mel Kutner. 2019. "Spinoza and the Affective Turn: A Return to the Philosophical Origins of Affect" (2018). *Qualitative Inquiry* 25, no. 2: 111–17.

Rogers, Arthur Kenyon. 1925. *A Student's History of Philosophy*. New York: Macmillan.

Rorty, Richard. 1982. "Dewey's Metaphysics." In *Consequences of Pragmatism*, 72–89. Minneapolis: University of Minnesota Press.

Rosenmeier, Christopher. 2017. *On the Margins of Modernity: Xu Xu, Wumingshi and Popular Chinese Literature in the 1940s*. Edinburgh: Edniburgh University Press.

Rousseau, Jean Jacques. 1997. *Julie, or the New Heloise: Letters of Two Lovers who Live in a Small Town at the Foot of the Alps* (1761). Translated by Philip Stewart and Jean Vaché. Lebanon, NH: University Press of New England.

Rousseau, Jean Jacques. 2004. *Discours sur les sciences et les arts* [Discourse on the arts and sciences, 1750]. Paris: Le Livre de Poche.

Russell, Bertrand. 1924. *Icarus: or, The Future of Science*. New York: E. P. Dutton & Co.

Russell, Bertrand. 1993. *The Problem of China* (1922). Nottingham: The Russell Press Ltd.

Rutt, Richard, trans. 2002. *The Book of Changes (Zhouyi): A Bronze Age Document*. Richmond, Surrey: Curzon.

Sakai, Hirobumi 坂井洋史, and Saga Takashi 嵯峨隆, eds. 1994. *Genten Chūgoku anakizumu shiryō shūsei* 原典中国アナキズム史料集成 [Chinese anarchism: Collection of original texts]. Tokyo: Ryōkuin shobō.

Sang, Yu. 2020. *Xiong Shili's Understanding of Reality and Function, 1920–1937*. Leiden: Brill.

Santayana, George. 1925. "Dewey's Naturalistic Metaphysics." *Journal of Philosophy* 22, no. 25 (3 December): 673–88.

Saussy, Haun, ed. 2006. *Comparative Literature in an Age of Globalization*. Baltimore, MD: Johns Hopkins University Press.

Schiller, Friedrich. 1982. *On the Aesthetic Education of Men in a Series of Letters* [Über die äesthetische Erziehung des Menschen, 1794]. Parallel text in English and German translated and edited by Elizabeth M. Wilkinson and L. A. Willoughby. Oxford: Clarendon Press.

Schwarcz, Vera. 1986. *The Chinese Enlightenment: Intellectuals and the Legacy of the May Fourth Movement of 1919*. Berkeley: University of California Press.

Shen, Congwen 沈從文. 2002. *Shen Congwen quanji* 沈從文全集 [Complete works of Shen Congwen]. Edited by Zhan Zhaohe 張兆和. Abbreviated as *SCWQJ*. Taiyuan: Beiyue wenyi chubanshe.

Shen, Yue 沈約. 1974. *Song shu* 宋書 [History of the Liu Song dynasty, 487 CE). Beijing: Zhonghua shuju.

Shi, Haitao 施海濤. 2013. "Shilun *Zhongguo xinwenxueshi* de duilixing yu weiqingxing 試論《中國新文學史》的對立性與唯情性 [On the polarity and affectivism in *A History of Modern Chinese New Literature*]. *Xueshu tantao* 12, no. 6 (June): 100–103.

Shiraishi, Kinosuke 白石喜之助. 1913. *Kirisutokyō no uchūkan oyobi jinseikan* 基督教の宇宙觀及び人生觀 [Christian universeview and lifeview]. Tokyo: Kyōbunkan.

Siku quanshu 四庫全書 [Complete library in four branches of literature, 1773–1781]. 1983–1986. Taiwan: Shangwu chubanshe.

Sima, Changfeng 司馬長風. 1976. *Weiqinglunzhe de duyu* 唯情論者的獨語 [Monologues of an affectivist]. Taipei: Yuanxing chubanshe.

Simmel, Georg. 1918. *Lebensanschauung: Vier metaphysische Kapitel* [Lifeview: Four metaphysical chapters]. München: Duncker & HNumblot.

Smith, Daniel W. 2012. "Deleuze and the History of Philosophy." In *The Cambridge Companion to Deleuze*. Edited by Henry Somers Hall and Daniel W. Smith, 13–32. New York: Cambridge University Press.

Smith, Olav Bryant. 2010. "The Social Self of Whitehead's Organic Philosophy." *European Journal of Pragmatism and American Philosophy* 11, no. 1 (December): 1–15.

Snow, Edgar, ed. 1937. *Mao Zedong zizhuan* 毛澤東自傳 [Autobiography of Mao Zedong]. Translated by Li Du 李杜. Hankou: Kangdi chubanshe.

Snow, Edgar. 1972. *Red Star Over China* (1937). Harmonsworth, Middlesex: Penguin Books.

Snow, Edgar, ed. 2001. *Mao Zedong zizhuan* 毛澤東自傳 [Autobiography of Mao Zedong]. Translated by Wang Heng 汪衡. Beijing: Jiefangjun Wenyi chubanshe.

Solomon, Robert C. 1983. *In the Spirit of Hegel*. Oxford: Oxford University Press.

Song, Gang. 2019. *Giulio Aleni, Kouduo Richao, and Christian-Confucian Dialogism in Late Ming Fujian*. New York: Routledge.

Song, Ming 宋溟. 2015. "Zhang Junmai 'renshengguan' de Deguo zhexue ziyuan" 張君勱 "人生觀" 的德國哲學資源 [The German philosophical resources of Zhang Junmai's theory of "lifeview"]. *Xiandai zhongwen xuekan* no. 36 (June): 81–89.

Song, Shengquan 宋聲泉. 2019. "'Kexueshi jiaopian' lanben kaolue" 〈科學史教篇〉藍本考略 [On the original text of "Lessons of the history of science"]. *Zhongguo xiandai wenxue yanjiu congkan* no. 1: 143–50.

Spencer, Herbert. 1870. *The Principles of Psychology*. London: Williams & Norgate.

Spinoza, Benedict de. 1952. *Ethics* (1677). Translated by W. H. White. Revised by A. H. Stirling. In *Descartes and Spinoza*. Edited By Robert Hutchins, 355–463. Chicago: Encyclopedia Britannica.

Spinoza, Benedict de. 1985. *Ethics*. In *The Collected Works of Spinoza*. Translated by Edwin Curley 1: 401–617. Princeton, NJ: Princeton University Press.

Spinoza, Benedict de. 1992. *The Ethics; Treatise on the Emendation of the Intellect; Selected Letters*. Translated by Samuel Shirley. Edited by Seymour Feldman. Indianapolis, IN: Hackett.

Spinoza, Benedict de. 2000. *Ethics*. Translated by G. H. R. Parkinson. Oxford: Oxford University Press.

Standaert, Nicolas. 2002. *Methodology in View of Contact between Cultures: The Chinese Case in the 17th Century*. Hong Kong: The Chinese University of Hong Kong Press.

Su, Xuelin 蘇雪林. 1980. "Yu Dafu ji qi zuopin" 郁達夫及其作品 [Yu Dafu and his works, 1932]. In *Ersanshi niandai zuojia yu zuopin* 二三十年代作家與作品 [Writers and their works in the 1920s and 30s], 298–309. Taipei: Guangdong chubanshe.

Sun, George Chi-sen 孫智燊. 1982. "Xuesheng shidai de Fang Dongmei xiansheng" 學生時代的方東美先生 [Professor Fang Dongmei during his student days]. In *Fang Dongmei xiansheng jinianji* 方東美先生紀念集 [Collection in commemoration of Professor Fang Dongmei]. Edited by Yang Shiyi 楊士毅, 155–75. Taipei: Zhengzhong shuju.

Sun, Jiang 孫江, and Liu Jianhui 劉建輝, eds. 2013. *Yazhou gainianshi yanjiu* 亞洲概念史研究 [Study of Asian history of ideas]. Beijing: Sanlian shudian.

Suzuki, Shigeo 鈴木重雄. 1942. *Sekaikan, kokkakan, jinseikan* 世界觀. 國家觀. 人生觀 [Worldview, stateview, and lifeview]. Tokyo: Daiichi kōronsha.

Swetz, Frank J. 2003. "Leibniz, the *Yijing*, and the Religious Conversion of the Chinese." *Mathematics Magazine* 76, no. 4: 276–91.

Tagore, Rabindranath. 1913. *Sādhanā: The Realization of Life*. New York and London: Macmillan.

Takahashi, Gorō 高橋五郎. 1909. *Eigozaso: taishō sōyaku* 英語雑俎: 対照双訳 [Miscellaneous English terms translated: A bilingual edition]. Tokyo: Kenbunkan.

Takamine, Hideo 高嶺秀夫, trans. 1886. *Kyōyiku shinron* 教育新論 [A new theory of education, 1878]. Tokyo: Tokyo Meikeikai.

Tan, Sitong 譚嗣同. 1898. "Yitaishuo" 以太說 [On ether]. *Xiangbao* no. 53: 209.

Tao, Yinghui 陶英惠. 2007. *Dianxing zai suxi: Zhuihuai Zhongyang Yanjiuyuan liuwei yigu yuanzhang* (shang) 典型在夙昔：追懷中央研究院六位已故院長（上）[Exemplary lives: Commemorating the six late presidents of Academia Sinica, vol. 1]. Taipei: Xiuwei Zixun Keji.

Taylor, Henry Osborn. 1920. *Thought and Expression in the Sixteenth Century*. New York: McMillan.

Terada, Rei. 2001. *Feeling in Theory: Emotion after the "Death of Subject."* Cambridge, MA: Harvard University Press.

Thiele, Leslie Paul. 1990. *Friedrich Nietzsche and the Politics of the Soul: A Study of Heroic Individualism*. Princeton, NJ: Princeton University Press.

Tian, Han 田漢, Zong Baihua 宗白華, and Guo Moruo 郭沫若. 1982. *Sanyeji* 三葉集 [Three-leaved clover, 1920]. Shanghai: Shanghai shudian.

Toscano, Alberto. 2010. "Everybody Thinks: Deleuze, Descartes and Rationalism." *Radical Philosophy* 162 (July/August): 8–17.

Tu, Wei-ming 杜維明. 1989. "Chaoyue er neizai—Rujia jingshen fangxiang de tese" 超越而內在—儒家精神方向的特色 [Transcendence in immanence: The spiritual characteristics of Confucianism]. In *Ruxue disanqi fazhan de qianjing wenti* 儒學第三期發展的前景問題 [The prospects of the development of the third generation Confucianism], 165–211. Taipei: Lianjing chuban.

Turner, Frank M. 2014. *European Intllectual History from Rousseau to Nietzsche*. New Haven, CT: Yale University Press.

Ulfers, Friedrich, and Mark Daniel Cohen. 2008. "Zarathustra, the Moment, and Eternal Recurrence of the Same: Nietzsche's Ontology of Time." In *Nietzsche's Thus Spoke Zarathustra: Before Sunrise*. Edited by James Luchte, 75–90. New York: Continuum International Publishing Group.

Vipassana meditation. As taught by S. N. Goenka in the tradition of Sayaghi U Ba Khin. https://www.dhamma.org/en-US/index.

Wadagaki, Kenzō 和田垣謙三, ed. 1881. *Tetsugaku jiyi: fu· shinkoku onpu* 哲學字彙：附 清國音符 [A dictionary of philosophy: With pronunciations of Chinese characters]. Tokyo: Tokyo daigaku sangakubu.

Wang, Ban. 2015. "Use in Uselessness: How Western Aesthetics Made Chinese Literature More Political." In *A Companion to Modern Chinese Literature*. Edited by Yingjin Zhang, 279–94. West Sussex, UK: Wiley Blackwell.

Wang, Changhuan 王昌煥, ed. 1999. *Liang Qichao Zhang Dongsun* 梁啟超 張東蓀. Beijing: Renmin ribao chubanshe.

Wang, David Derwei. 2015. *The Lyrical in Epic Time: Modern Chinese Intellectuals and Artists through the 1949 Crisis*. New York: Columbia University Press.

Wang, Donglin 汪東林. 1988. Liang Shuming wendalu 梁漱溟問答錄 [Liang Shuming: Questions and answers]. Changsha: Hunan renmin chubanshe.

Wang, Fansen 王汎森. 1985. *Zhang Taiyan de sixiang—jianlun qi dui Ruxue chuantong de chongji* 章太炎的思想—兼論其對儒學傳統的衝擊 [Zhang Taiyan's thought and its impact on traditional Confucianism]. Taipei: Shibao wenhua.

Wang, Fansen. 2017. *Sixiang shi shenghuo de yizhong fangshi: Zhongguo jindai sixiangshi de zai sikao* 思想是生活的一種方式：中國近代思想史的再思考 [Philosophy as a way of life: Rethinking modern Chinese history of ideas]. Taipei: Lianjing.

Wang, Futang 王福堂 and Sun Hongkai 孫宏開. 2010. "Yuan Jiahua xiansheng xueshu nianbiao" 袁家驊先生學術年表 [Mr. Yuan Jiahua's academic chronology]. In *Yuan Jiahua wenxuan* 袁家驊文選 [Selected works of Yuan Jiahua], 198–201. Beijing: Beijing University Press.

Wang, Guowei 王國維. 1993a. "Lun jiaoyu zhi zongzhi" 論教育之宗旨 [On the goal of education, 1903]. In *Wang Guowei zhexue meixue lunwen jiyi* 王國維哲學美學論文輯佚 [Collection of Wang Guowei's essays on philosophy and aesthetics], 251–53. Shanghai: Huadong shifan daxue chubanshe.

Wang, Guowei 王國維. 1993b. "Kongzi zhi meiyuzhuyi" 孔子之美育主義 [Confucius' principles of aesthetic education, 1904]. In *Collection of Wang Guowei's Essays on Philosophy and Aesthetics*, 254–57. Shanghai: Huadong shifan daxue chubanshe.

Wang, Hui 汪暉. 2010. "Sheng zhi shan'e" 聲之善惡：什麼是啟蒙？—重讀魯迅的〈破惡聲論〉[The voices of good and evil: What is enlightenment?—Rereading Lu Xun's "Toward a refutation of malevolent voices]. *Kaifang shidai* (October): 84–115.

Wang, Hui. 2011. "The voices of good and evil: What Is Enlightenment?—Rereading Lu Xun's 'Toward a refutation of malevolent voices.'" Translated by Ted Huters and Yangyang Zong. *Boundary 2* 38, no. 2: 67–123.

Wang, Jessica Ching-Sze. 2008. *John Dewey in China: To Teach and to Learn*. New York: State University of New York Press.

Wang, Mengzou 汪孟鄒. 1977. *Kexue yu renshengguan* 科學與人生觀 [Science and lifeview, 1923]. Taipei: Wenxue chubanshe.

Wang, Rongpei 汪榕培, trans. 1999. *Zhuangzi*. Oiginal Chinese text with English and modern Chinese translations. Changsha: Hunan renmin chubanshe.

Wang, Shiru 王世儒, ed. 1998. *Cai Yuanpei xiansheng nianpu* 蔡元培先生年譜 [Mr. Cai Yuanpei: A chronology]. Beijing: Beijing daxue chubanshe.

Wang, Tao 王韜, ed. 1889. *Gezhi Shuyuan keyi* 格致書院課藝 [The Shanghai Polytechnic Prize essays on science]. Shanghai: Gezhi shuyuan.

Wang, Xinggong 王星拱. 1920. *Kexue fangfalun* 科學方法論 [Scientific methodology]. Beijing: Beijing daxue chubanshe.

Wang, Yangming 王陽明. 1927. *Chuanxilu* 傳習錄 [Instructions for a practical living, 1518]. Edited with notes and punctuation by Ye Shaojun 葉紹鈞. Shanghai: Shanghai shangwu chubanshe.

Wang, Yangming. 1963. *Instructions for a Practical Living and Other Neo-Confucian Writings*. Translated by Chan Wing-tsit 陳榮捷. New York: Columbia University Press.

Wang, Yangzong 王揚宗. 2000. *Fu Lanya yu jindai Zhongguo de kexue qimeng* 傅蘭雅與近代中國的科學啟蒙 [John Fryer and the scientific enlightenment of modern China]. Beijing: Kexue chubanshe.

Wargo, Robert J. J. 2005. *The Logic of Nothingness*. Honolulu: University of Hawai'i Press.

Watson, Burton, trans. 1964. *Chuang Tzu: Basic Writings*. New York: Columbia University Press.

Whitehead, Alfred N. 1919. *The Concept of Nature*. Cambridge: Cambridge University Press.

Whitehead, Alfred N. 1978. *Process and Reality: Corrected Edition* (1929). Edited by David Ray Griffin and Donald W. Sherburne. New York: The Free Press.

Wright, David. 2000. *Translating Science: The Transmission of Western Chemistry into Late Imperial China, 1840–1900*. Leiden: Brill.

Wu, Charles Q. 2016. *Thus Spoke Laozi: A New Translation with Commentaries of Daodejing*. Honolulu: University of Hawai'i Press.

Wu, Hanquan 吳漢全. 2006. "Guxingshe, Zhuhun Xueshe, Zhongguo Shaonian Laodongdang—guanyu Zhongguo Shaonian Laodongdang de shuli 孤星社・鑄魂學社・中國少年勞動黨—關於中國少年勞動黨歷史的梳理 [Lone Star Society, Spirit Molding Society, Chinese Youth Labor Party—On the history of Chinese Youth Labor Party]. *Xinan daxue xuebao* 32, no. 1: 147–52.

Wu, Mengfei. 1920a. "Meiyu shi shemo?" 美育是什麼？[What is aesthetic education?, Part 1]. *Meiyu* no. 1 (April): 3–7.

Wu, Mengfei. 1920b. "Meiyu shi shemo? (Xu)" 美育是什麼？(續) [What is aesthetic education?, Part 2]. *Meiyu* no. 2 (May): 1–10.

Wu, Mengfei 吳夢非. 1920c. "Duiyu woguo banxuezhe de yige yiwen" 對於我國辦學者的一個疑問 [One question to the educators of our nation]. *Meiyu* no. 4 (July): 1–3.

Wu, Zhihui. 1977a. "Zhen yang baguhua de lixue" 箴洋八股化的理學 [Critiquing the Westernized eight-legged philosophy of Universal Order, 1923]. In *Science and Lifeview*. Edited by Wang Mengzou 2: 443–53. Taipei: Wenxue chubanshe.

Wu, Zhihui. 1977b. "Yige xin xinyang de yuzhouguan yu renshengguan" 一個新信仰的宇宙觀與人生觀 [The universeview and lifeview of a new faith, 1923]. In *Science and Lifeview*. Edited by Wang Mengzou 2: 489–653. Taipei: Wenxue chubanshe.

Wumingshi 無名氏. 1972. *Rensheng de aoyi* 人生的奧義 [The profound meaning of life, 1943]. Tainan: Kaishan shudian.

Wumingshi. 1982. "Luelun renlei weilai lixiang yu xinyang" 略論人類未來理想與信仰 [On the future ideals and faiths of human beings]. *United Daily* (21 and 24–25 December): 8.

Wumingshi. 1998–2002. *Wumingshu* 無名書 [The nameless book, 1945–1960]. Abbreviated as *NB*. Taipei: Wenshizhe chubanshe and jiuge chubanshe.

Xia, Xianzhun 夏咸淳. 1994. "Wanming zunqinglunzhe de wenyiguan" 晚明尊情論者的文藝觀 [The literary views of the advocates of *qing* in the late Ming]. *Tianfu xinlun* no. 3: 51–56.

Xiao, Ying 肖鷹. 2013. "Tang Xianzu weiqing wenxueguan de luoji jiexi" 湯顯祖唯情文學觀的邏輯解析 [A logical analysis of Tang Xianzu's affectivist view of literature]. *Hebei xuekan* 33, no. 4 (July): 71–75.

Xie, Yingxing 謝鶯興, ed. 2017. *Xu Fuguan Jiaoshou nianbiao chubian* 徐復觀教授年表初編 [Professor Xu Fuguan: Preliminary chronology]. Taizhong: Tunghai University Library.

Xu, Fuguan 徐復觀. 1974. *Zhongguo sixiangshi lunji* 中國思想史論集 [Collected essays on Chinese intellectual history, 1959]. Taipei: Taiwan xuesheng shuju.

Xu, Gaiping 徐改平. 2013. *Cong wenxue geming dao geming wenxue: yi wenxue guannian he hexin lingxiu de guanxi bianqian wei zhongxin* 從文學革命到革命文學：以文學觀念和核心領袖的關係變遷為中心 [From literary revolution to revolutionary literature: On the transformation of the relationships between literary views and core leaders]. Beijing: Zhongguo shehui kexueyuan chubanshe.

Xu, Jilin 許紀霖. 2011. *Dangdai Zhongguo de qimeng yu fanqimeng* 當代中國的啟蒙與反啟蒙 [Enlightenment and anti-enlightenment of contemporary China]. Beijing: Shehui kexue wenxian chubanbu.

Xu, Shuisheng 徐水生. 2007. "Daojia sixiang yu Riben zhexue de jindaihua—yi Xizhou, Zhongjiang Zhaomin, Xitian Jiduolang wei li" 道家思想與日本哲學的近代化—以西周、中江兆民、西田幾多郎為例 [Daoist thought and the modernization of Japanese philosophy: With Nishi Amane, Nakae Chōmin, and Nishida Kitarō as examples]. *Ehu yuekan* no. 379 (1 January): 42–50.

Xu, Wei 徐渭. 1983. *Xu Wei ji* 徐渭集 [Collected works of Xu Wei, Ming dynasty]. Taipei: Zhonghua shuju.

Xu, Zhimo. 1996. "Art and Life" (1923). In *Modern Chinese Literary Thought: Writings on Literature, 1893–1945*. Edited by Kirk A. Denton, 169–81. Stanford, CA: Stanford University Press.

Yan, Fu 嚴復, trans. 2012. *Tianyanlun* 天演論 [Evolution and ethics, 1897]. Edited by Wang Dawhwan 王道還. Taipei: Wenjing.

Yang, Bojun 楊伯峻. 1997. *Liezi jishi* 列子集釋 [Commentaries on *Liezi*, 1979]. Beijing: Zhonghua shuju.

Yang, Xiong 揚雄. 2010. *Maîtres mots* 法言 [Exemplary words, circa 10 BCE–18 CE]. Translated by Béatrice L'Hardon. Paris: Les Belles Lettres, Chinese-French bilingual edition.

Yang, Yongqian 楊永乾. 1993. *Zhang Junmai zhuan: Zhonghua Minguo xianfa zhi fu* 張君勱傳：中華民國憲法之父 [Biography of Zhang Junmai: The father of the constitution of the Republic of China]. Taipei: Tangshan chubanshe.

Yau, Kevin Ting Kit 丘庭傑. 2023. *Qinggan yu lixing de bianzheng yu shanbian: Yi qingmo minchu de Lu Xun, Chen Duxiu, Cai Yuanpei wei ge'an* 情感與理性的辯證與嬗變：以清末民初的魯迅、陳獨秀、蔡元培為個案 [Dialectic of affect and reason, variations: Lu Xun, Chen Duxiu, and Cai Yuanpei as case studies—from the late Qing to the early Republic]. Hong Kong: Shangwu yinshuguan.

Yu, Ning. 2007. "Heart and Cognition in Ancient Chinese Philosophy." *Journal of Cognition and Culture* 7: 27–47.

Yü, Ying-shih 余英時. 2014. "Jieju: neixiang chaoyue" 結局：內向超越 [Conclusion: Inward transcendence]. In *Lun tianren zhi ji: Zhongguo gudai sixiang qiyuan shitan* 論天人之際：中國古代思想起源試探 [Between Heaven and Earth: On the origin of ancient Chinese thought], 219–52. Taipei: Lianjing.

Yü, Ying-shih. 2016. *Chinese History and Culture*. Edited by Josephine Chiu-Duke and Michael S. Duke. New York: Columbia University Press.

Yuan, Jiahua 袁家驊. 1924. *Weiqing zhexue* 唯情哲學 [Affectivist philosophy]. Shanghai: Taidong shuju.

Yusa, Michiko. 2002. *Zen & Philosophy: An Intellectual Biography of Nishida Kitarō*. Honolulu: University of Hawai'i Press.

Zeng, Huanghai 曾黃海. 2018. *Zhongguo jindangdai zhexueshi* 中國近當代哲學史 [History of modern and contemporary Chinese philosophy]. Taipei: Wunan tushu.

Zhang, Dongsun 張東蓀. 1938. "Sixiang yuyan yu wenhua" 思想語言與文化 [Thought, language, and cuture]. *Shehui xuejie* 10 (June): 17–54.

Zhang, Dongsun (Chang Tung-sun). 1939. "A Chinese Philosopher's Theory of Knowledge" [Thought, language, and culture]. Translated by Li An-che 李安宅. *The Yenching Journal of Social Studies* 1, no. 2: 161–97.

Zhang, Dongsun (Chang Tung-sun). 1959. "A Chinese Philosopher's Theory of Knowledge." In *Our Language and Our World*. Edited by S. I. Hayakawa, 299–324. New York: Harper & Brothers.

Zhang, Dongsun (Chang Tung-sun). 1969. "*La Logique chinoise*" [the Chinese logic]. *Tel Quel* no. 38 (Summer): 3–21.

Zhang, Jingsheng. 2021. *Zhang Jingsheng ji* 張競生集 [Collected works of Zhang Jingsheng]. Abbreviated as *ZJSJ*. Beijing: Sanlian shudian.

Zhang, Junmai 張君勱 (Junmai 君勱). 1921a. "Woyikeng jingshen shenghuo zhexue dagai" 倭伊鏗精神生活哲學大概 [Outlines of Eucken's philosophy of spiritual life]. *Gaizao* 3, no. 7 (15 March): 1–18.

Zhang, Junmai. 1921b. "Faguo zhexuejia Bogesen tanhuaji" 法國哲學家柏格森談話記 [Report on the interview with the French philosopher Bergson]. *Gaizao* 3, no. 12 (15 August): 7–11.

Zhang, Junmai. 1981. "Renshengguan lunzhan zhi huigu—Sishi nian lai xifang zhexuejie zhi sixiangjia" 人生觀論戰之回顧—四十年來西方哲學界之思想家 [The Lifeview debate in retrospect: Western philosophers in the last forty years, 1963]. In *Zhongxiyin zhexue wenji* 中西印哲學文集 [Collected essays on Chinese, Western, and Indian philosophy]. Edited by Cheng Wenxi 程文熙, 2: 1041–1087. Taipei: Taiwan shuju.

Zhang, Junmai. 1977. "Renshengguan" 人生觀 [Lifeview, 1923]. In *Science and Lifeview*. Edited by Wang Mengzou, 1: 1–13.

Zhang, Taiyan 章太炎. 2014. *Zhang Taiyan quanji* 章太炎全集 [Complete works of Zhang Taiyan]. Abbrieviated as *ZTYQJ*. Shanghai: Renmin chubanshe.

Zhang, Zhaojun 張昭軍. 2011. *Ruxue jindai zhi jing: Zhang Taiyan sixiang yanjiu* 儒學近代之境：章太炎思想研究 [Confucianism in a modern context: On Zhang Taiyan's thought]. Beijing: Beijing shifan daxue chubanshe.

Zheng, Boqi 鄭伯奇. 1982. "Yi Chuangzaoshe" 憶創造社 [Memories of the Creation Society]. In *Yi Chuangzaoshe ji qita* 憶創造社及其他 [Memories of the Creation Society and other essays]. Hong Kong: Sanlian shudian.

Zheng, Xuejia 鄭學稼. 1953. *Yiu wenxue geming dao ge wenxue de ming* 由文學革命到革文學的命 [From Literary Revolution to revolutionizing literature]. Hong Kong: Yazhou chubanshe.

Zhou, Limin 周立民. 2011. *Ba Jin pingzhuan—Wusi zhi zi de shiji zhi lü* 巴金評傳—五四之子的世紀之旅 [A Critical biography of Ba Jin, son of the May Fourth: Voyage of a century]. Taipei: Xiuwei zixun keji.

Zhou, Lingsun 周玲蓀. 1920. "Xinwenhua yundong he meiyu" 新文化運動和美育 [The New Culture movement and aesthetic education]. *Meiyu* no. 3 (June): 1–16.

Zhou, Yuefeng 周月峰. 2019. "Ling yichang Xinwenhua yundong—Liang Qichao zhuren de wenhua nuli yu Wusi sixiangjie" 另一場新文化運動—梁啟超諸人的文化努力與五四思想界 [Another New Culture movement—The cultural endeavors of Liang Qichao's circle and May Fourth world of ideas]. *Jindaishi yanjiusuo jikan* no. 105 (September): 49–89.

Zhu, Jiancheng 朱建成. 1996. "Gu Shouchang" 顧綬昌. In *Zhonghua Renmin Gongheguo xiangshou zhengfu teshu jintie zhuanjia, xuezhe, jishu renyuan minglu* 中華人民共和國享受政府特殊津貼專家、學者、技術人員名錄 [Directory of experts, scholars, and technicians enjoying government special subsidies in the People's Republic of China]. Edited by Zhuang Yi 莊毅, 131–33. Beijing: Zhongguo guoji guangbo chubanshe.

Zhu, Linlin 朱林林. 2013. "Zhuhun Xueshe shimo" 鑄魂學社始末 [History of the Spirit Molding Society]. *Wenshi jinghua* no. 278: 68–71.

Zhu, Qianzhi 朱謙之. 1932. "Reqing zhansheng yiqie" 熱情戰勝一切 [Passions conquer all]. *Daxiahun* 1, no. 8: 4–5.

Zhu, Qianzhi. 2002. *Zhu Qianzhi wenji* 朱謙之文集 [Collected works of Zhu Qianzhi]. Edited by Huang Xianian 黃夏年. Abbreviated as *ZQZWJ*. Fuzhou: Fujian jiaoyu chubanshe.

Zuo, Qifu 左其福. 2001. "Tang Xiangzu de 'weiqing' wenxueguan" 湯顯祖的「唯情」文學觀 [Tang Xianzu's "Affectivist" view of literature]. MA thesis, Xiangtan University.

Zuo, Yuhe 左玉河, ed. 2013. *Zhang Dongsun nianpu* 張東蓀年譜 [Zhang Dongsun: A chronology]. Beijing: Qunyan chubanshe.

Index